"Good Coup" Gone Bad

The **Institute of Southeast Asian Studies (ISEAS)** was established as an autonomous organization in 1968. It is a regional centre dedicated to the study of socio-political, security and economic trends and developments in Southeast Asia and its wider geostrategic and economic environment. The Institute's research programmes are the Regional Economic Studies (RES, including ASEAN and APEC), Regional Strategic and Political Studies (RSPS), and Regional Social and Cultural Studies (RSCS).

ISEAS Publishing, an established academic press, has issued more than 2,000 books and journals. It is the largest scholarly publisher of research about Southeast Asia from within the region. ISEAS Publishing works with many other academic and trade publishers and distributors to disseminate important research and analyses from and about Southeast Asia to the rest of the world.

"Good Coup" Gone Bad

Thailand's Political Developments
since Thaksin's Downfall

edited by
Pavin Chachavalpongpun

ISEAS

INSTITUTE OF SOUTHEAST ASIAN STUDIES
SINGAPORE

First published in Singapore in 2014 by
ISEAS Publishing
Institute of Southeast Asian Studies
30 Heng Mui Keng Terrace
Pasir Panjang
Singapore 119614

E-mail: publish@iseas.edu.sg
Website: http://bookshop.iseas.edu.sg

The responsibility for facts and opinions in this publication rests exclusively with the authors and their interpretations do not necessarily reflect the views or the policy of the publishers or their supporters.

ISEAS Library Cataloguing-in-Publication Data

"Good coup" gone bad : Thailand's political development since Thaksin's downfall
/ edited by Pavin Chachavalpongpun.
  1.   Thailand—Politics and government—21st century.
  2.   Thailand—History—Coup d'état, 2006.
  3.   Democracy—Thailand.
  4.   Monarchy—Thailand.
  5.   Peasants—Thailand—Political activity.
  6.   Thailand, Southern—Politics and government.
  7.   Thailand—Foreign relations—Cambodia.
  8.   Cambodia—Foreign relations—Thailand.
  I.   Pavin Chachavalpongpun.
DS586 G64   2013

ISBN 978-981-4459-60-0 (soft cover)
ISBN 978-981-4459-61-7 (e-book, PDF)

Cover design by Wasin Pathomyok

Typeset by Superskill Graphics Pte Ltd
Printed in Singapore by Markono Print Media Pte Ltd

CONTENTS

LIST OF TABLES & FIGURES

FOREWORD

Even at the best of times Thai politics has not been easy to understand, and now, late in the reign of a revered and activist monarch, it is even more difficult to comprehend. Constitutions, sometimes written by the winning side that has taken power by extra-constitutional means, come and go with astonishing frequency. Since the end of the absolute monarchy in 1932 military coups have intervened so frequently (eighteen times) that regime change by force seems to be an integral part of the political process. Bloodshed often attends Thailand's political struggles. In the past four decades, the military has taken its arms into the streets several times, and national elections see a fair number of vote canvassers and journalists murdered. Little wonder that turbulence, polarization and violence describe Thai politics all too well.

The motivation for the army to cut short the electoral cycle is its self-appointed responsibility to protect the monarchy if it deems the supreme institution to be threatened. The army is jealous of its prerogatives especially with regard to promotions in the upper echelon of the officer corps. Wary of the slightest political interference, it insists on control over its own line management. Thai governments that have attempted to reform the military's relationship with the parliamentary system have been promptly dispatched, as happened in 1991 and 2006. As a result of the violent crackdown and arson attacks in Bangkok in April–May 2010, the army's reputation briefly plummeted, but this was reversed by its civic activism in offering a helping hand to communities affected by the floods in late 2011. Once again, the army proved its ability to adapt and respond to changed circumstances in a popular way.

The 1997 constitution, which was abrogated in 2006, may have been as flawed as its critics have charged, but it held promise. Crafted during the 1997 Asian financial crisis after a string of shaky coalition governments, it aimed to reform the political system, curtail money politics and establish a strong executive. In response to the conditions for "good governance" attached to the IMF loan programme that aimed to lift the country out of the financial crisis, Thai public intellectuals seized on "good governance" and translated it as *thammarat*. For its architects and many of its advocates, the concept of *thammarat* would imbue politics and government with moral righteousness, truth and law. Good governance Thai-style was supposed to discipline the Thai state and create a legitimate space for civil disobedience against it.

Alas, as events unfolded, good governance Thai-style had an authoritarian strand as well as communitarian and liberal ones. Thaksin's massive electoral victory in 2005, which led to dominance of the parliament by his Thai Rak Thai party, attracted the charge that he had created a parliamentary dictatorship. Running the country as if he were running a corporation, as he once said, did not mean he would consult widely or nourish a participatory politics. The command-and-control style of leadership that he was comfortable with did not sit well with all constituencies and powerful interests. When reporting on his activities, the Thai-language press is fond of including his rank in the police force, Police Lieutenant Colonel, as if to remind readers of his background in the security services. Although Thaksin had phenomenal electoral success, his leadership style often smacked of anti-democratic methods.

The root meaning of democracy is empowerment of people. Like democracy everywhere it has flourished, Thai democracy had a rocky start and has suffered many setbacks. If dated from 1932, Thai democracy has had a mere eighty years to evolve. In its early decades, it was handed down from above, an elite project in which the people were asked to abide by certain rules in exchange for their citizenship. This democracy-from-above was more about bureaucratic control and the legitimacy of authoritarian government than about empowerment of people. Even in the relatively liberal period following a new constitution in 1974, democracy was propagated through manuals "taught" by officials in public education programmes. The liberal winds of this period subsided long ago, and nowadays, once again, democracy has been thwarted by state institutions, powerful interests, and elite attitudes that discount the value of rural and subaltern votes.

Many upper class Thais hold rural voters in contempt, even as they cling to mythical memories of village society as a haven of tranquillity and self-reliance. Economic growth over the past generation has brought prosperity to many households, but it has also increased the inequalities. Class cleavages, the rural-urban divide, and regional disparities have given rise to new social forces that the political system in its present configuration is unable to accommodate. Yet, it is worth remembering that the mass mobilizations and street rallies that have captured international attention in the past two decades are not new. The political conflicts that escaped from the parliament as the People's Alliance for Democracy and the red shirts took their campaign into the streets from late 2005 have long featured in Thai politics.

The expert authors in this book have chosen to study the social forces and mass mobilizations unleashed by economic change against the backdrop of a familiar political system that has been dysfunctional since the 2006 coup. Mistranslated often as "constitutional monarchy", the official designation of the political system is best translated as "a democratic system headed by the king". In that literal translation lie both expectation and limitation. The fervent, pro-monarchy, ultranationalism that has gripped Thailand in recent years has pressured state institutions to remain vigilant about the kingdom's territorial integrity and sovereignty, a topic taken up by three essays on the Cambodian border dispute, the Deep South and the increase in surveillance by the security services in their pursuit of *lèse-majesté* cases.

It is striking that electoral politics has faded from view in this collection of essays. Political leadership also receives little attention, another sign of how the political system was damaged by the events of 2006. At the time of writing, Thai political development has arrived at a new normal condition described eloquently in the following pages. Who knows how long it will last?

Craig J. Reynolds
Australian National University
Canberra, July 2012

CONTRIBUTORS

Marc Askew is currently Senior Fellow in Anthropology, School of Social and Political Sciences, The University of Melbourne, Australia. He has taught and researched in Thailand for over twenty years, with a focus on urban and political culture. Since 2003 he has undertaken sustained periods of fieldwork in Thailand's south. In addition to newspaper and academic journal articles, his recent publications include *Performing Political Identity: The Democrat Party in Southern Thailand* (2008), (as editor and contributor) *Legitimacy Crisis in Thailand* (2010) and, with Sascha Helbardt, "Becoming Patani Warriors: Individuals and the Insurgent Collective in Southern Thailand", *Studies in Conflict & Terrorism* 35, no. 11 (2012).

Federico Ferrara, receiving his PhD from Harvard University, is assistant professor at the City University of Hong Kong, Department of Asian and International Studies. He previously taught at the Department of Political Science, National University of Singapore. He is the author of *Thailand Unhinged: The Death of Thai-Style Democracy* (2011) and a number of articles on comparative elections and party systems.

Michael H. Nelson is with the Southeast Asian Studies Program, Walailak University, Nakorn Si Thammarat. His research has focused on Thai politics, comparative sub-national government and decentralization, and globalization in Southeast Asia. He published *Central Authority and Local Democratization in Thailand* (1998), and co-authored (with Jürgen Rüland, Clemens Jürgenmeyer, and Patrick Ziegenhain) *Parliaments and Political Change in Asia* (2005). He has also edited the two volumes *Thailand's New Politics* (2002), and *Thai Politics: Global and Local Perspectives* (2005). His current research interests concern the development of Thailand's parliamentary system, general elections and voting behaviour, and provincial-level political structures.

Nick Nostitz, originally a photographer, has followed closely the red/yellow conflicts since late 2005 with his camera. Not until 2008 has he begun to write articles on the subject more seriously, which could be found on the website *New Mandala*. He is the author of a series of books entitled *Red vs. Yellow, Volume 1: Thailand's Crisis of Identity* (2009) and *Red vs. Yellow, Volume 2: Thailand's Political Awakening* (2011). Currently, Nostitz is working on Volume 3 of the series, dealing more profoundly with the violent conflicts on 2010 and their impact on today's political life of Thailand.

James Ockey is associate professor at the School of Social and Political Sciences at the University of Canterbury, New Zealand. His main interest is in comparative politics of Southeast Asia. His recent publications include "Individual Imaginings: The Religio-Nationalist Pilgrimages of Haji Sulong Abdulkadir al-Fatani" in *Journal of Southeast Asian Studies* (2011), "Political Parties, Factions and Corruption in Thailand", in *Politics of Modern Southeast Asia: Critical Issues in Modern Politics, Vol. III Regimes and Institutions* (2010), and "Red Democracy, Yellow Democracy: Political Conflict in Thailand", in *New Zealand International Review* (2010).

Pavin Chachavalpongpun is associate professor at the Centre for Southeast Asian Studies, Kyoto University, Japan. Previously, he had worked as a fellow at the Institute of Southeast Asian Studies (ISEAS), Singapore, and a lead researcher for Political and Strategic Affairs at ISEAS's ASEAN Studies Centre. Earning his PhD from the School of Oriental and African Studies, Pavin has written two books: *A Plastic Nation: The Curse of Thailand in Thai-Burmese Relations* (2005) and *Reinventing Thailand: Thaksin and His Foreign Policy* (2010). Pavin is also an editor of *Kyoto Review of Southeast Asia*.

David Streckfuss is an honorary fellow with the University of Wisconsin-Madison who has lived in Thailand for more than twenty years. He is interested in legal history, nationalism, and ethnic identities. His book, *Truth on Trial in Thailand: Defamation, Treason, and Lèse-majesté*, was published in 2011, and he was a contributor to the recent biography, *King Bhumibol: A Life's Work*. He also occasionally has pieces published in the *Bangkok Post* and the *Asian Wall Street Journal*.

Thongchai Winichakul is Professor of History at University of Wisconsin-Madison, and a Research Fellow at Asia Research Institute (ARI), NUS in

2010 when this conference took place. His book, *Siam Mapped* (1994) was awarded the Harry J Benda Prize from the Association for Asian Studies (USA) in 1995. He currently works on the intellectual foundation of modern Siam (1880s–1930s) and also a book on the memories of the 1976 massacre in Bangkok. He also writes in Thai on contemporary political issues.

Andrew Walker is an anthropologist in the College of Asia and the Pacific at the Australian National University. He is co-founder of the blog *New Mandala* which provides anecdote, analysis and new perspectives on Mainland Southeast Asia. His new book, *Thailand's Political Peasants*, was published in 2012.

ABBREVIATIONS

ACD	Asia-Dialogue Cooperation
ACMECS	Ayeyawady–Chao Phraya–Mekong Economic Cooperation Strategy
ASEAN	Association of Southeast Asian Nations
CDA	Constitution Drafting Assembly
CDR	Council for Democratic Reform
CEO	Chief Executive Officer
CMC	Cluster Munition Coalition
CNS	Council for National Security
CPB	Crown Property Bureau
CPMC	Civilian-Police-Military Command
DAAD	Democratic Alliance against Dictatorship
FBA	Foreign Business Act
GBC	General Border Committee
ICG	International Crisis Group
ICJ	International Court of Justice
ISOC	Internal Suppression Operations Command
NESDB	National Economic and Social Development Board
NLA	National Legislative Assembly
NPP	New Politics Party
PAD	People's Alliance for Democracy
PPP	People's Power Party
NRC	National Reconciliation Commission
PTV	People's Television
SBPAC	Southern Border Provinces Administrative Centre
SBPPPC	Southern Border Provinces Peace Promotion Command
TRT	Thai Rak Thai Party
UDD	United Front for Democracy against Dictatorship
UNESCO	United Nations Educational, Scientific and Cultural Organization

Section I

The 2006 Military Coup: Impact on the Thai Political Landscape

1

"GOOD COUP" GONE BAD
Thailand's Political Developments since Thaksin's Downfall

Pavin Chachavalpongpun

In the evening of 19 September 2006, the military staged the eighteenth coup since the abolition of absolute monarchy in 1932, overthrowing the elected government of Thaksin Shinawatra. Although Thailand adopted a democratic model of governance to replace the *ancien régime*, the military has imposingly dominated the Thai political space throughout the past eighty years. It has worked intimately with the monarchy in cultivating a particular kind of politics whereby civilian governments are kept vulnerable, or face the possibility of being toppled should they pose a menace to the power position of the traditional elite. Under these conditions, coups were therefore not uncommon, especially as a tool to undermine a strong civilian government. The military's political intervention has become part of Thai political culture. Often, there have been attempts on the part of the military to legitimize the coups as a moral instrument in the riddance of immoral civilian regimes. From 2001 to 2006, Prime Minister Thaksin Shinawatra enjoyed electoral popularity, and thus managed to firmly consolidate his grip on power. He won two landslide elections, in 2001 and 2005, becoming the only prime minister who had ever served a full four-year term in Thai history. But his intensifying political strength gravely worried the traditional elite. They perceived him as a threat to their long-held political influence. With political interests in jeopardy, and in exercising the old trick, the traditional elite removed the Thaksin regime with the bluntest of tools; a military coup. They accused Thaksin of displaying disrespect for the King and committing corruption, among other things. These accusations served to justify the unlawful coup as a necessity to punish the fraudulent government of Thaksin. A large number of middle-class Bangkok residents came out to lend their support for the coup; they were seen offering food and flowers to Thai soldiers who seized power on that ill-fated night. Tanks which rolled onto the streets were decorated with yellow ribbons — the colour that represents the Thai monarchy. A sense of jubilation was felt in the Thai capital, a rather strange sentiment in a country known as the "Land of the Free".

But as it turned out, this time, the effects of the coup were different. The coup that was meant to protect the political interests of the military and to safeguard the royal prerogatives gave birth to an anti-establishment movement whose members identify themselves in red shirts. That coup, initially staged to solidify the monarchy's position in politics, also stirred up an anti-monarchy reaction among many Thais. They became aware of the extent to which the monarchy had long been actively involved in politics, with the backing of the army, despite its confined role under the constitution. While other studies tend to concentrate on Thaksin's authoritarian behaviour and his corrupt policies as the root causes of the Thai crisis, this book, based on the above context, argues that the Thai establishment, which comprises of the monarchy, the military, the judges and their defenders, has played a large part in instigating and deepening the political conflict and that blaming Thaksin alone would be immeasurably misleading. Not just Thaksin, but the Thai monarch is an equally divisive figure. More importantly, the royal institution itself has increasingly become estranged with the ongoing democratization. In fact, it has acted as an obstacle to the country's democratic development. As political scientist Thitinan Pongsudhirak succinctly said, "In Thailand, there is more monarchy among the democrats than there is democracy among the monarchists."[1] Such a statement suggested a stark incompatibility between the royal and the democratic institutions. The military, in the meantime, has continued to take advantage from the crisis it created, and at times exploit the monarchy, in order to ensure its position in politics, with the support of the royalists. The ongoing southern crisis and the Thai conflict with Cambodia have provided the military a much-needed legitimacy for its continued domination of security policy which has been greatly independent from that of a series of Thaksin-backed governments.

But first, it is imperative to briefly discuss the nature of Thai politics over the past years. Duncan McCargo argued that the best way to understand Thai politics was to look at it through political networks. And the most influential network has been the network monarchy with King Bhumibol Adulyadej situating on top of the political structure.[2] The real driving force behind the network monarchy however, is not the King. It has been General Prem Tinsulanonda, former prime minister and now President of the Privy Council. Thus, the King is not the only component of the network monarchy; it includes various actors within the Thai establishment. Network monarchy has functioned both as a powerful interest group as well as a separate political entity outside the parliamentary system. Despite having no position within the formal political system, network monarchy has effectively controlled the fate of Thai politics because of the intimate association it has with the King and the support from the army. Network monarchy was actively in operation throughout critical periods in Thai history, ranging from the Cold War when the threat of communism was imminent to the post-Cold War era during which the diminishing role of the military in domestic and foreign policies and the expansion of the middle class began to contest the monopoly of power in the hands of the traditional elite. Thus, as Thaksin strolled to the premiership in 2001 with overwhelming confidence and an indisputable electoral triumph, he threatened to recast the old political equation long dominated by the network monarchy. The result of this was the 2006 military coup. In this book, it adopts McCargo's concept to explain the interconnection between members of the Thai establishment subsumed within this network monarchy and their need to maintain their power position even when their behaviour has severely deepened the political crisis.

Perceiving that Thaksin was scheming to construct his own network with mass support made possible by his populist policies, self-proclaimed royalists, in the name of the People's Alliance for Democracy (PAD), embarked on a plot to overthrow Thaksin in 2005 by creating a situation of ungovernability so as to invite the military to intervene in politics. The PAD employed royal symbols as part of its campaign, successfully polarizing society by cooperating with the network monarchy to attack political enemies. It erected a protective wall against Thaksin encapsulated within the notion of the King as the ultimate moral ruler of the country. Slogans propagated by the PAD like "Fight for the King" and "Loyalty to the Chakri Party" (Chakri is the name of the current dynasty) signified the network monarchy's consent to the removal of Thaksin from power by extra-constitutional means. There are at least three incidents that indicate the continued active involvement in Thai politics of the country's monarchy: the coup-makers' meeting with the King on the night of the coup — apparently to seek the royal approval of the coup; the Queen's attendance at a funeral of a yellow-shirt member, Angkhana "Nong Bo" Radappanyawut, in October 2008, and; the exclusive interview of Princess Chulabhorn with Woody Milintachinda, a talk-show host, in April 2011 in which she openly condemned the red shirts for the deepening crisis which greatly affected the health of the King. Such open intervention in politics suggested a sense of desperation among people close to the monarchy. But such practices of indiscreet political intervention went against the usual modus operandi of the network monarchy, that of operating mostly behind the scenes. And this surely was responsible for the rise of anti-monarchy sentiment and as a result the rapid decline of the royal reverence which had been carefully built up over past decades.

Instead of stepping back from politics to re-establish their authority, the network monarchy and its defenders have chosen to further permeate themselves into the political mess in response to the continued challenges from their opponents. This was particularly evident after Samak Sundaravej, a Thaksin crony, won the election in December 2007 replacing the military regime of General Surayud Chulanont. Just when the traditional elite thought that they had eliminated Thaksin and his political stooges by a military coup, they were proven wrong. The premiership of Samak tremendously irritated the royalists and the supporters of the network monarchy. They sought to discredit Samak and his successor Somchai Wongsawat, also Thaksin's brother-in-law, by creating a conflict with Cambodia over the Preah Vihear Temple, as well as using the Thai court to end their premiership. In the case of Samak, the dispute with Cambodia failed to destabilize his government. But in the end, Samak was forced to step down by the Constitutional Court which considered his appearance on the television as a celebrity chef while serving as prime minister as a case of conflict of interest. Next, to oust Somchai, the PAD seized Suvarnabhumi and Don Muang Airports in late November 2008, virtually closing down Thailand from the outside world for about a week. At the occupied airports, the PAD members held the portraits of the King and Queen while shouting, "Somchai, Get Out!". Shortly after that, Somchai had to resign at the order of the Constitutional Court on the grounds that one of the executive members of his People's Power Party (PPP) committed electoral fraud.

Meanwhile, hyper-royalism had taken root and it proliferated into other social units, including in the entertainment industry. Just three days before the deadly crackdown on the red-shirt protesters at Rachaprasong intersection, famous actor Pongpat Wachirabanchong, upon collecting his best actor accolade at the Nataraja awards on 16 May 2010, delivered his acceptance. It was perceived to be the fiercest defence of the monarchy in public and reflected the general attempt to initiate a new discourse of Thailand as an exclusive place for monarchists. He said,

> This is an award I received for playing a father role. I would like to seek your permission now to talk about our father (the King of Thailand) briefly. A father is a pillar to a house (which he meant "Thailand"). My house is very big. We have many people living together. Since I was born, this house was very beautiful and homely. For it to be like this, the ancestors of our father lost sweat and blood and sacrificed their lives to be able to build this house. Up to this point, this father is still working tirelessly to look after this house and to care for the happiness of anyone under this roof. If someone is angry at another, whoever, and then passed that anger down to our father, hate our father, insult our father, and have thoughts about chasing our father out of this house, I would have to walk up to that person and say, if you hate our father, and do not love our father anymore, you should leave, because this is our father's house, because this is our father's kingdom. I love our King. I believe that everyone here loves our King too. We are the same colour. This crown on my head I bestow for the King. Thank you.[3]

Such a discourse of the country being an exclusive place for monarchists has become popular and authoritative, being repeatedly referred to by defenders of the network monarchy to justify their actions and policies against their opponents, even when those actions and policies are incompatible with democratic principles. At the height of the campaign to amend the draconian *lèse-majesté* law by a group of young law professors — Nitirat — at Thammasat University, Army Chief General Prayuth Chanocha, a confidant of the Queen, harshly condemned the young professors and asked them to "leave Thailand" because every Thai was supposed to love the King. Prayuth also said, "Will Nitirat be tolerable if their parents were insulted by others?"[4] The social alienation of those with different political opinions and attitudes has indeed pulled the King from his subjects and intensified a sense of resentment which now represents a source of anti-monarchy sentiment in Thailand. Seven years after the coup, the debate over whether the monarchy should readjust itself for the sake of its own survival in a new climate of political openness has become more vigorous as well as divisive. Some hyper-royalists never hide their aspiration to take Thailand back to the old days under absolute monarchy, as Sondhi Limthongkul, a core PAD leader, famously said, "Let's return power to the King. His Majesty is a Dhammaraja King. This is the only way we can prevent Thailand from falling into becoming a failed state."[5] But in another reality in rural areas, most residents who lent their support to both Thaksin and the red shirts explicitly detest the political involvement of the network monarchy. Many removed the portraits of the King and Queen which once adorned the walls in many households.[6] It seems that monarchists are the ones who breed anti-monarchists.

Unfortunately, there are no signs of the network monarchy's willingness to negotiate with democracy. To counter growing critical views of the monarchy, powerful royalists have exploited the *lèse-majesté* law as a direct weapon. *Lèse-majesté*, or the crime of injury to royalty, is defined by Article 112 of the Thai Criminal Code, which states that defamatory, insulting or threatening comments about the King, Queen, Heir-Apparent and Regent are punishable by three to fifteen years in prison. Charges against Thais are usually grave and the investigation and prosecution process is by nature opaque. With King Bhumibol's frail health signalling the autumn of his reign, the royalists have launched an ever more aggressive campaign against critics of the monarchy. Prosecution has become more pervasive, virtually against anyone. The manipulation of the *lèse-majesté* law has severely impacted the human rights cause. In retrospect, cases of *lèse-majesté* have multiplied since the last coup. In 2005, 33 charges came before the Court of First Instance, which later handed down 18 decisions in these cases. By 2007, the number of charges increased almost fourfold to 126. This number jumped to 164 in 2009, and then tripled to 478 cases in 2010. The most dramatic increases occurred under the Democrat Party-led government of Abhisit Vejjajiva, which adopted a royalist line strongly backed by the military. Under the current Yingluck Shinawatra government, the cases going to the court have gone up slightly, but they may have been initiated during the last government. The number of recent high-profile cases underscores the misuse of *lèse-majesté* law in the name of defending the monarchy and the display of loyalty of the government for the royal institution. The arrest of a sixty-two-year-old Thai-Chinese man, Amphon Tangnoppakul, also known as Akong (or grandfather) who was sentenced to twenty years in prison, shocked Thai society. He allegedly sent four text messages insulting the Queen. Amphon always maintained his innocence. He died in prison of terminal cancer on 8 May 2012 after several requests for bail were turned down before being sentenced by the Thai court.

Joe Gordon, or Lerpong Wichaikhammat, a Thai-born American, was jailed for two-and-a-half years in Thailand after posting online excerpts from a banned book, *The King Never Smiles* authored by Paul Handley, while living in the United States. The U.S. government criticized the *lèse-majesté* law, but was taken aback by the response of Thai hyper-royalists, who called for the expulsion of the U.S. Ambassador to Bangkok. More staggeringly, Abhinya Sawatvarakorn, nicknamed Kantoop, or "Joss Stick", a nineteen-year-old student at Thammasat University, could be charged with a *lèse-majesté* violation over comments she made on Facebook years ago. Kantoop was accused of committing *lèse-majesté* in April 2009 while she was still in high school. She would be one of the youngest ever to be charged under the law, and has already undergone a catalog of social punishments. For example, she was reportedly refused admission into Silpakorn University, where some professors painted her as an anti-monarchist. She also had a shoe thrown at her by a student at the esteemed Thammasat University, where she currently studies, and has been forced to change her name to avoid being recognized — and possibly attacked. Also, the case against Chiranuch Premchaiporn, director of the on-line newspaper Prachatai.com on the grounds that she allowed Web-board comments with *lèse-majesté* content, is still pending. Chiranuch was among three female journalists who won the 2011 Courage in Journalism Award given by the International Women's Media Foundation. At the same time as the arrests have continued, the glorification of King Bhumibol has been religiously carried out by royalists as a way of legitimizing the overpowering royal influence on politics and demoralizing the anti-monarchy elements.

The 2006 coup that was staged amid joy among many Bangkok residents — some even calling it a "good coup" — has turned out to be disastrous to the position of key members of the network monarchy, including the King and the military. More devastatingly, it has caused a tremendous impact on the country's democratization process which has to be slowed down owing to the continuing face-offs between the pro-monarchy and pro-democracy groups as well as between those who support the shift of the political order and those who prefer to conserve the status quo. The coup has revealed the ugly reality in Thai politics in which the long domination of power in the hands of the traditional elite using illegitimate tools to eliminate successive elected governments has refused to subside. As members of society have become more conscious about the unfair distribution of power, they have begun to fight back to defend their rights and more importantly the spirit of democracy. As the monarchy has defended its political territory, the military has worked indefatigably in tandem to maintain its footprint in politics. The consistent interference in policy by the current army chief is testimony of the typical attitude that prevails among top royalist generals; they have sought to exploit the monarchy in order to sustain their own political advantages. This explains why the military always claims that it is in its duty to protect the monarchy just as it is protecting Thailand's national security. Yet, the direct political involvement of the military has greatly alleviated the professionalism and the corporateness of the army. But military-monarchy relations can sometime be volatile. This is because the network monarchy possesses its own particular clients in the army. Accordingly, it has caused disintegration within the military. The case of the "watermelon soldiers" — green only on the uniform but red at heart — indicates serious disunity of the army. The last coup partly brought about this split; some of the soldiers came from the poorest regions in Thailand where the elite's control of power did not benefit them and their families. My own conversations with a number of military officers confirmed that not all soldiers are fond of the monarchy.[7]

So, what did the 2006 coup tell us? It tells us that the crux of the Thai crisis is far more severe and much wider in scope than we previously thought. The network monarchy is surely not the victim in the protracted political conflict. Rather, it represents both a root cause and a factor that has made the political situation more fragile. The coup has instigated more unjust uses of the *lèse-majesté* law, and in the process, led to more political prisoners. This unswervingly worsened the human rights condition in the kingdom. With the looming end of the current reign, more questions are being asked, including those about the future of Thailand without the supposedly benevolent King, the competency and legitimacy of his successor, the survival of the monarchy as an institution, and the future role of the military. It might be seen as a harrowing close of the Bhumibol reign — for the King to witness the waning royal institution — the institution that he had constructed throughout his lifetime by working personally with a series of despotic regimes and corrupt Western governments. The coup has also shredded the military into pieces, turning generals into desperate royalists who continue to live on the monarchical institution and political crises, as seen in the case of the conflict in the restive south, in order to survive. Moreover, the coup produced a unique phenomenon in Thailand, the so-called "colour-coded politics". The emergence of the yellow- and red-shirt movements has certainly complicated the Thai crisis. It unveiled another aspect of Thai politics in which non-state actors came to influence and manipulate the political process on a larger scale. The PAD and its yellow-shirt supporters transformed themselves into hyper-royalists and extreme nationalists. Domestically, they expressed their nostalgia for the absolute monarchy. Externally, they demanded a war with Cambodia over the Preah Vihear conflict not only to discredit the Thaksin faction (because of Thaksin's cosy ties with the Cambodian leadership) but also to prove that they were more Thai than their nemeses. On the other hand, the coming to the scene of the red shirts is not unexpected. As emphasized earlier, not all members of the red-shirt movement are supporters of Thaksin. Many of them are simply pro-democracy. But the fact that there remains an inexorable association between the red shirts and Thaksin and the outstanding allegation against them over the arson attack (against the Central World Department Store in Bangkok supposedly in response to the state's brutal crackdown in May 2010) has become their inevitable stigma. Briefly put, the red shirts have been held hostage by Thaksin and the conflict he has with the traditional elite. This pro-Thaksin image has been lumped together with another image of being an anti-monarchy movement. Thus, there is a limit on what the red shirts can do without being accused by their opponents and misjudged by the society.

Thailand has suffered from a legitimacy crisis which was first ignited by the 2006 military coup. I am proud of this collection of essays by leading experts in Thai studies who contributed their views on the effects of the coup on Thailand's political landscape. This volume is a product of an international conference titled "Five Years after the Military Coup: Thailand's Political Developments since Thaksin's Downfall", organized by Singapore's Institute of Southeast Asian Studies (ISEAS), on 19 September 2011, marking exactly the fifth commemoration of the

2006 coup. I am grateful for the unfailing support for this project of Ambassador K. Kesavapany, then director of ISEAS. The conference was well received by the Singaporean public, international media, as well as participants from different countries mostly in the Southeast Asian region. The primary aim of the conference was to discuss the lessons learnt, and not learnt, from the coup, to explore Thai political developments, the role of the key players — the military, the monarchy, the yellow shirts, the red shirts — and to investigate issues that generated the legitimacy crises in Thailand, including the southern conflict and Thai-Cambodian relations. The conference highlighted the dramatic state of Thai politics which was both ironic and brutal. Undoubtedly, Thailand has produced the longest-running soap opera in the whole of Southeast Asia. The Thai crisis has offered all sorts of incredible, and somewhat disturbing, tales, ranging from deadly crackdowns, plotted assassinations, war with a neighbour, irredentism and separatism, rainbow politics, foreign leaders evacuating via a hotel's roof, international airport occupations, House of Government intrusions, two prime ministers being removed through judicial coups, a former prime minister becoming a fugitive, more people being arrested for *lèse-majesté*, thousands of websites being closed down, an army chief acting as if he was a prime minister — and then, issues related to the monarchy — the anxiety over the succession, the anti-monarchy movement, the political domination of the Privy Council, the self-politicization of the monarchy to the many dark secrets within the royal family.

This book is divided into four sections: first, lessons learnt from the coup; second, defending the old political consensus: the military and monarchy; third, new political discourse and the emergence of the yellows and reds, and; fourth, crises of legitimacy — south of Thailand and Thai-Cambodian conflict. Apart from this introductory chapter, Federico Ferrara summarized key political developments in the post-coup period. In his opinion, the seven years since the coup have exposed the fatal flaws of Thailand's "formal democracy with the King above the constitution". The coup set in motion a series of events that plunged the country into unprecedented political instability and prolonged civil strife. The actions necessary for the removal of Thaksin and his proxies gave rise to a severe crisis of legitimacy marked by a hitherto unseen measure of resentment for the network monarchy that would have been unthinkable just seven years ago. Indeed, the political crisis that has gripped Thailand for the last seven years could be said to be the expression of the cleavage that has variously defined political struggles since the days of the absolute monarchy — the conflict over whether sovereignty, or "constituent power", rests with the people or the King. Chapters by James Ockey, Thongchai Winichakul and David Streckfuss deal with the role of the network monarchy in the Thai crisis. Ockey argues that the coup of 2006 was a part of the military yearning to consolidate the position of the network monarchy. But it also unveiled the struggle within the military to survive under a new political climate brought about by the Thaksin regime. When the military leadership is itself so politicized, the struggle within the military also becomes political. This struggle has partly driven violence within society in the post-coup period.

As for the role of the monarchy, the 2006 coup and its subsequent political crisis is the consequence of many deep holes into which Thailand has dug itself for many years before the coup. Instead of the institutionalization of a political system with less interference by the monarchy, royalist democracy has hindered such institutionalization of democracy and headed in the opposite direction, once again, for the purpose of defending the network monarchy. Royal democracy is an oxymoron that is unstable and essentially anti-democratic. Thongchai emphasized that the many achievements of King Bhumibol will not be transferable to the next monarch. And this will surely represent a major challenge for the network monarchy. Streckfuss's chapter looks into the increasing cases of *lèse-majesté*. He discusses extensively the extent to which the rule of law in Thailand has been shattered within an entrenched culture of impunity; and in this, the *lèse-majesté* law has thrived as never before. As a surviving remnant of absolute monarchy and a living legacy of military dictatorship, *lèse-majesté* is an expression of "the state of the exception" under which the rule of law and democratic accountability has no role. In the current political context, *lèse-majesté* is a perfect, yet brutal, tool in undermining opponents of the network monarchy.

In the third section, two major themes are examined: the colour-coded politics and the emergence of the new middle-income peasant class. These are quintessential factors which either help empower or weaken the network monarchy. Michael Nelson argues that it is too soon to write an "obituary" for the yellow-shirt PAD. The group's strength may have declined in the past year; but the Thai crisis has been portrayed as a crisis triggered by Thaksin. The fact that Thaksin is very much pulling the strings behind the scenes may allow the yellow shirts to return. The societal infrastructure and its political culture out of which the PAD arose in interaction with their perception of the "Thaksin regime" are still there. They might well produce another round of political opposition — with or without the PAD — if their relationship with the Yingluck government seriously deteriorates. On the contrary, as Nick Nostitz reiterated, the red shirts, born out of the 2006 coup, have grown in strength. Now that Yingluck is in power, the government may help elevate the role and status of the reds to become a more important stakeholder in politics. But doubts have also grown whether the Yingluck government is really interested in promoting that role of the red shirts if this would further jeopardize its relations with the Thai establishment. Andrew Walker focuses mainly on the question of whether peasant politics in Thailand is civil. He then states that the answer is straightforward: no. Peasant politics in Thailand is not civil if it is judged by many of the established standards which define contemporary civil society, especially its institutionalization and relative autonomy from the state. Rather, Walker prefers to describe Thailand's modern peasantry as being involved in an active political society in which the primary desire is to draw state power into local circuits of exchange by means of diverse, informal and pragmatic relationships. The 2006 coup attempted to negate the influence of this non-civil rural politics. It was a failed attempt because it was impossible to reverse the powerful economic, social and political developments that have been unfolding over the past fifty years. Such developments have long been denied by the Thai establishment which continues to portray the economy, society and politics as somewhat underdeveloped. In order to understand Thailand's tumultuous politics over the past seven years, it is necessary to understand the politics of Thailand's new peasantry.

The last two chapters discuss issues that led to the legitimacy crises in Thailand. In Marc Askew's chapter, despite the adoption of a more politically correct rhetoric by the Surayud administration, the post-coup years saw more stringent security arrangements and increases in military force in the region, a spike in violence from 2006 to 2007, and a transfer of blame for continuing violence from Thaksin to the military and post-coup civilian governments. In the context of the rising civil conflict between anti- and pro-Thaksin forces during 2008–10, Askew elaborates that one simplistic explanation for persisting southern violence and lack of decisive progress has been based on the thesis of "government distraction". A popular argument to explain the persistence of the violence over this period of profound national conflict has been to claim that governments have been "distracted" from attending fully to the southern crisis. This would appear to be fallacious and too simplistic. Certainly, the increase of the military's presence in the deep south after the 2006 coup does not necessarily mean the increase of legitimacy on the part of the Thai security forces. In fact, it has led to a question of legitimacy of the military regarding its inability to solve the conflict in the three southern provinces. As for the last chapter, I as the author write that in the context of Thai-Cambodian relations, the military's domination of foreign policy is not a new phenomenon. Clearly, the Thai army exploited the Cambodian border conflict to preserve its hegemony in Thai politics: it indicated an increasingly agonized state of Thai domestic politics from which the military refused to withdraw itself. Numerous clashes provided much-needed opportunity for the Thai military and its defenders within the network monarchy to take full control of foreign policy vis-à-vis Cambodia.

In this final paragraph, I would like to express my sincere thanks to all the contributors for their unfailing commitment. My thanks also go, once again, to Ambassador K. Kesavapany, then ISEAS Director, current director Ambassador Tan Chin Tiong, and the ISEAS Publications Unit for making this manuscript now a publication that will make a contribution to Thai studies, as well as to esteemed moderators (during the conference in September 2011) — Charnvit Kasetsiri, Michael Montesano and the late Pattana Kitiarsa. I wish to thank Nick Potts and Amy V.R. Lugg for editing the first draft of this manuscript. I am appreciative of the generous support from the Centre for Southeast Asian Studies, at Kyoto University, which has allowed me to complete this book following my move from Singapore's ISEAS to Kyoto. Finally, I take all the responsibility for any mistakes in this publication.

Notes

1. Thitinan Pongsudhirak, "Shifting Political Tides Portend Turmoil", *Bangkok Post*, 6 January 2012.
2. See Duncan McCargo, "Network Monarchy and Legitimacy Crises in Thailand", *Pacific Review* 18, no. 4 (December 2005): 499–519.
3. Watch his acceptance speech at <http://www.youtube.com/watch?v=_CA0QY9Vdy4>.
4. "Prayuth Yontham Nitirat Thondairuemai Thookkhondhawha Por Mae Pee

Yat Pee Nong" [Prayuth Asked Nitirat if They will be Okay if their Fathers, Mothers, Relatives, Brothers and Sisters were Insulted], *Kloomsue Prachachon* [*Group of People's Media*], 6 February 2012 <http://www.google.co.jp/url?sa= t&rct=j&q=&esrc=s&source=web&cd=18&ved=0CHUQFjAHOAo&url=http% 3A%2F%2Fwww.tfn5.info%2Fboard%2Findex.php%3Ftopic%3D34663.0&ei=n RStT-eZDKHPmAWu-qm7DA&usg=AFQjCNGiOuOyyyeWpHOKSyvjauwgs-EK5w> (accessed 11 May 2012).

5. Mai Koraja, "Sam Khon Sam Khom Khuen Praraja Amnaj" [Three Wise Men: Return Power to the King], *Manager Online*, 22 May 2010 <http://www. manager.co.th/Daily/ViewNews.aspx?NewsID=9530000070492> (accessed 11 May 2012).

6. My own reservation during my fieldtrip to the Northeast region of Thailand, June 2012.

7. Interview with a number of unnamed military officers, Nakhon Nayok, Thailand, December 2011.

References

Mai Koraja. "Sam Khon Sam Khom Khuen Praraja Amnaj" [Three Wise Men: Return Power to the King]. *Manager Online*, 22 May 2010. <http://www. manager.co.th/Daily/ViewNews.aspx?NewsID=9530000070492> (accessed 11 May 2012).

McCargo, Duncan. "Network Monarchy and Legitimacy Crises in Thailand". *Pacific Review* 18, no. 4 (December 2005): 499–519.

Pavin Chachavalpongpun. "If You Don't Think the King Deserves to be Feted, Don't Say So in Thailand". *Japan Times*, 3 May 2012.

Thitinan Pongsudhirak. "Shifting Political Tides Portend Turmoil". *Bangkok Post*, 6 January 2012.

2

UNFINISHED BUSINESS
The Contagion of Conflict
over a Century of Thai Political
Development

Federico Ferrara

INTRODUCTION

Just over an hour after announcing on television that the military had seized power on the evening of 19 September 2006, Army Commander-in-Chief Sonthi Boonyaratglin was photographed on his knees at Chitralada Palace, seeking the blessing of King Bhumibol Adulyadej. By then, the generals' every move had been painstakingly choreographed to impress upon the public the idea that the coup had been staged in the King's name. Yellow ribbons and flowers adorned tanks, uniforms, and assault rifles. Giant portraits of the King and Queen served as the background for major announcements. Royal Commands were read before ornate shrines to their Majesties. The junta's studiously verbose name, the "Council for Democratic Reform under the King as Head of State", was officially changed more than ten days after the coup, but not before making sure that the people had heard the message loud and clear. Thailand, to be sure, had seen "royalist coups" before, but none as awash in royal symbolism. Then again, the military had never removed a prime minister as popular as Thaksin Shinawatra. As life quickly returned to normal, it was evident that only the appearance of royal sanction could have muted public opposition to the coup, or staved off the possibility that the deposed prime minister might put up any resistance.

The argument made by royalists in support of the legitimacy of the illegal seizure of power springs from a conception of the nation fundamentally at odds with that common to modern constitutional monarchies. Nowhere in particular was the fight against Thaksin defined in more memorable terms than in a speech delivered by General Prem Tinsulanonda — a former prime minister (1980–88) and current president of the Privy Council — at the Chulachomklao Royal Military Academy two months before the coup. Prem famously likened the military to a "horse", and hastened to add that governments, unlike the horse's actual "owner", come and go like mere "jockeys". As if to dispel any doubt, Prem reminded his audience: "You belong to the nation and His Majesty the King."[1] In Prem's formulation, sovereignty rests with the King, as well as an idea of "the nation" quite distinct from "the electorate" that had selected the "jockey" — twice, and by crushing margins. To the "jockey", and to the majority of the electorate, the "horse" must pay no heed, if the "owner" thus commands. Elections, after all, weigh each person's vote equally, thereby distorting the will of a nation whose very essence, whose main claim to exceptionalism and uniqueness, is a hierarchy of merit, status, and power atop which sits His Majesty the King.

Each of the eighteen constitutions the country has lived under since 1932 has made variously contrived references to the idea of popular sovereignty. In Thailand, however, the monarchy's authority exists quite independently of what the constitution happens to provide.[2] Noted royalist Pramuan Ruchanaseri argued as much in a best-selling book published before the coup, where he argued — correctly, as a matter of empirical observation — that "the constitution is not above the King in any way […] the status of the King does not come under the constitution".[3] Indeed, whereas the stated intent of the revolution that overthrew the absolute monarchy on 24 June 1932 had been to place the King "under the Constitution", the result of the *ancien régime*'s partial restoration in the late 1950s was not only to elevate the King above the constitution, but to confer upon those claiming the mantle of the monarchy's protection the authority to undo, through extra-constitutional means, the results of processes conducted in accordance with the constitution. In addition, whereas the "promoters" of the 1932 revolution had vested "supreme power" in "the people", and guaranteed each member of the national community the enjoyment of equal rights, over the past five decades "the people" have been most commonly understood to enjoy their political rights not as full members of the national community — per T.H. Marshall's classic definition of citizenship, "equal with respect to the rights and duties with which the status is endowed"[4] — but as "subjects" or "children" to whom rights are delegated by a higher sovereign power in measures commensurate with their social status.

The seven years since the coup have exposed the fatal flaws of a system of government — sometimes known as "Thai-style democracy" — founded on the denial of popular sovereignty, the repudiation of majority rule, and the advocacy of hierarchical over egalitarian understandings of "the nation". Not only did the coup set in motion a series of events that plunged the country into seemingly intractable political instability and prolonged civil strife. The actions necessary to the removal of Thaksin and his proxies have given rise to a severe crisis of legitimacy marked by a hitherto unseen measure of resentment for traditional institutions, complete with expressions of public dissent that would have been unthinkable just a few years ago. Ironically, it was thanks to royalists like General Prem that the fight became, at least implicitly, about the unfinished business of the 1932 revolution, returning to the foreground a century-old cleavage over alternative conceptions of nationhood that royalists had struggled to suppress over the past several decades. To borrow Prem's imagery, the "horse" effortlessly dismounted the "jockey", as Thaksin proved powerless to either prevent the coup or challenge its legality *ex post facto*. Unlike most of his predecessors, however, Thaksin failed to roll over and die, and struck back by leveraging his supporters' ambition to be recognized as equal citizens, to be acknowledged as "the nation's rightful owners", to turn much of the audience in the stands against those lounging in the owners' box. The riot in the stands eventually transcended demands for the jockey's reinstatement, as the crowd in the cheap seats went so far as to claim ownership of the horse — indeed, the entire racetrack.

Accounts of the political crisis triggered by the 2006 coup are dominated by narratives that alternatively describe the ongoing conflict as a fight between democracy and dictatorship, the juxtaposition of two visions of "democracy", or a choice between different forms of authoritarianism.[5] This chapter sketches out an integrated approach, one that emphasizes the multi-dimensional nature of the conflict, examining the historical process by which the conflict between "royalist" and "popular" strands of nationalism, as well as the prevailing alignments on both sides of the fight that have developed over the past century.

During this time, debates over alternative conceptions of sovereignty and citizenship have spilled over from a highly exclusive circle in the court of King Chulalongkorn (1868–1910) and a few urban intellectuals to increasingly broad and varied constituencies. The gradual "contagion" of conflict[6] was made possible by socio-economic change, which made various groups excluded from the original debate increasingly likely to join the fight, often in response to appeals to their desire for political or economic empowerment. What accounts for the uneven, non-linear nature of the contagion is that these constituencies had to be awakened, galvanized, and mobilized by one side of the other before they could themselves turn into "active participants". Given the multiplicity of cleavages in Thai society, and the internal diversity of all major constituencies, different groups did not always enter the fray as blocks, nor were their allegiances necessarily fixed. At different times, moreover, different sides were variously successful in their attempt to define the terms of the fight in more favourable terms, and to either "socialize" or "privatize" the conflict by expanding or restricting the number of active participants as it best suited their ambitions. For decades, royalists managed largely to remove the foundational fight over different ways of conceiving the Thai nation from the public arena, limiting the debate to whether the Thai people should enjoy more or less rights within the existing framework. The conflict's explosive re-emergence after the 2006 coup was driven by a combination of reasons of both a structural and contingent nature.

While acknowledging the salience of an intra-elite struggle in which naked power is a far stronger motive, for royalists and Thaksinites alike, than the ideals in which both sides generally couch their appeals for popular support, this essay takes Thailand's political crisis to be more than a simple "conflict between different elements of the Thai elite, who have mobilized rival patronage-based networks of supporters".[7] Like most political fights, private and public motives are far from mutually exclusive, as movements or causes most often amalgamate a multiplicity of motivations. As Lipset and Rokkan put it, the fact that on some level political cleavages are "nothing more than direct struggles among competing elites for central power" in no way precludes the possibility that "they might also reflect deeper differences in conceptions of nationhood, over domestic priorities, and over external strategies".[8] After all, as Schattschneider pointed out, each sizeable increase in the number of participants must be "about something", beyond simple elite interest, as "newcomers have sympathies and antipathies that make it possible to involve them".[9] In other words, while stipulating Thaksin's self-interest and authoritarian proclivities, this essay recognizes that the reasons for his removal were others, and interprets the backlash against the repeated subversion of the electoral process as visceral and principled, not just "patronage-based".

FAIT (IN) ACCOMPLI

Thailand's (then Siam) absolute monarchy came to an end with a pre-dawn coup d'état staged on 24 June 1932 by a group of mostly young, foreign-educated military officers and civil servants. Upon seizing power, the promoters mapped out a ten-year transition to full representative democracy. The 1932 coup, however, had been less about "democracy" than it had been about "constitutionalism",[10] the ambition to limit royal authority and place the King under a constitution. The six principles spelled out in the "First Announcement of the People's Party" included "freedom" (*seriphap*) and "individual autonomy" (*khwam pen itsara*) as well as the provision of "equal rights" (*sitthi samoe phak kan*), such that "the royal class does not have more rights than the people" (*mai chai phuak jao mi sitthi ying kwa ratsadon*). Crucially, the promoters declared: "the country belongs to the people, not to the King, as he has fraudulently claimed" (*prathet rao ni pen khong ratsadon mai chai khong kasat tam ti khao lok luang*). The temporary constitution promulgated within days of the coup vested "supreme power" in "the people" (Article 1) and specified that the King, together with the legislature, the executive, and the courts, would "exercise power on behalf of the people" (Article 2).

The conflict between alternative conceptions of nationhood had emerged in the early period of "National Revolution"[11] set in motion in Siam by the sweeping bureaucratic reforms enacted by King Chulalongkorn in the late nineteenth century. The debate over limitations to monarchical power is customarily traced back to 1885, when eleven members of the Siamese royal elite in Europe, led by Prince Prisdang, wrote to the King to suggest that the threats to Siam's independence could be defused by reforming the country's political institutions in an attempt to make Siam appear more civilized, just, and thereby more worthy of its independence as "a country owned by its people" (*mueang khong ratsadon*).[12] The significance of the appeal lies in the identification of the "nation", and the national interest, not with the preservation or expansion of royal authority, but rather with ideas of constitutionalism, popular sovereignty, equality under the law, social justice, and the respect of civil and political rights.[13] This marked the beginning of a debate, by all accounts still ongoing, for the soul of an incipient nation-state — the earliest bifurcation of a nascent nationalist ideology into more "popular" and "royalist" strands.

By the time the possibility of transitioning to constitutional monarchy was put to the King, the conflict had already been spreading through the ranks of the expanding bureaucracy, especially the new "bureaucratic bourgeoisie" recruited from among commoners who had received a Western or "Western-style" education. Their concerns were private and public, their motivations both instrumental and ideological. On the one hand, the exposure that these officials had received to Western liberal ideas — articulated in Siam by a growing number of books and periodicals published by foreigners as well as local mavericks such as Thianwan (T.W.S. Wannapho) and K.S.R. Kulap Kritsananon — provided ideological content to their discontent over arbitrary royal power and privilege, fostering a growing identification with an idea of "the nation" dissociated from the person of the King.[14] The destabilizing potential of these grievances was only amplified by cultural change among educated commoners, many of whom, as Charnvit[15] puts it, now held "views that questioned the old system's traditional beliefs of *chat kamnoet* (birthright) or *bun-barami* (merit and charismatic authority)". On the other hand, the coexistence of a salaried, modern bureaucracy with a system of patronage designed to preserve the privilege of the old nobility stifled opportunities for career advancement for those whose lineage lagged behind their educational achievement. These officials soon came to pose a serious insurrectionary threat to the regime. In 1912, junior military officers dominated the group of conspirators involved in a thwarted rebellion. The promoters of the 1932 Revolution were drawn from the same "bureaucratic bourgeoisie", whose discontent had only deepened during the profligate reign of King Vajiravudh (1910–25) and the dithering rule of King Prajadhipok (1925–35).

Having only recently succeeded in wresting power away from more conservative princes within his own court, King Chulalongkorn had initially responded to the request put to him in 1885 by arguing that limitations to his authority would have actually compromised the implementation of reforms necessary to protect Siam's independence. In the ensuing years, however, the King moved from reasoning exclusively on grounds of expediency to sketching out a more ideological defence of his personal power aimed at cementing the loyalty of the bureaucracy. In a series of speeches, Chulalongkorn elaborated on his opposition to liberal reforms by emphasizing the differences between European and Siamese conceptions of kingship, thereby asserting the incompatibility of "Western political institutions" with local traditions.[16] His son and successor, King Vajiravudh, fleshed out the defence of royal absolutism more fully, providing more content to an "official nationalism"[17] that stressed the identification of "nation" and "king". Among other things, Vajiravudh's vision of Thai society entailed a by now familiar distinction between *phu yai*, "big men", tasked with the responsibility to rule, and *phu noi*, "little people", whose service to the nation was to be measured in terms of their submission and compliance.[18]

While King Vajiravudh's ideas proved quite influential, in the long run, to the development of Thailand's state-sanctioned nationalist ideology, in the short-to-medium term they had little effect on shoring up the loyalty of the country's officialdom. In fact, Vajiravudh's reign was distinguished by the further contagion of conflict. This took place as a result of the diffusion of ideas of progress and individual equality as well as contingent factors, particularly the growing dissatisfaction with the self-indulgence of prominent members of the royal family. By the end of the Sixth Reign, the boom of popular newspapers catering to a bourgeois and upper-middle class readership led to the popularization of verbal and visual content that routinely portrayed royals and noblemen as a corrupt, debauched, parasitic elite.[19] When Vajiravudh was succeeded by his brother, Prajadhipok, in 1925, threats to the monarchy's continued existence figured prominently in the new King's willingness to consider promulgating a constitution. Ultimately, the failure to enact one reflected unresolved doubts in Prajadhipok's court over whether the delegation in some of his powers, instead of defusing the potential for the monarchy to succumb to a rebellion, could have in fact accelerated the conflict's contagion by raising further questions about the King's strength, competence, and commitment.

Not unlike Western Europe, where the competition between liberals and conservatives had dominated the political scene throughout the nineteenth century, the main political cleavage in the aftermath of Siam's 1932 coup placed liberal-radical proponents of popular sovereignty, constitutionalism, and gradual democratic reforms against conservative-royalist elements intent on restoring royal authority. In Western Europe, however, liberals and conservatives largely fought out their differences in the electoral arena, such that by the time universal (male) suffrage was granted in the aftermath of World War I, conservative parties almost everywhere had given up on advocating for a return to the *ancien régime*.[20] Things turned out quite differently in Siam, where royalists ultimately managed partially to roll back the 1932 revolution.

Whereas the nineteenth-century Western European struggle for civil and political rights intersected with the Industrial Revolution, which ushered in the era of mass politics, Siam's National Revolution took place well before the emergence of any working class movement, or for that matter any form of mass mobilization. The coup staged on 24 June 1932 was broadly welcomed by Bangkok's small upper-middle class, but much of the rest of the country reacted with indifference to the events in the capital. While the absence of popular involvement may have helped ensure the smoothness of the operation, the masses' indifference and backwardness discouraged the promoters from attempting to broaden their fight against the old royalist establishment.[21] The timing of the coup, moreover, aided the royalists' initial counter-revolutionary effort, which exploited the spectre of communism to undermine the public's trust in the new government and drive a wedge between more conservative/ authoritarian and progressive/radical factions of the People's Party.[22] The counter-revolution failed to dislodge the promoters, or restore any of the King's old prerogatives in the short term. But the resulting instability, and the authoritarian measures taken in response, created an opening for the subsequent reassertion of the monarchy's status and power.

Months before his abdication, King Prajadhipok issued a stern warning to the government of Phya Phahon Phonphayuhasena. "There are those who still believe in the absolute monarchy because of its long history", he wrote, "but nobody will stand for the absolute rule of the *khana*."[23] In fact, the People's Party never came close to exercising "absolute rule". But the King had nonetheless correctly identified the regime's Achilles' heel in its conferral upon those in power the role of sole protectors of the constitution and only true representatives of "the people". Still in office but shaken by the failed counter-revolution and less than confident in their own pull with the electorate, the promoters opted to manage the conflict instead of broadening it, and chose to control civil society rather than take a chance on its mobilization. In the years comprised between Prajadhipok's abdication in 1935 and the Japanese invasion in 1941, Field Marshal Phibun Songkhram presided over the country's slide into military dictatorship, as well as the development of a virulent form of nationalism that emphasized social conformity and "state identity" over "constitutionalism".[24]

The People's Party's departure from ideals of constitutionalism and democracy aggravated the internal rifts and deficit of legitimacy that royalists successfully exploited to regain their ascendancy in the 1940s and 1950s. Thailand's reversal into authoritarianism gave rise to new, unstable alignments. Royalists joined forces with civilian promoter Pridi Banomyong to oust Phibun in 1944, but the anti-Phibun, anti-Japanese movement Seri Thai fractured in the aftermath of World War II. Pridi's supporters and royalists organized in different political parties, which fought bitterly for political power. Outnumbered in parliament, royalists took the opportunity to accuse Pridi of King Ananda Mahidol's still unresolved death in 1946, then helped the "Coup Group" nominally led by Phibun seize power in 1947, leading to the promulgation of a new constitution complete with a set of expanded royal prerogatives. The "Coup Group" later stripped away most of the powers the monarchy had recently regained in the "Radio Coup" staged in late November 1951, introducing an amended version of the 1932 constitution.

Throughout his second stint as prime minister from 1948 to 1957, Phibun struggled to overcome two major threats to his power. The first was posed by royalists (including princes, senior civil servants, and Democrat Party politicians) who had benefited from their post-war reorganization as well as the campaign carried out between 1946 and 1951 to bolster the popularity of the young King Bhumibol. The second was posed by the other members of his own governing triumvirate, Field Marshal Sarit Thanarat and Police Director-General Phao Sriyanond. To counter these threats, in the mid-1950s Phibun made a strategic decision to "socialize" his power struggles, liberalizing political speech and legalizing the formation of political parties in an attempt to establish an independent base of power. Phibun's gambit, however, failed to produce the intended effects. On the one hand, the long-serving Prime Minister had underestimated the educated public's dissatisfaction with the government, as well as Sarit's growing popularity with public opinion leaders, students, and members of parliament.[25] On the other hand, Phao's diminished credibility deprived Phibun of an effective ally with whom to counter Sarit's rise. With the support of the palace, Sarit exploited the discontent with Phibun's fraudulent victory in the February 1957 elections by further undermining the government in parliament as well as with public opinion in Bangkok. Sarit ultimately seized power in September 1957, forcing Phibun and Phao to leave the country for good.

THAI-STYLE "DEMOCRACY"

Field Marshal Sarit quickly tired of the more liberal climate fostered by Phibun's reforms, which had helped propel his rise, and within a year implemented measures designed to prevent any further contagion of conflict. Deeply dissatisfied over the fact that "there still existed a parliament, political parties, a free press system that could criticize the government", and "labour unions that could go on strike whenever they were unhappy with their employers",[26] Sarit staged another coup on 20 October 1958. Political rights like freedom of speech and association were rescinded under Sarit's iron-fisted dictatorship, while the recurrent election of legislative representatives was scrapped altogether. Civil liberties like those that guaranteed criminal defendants a measure of due process were supplanted by illiberal provisions like Article 17 of the 1959 constitution, which allowed the prime minister to order the execution without trial of anyone he deemed a threat to national security. The egalitarian ideals formerly championed by some People's Party officials were superseded by the government's unabashed attempt to perpetuate existing inequalities. The country's most powerful domestic capitalists were nurtured by the state and protected from competition. While entire sectors of Thailand's economy were sold off to foreign and domestic oligopolists in exchange for billions — paid on the condition that the generals make life difficult for smaller, local competitors and repress any labour movement that might seek better pay and work conditions for millions of Thai workers[27] — the military government now insisted that the rural population should remain forever content to eke out a simple existence upcountry, the refusal of many to embrace their station in life portending the "deterioration" of Thai society.[28]

The elevation of the King above the constitution, and the nationalist ideology that substituted "hierarchical" for "egalitarian" understandings of "the nation", are legacies of the dictatorship of Field Marshal Sarit Thanarat. Having suffered considerable erosion in the first twenty-five years since the 1932 revolution, it was during this time that the principles spelled out in the "First Announcement of the People's Party" came to be subverted entirely. Most importantly, perhaps, as Sarit sought to establish the absolute rule of his own *khana*, he saw in the restoration of the monarchy's mystique, prestige, and power a source of legitimacy more potent than the pretence of constitutionalism and elections — one that would afford him, and some of his successors, the opportunity to dress up harsh dictatorial measures in a benign, paternalistic attire. With the enthusiastic backing of the American government, Sarit went about resacralizing the monarchy and deifying the young King. Meanwhile, his ideologues — men like Luang Wichit Wathakan and Kukrit Pramoj — repurposed the "official nationalism" originally crafted under the absolute monarchy and conceived a model of governance ("Thai-Style Democracy") that could be described as a form of "Platonic guardianship with Theravada characteristics".[29] At first only figuratively, the multi-talented "philosopher-king" sat atop a hierarchy of supposedly "natural" inequalities of wealth, power, and status — legitimized, in place of Plato's "noble lie", by Buddhist superstitions of karma, merit, and charismatic authority. The King's military "auxiliaries" were put in charge of running the country and effectively elevated above the law. What was demanded of "the people", once again equated with "children", not "citizens", was mere reverence and obedience.

The palace-military alliance forged under Sarit reconciled two institutions that had been mostly at loggerheads over the previous quarter century. At least initially, the new alliance did not find it especially difficult to consolidate power and manage conflict. Part of this had to do with the weakness of the opposition, deprived of many of its leading personalities through arrest, exile, and murder. By then, moreover, most of the country's population was not appreciably more involved or politicized than it had been at the time of the 1932 coup. In fact, while much of the country had experienced significant economic change since the signing of the Bowring Treaty in 1855, the increased economic insecurity produced by the commercialization of the agricultural sector and explosive population growth had not been accompanied by the emergence of a strong political consciousness, perhaps primarily because economic change had failed to trigger much in the way of actual development or modernization.[30] As noted, one of the reasons why the end of the absolute monarchy did not settle the issues of popular sovereignty and citizenship is that Thailand's National Revolution did not intersect, as it did in Western Europe, with the "massification" of politics set in motion by the Industrial Revolution. An economic transformation of comparable import did take place in Thailand beginning in the late 1950s and 1960s. Once again, however, the decoupling of Thailand's National and Industrial Revolutions, and the occurrence of the latter at a time when the power of the monarchy and the military was deeply entrenched, accounts for the contradictory effects exerted by the subsequent political awakening of new constituencies.

In retrospect, it is somewhat ironic that the power and prestige of the monarchy reached its zenith as Thailand entered the era of mass politics — just as more and more people entered the system and demanded "democracy", some of the main ideas in which the People's Party had grounded its seizure of power in 1932 were effectively muted. Part of the reason is that by the time Thailand experienced mass participation in the early 1970s, the palace had benefited from a fifteen-year head start in promoting its image through modern means of mass communication. For most mainstream political actors, the mere appearance of a "universally revered" monarch was strong enough incentive to frame political demands in a manner that did not challenge the palace or its extra-constitutional prerogatives. Failing that, Thailand's *lèse-majesté* law effectively restricted the range of political contestation by punishing, harshly, the few inclined to test the limits of the institution's popularity. By the 1970s, the 1930s-era fight to place the King under the constitution had morphed into mere demands for a constitution, while the struggle for democracy waged by increasingly sizeable constituencies between 1973 and 1992 did not result in the mainstreaming of more radical critiques of the monarchy's role and constitutional status. Most of the movements and organizations that came onto the scene beginning in the 1970s saw it fit not to challenge the role of the King as sovereign, but rather chose to frame appeals for civil rights and democracy in royal symbolism. Whenever the palace felt that its image was threatened by events on the streets, moreover, King Bhumibol's public interventions served to "privatize", manage, or steer the course of conflict in less menacing directions. The King's interventions in 1973 and 1992, in turn, further elevated the status of the monarchy, providing some cover for the royalist establishment's support of the mob violence in the mid-1970s as well as military coups in 1976 and 1991.

The palace's success, however, was also in part a function of its willingness to adapt, learn from its mistakes, and eventually allow the country to democratize insofar as the process did not encroach on its prerogatives. While the 1973 protests definitively brought the era of outright military dictatorship to a close, the palace played a major role in the effort to contain the rapid contagion of conflict that characterized the ill-fated period of "real" democracy comprised between 1973 and 1976. The nationalist hysteria and fears of communist takeover hyped by royalists during that time intensified the social hostilities that had emerged as a result of the economic transformation the country had recently experienced, securing the support of the disaffected, the insecure petty bourgeoisie, and traditionalist elites who felt threatened by the mobilization of students, workers, and peasants for the drastic measures taken in 1976.[31] After a brief period of extreme repression following the 1976 massacre at Thammasat University, the royalist establishment remained determined to preserve its dominance over Thailand's political system. The premiership of General Prem Tinsulanonda, however, was also marked by the development of functioning representative institutions, and increased emphasis on electoral participation and competition. Thailand was allowed to transition from a version of "pseudo-democracy" to "electoral democracy"[32] upon Prem's retirement in 1988, and again after the state violence of "Black May" in 1992.

The ouster of General Suchinda Kraprayoon in 1992 resulted from a botched attempt made by military and the palace to restore Thailand to the days of "Premocracy", to turn the clock back to a time when an unelected military man could run the country, legitimized by the existence of a functioning parliament but not meaningfully encumbered by any changes elections might bring to its composition. The failure of Suchinda's restoration gave way to a new adaptation. The military was effectively sidelined, the Thai people's wish to elect their own governments begrudgingly granted. Still, as a result of the King's intervention, the palace preserved much of its influence and standing. The network of "good men" Prem had built in most state institutions was leveraged throughout the 1990s to shape national policy, as well as manipulate or actively undermine elected governments notorious for their weakness, fragmentation, and corruption.[33] At the same time, the efforts made to discredit elected politicians and prevent the aggregation of political forces capable of challenging its extra-constitutional authority softened the public's confidence in democratic institutions, weakened elected governments, and favoured a style of politics founded on patronage and corruption. This allowed the palace to conserve the moral high ground, protect the legitimacy of its routine interferences, and maintain its role as the "ultimate arbiter of political decisions in times of crisis".[34]

As it turns out, the military and the palace were quite successful in their efforts to stem the tide of the new "popular nationalism" that Benedict Anderson had credited in the mid-1970s for the acceleration in the "secular demystification of Thai politics" — an observation accompanied by the prediction that "direct and open attacks on the monarchy loom imminently".[35] At the same time, while the debate over the monarchy's role was effectively "organized out of politics" as King Bhumibol reached the apogee of his power and popularity, the prevalence of ideas of popular sovereignty around the world made it almost inevitable that the question would be revisited at some point. It was a constellation of factors of both a structural and contingent character, and the confluence of historical processes of both a long- and short-term nature, that accounts for the rapid and explosive re-emergence of the unresolved fight over alternative conceptions of nationhood in the wake of the 2006 coup.

Perhaps the most profound reason for the system's inherent instability — beyond the diffusion of new technologies that make it more difficult to control the flow of information without resorting to conspicuous repressive measures — was the ongoing nature of the transformations Thailand's social structure has undergone since the late 1950s. The socioeconomic transformations in question transcended the numerical growth of the urban middle class, which had formed the basis for mass demonstrations in 1973 and 1992. At the top level, continued economic growth spurred the rise of new business elites far less connected with, and hence less invested in, the palace's networks of power in the military and the civil service.[36] This class did not exhibit any particular ideological aversion to the old order. Nonetheless, the capital available to this new business elite created conditions for the emergence of networks of power alternative to those commanded by the palace.[37] Possibly more momentous was the transformation that had taken place at the bottom of Thailand's social hierarchy, undermining its foundations. On the one hand, development and modernization transformed rural livelihoods, giving rise to a more educated, more worldly, more consumption-minded mass of "middle income peasants"[38] — an increasingly large percentage no longer involved in agriculture at all — less likely to exhibit the "inarticulate acquiescence" and "indifference to national politics" that were once identified as essential to the stability of the old order.[39] On the other hand, the persistence of extreme levels of inequality[40] rendered this vast segment of the population decidedly more receptive to a discourse of empowerment. Though neither political consciousness nor economic grievances automatically translate into political mobilization, the "struggles for the right to have rights"[41] waged by groups representing farmers and workers in the 1980s and 1990s offered glimpses of the potential held by the mobilization of the provincial masses, now more inclined to view themselves as "citizens" than "children".

The royalist camp made things worse in at least two ways. First, royalists continued to speak in terms that evidenced their failure to accept the implications of the country's socioeconomic transformation. The King's own rejection of "progress", his pleas to "walk backwards into a *khlong*", his equation of the desire for self-advancement with "greed", and eventually his "new theory" centred on economic "sufficiency"[42] offered a vision of the future at variance with the aspirations of upward mobility increasingly harboured by much of the population. Given the King's fatherly image and well-intentioned presentation, that generated no opposition in and of itself, but placed the palace at a risk of fading rapidly into irrelevance, should someone ever come along with an alternative, potentially more empowering vision. Second, in the absence of an imminent, majoritarian threat to the status quo, "royal liberals"[43] close to the palace felt comfortable enough to spearhead the effort that culminated in the promulgation of a constitution, in 1997, that was not only more "liberal" than its forerunners, but also more protective of the stability of the executive against the vagaries of Thailand's fragmented legislature. This, in turn, constituted something of a unilateral disarmament on the part of the royalist establishment. Should a government ever develop the electoral popularity and ambition to challenge the "network monarchy", the new rules of the game limited the ability of unelected institutions to deter, undermine, or eject it through means other than brute military force.

THE EARTH AND THE SKY

There is considerable merit to the argument that Thaksin had sought to establish an "elected dictatorship" during his five years in office. While Thaksin proved singularly capable of reducing the fragmentation of Thailand's political system, that is, the unprecedented concentration of powers in the hands of an elected civilian leader also allowed his administration to pursue policies that eroded several aspects of the country's electoral democracy. The rule of law was weakened by corruption and, especially, by the state violence unleashed in the context of the "War on Drugs" in 2003 and the response to the southern insurgency beginning in 2004. Government accountability was undermined by the attempts made to vanquish independent state agencies. Freedom of the press declined sharply as a result of legal measures taken against critics of the administration as well as informal pressures placed on the print and broadcast media to provide favourable coverage. After the 2005 elections, where Thaksin's Thai Rak Thai party took three quarters of the lower house seats, Thailand seemed well on its way to developing a form of "democracy" with a much stronger "delegative"[44] than "liberal" flavour.

Far more determinative of his eventual removal is the fact that Thaksin's electoral popularity placed him in a position to mount a historic assault on the reserve domains of unelected institutions such as the palace, the military, and the bureaucracy.[45] Unlike most of his predecessors, Thaksin had ambition and hubris in large enough supplies to actually take them on, if only to maximize his own standing and power. Aside from the troubling possibility that Thaksin might be in office in the event of royal succession, what appears to have most threatened the royalist establishment was the prospect that the popularity Thaksin enjoyed in the provinces might have begun to rival, in the space of a few years, the cult of personality the state had built for King. Such fears were rendered particularly acute by the recognition that Thaksin's vision of "capitalist revolution" were not only proving far more in step with the provincial electorate's aspirations, but also that the ambitions of upward mobility even the poorest Thais were now encouraged to embrace threatened to scramble the social hierarchies upon which "Thai-Style Democracy" had once been founded.[46] Indeed, whereas critics often justify their distaste for Thaksin on the grounds that his support is bought and paid for, Thaksin's popularity with provincial voters and the urban working class has never been primarily about the material benefits he was able to provide. By and large, Thaksin remains popular with these constituencies for reasons of a more psychological or emotional nature — in Thaksin, these voters found a national leader who did not tell them it was their patriotic duty to accept their station in life, but encouraged them to imagine a different future for themselves and their families. In essence that is what made Thaksin dangerous, the capacity he had demonstrated to involve in his largely private struggle for political power a whole new mass of "active participants".[47]

Given Thaksin's strength and staying power, the only card his enemies had left to play was military force, backed by the monarchy's prestige. The task, however, was far more complex than simply removing a prime minister. Indeed, the complexity of the task, and the determination with which Thaksin fought back, transformed the attempt to stamp out his influence into something of a bottomless pit, down which royalists ended up flushing much of the political capital accumulated over decades. While the junta set the groundwork for Thaksin's prosecution, confiscated his assets, dissolved Thai Rak Thai, and dismantled the constitutional provisions that protected his dominance, all that did not prevent the Thaksin-backed People's Power Party from winning a large plurality in the 2007 elections. Nor did the desperate measures launched in 2008 by the People's Alliance for Democracy (PAD), the military, and the judiciary accomplish much more than further compromise the stability of the country and the legitimacy of the royalist establishment. Abhisit Vejjajiva was made prime minister in December 2008, on the strength of a motley legislative coalition patched together with the assistance of the military and the palace, if only to suffer a crushing defeat at the hands of Thaksin's youngest sister Yingluck in the 2011 elections. The intervening thirty months ranked among the most tumultuous in King Bhumibol's sixty-eight-year reign.

In response to a series of protests staged against his administration in late 2005, Thaksin boasted that he was immune to the recurrence of a historical pattern that had seen governments elected by the countryside removed by (or with the support of) Bangkok, as he had the backing of both. Based on the results of the 2005 elections, that assessment was largely accurate. Thai Rak Thai dominated not only the North and Northeast of the country, but also the more prosperous Central region as well as much of Bangkok. That had changed by the time of the coup, to which Bangkok residents exhibited little overt opposition, and especially in the 2007 elections, when the People's Power Party lost considerable ground to the Democrats in the capital. In the intervening time, it seems, royalists had successfully dented Thaksin's support among urban middle class voters. Taking a page out of the playbook from the mid-1970s, the PAD had successfully aroused the insecurities and fears of urban middle class voters, warning that Thaksin's populism would come largely at the expense of their economic well being and social status.[48] The PAD, moreover, was joined by military generals, royalist academics, Democrat Party politicians, and parts of the national press in appealing to the sense of moral superiority of middle-class voters, playing up crude cultural stereotypes such as the notion that the provincial electorate's ignorance, credulousness, and moral corruption required the derogation of majority rule, and the placement of the majority of the population under the tutelage of the usual set of "good men". According to royalist rationalizations of the coup, the problem was not just Thaksin, but those who elected him.

This rhetorical strategy may have earned the urban middle class' support for, or acquiescence to, the 2006 coup and the removal of two People's Power Party governments in 2008. But the invalidation of clear electoral choices, and its justification in terms so offensive, elitist, and occasionally dehumanizing, had the effect of radicalizing a sizeable portion of Thaksin's supporters among provincial voters and the urban working class, making many of them receptive to arguments denouncing the fundamental injustice of Thailand's traditional hierarchies of status and power. This, in turn, facilitated Thaksin's effort to "socialize" the conflict by linking the grievances of his constituents to his own, as well as by fostering among his diverse supporters something of a common identity as second-class citizens. The host of illiberal measures taken by the royalist establishment to obliterate Thaksin's influence, moreover, not only marked a radical departure from "royal liberalism", exposing a decidedly less benevolent side to the royalist hierarchical worldview, but also revealed the hypocrisy of much of the criticism that had been levelled against Thaksin's own administration.

This is the basis of resentment and frustration that accounts for the rapid growth of the red-shirt movement in the months following Abhisit's rise to prime minister. There can be little doubt that the establishment of the National United Front for Democracy against Dictatorship (UDD) reflected an attempt by Thaksin and his allies to "socialize" their struggle for power by involving constituencies that could tip the balance in their favour. Thaksin's call for a "people's revolution" during the red shirts' failed uprising in April 2009 contrasted starkly with his "pluto-populist" governing philosophy — as one commentator put it early in his first term, "the plutocrats make big money, and the people don't make big trouble".[49] For "the people" to now make "big trouble", however, Thaksin had to make the fight about more than himself. And, on this count, recent Thai history offered a rich repertoire of issues and symbols that fit the circumstances and mood of his supporters. It was thus that the 1930s-era fight for equal citizenship and popular sovereignty was unearthed, albeit now married to a political vision that emphasizes "electoralism" over "constitutionalism". On the one hand, UDD leaders spoke to the issue of citizenship by appealing to their supporters' desire to be recognized as fully "Thai" — to be considered full members of the community, irrespective of wealth, status, or karmic stock, and to be treated as equal under the law without "double standards". On the other hand, by training its sights on the *ammat* — the King's mandarins and praetorian guards — for the first time in decades the UDD combined a campaign for "democracy" with the demand that no unelected institution, no matter how close its affiliation with the palace, should have the authority to overturn the electorate's decisions, or interfere with the activities of an elected government.

As the red shirts stepped up their activities and mobilization, it is not altogether surprising, given the issues at stake, that the fight was increasingly presented through imagery hearkening back to the days of the absolute monarchy. Dismissed by pundits as anachronistic, the adoption of the word *phrai* as an identifier served to both redefine the nature of the fight and bring into sharper focus just how radical a challenge the red shirts had grown to present, by 2010, to Thailand's entrenched structure of power. Up until 1905, the designation *phrai* referred to the lowest commoners in Siam's feudal hierarchy (*sakdina*) — freemen subject to corvée in the service of the King, or individual landlords. The embracement of their identity as modern-day *phrai* reflected not only the red shirts' newfound sense of pride in their status as commoners, but perhaps most ominously their rejection of an entire social order founded upon supposedly "natural" hierarchies of status and merit. Taking pride in low social status, in particular, highlighted the fact that many among them no longer accepted the myth that high status means "goodness", and "goodness" legitimizes privileged access to political power.

Thaksin and the red shirts have been frequently accused of harbouring ambitions to overthrow the monarchy. Far greater damage to the monarchy, however, has been done by the continued exploitation of the need to "protect the institution" to justify the series of ineffectual anti-democratic actions supposed "royalists" have carried out since the coup. The conspicuous use of royal symbolism may have helped the generals outmanoeuvre Thaksin on the night of 19 September 2006. But Thaksin's comeback forced his enemies to fall back on the need to protect the monarchy so often, and to justify measures so distasteful, as to not only diminish the power of the argument, but also effectively devalue the institution itself. The airport occupations, the censorship of the Internet, the arrests for *lèse-majesté*, the recourse to emergency powers, and even the killings of some eighty red-shirt protesters in April–May 2010 were all justified on the basis of defending the King from a tenebrous conspiracy. While Thaksin, as most red-shirt leaders, have continued to publicly profess their loyalty, the royalist establishment's constant misuse of the monarchy's supposed endangerment invited a measure of scrutiny, by the international media and ordinary citizens, which compromised the palace's inviolateness and carefully managed image. The heavy crackdown on freedom of expression launched as a result has only attracted greater scrutiny in turn. In these circumstances, further attempts by professed royalists to use the monarchy as justification for the suspension of electoral democracy threaten irreparably to compromise the institution's future viability.

RUNNING ON EMPTY

On 24 June 2012, Thailand marked the eighty-year anniversary of the end of the absolute monarchy. As it has been the case for over five decades, no event was organized by the state on a date that had once served as National Day, between 1939 and 1960. In the time since, royalists have done what they could to rewrite history and attribute the country's shift towards constitutionalism and democracy to benevolent Chakri monarchs, claiming among other things that the transition from absolutism took place thanks to, or at any rate in accordance with the wishes of, King Prajadhipok. Still, Thailand's royalist establishment has little reason to commemorate, much less celebrate, an event that temporarily saw the monarchy stripped of most of its power, property, and prestige. When Field Marshal Sarit decreed that National Day be observed not on 24 June, but on the current King's birthday on 5 December, the act symbolized the triumph of royalist forces over the personalities and ideas that had powered the 1932 revolution.

This time the anniversary did not come and go unnoticed, for in 2012 the small commemorations generally organized on 24 June were replaced by a large demonstration staged by at least 35,000 red shirts who gathered at the Democracy Monument in Bangkok. The red shirts, however, were not there to celebrate. They were there to denounce the fact that, eighty years on, Thailand remains no real democracy, and to reaffirm their commitment to finish the job. From the rally stage, UDD leader Nattawut Saikua told supporters that the red shirts' struggle is nothing new, tracing its roots all the way back to the failed rebellion of 1912, and indeed to the proposals contained in the letter that Prince Prisdang and others sent to King Chulalongkorn in 1885. Nattawut delivered the speech in a red t-shirt emblazoned with the word *phrai*, another symbol the UDD has drawn from that era to refer to the people's unfinished struggle for full and equal citizenship. The event underscored the fact that the royalist triumph is not only under threat, in the most explicit terms the point could be made without incurring a charge for *lèse-majesté*, but appears closer to unravelling than at any point since the days of Sarit.

While Thailand's process of political development has experienced bloody and traumatic disruptions several times over in the past five decades, there appears to be an emerging consensus among scholars and observers that the events since the military coup of 19 September 2006 harbour something of the end of an era. Indeed, it is increasingly commonplace for journalistic and scholarly accounts to describe the special significance of these events through metaphors that conjure up images of death, cataclysm, and dramatic breaks with the past — to cite but a few, the "death of Thai-Style Democracy",[50] the "death of Thainess",[51] a "moment of truth",[52] and "walls crumbling down".[53] Each of these accounts emphasizes different aspects of the crisis, but three dimensions are regularly identified as defining the *fin-de-siècle* nature of Thailand's current political context. The first is the awakening of constituencies that had not been especially active participants in previous political fights. The second is the possibly fatal decline in the legitimacy accorded by much of the population to the extra-constitutional role played by institutions whose power has ebbed and flowed over the past eight decades, but which had previously always found a way to recover from periodic reversals of fortunes. The third is the increased questioning of an official ideology that emphasizes "unity in hierarchy" — as reflected in the concepts of "Thainess" and "Thai-Style Democracy".

The significance of these developments notwithstanding, one cannot fail to note that the workings of Thailand's political system exhibit, in many respects, very little change. Perhaps most obviously, the royalist establishment retains much of its power to undermine and, potentially, remove elected governments, whose range of action continues to be limited by the extra-constitutional authority of unelected institutions. Indeed, at the root of this dissonance is the fact that the 2006 coup, and the events since, are less significant in terms of changes they already have wrought on Thailand's politics and government than for the new possibilities these transformations have opened up moving forward, or perhaps better yet the developmental trajectories they have likely foreclosed. More than its actual power, what the royalist establishment appears to have now lost is the authority that once allowed unelected institutions to impose their will without the sustained application of physical coercion. The recent recourse to bullets and emergency rule, as well as the hundreds of arrests for *lèse-majesté*, are in this sense symptomatic of the diminished effectiveness of their myths, their ideology, and their moral authority. At the same time, if the repressive measures introduced in recent years have enjoyed a modicum of support in key segments of the population, especially among southerners and portions of Bangkok's (upper-) middle class, that support is itself threatened by the succession of the eighty-six-year-old King. After King Bhumibol, there is little chance that large or significant enough constituencies will accept "protecting the monarchy" as the justification for more coups, the periodic suspension of their civil and political rights, or the draconian measures that currently strangle freedom of expression.

For a variety of reasons, that itself will not suffice to bring about a "real" democracy. On the one hand, whether or not the excuse of "protecting the monarchy" is still available, the military will remain a threat to the stability of the country and its democratic prospects for some time to come. On the other hand, if ultimately allowed to take place, the reassertion of Thaksin's electoral dominance might simply amount to the revival of his illiberal brand of plebiscitarian or delegative democracy, possibly in a form imposing checks on his powers even more casual than in Thai Rak Thai's heyday. Either way, the events that took place since the 2006 coup speak rather clearly to the failure of the royalist project of unity in hierarchy and cultural conformity. As hard as royalists might try to restore its viability, the moribund state-sanctioned ideology responsible for denying the majority of the population's inclusion as full and equal members of the national community will not survive the Ninth Reign. Should its supporters fail to make peace with reality, cease standing in the way of the country's democratization, and agree to take part in a process of genuine reform, the monarchy's own future could soon be in the balance.

Notes

1. See *The Nation*, 15 July 2006.
2. For an account of how the drafters of the 1997 constitution managed the ambiguity, see Michael K. Connors, "Article of Faith: The Failure of Royal Liberalism in Thailand", *Journal of Contemporary Asia* 38 (2008): 143–65, pp. 150–51.
3. Cited in Pasuk Phongpaichit and Chris Baker, *Thaksin* (Chiang Mai: Silkworm Books, 2009), pp. 255–56.
4. T.H. Marshall, ed., *Class, Citizenship and Social Development* (New York: Doubleday, 1964 [1949]), p. 84.
5. For a rich sampling, see Michael J. Montesano, Pavin Chachavalpongpun and Aekapol Chongvilaivan, eds., *Bangkok, May 2010: Perspectives on a Divided Thailand* (Singapore: Institute of Southeast Asian Studies, 2012). Thongchai demolishes a fourth narrative of Thailand's political crisis, which describes the 2006 coup as a coup *for* democracy. See Thongchai Winichakul, "Toppling Democracy", *Journal of Contemporary Asia* 38 (2008): 11–37.
6. In a classic book, E.E. Schattschneider argued that political conflicts are as "contagious" as street fights, such that a particular conflict originating from a dispute limited to a small, exclusive group of "active participants", both the nature and the outcome of the fight change dramatically as a larger "audience" joins in. Schattschneider examines strategies deployed by political actors seeking to "socialize" or "privatize" conflict, singling out the capacity to define alternatives, to shape the definition of what conflict is about, "the supreme instrument of power". See E.E. Schattschneider, *The Semisovereign People: A Realist's View of Democracy in America* (Boston: Wadsworth, 1988 [1960]).
7. Duncan McCargo, "Thailand's Twin Fires", *Survival* 52 (2010): 5–12, p. 9.
8. See Seymour Martin Lipset and Stein Rokkan, "Cleavage Structures, Party

Systems, and Voter Alignments: An Introduction", in *Party Systems and Voter Alignments: Cross-National Perspectives*, edited by Lipset and Rokkan (New York: Free Press, 1967), p. 10.

9. Schattschneider, *The Semisovereign People*, p. 4.

10. For greater insight into this distinction, see Jon Elster, "Introduction", in *Constitutionalism and Democracy*, edited by Jon Elster and Rune Slagstad (New York: Cambridge University Press, 1993).

11. National Revolutions entail the "growth of national bureaucracies", the "widening of the scope of governmental activities", as well as an effort by the state to foster the emergence of a single national identity through cultural, linguistic, and sometimes religious standardization. Among other things, the process tends to generate oppositions between different groups of "nation-builders" over the organization of the state, particularly over issues of popular sovereignty, rights, secularism, constitutionalism, and democracy. See Lipset and Rokkan, "Cleavage Structures, Party Systems, and Voter Alignments", p. 13. For an earlier application to Siam/Thailand, see James Ockey, "Variations on a Theme: Societal Cleavages and Party Orientations through Multiple Transitions in Thailand", *Party Politics* 11 (2005): 728–47.

12. See Prisdang et al., "*Chao nai lae kha ratchakan krapbangkhomthun khwam hen chatkan kan plian plaeng rabiab ratchakan paendin Ro.So. 103*" [The Presentation of Opinions on Governmental Reforms Submitted to the King by the Royal Princes and the King's Servants in 1885], in *Ekkasan kan mueang kan pokkhrong thai Pho. So. 2417–2477* [Thai Political and Administrative Documents, B.E. 2417–2477], edited by Chai-anan Samudavanija and Khattiya Kansut (Bangkok: Sathaban sayam sueksa samakhom sangkhomsat haeng prathet thai, 1989).

13. See Eiji Murashima, "The Origin of Official State Ideology in Thailand", *Journal of Southeast Asian Studies* 19 (1988): 80–96, p. 84.

14. See Kullada Kesboonchoo Mead, *The Rise and Decline of Thai Absolutism* (New York: Routledge/Curzon, 2004), pp. 154–78.

15. Charnvit Kasetsiri, *2475 kan pattiwat Sayam* [The 1932 Revolution in Siam] (Bangkok: The Foundation for the Promotion of Social Sciences and Humanities Textbook Project, 2000), p. 34.

16. See Murashima, "The Origins of Official State Ideology in Thailand", pp. 84–89.

17. The distinction between "popular" and "official nationalism" was introduced by Benedict Anderson. Nationalism of the "popular" or "authentic" variety emerges from below and conceives of the nation, however exploitative or unequal its social structure, as a "deep, horizontal comradeship" of equal citizens. "Official nationalism", by contrast, is defined as an "anticipatory strategy adopted by dominant groups which are threatened with marginalization or exclusion from an emerging nationally-imagined community", typically designed to

defeat challenges to dynastic rule presented by the "fraternizing" qualities of nationalism. See Benedict Anderson, *Imagined Communities: Reflections on the Origin and Spread of Nationalism* (London: Verso, 1991 [1983]), pp. 15 and 101.

18. Scot Barmé, *Luang Wichit Wathakan and the Creation of a Thai Identity* (Singapore: Institute of Southeast Asian Studies, 1993), p. 31.

19. Scot Barmé, *Woman, Man, Bangkok: Love, Sex, and Popular Culture in Thailand* (London: Rowman & Littlefield Publishers, 2002), Ch. 4.

20. Daniele Caramani, *The Nationalization of Politics: The Formation of National Electorates and Party Systems in Western Europe* (New York: Cambridge University Press, 2004), pp. 199–204.

21. The fact that the country's tiny industrial/commercial bourgeoisie was dominated by ethnic Chinese, who also accounted for at least half of Bangkok's small urban working class, served to further caution the promoters against the prospect of mobilizing these constituencies.

22. Nattapoll Chaiching, "The Monarchy and the Royalist Movement in Modern Thai Politics, 1932–1957", in *Saying the Unsayable: Monarchy and Democracy in Thailand*, edited by Søren Ivarsson and Lotte Isager (Copenhagen: NIAS Press, 2010).

23. These words appear in a Royal Note transmitted to the government in December 1934. See *Thalaeng kan rueang phrabat somdet phra poramintharamaha Prajadhipok phra pokklao chao yu hua song sala ratchasombat* [Official Report on the Abdication of King Prajadhipok] (Bangkok: Rong phim prajant, 1935), p. 105.

24. Chai-anan Samudavanija, "State-Identity Creation, State-Building and Civil Society, 1939–1981", in *National Identity and Its Defenders: Thailand Today*, edited by Craig J. Reynolds (Chiang Mai: Silkworm Books, 2002), p. 58.

25. Thak Chaloemtiarana, *Thailand: The Politics of Despotic Paternalism* (Chiang Mai: Silkworm Books, 1979), p. 73.

26. Ibid., p. 95.

27. Suehiro Akira, *Capital Accumulation in Thailand, 1855–1985* (Chiang Mai: Silkworm Books, 1996), pp. 179–80.

28. Thak, *Thailand: The Politics of Despotic Paternalism*, pp. 105–106 and 122.

29. The concept of "guardianship" is contrasted with "democracy" in Robert A. Dahl, *Democracy and Its Critics* (New Haven: Yale University Press, 1991), pp. 52–64.

30. For an argument about the failure of economic change to bring about development between 1850 and 1950, see James C. Ingram, *Economic Change in Thailand 1850–1970* (Stanford: Stanford University Press, 1971), pp. 216–17. Part of the reason is that the expansion in economic activity had largely followed an exploitative, quasi-colonial model founded on the extraction of wealth from the countryside and its reinvestment in Bangkok. See Chatthip Nartsupha,

The Thai Village Economy in the Past (Chiang Mai: Silkworm Books, 1999), pp. 51–59.

31. See Benedict Anderson, "Withdrawal Symptoms: Social and Cultural Aspects of the October 6 Coup", *Bulletin of Concerned Asian Scholars* 9 (1977), p. 24.

32. Larry Diamond, "Is the Third Wave Over?", *Journal of Democracy* 7 (1996): 20–37, p. 25.

33. Duncan McCargo, "Network Monarchy and Legitimacy Crises in Thailand", *Pacific Review* 18 (2005): 507–15.

34. Ibid., p. 501.

35. Anderson, "Withdrawal Symptoms", p. 24.

36. See Anek Laothamatas, *Business Associations and the new Political Economy of Thailand: From Bureaucratic Polity to Liberal Corporatism* (Boulder: Westview Press, 1992).

37. For how this new network subsequently coalesced around Thaksin Shinawatra, see Duncan McCargo and Ukrist Pathmanand, *The Thaksinization of Thailand* (Copenhagen: NIAS Press, 2005), Ch. 6.

38. See Andrew Walker, "Thailand's Farmers Have Stood Up", *Wall Street Journal*, 19 May 2010.

39. See David Wilson, *Politics in Thailand* (Ithaca: Cornell University Press, 1962), pp. 57–58.

40. For a concise explanation of why Thailand's growth required extreme levels of inequality, see Michael J. Montesano, "Four Thai Pathologies, Late 2009", in *Legitimacy Crisis in Thailand*, edited by Marc Askew, pp. 273–302 (Chiang Mai: Silkworm Books, 2010), p. 279.

41. See Somchai Phatharathananunth, *Civil Society and Democratization: Social Movements in Northeast* Thailand (Copenhagen: NIAS Press, 2006). Also see Bruce D. Missingham, *The Assembly of the Poor in Thailand: From Local Struggles to National Protest Movement* (Chiang Mai: Silkworm Books, 2004).

42. See Andrew Walker, "Royal Sufficiency and Elite Misrepresentation of Rural Livelihoods", in *Saying the Unsayable: Monarchy and Democracy in Thailand*, edited by Søren Ivarsson and Lotte Isager (Copenhagen: NIAS Press, 2010).

43. See Connors, "Article of Faith".

44. Guillermo O'Donnell, "Delegative Democracy", *Journal of Democracy* 5 (1994): 55–69, p. 59.

45. See Thitinan Pongsudhirak, "Thailand Since the Coup", *Journal of Democracy* 19 (2008): 140–53.

46. For a more detailed discussion, see Kevin Hewison and Kengkij Kitirianglarp, "'Thai-Style Democracy': The Royalist Struggle for Thailand's Politics", in *Saying the Unsayable*, edited by Ivarsson and Isager, pp. 179–202, pp. 194–96.

47. The irony is that Thaksin himself may not have initially realized the historical import of what he was doing. After all, while his policies may have been designed in part to earn the support provincial voters and the urban poor, the largest beneficiaries had been large corporations, particularly those in his own network (see McCargo and Ukrist, *The Thaksinization of Thailand*, p. 218). By the end of his first term, however, Thaksin had clearly realized the potential trump card he held, and sought to rebrand himself as something of a plebeian tribune (see Pasuk and Baker, *Thaksin*, pp. 232–33).
48. Pasuk and Baker, *Thaksin*, pp. 264–66.
49. See Chang Noi, "Understanding Thaksin's Pluto-Populism", *The Nation*, 18 February 2002.
50. See Federico Ferrara, *Thailand Unhinged: The Death of Thai-Style Democracy* (Singapore: Equinox, 2011).
51. See David Streckfuss, *Truth on Trial in Thailand: Defamation, Treason, and Lèse-Majesté* (London: Routledge, 2012).
52. See Andrew MacGregor Marshall, "Thailand's Moment of Truth: A Secret History of Twenty-First Century Siam", <zenjournalist.com>, 2011.
53. Michael K. Connors, "When the Walls Come Crumbling Down: The Monarchy and Thai-Style Democracy", *Journal of Contemporary Asia* 41 (2011): 657–73.

References

Akira, Suehiro. *Capital Accumulation in Thailand, 1855–1985*. Chiang Mai: Silkworm Books, 1996.

Anderson, Benedict. "Withdrawal Symptoms: Social and Cultural Aspects of the October 6 Coup". *Bulletin of Concerned Asian Scholars* 9 (1977): 13–30.

———. *Imagined Communities: Reflections on the Origin and Spread of Nationalism*. London: Verso, 1991 [1983].

Anek Laothamatas. *Business Associations and the New Political Economy of Thailand: From Bureaucratic Polity to Liberal Corporatism*. Boulder, CO: Westview Press, 1992.

Barmé, Scot. *Woman, Man, Bangkok: Love, Sex, and Popular Culture in Thailand*. London: Rowman & Littlefield Publishers, 2002.

———. *Luang Wichit Wathakan and the Creation of a Thai Identity*. Singapore: Institute of Southeast Asian Studies, 1993.

Caramani, Daniele. *The Nationalization of Politics: The Formation of National Electorates and Party Systems in Western Europe*. New York: Cambridge University Press, 2004.

Chai-anan Samudavanija. "State-Identity Creation, State-Building and Civil Society, 1939-1981". In *National Identity and Its Defenders: Thailand Today*, edited by Craig J. Reynolds. Chiang Mai: Silkworm Books, 2002.

Chang Noi. "Understanding Thaksin's Pluto-Populism". *The Nation*, 18 February 2002.

Charnvit Kasetsiri. *2475 kan pattiwat Sayam* [The 1932 Revolution in Siam]. Bangkok: The Foundation for the Promotion of Social Sciences and Humanities Textbook Project, 2000.

Chatthip Nartsupha. *The Thai Village Economy in the Past*. Chiang Mai: Silkworm Books, 1999.

Connors, Michael K. "Article of Faith: The Failure of Royal Liberalism in Thailand". *Journal of Contemporary Asia* 38 (2008): 143–65.

———. "When the Walls Come Crumbling Down: The Monarchy and Thai-Style Democracy". *Journal of Contemporary Asia* 41 (2011): 657–73.

Dahl, Robert A. *Democracy and Its Critics*. New Haven: Yale University Press, 1991.

Diamond, Larry. "Is the Third Wave Over?". *Journal of Democracy* 7 (1996): 20–37.

Elster, Jon. "Introduction". In *Constitutionalism and Democracy*, edited by Jon Elster and Rune Slagstad. New York: Cambridge University Press, 1993.

Ferrara, Federico. *Thailand Unhinged: The Death of Thai-Style Democracy*. Singapore: Equinox, 2011.

Hewison, Kevin and Kengkij Kitirianglarp. " 'Thai-Style Democracy': The Royalist Struggle for Thailand's Politics". In *Saying the Unsayable: Monarchy and Democracy in Thailand*, edited by Søren Ivarsson and Lotte Isager. Copenhagen: NIAS Press, 2010.

Ingram, James C. *Economic Change in Thailand 1850–1970*. Stanford: Stanford University Press, 1971.

Kullada Kesboonchoo Mead. *The Rise and Decline of Thai Absolutism*. New York: Routledge/Curzon, 2004.

Lipset, Seymour Martin and Stein Rokkan. "Cleavage Structures, Party Systems, and Voter Alignments: An Introduction". In *Party Systems and Voter Alignments: Cross-National Perspectives*, edited by Seymour Martin Lipset and Stein Rokkan. New York: Free Press, 1967.

McCargo, Duncan. "Network Monarchy and Legitimacy Crises in Thailand". *Pacific Review* 18 (2005): 499–519.

———. "Thailand's Twin Fires". *Survival* 52 (2009): 5–12.

——— and Ukrist Pathmanand. *The Thaksinization of Thailand*. Copenhagen: NIAS Press, 2005.

Marshall, Andrew MacGregor. "Thailand's Moment of Truth: A Secret History of Twenty-First Century Siam". Available at <http://www.zenjournalist.com/>. 2011.

Marshall, T.H. "Citizenship and Social Class". In *Class, Citizenship and Social Development*, edited by T.H. Marshall. New York: Doubleday, 1964 [1949].

Missingham, Bruce D. *The Assembly of the Poor in Thailand: From Local Struggles to National Protest Movement*. Chiang Mai: Silkworm Books, 2004.

Montesano, Michael J. "Four Thai Pathologies, Late 2009". In *Legitimacy Crisis in Thailand*, edited by Marc Askew. Chiang Mai: Silkworm Books, 2010.

————, Pavin Chachavalpongpun and Aekapol Chongvilaivan, eds. *Bangkok, May 2010: Perspectives on a Divided Thailand*. Singapore: Institute of Southeast Asian Studies, 2012.

Murashima, Eiji. "The Origin of Official State Ideology in Thailand". *Journal of Southeast Asian Studies* 19 (1988): 80–96.

Nation, The. "Military 'Must Back King' ". 15 July 2006.

Nattapoll Chaiching. "The Monarchy and the Royalist Movement in Modern Thai Politics, 1932–1957". In *Saying the Unsayable: Monarchy and Democracy in Thailand*, edited by Søren Ivarsson and Lotte Isager. Copenhagen: NIAS Press, 2010.

Ockey, James. "Variations on a Theme: Societal Cleavages and Party Orientations through Multiple Transitions in Thailand". *Party Politics* 11 (2005): 728–47.

O'Donnell, Guillermo. "Delegative Democracy". *Journal of Democracy* 5 (1994): 55–69.

Pasuk Phongpaichit and Chris Baker. *Thaksin*. Chiang Mai: Silkworm Books, 2009.

Prisdang, Prince and ten additional signatories. "Chao nai lae kha ratchakan krapbangkhomthun khwam hen chatkan kan plian plaeng rabiab ratchakan paendin Ro.So. 103" [The Presentation of Opinions on Governmental Reforms Submitted to the King by the Royal Princes and the King's Servants in 1885]. In *Ekkasan kan mueang kan pokkhrong thai Pho.So. 2417-2477* [Thai Political and Administrative Documents, B.E. 2417-2477], edited by Chai-anan Samudavanija and Khattiya Kansut. Bangkok: Sathaban sayam sueksa samakhom sangkhomsat haeng prathet thai, 1989 [1885].

Schattschneider, E.E. *The Semisovereign People: A Realist's View of Democracy in America*. Boston: Wadsworth, 1988 [1960].

Somchai Phatharathananunth. *Civil Society and Democratization: Social Movements in Northeast Thailand*. Copenhagen: NIAS Press, 2006.

Streckfuss, David. *Truth on Trial in Thailand: Defamation, Treason, and Lèse-Majesté*. London: Routledge, 2010.

Thak Chaloemtiarana. *Thailand: The Politics of Despotic Paternalism*. Chiang Mai: Silkworm Books, 2007 [1979].

Thalaeng kan rueang phrabat somdet phra poramintharamaha Prajadhipok phra pokklao chao yu hua song sala ratchasombat [Official Report on the Abdication of King Prajadhipok]. Bangkok: Rong phim prajant, 1935.

Thitinan Pongsudhirak. "Thailand Since the Coup". *Journal of Democracy* 19 (2008): 140–53.

Thongchai Winichakul. "Toppling Democracy". *Journal of Contemporary Asia* 38 (2008): 11–37.

Walker, Andrew. "Thailand's Farmers Have Stood Up", *Wall Street Journal*, 19 May 2010.

———. "Royal Sufficiency and Elite Misrepresentation of Rural Livelihoods". In *Saying the Unsayable: Monarchy and Democracy in Thailand*, edited by Søren Ivarsson and Lotte Isager. Copenhagen: NIAS Press, 2010.

Wilson, David. *Politics in Thailand*. Ithaca: Cornell University Press, 1962.

Section II

Defending the Old Political Consensus: The Military and the Monarchy

3

BROKEN POWER
The Thai Military in the
Aftermath of the 2006 Coup

James Ockey

> The notion of a "politicized" military most often evokes images of ... men
> in uniforms issuing ultimatums to cowering civilian politicians.
>
> *Meyer, 1991–92, p. 5*

In 2006, the Thai military carried out a coup against the Thai Rak Thai
party government of Thaksin Shinawatra, a government that had won
two landslide elections within a two-year period, an unprecedented
achievement in Thai history. Since that time, the military has governed
Thailand for a year, it has exerted its influence to break up one coalition
government and create an alternative coalition more to its liking, designed
a new internal security law giving it wide-ranging domestic powers, and
forcibly cracked down on large-scale demonstrations in Bangkok, with
many lives lost in the suppression. Certainly this indicates the military
has tremendous political power. Yet, the military as an institution today
is broken. As a military institution it is at a nadir, politicized, internally
divided, unprofessional, and therefore weak. In this chapter, it will be

argued that, while seemingly powerful, the Thai military contains all the divisions and conflicts inherent in Thai society. It will be argued further that, if the military wishes to be institutionally strong, rather than politically strong, the only way out of this internal weakness is to leave politics behind, and embrace merit-based promotion and professionalism in its place.

MILITARIES AND SOCIETIES

In analysing the collapse of the 1991 attempted coup in the Soviet Union, Stephen Meyer set out to explain why the Soviet military did not unite behind the coup plotters, when it had much to gain in the event of success.[1] The 1991 coup, which would spell the end of the Soviet Union, failed, according to Meyer, because the military was so divided by its involvement in politics, both as an institution and individually, that it could not unite, even under such circumstances. Under *Glasnost*, the military had been the focus of much criticism, and as the political system opened up, ambitious officers began to seek political office. The military was also divided by factionalism, particularly between junior and senior officers. Consequently, even institutional loyalties could not bring soldiers to unite behind the coup.

Meyer takes it as axiomatic that a military will always reflect the divisions in society; he thus focused on the depth of the divide in civilian society as the key factor in the emergence of the coup, and in its failure, noting, "the impact of Soviet domestic politics on the military establishment has been far greater than that of the military on domestic politics ... the key to understanding the evolution of Soviet military power in the years ahead lies in an analysis of the political and social revolution underway in that country and its impact on the military establishment."[2] Meyer would thus have us focus our analysis primarily on society, with the internal workings of the military dependent on events taking place in society. However, it is not at all clear that militaries always reflect societal divisions, and indeed they were designed, in part, to maintain some separation from parent societies, in order to minimize such internal divisions.[3] It is thus important to consider carefully when militaries are most vulnerable to the divisions evident in civilian society.

In analysing the Nigerian military coups in the 1960s, Robin Luckham took up this question.[4] Seeking to explain how the politicized ethnic divisions inherent in Nigerian society came to play the leading role in military politics, he undertook an extensive study of the internal structure of the military. In part, he focused on the promotion structure, exploring bottlenecks, age distortions, and class cohorts, and the stresses and strains they placed on the military as an institution. He argued, "How did these uncertainties [regarding violence based on ethnic differences] permeate the military? It seems clear that they were only able to do so because of conditions of acute strain within the military organization itself."[5] In other words, for Luckham, the problems inherent in society were able to penetrate the military because it was under strain and weakened internally. Once the societal divisions entered the military, he argued, they interacted with those existing internal strains, leading to the series of coups and killings in Nigeria. He concluded:

> It is rather hard to account for the burgeoning of conflict in the army in 1966 by reference purely to existing sources of cleavage. Ethnic and regional bonds ... did not have the strength or compulsiveness in and of themselves to stimulate overt expressions of antagonism within the military in the face of the well-enforced and internalized fraternal norms of the officer corps.... One major source of tension was political ... Not only had the officer corps exposed itself by virtue of its newly acquired political role to unaccustomed political demands and pressures; it had done so under circumstances which increased the intensity of those pressures... Secondly, there were the purely organizational sources of strain ... as Karl Deutsch has put it, the impact of new information on a system is related "to the extent of the instabilities that already exist there."[6]

More recent literature on civil-military relations, most notably the work of Rebecca Schiff, has highlighted the need to look more carefully at a third partner in civil military relations, the citizenry.[7] In the past, most work on civil-military relations has assumed the state is representative of the citizenry, and has thus ignored its role in the relationship. However, the state may not represent the citizenry. Furthermore, the military may interact directly with civilians in ways the state cannot control. In Thailand, the military has interacted directly with civilians since it first successfully intervened in domestic politics in 1932, and has expanded its interactions through its war on communism and its promotion of democracy. In interacting with civilians, it is exposed directly to their views and opinions, even as it seeks to reshape them into the views it deems most desirable. In a divided society, a divided military seeking to reshape public opinion may inevitably provoke further resentment. Schiff also argued that previous models of civil-military relations had been based on the American experience. She contended that this was a mistake, that civil-military relations in any state will depend on the historical and cultural context. In my own earlier study, I further noted that militaries have strong institutional memories, embedded in socialization and ritual, and shaped by both the mission orientation and self-reflective learning process applied to previous missions as they glorify their successes and explain their defeats.[8] It is therefore necessary to ground any analysis of civil-military relations in a particular country in its historical and cultural context.

Thus, following a brief summary of the historical development of civil-military relations in Thailand, this chapter will turn to the internal weaknesses of the military, focusing on budget, role, structure, promotion, and factionalism. It will examine the relationship between the military and society, in particular the ways that the military seeks to shape political opinion. Last, it turns to the question of easing the conflict within the military, arguing that only the strengthening of military corporateness will ultimately cure the divisions.

CIVIL MILITARY RELATIONS IN THAILAND

Prior to 2005, few, if any, civilians thought of the military as a force for democracy. Many in the military felt differently. The military could point to its role in the 1932 uprising, which overthrew the absolute monarchy, opening the way for parliamentary rule. Young officers executed a coup a year later to restore a parliament that had been abrogated. Thus the military helped bring about and preserve democracy in this early period. This politicization also brought them into contact with civilians in new ways, though primarily at this time with the civilians in what was a military/civilian coalition government, the beginning of a strong military role within the state that has, over time, evolved, but never disappeared. By the late 1930s, the military was forging a direct relationship with ordinary citizens, as the leader of the army, Field Marshal Phibun Songkhram, competed with civilian leader Pridi Banomyong for support in the countryside, a competition that took on aspects of anti-communism quite early. World War II provided further justification for a militarization of society, and by the end of the war, a wide range of paramilitary groups had been organized and trained by the military, giving it a direct link to many Thai citizens.

After the war, the Thai military soon returned to its position of authority in the state, and, for a time, managed to institutionalize it, as the generals governed either directly or indirectly for most of the period from 1947 to 1973. However, during this period, the relationship with Thai citizens changed profoundly. While paramilitary groups were retained, and even expanded, Thai citizens also became potential enemies, vulnerable to the lure of communism, and over time, a large internal security institution was developed to prevent such behaviour. Beginning as the Communist Suppression Operations Command, as parliamentary rule approached, its role would widen and its name change accordingly to Internal Suppression Operations Command (ISOC) in 1974. Through ISOC, the military not only kept a careful watch on Thai citizens, it also sought to shape their beliefs and behaviour. In addition, the Thai military began its involvement in development projects; in this period, much of the focus was on building infrastructure that would facilitate military operations. However, over time, development became an important part of the counter-insurgency process, as the military sought to win over the hearts and minds of rural Thais through development.[9]

Parliamentary rule became more firmly established in the 1980s, when the military decided to promote democracy as a part of its counter-insurgency strategy. The Thai military, working through ISOC, came to see itself as a mentor in the development of "democracy", a carefully shaped and controlled "democracy", but one that mostly preserved parliamentary rule.[10] By the time of the 2006 coup, the military played only an indirect role in government, and saw itself as a positive force for democracy, especially for uneducated rural Thais. It had developed close relationships with a wide variety of citizens through paramilitary units, including Thai National Defence Volunteers and *Thahan Phran* and through its efforts to propagate its own version of "democracy".[11] While these relationships were organized by the military as an institution, in practice, they were assigned to specific units and their commanders, so that the relationships established were sometimes linked to individual soldiers, often soldiers with political ambitions.

THE MILITARY AND THE 2006 COUP

The military coup in 2006 has sometimes been characterized in the press and in academic writing as a political coup, or as a royalist coup, with generals in the military working with generals on the Privy Council to remove the Thaksin government from power. While politics certainly played a part, many of the causes of the coup were internal to the military.[12] The military by 2006 had concerns about its budget, and its role in the aftermath of the Cold War and the emergence of the "global war on terror". It was also struggling with factionalism and promotion blockages.

According to Stockholm Institute of Peace Research Institute figures,[13] between 1988 and 1996, the Thai military budget more than doubled from an estimated 44.7 billion baht in 1988 to 102 billion baht.[14] Then in 1997, the Asian financial crisis led to sweeping budget cuts for the Thai state. The military budget declined by nearly 30 per cent over the next four years, falling to 72.2 billion baht by 2000, as the military was convinced to sacrifice for the good of the national economy. In 2001, the Thai Rak Thai party was elected to office as the Thai economy, in line with other Asian economies, began to recover. The Thaksin government encouraged economic growth through stimulus policies; however, government largesse did not extend to the military as the military budget rose only marginally from 76.4 billion baht in 2001 to 78.1 billion baht in 2005, the year before the coup, a level still more than 20 per cent below the 1996 military budget. A military budget set at levels that did not keep up with inflation, and still well below pre-financial crisis levels, despite the return of violence in the southern border provinces, was a source of dissatisfaction for many in the military. The level of dissatisfaction is evident in the large increases after the coup, discussed further below.

Dissatisfaction over the military budget was compounded by confusion over the changing role of the military, associated with the emergence of the "global war on terror" after 11 September 2001, the same year that the Thaksin administration took office. As the American military and other militaries geared up to fight the "global war on terror", the Thai military found that its role in the Muslim South was being turned over to the police force, most notably with the elimination of the Southern Border Provinces Administrative Centre in 2002. Not only did this lead to confusion about the role of the military, it severed many of the direct ties between the military and citizens in the South. When the long-standing insurgency was reignited in 2004, the military was given greater responsibility, but still not the level of authority it believed necessary to end the insurgency.

The concerns over budget and role were exacerbated by promotion blockages, which intensified conflict between factions within the military.

Over the years, the size of classes admitted to the military academy has trended upward, but not gradually; at certain times, there have been large increases in class size.[15] Such large increases mean more soldiers competing for the same number of promotions, which has often led to the creation of strong horizontal factions, based on military academy classes (most notably Class 5 and its younger rivals, Class 7, The Young Turks), and has sparked conflict and coups. In Table 3.1, we can see such a bulge in class sizes, with the soldiers from these large classes reaching the normal age for promotion through the ranks of general in the period leading up to the 2006 coup.

Between 1960 and 1969, despite some variation and a slight upward trend, numbers of admissions were relatively stable, just twenty more in 1969 than in 1960. However, in 1970, class sizes increased quite dramatically, with more than a 25 per cent increase in admissions. In 1973, admissions jumped a further 20 per cent, and in 1975, admissions peaked at more than 50 per cent higher than 1970. While this huge increase in admissions to the officers corps seemed necessary at the time, with the drawdown of U.S. troops in Thailand amidst the ongoing war in Vietnam, by the time of the Thaksin regime, there was little need for so many officers, and the Thai military found itself with far more officers at the top than necessary, with a large number of officers in inactive posts or with ranks not commensurate with responsibility, so that competition for top positions was fierce, with factions strongly advocating promotion for their own members. With

TABLE 3.1
Military Academy Class Sizes

1946	159	1956	139	1966	196	1976	277
1947	19	1957	165	1967	192	1977	311
1948	6	1958	137	1968	198	1978	283
1949	28	1959	135	1969	188	1979	268
1950	33	1960	168	1970	240	1980	365
1951	57	1961	147	1971	238	1981	257
1952	59	1962	178	1972	276	1982	333
1953	148	1963	141	1973	267	1983	314
1954	170	1964	181	1974	286	1984	329
1955	136	1965	183	1975	371	1985	325

Source: Counted from *100 Pi Rongrian Nairoi Phrachulachomklaeo* [100 Years of the Chulachomklaeo Military Academy], (Bangkok: Royal Thai Army, n.d.), originally published in Ockey 2001.

another large increase in 1975, the intense competition is likely to continue. These admissions patterns meant the rational structure of the military was under strain, and contributed to a breakdown in corporateness and, eventually, discipline in the military.

The factional struggle over promotion was closely linked to a struggle over control of the military. Within the military, the struggle was taking place primarily between a vertical faction, which distinguished itself through its belief in its superior professionalism, and a horizontal faction, based on military academy Class 21 (1969) more generally known by their Armed Forces Academies Preparatory School number, where they comprised Class 10. The vertical faction had grown out of two factions active in the 1970s, the Democratic Soldiers, a faction drawn largely from ISOC and its promotion of democracy to counter the communist insurgency, and the Thai Young Turks, officers from military academy Class 7 (1955).[16] These two factions found common cause in their support for army commander General Prem Tinsulanonda as prime minister in the early 1980s, and General Prem would later become the key figure in this faction, which I have elsewhere dubbed the "Professional" soldiers, not because they were professional, but because they believed themselves professional.[17] They were largely responsible for the military support for a carefully controlled democracy beginning in the 1980s. By 2006, General Prem was long retired, but retained considerable influence through a network of patron-client ties in the military, and through his influence over the promotion list, which had to be signed by the King, and thus was subject to his perusal in his role as president of the Privy Council. The Class 21 faction found its own champion in Thaksin, who attended the Armed Forces Academies Preparatory School with many members of Class 21, and, as prime minister, also reviewed the promotion list. Where the "Professional" soldiers comprised an "old guard", Class 21 represented a new generation of officers, with new ideas and a desire for change. With Prem and Thaksin both reviewing promotion lists, and both powerful factions strongly advocating promotion of their members, the promotion list each year during Thaksin's premiership proved a delicate balancing act, but one that, slowly, was shifting power to Class 21, as more of its members rose up through the ranks.

The 2006 coup came about as all these tensions within the military combined with a political crisis, as Thaksin struggled to retain his position amidst widespread protest. During the year, General Prem donned his uniform, marshalled support from his allies, both retired and active duty soldiers, and visited each of the military academies to proclaim to troops that their client was not the elected government, but the King.[18] Yellow-shirt demonstrators called on the military to step in and end the chaos. In the July promotion round of mid-ranking officers (under the control of the army commander), supporters of Class 21 were transferred out of Bangkok. In September, just before the promotion list was issued, the coup was carried out; the promotion list was recalled and rewritten so that Thaksin supporters were sidelined, while the "Professional" soldiers were promoted. Prem's protégé, Surayud Chulanont, stepped down from his position on the Privy Council to serve as prime minister of the new government, while a protégé of Surayud, Sonthi Boonyaratglin, the leader of the coup group, retained his position as army commander. Soldiers were cheered by the yellow-shirt demonstrators, who had called for intervention. However, Thaksin supporters and many pro-democracy activists spoke out against the coup, and organized protests of their own. The coup thus placed the military on one side of the political conflict, putting strain on the ties that the military had had with many segments of the population, especially in rural areas, in the northeast, and in the north.

After the coup, military leaders set out to change the political system. At the same time, they set out to resolve the problems within the military that had contributed to the decision to carry out the coup. They also sought to reshape the relationship between the military and the people, particularly those who had supported Thaksin, relying, for the most part, on the same tools that had been used during the Cold War against the communist insurgency.

AFTER THE COUP: BUDGET

In the aftermath of the coup, military spending increased rapidly. Reports indicated that some 1.5 billion baht were spent on the coup itself, much of it going to the officers who supported the putsch.[19] Shortly thereafter, 556 million baht was allocated to create a new special unit to be comprised of 14,000 troops to handle anti-government protests.[20] In ensuing years, the budget increased rapidly, easily surpassing the 1996 peak in 2007, as it grew by 9 per cent in 2006, followed by increases of 35 per cent in 2007, 23.5 per cent in 2008, and 18.3 per cent in 2009, before stabilizing at this new level, nearly double the amount spent before the coup. See Table 3.2.

The military also leveraged its more powerful role in politics in seeking to purchase a wide array of new weapons systems. After it played a key role in installing a Democrat Party-led coalition government in 2008, the military convinced the government to allow it to draw up plans for weapons procurement of up to 500 billion baht, to be spread out over ten years. Included in the plan are helicopters and jet fighters, some of which have already been delivered, and tanks, armoured personnel carriers, and second-hand submarines, as all branches of the armed forces have sought to gain a share.[21] The plan was sent to the Democrat Party government at the same time the military issued a denial that it was planning a coup.[22] The military also attempted to entrench budget support in the 2007 constitution, through a policy provision requiring that future governments allocate adequate funding for the military, including funding for weapons,

TABLE 3.2
Military Budgets

Year	Billion Baht	Constant Million US$ (2009)	Percent of GDP
1996	102	4,311	2.2
1997	99.5	3,999	2.1
1998	87.3	3,249	1.9
1999	75.8	2,813	1.6
2000	72.2	2,638	1.5
2001	76.4	2,747	1.5
2002	77.2	2,755	1.4
2003	79.9	2,802	1.3
2004	74.1	2,528	1.1
2005	78.1	2,547	1.1
2006	85.1	2,654	1.1
2007	115	3,498	1.3
2008	42	4,115	1.6
2009	168	4,907	1.9
2010	154	4,336	1.5*
2011	168		1.6**

Sources: Stockholm International Peace Research Institute (SIPRI) Military Expenditure database, online at <www.sipri.org> (Constant US$, 1996–2010 figures); Bureau of the Budget [Thailand] *Budget in Brief, Fiscal Year 2011* <http://www.bb.go.th/bbhomeeng/> (2011, is the allocated figure).
* Calculated based on the Bank of Thailand GDP figure for 2010.
** This percentage is based on the GDP figure used by the Bureau of the Budget in its calculations.

equipment, and technology.[23] While the provision will have limited practical effect, it does indicate the degree of dissatisfaction of senior officers with the military budget in the lead-up to the coup.

THE ROLE OF THE MILITARY AFTER 2006

The military also moved quickly to restore, and to expand, its role. While restoring the budget was relatively straightforward, establishing parameters for a new role was more complicated. In the South, the Surayud government re-established the Southern Border Provinces Administrative Centre, and returned authority for counterinsurgency policy to the military. Leadership and coordination was given over to ISOC, with a new Region 4 Forward Command created for the southern border provinces. Under the leadership of Pranai Suwanrath, brother of a privy councillor, the strategy was based on the recruitment of grassroots volunteers to support the work of ISOC, which would establish new relationships with both volunteers and the wider community, although, Marc Askew noted, they experienced little success.[24] The coup government also reinvigorated its democracy promotion campaigns, most notably through the Democracy Development Volunteer project, established under the Ministry of the Interior to promote the ratification of the constitution in a national referendum in August 2007, and extended through the December election.[25]

However, reviving and reinvigorating such programmes was only the beginning. The military set out to define for itself new roles, and to institutionalize those new roles. The first and most important step in that process was the recreation and expansion of ISOC, in one of the last pieces of legislation passed by the coup government, promulgated as the Internal Security Act of 2551 (*Phrarachabanyat Kanraksa Khwammankhong Phainai Racha-anajak*, 2008).[26] Originally the military wished to make the army commander the head of the new ISOC; however, following resistance, ISOC was placed under the direct control of the prime minister, with the army commander as deputy director. ISOC was territorially organized, with units at the regional and provincial level, with the military in control of those territorial units. In addition to a broad range of powers in undeclared periods of crisis, ISOC was given the mandate to:

> Develop the people's awareness of their responsibility to protect the nation, religion, and King. Build love and unity of the people in the

nation, including supporting the people's participation in preventing
and solving various problems that impact on the internal security and
stability of society.[27]

Led largely by General Anupong Paochinda and General Prayuth Chan-
ocha, close friends, and each an army commander in turn, the military
turned its attention to solidifying that new role, and justifying it, as far
as useful and necessary, by reference to developments in other nations.
In 2007, then Lieutenant General Prayuth, commander of the First Army
Region, produced a thesis at the National Defence College for a Joint
Public Private Sector degree with the English language title, "Roles and
Responsibilities Reform of the Royal Thai Armed Forced Against the
Non-traditional Threats" (sic, the Thai is "Reforming the Role of the Thai
Military to Prepare for New Types of Threats"). Prayuth identified seven
types of new threats the military needed to counter through "Military
Operations Other Than War": (1) security in the southern border provinces,
(2) international insurgency and transnational crime, (3) drug trafficking,
(4) foreign labourers and illegal migrants, (5) disasters resulting from
climate change and disease, (6) loss of natural resources, and (7) poverty.
The first four comprised short-term threats, the fifth and sixth medium-
term threats, and the last a long-term threat, and an underlying cause of
some of the other threats.[28] This opens up a wide range of roles for the
military. Prayuth further argued that the military should play the role of
mentor (philiang) to other institutions in countering such threats, working
primarily through ISOC.

In addition to outlining the nature of non-traditional threats and
the policies of recent Thai governments regarding those threats, Prayuth
compares Thai, United States, Russian, and United Kingdom structures
for countering non-traditional threats, in this way justifying the new roles
of the military in the international context, and justifying it in line with
powerful technologically advanced Western militaries rather than more
similar nations. In writing the report, Prayuth interviewed a range of
top generals, including then army commander Anupong, indicating not
only his leadership in this area, but also the emerging consensus among
top generals around military operations other than warfare.[29] After his
time as commander of the First Army Region, Prayuth was promoted
to Deputy Army Commander, where he was made assistant director for
ISOC, a position created for him, and given a powerful role in shaping and

managing the new ISOC.[30] While many of these roles had been undertaken for some time, formalizing them under ISOC has reshaped the way that the military interacts with civilians, as we will see below.

THE MILITARY AFTER 2006: STRUCTURE, FACTIONS, PROMOTIONS

During its brief period in power, the military made changes to take control of the promotion process from politicians. Rather than refer promotions successively up the chain of command, and eventually through the civilian minister of defence (in practice generally a retired general), a new Defence Committee was established to finalize promotion lists, making changes by politicians much more difficult. The new Defence Committee consists of the minister of defence, a deputy minister, the permanent secretary for defence, the supreme commander, and the commander of each of the three branches of the military (army, navy, air force), so that civilians (again, in practice, usually retired generals) are outnumbered five to two on the committee. If active duty officers unite on the list, as they did for the October 2011 reshuffle, the minister of defence is left with no authority to influence promotions.[31] While the stated goal of the change, removing political interference from the promotion process, would be a positive development, when the military itself has taken a side in the political conflict, and merit takes second place to political loyalties, this goal cannot be achieved.

As noted above, the military is currently confronting conditions of acute strain around the promotions process, with a much larger numbers of candidates vying for the top positions than previously, which has contributed to the factionalism in the military, especially along academy class lines. Further compounding the problem is the long-standing military faction that has considered itself "professional", but which has been centred on General Prem and his protégés. Prior to the coup, while the "Professional" soldiers had generally managed to maintain control at the top, Class 21 members had been promoted to positions where they were poised to take over. The coup occurred just before the annual promotion round, and the promotions list was immediately recalled for further consideration.

The "Professional" soldiers faced two problems, if they were to retain control of the military. First, as Prem had retired some thirty years earlier, in 1981, there were few if any in the military who had worked closely with him. Consequently, he was in the position of relying on protégés of protégés. In addition, as horizontal factions and their struggles became increasingly important, due to the promotion blockages, it was necessary to reach further down into the military to secure support. The search for reliable allies had to turn in a new direction.

When the new promotions list emerged, most Class 21 members had been sidelined, with the exception of Anupong, who, despite his class ties, was a member of the coup group. Anupong had commanded the 21st Regiment, the Queen's Guard,[32] a battalion in the Second Army Region, covering the Northeast. The Queen's Guard is responsible for protection of the queen, and the Privy Council, and, according to *Jane's Intelligence Review*, it has historically been "informally under the king, rather than following the formal chain of command".[33] Anupong had also commanded the 2nd Infantry Division (known colloquially as Burapha Phayak), which contains the Queen's Guard. It was to this group that Prem and the "Professional" soldiers turned in order to secure reliable allies. In addition to Anupong, former army commander Prawit Wongsuwon (Class 19/AFAPS Class 8) had commanded both units, as had General Prayuth (Class 23/AFAPS Class 12). General Prayuth had worked with the Queen from a young age, and, although too young to have worked with Prem while the latter was on active duty, he had worked closely with Prem in his role on the Privy Council, making him one of the youngest soldiers with a link to Prem.[34] In subsequent promotion rounds, Anupong was promoted to army commander-in-chief (2008), and in turn was succeeded by Prayuth (2010), with others in line to follow the same path. In this way, the "Professional" soldiers became a new type of faction, one linked to Prem in his role as president of the Privy Council, one linked to a specific military unit, the Queen's Guard.

This unusual arrangement was born of the desire to ensure the loyalty of the top military leadership to the goals of the coup group, but more importantly to the goals of the coup government, led by Prime Minister Surayud, a Prem protégé and member of the Privy Council. While it has achieved that purpose, at least for now, it has come at the cost of merit-based promotion, and in the process undermined the corporateness and professionalism of the Thai military. Promoting top generals on the basis of such personal ties and political loyalties has led to tensions within the military, so that while some units are staunchly loyal, others have been alienated and become disaffected.[35] This has been evident in the relationship between the military and the people as well.

AFTER THE 2006 COUP: THE MILITARY AND THE PEOPLE

The 2006 coup was unusual for Thailand. While soldiers were welcomed by yellow-shirt crowds in Bangkok, the military had intervened in a mainstream political conflict, and had intervened on behalf of the minority, against an elected majority government. Many soldiers were themselves sporting yellow ribbons, or had attached yellow ribbons to their tanks. Further, the military had intervened against the interests of those in the rural northeast, where it had spent so much time cultivating ties during the campaign against the Communist Party of Thailand. The military was thus seen by the majority at the time as a pro-yellow-shirt institution as well as an anti-democratic institution. The military subsequently sought to legitimize the coup by linking it to the monarchy, calling itself the "Council for Democratic Reform under the Constitutional Monarchy", and to the Privy Council, by appointing a privy councillor as the new prime minister. Repairing the relationship between the military, the military government, and citizenry became a high priority for the military leadership.

The military sought to mend its relationships by winning over the people politically, launching a number of large-scale campaigns even before ISOC was reinvigorated. According to Chairat, the military, working through a secret army unit under the direction of General Prayuth, spent some 319 million baht to win support for the coup government.[36] The military government launched a large campaign to win support for its new constitution, sending volunteers door-to-door to gain support. After the referendum, which demonstrated the discontent in the northeast and north, a "Centre for Poverty Eradication and Rural Development under the Philosophy of Self-Sufficiency Economy" was established under aegis of ISOC, as the military sought to compete with the Thai Rak Thai party directly for the hearts and minds of the people of the two regions by improving the economy.[37] After the Internal Security Act was promulgated giving shape to ISOC, 1 billion baht was allocated through the agency to rural projects, with the same purpose in mind.[38] In a continuation of this programme following the violent crackdown on red-shirt protests in 2010, ISOC sent some 1,200 staff out to meet with people, to promote sufficiency economy, and to explain the reasons armed troops had suppressed the demonstrations.[39] ISOC also sent out 2,000 troops to villages in the north and northeast prior to the January 2009 by-elections.[40]

While ISOC competed directly with Thai Rak Thai on poverty alleviation, it took a different tack when it came to the promotion of democracy. Since Thaksin's Thai Rak Thai party and its successor Phalang Prachachon party had won elections both before and after the coup, and the military had overthrown an elected government, it was quite vulnerable on its support for democracy. Thus, although it was originally tasked to promote democracy to fight communism, by 2009, ISOC had instead turned to promotion of the monarchy. We can see the extent of this shift in the focus of ISOC in the published transcripts of its *Sayamanusati* radio series (Ko Or Ro Mo No [ISOC], 2008, 2009). In 2008, of the fifty-three published transcripts, only fifteen allude to the monarchy in the title, with nine of those in a section titled, "The King and Development". A year later, thirty-seven of the forty-four published transcripts referred to the monarchy in some way in the title, including all twelve in a section titled "Politics and Administration". Neither democracy nor any similar word appears in any of the titles in 2009. ISOC also absorbed taskforce 6080, taking over its responsibility for monitoring lèse-majesté cases and Thais thought to be anti-royalist.[41] ISOC has pursued such cases zealously. In one instance Army Commander General Prayuth, on behalf of the army, quite publically lodged a complaint against some red-shirt leaders.[42]

Perhaps the best measure of the very limited success of these measures to reshape popular opinion is the election results of 2011. In the lead-up to the election, army commander Prayuth called on voters to elect "good" people to protect the monarchy. He claimed that the campaigns of some parties had an "anti-monarchist" tone, and that intelligence agencies had uncovered "rampant" evidence of lèse-majesté, especially among overseas Thais, promising prosecution.[43] This was widely seen as a call for voters to choose coalition parties. ISOC was also active on the ground in the northeast. Villagers in a community that declared itself a "Red-shirt Village for Democracy" give us a picture of ISOC activities:

> Yesterday we were visited by ISOC people... They came to repair [two] houses, yet even after completing the job, they kept coming back. It's not normal having the Army come to the village so regularly.[44]

Reporter Pravit Rojanaphruk further notes:

> We soon pass one of the two houses recently repaired by the Army. I notice that a brand new portrait of the King and Queen is attached to the wall of the house. It is not shielded from the sun or rain and [is] very

visible from the roadside... [The householder] says the picture came part
and parcel with the repair job by the ISOC Army officers.[45]

Despite such efforts, the village remained "red", and what was originally
expected to be a close contest between Thaksin's party, now reincarnated
as Pheu Thai, and the coalition partners, turned out to be a landslide
victory for Pheu Thai.

AFTER THE 2006 COUP: A BROKEN INSTITUTION

I noted at the beginning that Robin Luckham has argued that the stresses
and strains introduced into the military by promotion blockages contributed
to the coup and the associated violence in Nigeria in 1966. Some have
argued that the promotion of troops from the Queen's Guard and Burapha
Phayak units to the leading positions in the military has "achieved a high
degree of unity" for the military.[46] While there is unity at the top, and
within those chosen units, to focus only on those handpicked troops is to
ignore very real dissension within the military. Much of that dissension
results from overreliance on those units, and on the promotions of their
members, along with the members of Class 19 and 23 (AFAPS Classes 8
and 12) to positions of power at the expense of other qualified soldiers.
These promotion stresses have exacerbated the red-yellow conflict within
the military. The military has sought to convey an image of unity, so that
evidence is fragmentary, but nevertheless, that conflict can be seen in a
variety of ways, from voting patterns to violence.

The red-yellow conflict within the military began before the coup, where
it had a powerful impact on the promotions and career prospects of a wide
range of soldiers. As noted, supporters of Class 21 were transferred out
of Bangkok prior to the coup, and then sidelined when the promotion list
was recalled immediately after the coup. At the time of the coup, and for
some time afterward, coup leaders were closely associated with the yellow
shirts, with soldiers sporting yellow ribbons during the coup. Military
leaders consistently refused to suppress yellow-shirt demonstrations
against the pro-Thaksin Phalang Prachachon government throughout
2008, and remained idle even after the takeover of Bangkok's international
airport. When the courts ended the dispute with a decision to dissolve
the Phalang Prachachon party and ban executives, including the prime
minister, from office, army commander Anupong hosted a meeting in his

home where a new governing coalition was formed under the leadership of the Democrat Party.[47] Subsequently, Prawit Wongsuwan, Anupong's close ally, was named Defence Minister. Through these events, the military leadership had placed itself firmly on one side in the political conflict, initially the yellow-shirt side, then as the yellow shirts and the Democrat party grew apart, it supported Democrat party rule. I have noted above the impact this had on the military relationship with the people, with the majority of the population having voted for pro-Thaksin parties in recent elections, and the Democrat party, like the yellow shirts, representing a political minority. It should be kept in mind that soldiers are themselves recruited from that same population; many are from the northeast, and many had the same political sympathies. While their loyalty to the military as an institution has to be weighed up against those sympathies, as the stresses on the promotion system eroded corporateness and strengthened factionalism, as the military leadership introduced political criteria into the institution, that institutional loyalty became increasingly fragile.

Much of the attention paid to divisions in the military has focused on the mildest form of dissent among the enlisted. The enlisted are often from poor rural families, and have less socialization than do officers who go through four years of training. Both the red shirts and the army have acknowledged the presence of "watermelon" soldiers, green-uniformed on the outside, red politically on the inside, among the enlisted with the red shirts hoping the army will split as a result, and the army downplaying their importance.[48] We can get a sense of the scope of such dissent, perhaps, by considering the 2011 election results. Army leaders, particularly the commander General Prayuth, called on people to vote, and soldiers were bussed to the polls in some places to encourage them to vote. As noted above, Prayuth urged citizens to vote for "good" people, who would protect the monarchy, a message that was quite clear, particularly since Prayuth had also levelled lèse-majesté charges against red-shirt leaders at about the same time. Nevertheless, Pheu Thai candidates won seats in the house in three military-dominated constituencies in Bangkok, including the district comprising the 11th Infantry Regiment, which hosted the government during the red-shirt protests.[49] Concerns about the loyalty of troops appear to have had an impact on military decision-making. During the red-shirt protests in 2010, the military sought to remove any soldiers with red-shirt sympathies from positions of authority,[50] and all the crackdowns on red-shirt demonstrations were led by the Queen's Guard and other units with close relationships to the military leadership.

While concerns about the loyalty of the enlisted reveal some of the divisions in the military, it is when we turn to the demonstrations themselves that we can see the extent of the divide.[51] There is evidence that a few highly trained well-armed warriors fought on the side of the red shirts. At the most public level, Major General Khattiya Sawasdiphol (Seh Daeng) openly supported the red shirts, training some of their guards. Major General Khattiya had spent much of his career in ISOC, so perhaps it is not surprising that he was strongly politicised. At ISOC, he had been close to the paramilitary rangers, the *Thahan Phran*, in his duties, and he had the respect and sometimes personal loyalty of some. Major General Khattiya and his aides were suspected of involvement in a rocket-propelled grenade attack on the offices of army commander Anupong, which the army tried to conceal.[52] He participated in the red-shirt uprisings politically, appearing on the stage, as well as providing leadership to some red-shirt guards. Just prior to the crackdown, he was assassinated, apparently by a trained sniper from long range, shortly after the army spokesman announced that snipers were being brought in.[53]

While Major General Khattiya and his aides were quite visible, other highly trained warriors, the "black shirts" or "men in black" were more heavily engaged in the battle. No doubt aware of the dangers of disunity, the army and the Democrat coalition government carefully conflated the "men in black" with the red-shirt guards, despite the evidence that they were highly trained effective warriors, not young men quickly trained to provide security at demonstrations. The most detailed study of the protests and the suppression was undertaken by Human Rights Watch, which interviewed many people at the protests, on all sides, including soldiers. Human Rights Watch notes that the men in black can be seen in photos with military weaponry, including assault rifles and grenade launchers. They had a separate line of command from the red-shirt guards, and were experienced and highly trained. Journalist Olivier Sarbil observed:

> I met about 17 or 18 of them, but they said they were part of a group of 30.... They were all ex-military, and some of them were still on active duty. Some of them were paratroopers, and at least one was from the Navy.... They took their work very seriously. The guys I met, they knew how to move and shoot. They also had experience handling explosives.... The black shirts didn't come to try and take territory — they shoot and then they leave, they hit [the soldiers] and retreat.[54] (Human Rights Watch 2011, p. 45).

A Thai journalist added:

> The way they operated reminded me of those with military training....
> Their operations seemed to be coordinated by a man who always had
> sunglasses on. At one point, I heard him giving orders to the black shirts
> to fire M79 grenades at the bunkers and sniper posts of soldiers. But when
> I asked the black shirts about that man, they told me I should not raise
> that question again if I want to stay behind their line. The red shirts that
> I talked to said they did not know who that man was either.[55]

If these reports are accurate, and they do appear to be carefully documented,
the black shirts were individuals trained as soldiers of some sort, with at
least a few coming from active ranks, and much of the violence was thus
between soldiers. Whether accurate or not, the attack on the office of the
army commander, the role of Seh Daeng in organizing red-shirt guards, the
assassination of Seh Daeng, and other incidents indicate that at least a part
of the violence was soldiers engaging in battles against soldiers. Although
such violence has been confined to a limited number of individuals, it does
indicate the extent of the dissension and the degree of the erosion of both
military corporateness and discipline.

AFTER THE 2006 COUP: RED, YELLOW AND BLUE

The mutual support between the military and the Democrat coalition it
helped establish meant that the military leadership was able to act relatively
independently, controlling its own promotions and obtaining a very high
level of budgetary support, as long as the coalition remained in power. As
Thailand prepared for elections in 2011, the military continued to support
the Democrat Party and its coalition partners, as noted above. At the same
time, the military leadership began to consider how to protect itself, and
its new-found prerogatives, under a Pheu Thai government. The Pheu Thai
party was equally aware of the need to gain the acquiescence of the military,
if it was to govern — it had been forced from power in 2006 and again in
2008 by the military. With each side publicly signalling its willingness to
reach an accommodation as the election neared, at least a tacit agreement
seems to have been reached: Pheu Thai would not transfer Prayuth, would
not interfere in the October reshuffle, nor seek revenge,[56] and in turn,
that there would be no coup, the military would respect the results of the
election.[57] Perhaps as a sign of good will and cooperation, immediately
after the election, the army withdrew from an ISOC anti-narcotics task

force that had been criticized by Pheu Thai candidates for intimidating its supporters during the campaign; ISOC also suspended a crackdown on community radio stations, which had predominantly supported Pheu Thai and the red shirts.[58] Subsequently, Pheu Thai appointed retired General Yuthasak Sasiprapa as minister of defence. Yuthasak was a careful choice; while he was a Pheu Thai supporter, he was from a military family and had good relations with a wide range of military officers.

While the new Pheu Thai government generally sought accommodation with the military, it did seek to assert some control over the military's attempts to create a political relationship with the people. As prime minister, Yingluck became the statutory leader of ISOC. Where Abhisit had delegated this authority to military leaders, Yingluck sought to delegate it to retired general Panlop Pinmanee. Panlop, a member of military academy Class 7 (the Young Turks), has been at the centre of many controversies. In April 2004, when insurgents took over Krue Se Mosque in Pattani, he disobeyed a direct order to negotiate, and instead had troops attack the mosque, resulting in the death of thirty-two insurgents and three soldiers. In 2006, his driver was arrested after police defused a car bomb near the residence of Thaksin. He was appointed to an advisory position at ISOC by the coup group, joined the yellow-shirt movement, and then later supported the red-shirt movement, calling for the formation of a People's Army during the 2010 demonstrations.[59] Controversy aside, he had long experience working at ISOC, and thus had a good knowledge of its workings, and perhaps could have exerted some influence there to rein in some of the political activities carried out by the military through ISOC. The military managed to stymie this attempt, as Panlop was not eligible for the position under the Internal Security Act — only a director of a government agency can fill the director role in place of the prime minister. At any rate, the structure of ISOC, particularly at the provincial level, where the directors are army commanders, would make it difficult for the prime minister or her designee to exert more than cursory supervision. Pheu Thai reportedly made a second attempt to gain some control over ISOC in the October 2011 military reshuffle, seeking to have Thaksin classmate Prin Suwannathat promoted to the position of army chief of staff, where he would also serve as ISOC chief of staff.[60] Again, the military leadership successfully resisted.

The level of autonomy from political leaders achieved by the current military leadership became apparent when the October 2011 promotion list emerged. Thaksin's four remaining classmates from AFPAS Class

10 were further marginalized, while Pracha's Class 12 mates, Burapha Phayak commanders, and members of the Queen's Guard, including those responsible for suppressing the red-shirt demonstrations, were promoted to positions of influence. Former Queen's Guard and Burapha Phayak commanders were placed in positions where they are in line for promotion to army commander in the future. Defence Minister Yuthasak was ultimately unable to change even the appointment of the permanent secretary position at the ministry,[61] leading to calls from Pheu Thai MPs for a change to the law. Had the military used its independence from political control to reward merit, this might have represented a step forward; instead, the military leadership rewarded favoured troops for personal and political loyalties, sometimes at the expense of more meritorious soldiers. This tendency was, according to Cole and Sciaccitano, most pronounced in the army, "with only one officer who truly met the required criteria to be chosen for a key position".[62] While merit in individual cases can be difficult to assess, and opinions might well vary, the general pattern is quite clear, and readily apparent to observers, and to Thai soldiers. In choosing loyalties above merit, the military leadership ensured a degree of unity at the top, and among favoured classes and factions, at the risk of further undermining military corporateness.

Unhappy with its inability to influence military promotions, in a cabinet reshuffle in January 2012, Pheu Thai named retired air force General Sukhampol Suwanathat as the new defence minister. Sukhampol had been a classmate of Thaksin at the Armed Forces Preparatory School. In the annual reshuffle in October 2012, Sukhampol demonstrated his political acumen, allowing each service to control its own promotions, while asserting personal control over promotions in the defence ministry. To seal the arrangement, he created about 210 new senior positions in the defence ministry and promoted an unprecedented 300 officers to the rank of general, taking the total number of generals to some 1,600,[63] increasing the number without appropriate responsibilities. On his part, General Prayuth sought to ease factionalism in the army, administering a test to middle-ranking officers to determine their concerns and attitudes, and then meeting personally with some. He also began to allocate promotions to a wider group of officers, where previously promotions had tended to go to his own academy classmates.[64] At the same time, in the October 2012 reshuffle, General Prayuth again rewarded loyalists, exerting his influence to promote officers who had commanded the units responsible for the 2010 crackdown. While tensions within the military may have been temporarily eased by creating new positions to alleviate some promotion blocks, the factions remained in an uneasy relationship, with contention over promotion at issue.

CONCLUSIONS

Pro-democracy activists frequently, and rightly, remind us of the political problems that result when the military interferes in politics. Often overlooked is the damage that interference can do to the military itself. When militaries become involved in politics, they are often broken; with political involvement comes the need to assess political loyalties, and that comes at the expense of corporate loyalties. Promotion patterns become warped by a focus on politics, rather than merit. Robin Luckham has argued that politics can have a particularly devastating impact on militaries when they are already under structural strain, such as that created by promotion blockages. The Thai military today finds itself in exactly that state, as, following a long period of relatively stable admissions to the military academy, rapid expansion took place beginning in 1970. That has placed tremendous stress on the system, as soldiers and factions struggle for scarce promotion opportunities. With another bulge in admissions set to flow through soon, the stress will increase. The potential for further division and further violence remains high. The military leadership is clearly aware of the problem, and has struggled to portray an image of unity, with limited success. Army commander General Anupong acknowledged this difficulty, even as he downplayed it, stating, "No matter what colour your heart is or what doctrine you subscribe to, you do your duty as a soldier when you are deployed. Do not bring the colour in your heart into your duty."[65] There followed an attempt to vet the politics of soldiers and remove those with the wrong politics from positions of authority. When the military leadership is itself so politicized, and promotions are based on political loyalties, the struggle within the military becomes political. Any violence within the military may exacerbate the violence within society. Despite denials, the death of General Khattiya, killed by a sniper bullet shortly after the government announced it had brought in snipers, appears to be a case of a soldier killing another soldier, a higher ranking soldier. The greatest violence in the 2010 uprisings came as black shirts, allegedly trained soldiers — whether active duty, retired, paramilitary, or some combination and clearly acting outside the chain of command — fought with the army. While we may never know the full story behind this violence, it may be that the military can best contribute to a more stable and peaceful society by solving its own internal problems.

The entry of the military into politics has also eroded its relationship with the people. It finds itself struggling not against a communist threat, but struggling to support one political party over another and a minority party at that. The military thus finds itself expending resources to win over the majority of the Thai people. This is a costly endeavour, and despite the resources devoted, the 2011 election results indicate the lack of success. Furthermore, the distrust created between soldiers and citizens will make it more difficult for the military to carry out its mission, particularly when it comes to Military Operations Other than Warfare. Many of these operations, such as drug suppression or conserving natural resources, depend on the support of the people. As long as the military is expending resources seeking to convert people to a political point of view, rather than win trust for military operations, it will struggle to achieve these objectives.

While the military currently plays a powerful role in politics, from an institutional point of view, the military is broken, as is perhaps inevitably the case when a military engages in political activism. When loyalty replaces merit in promotions, the corporateness and expertise of the military are inevitably eroded. And yet, the very nature of politicization makes it difficult for military leaders to take an institutional point of view. Current military leaders have been promoted, in large part, precisely because of their political, factional, and personal loyalties, at a time when promotions are at a premium. Unless the military leadership can shift its attention from politics and personalism to the restoration of military corporateness, it will remain broken, divided, and dangerous both to itself and to others. Unfortunately with promotion and career stakes so high, placing the military institution first may prove impossible.

Notes

1. See Meyer, "How the Threat (and the Coup) Collapsed", *International Security* 16 (Winter 1992).
2. Ibid., p. 6.
3. To take just the two most obvious examples, basic training isolates soldiers from society, restricting access by keeping them on base without leave in early weeks, usually in remote locations and often limiting contact by phone or email. Later, soldiers and their families live together in military bases, fenced

off from civilian society, socializing almost entirely with each other through clubs and societies on the base, though this later type of separation has been eroded in recent years, perhaps to the detriment of professionalism.

4. See A. R. Luckham, "The Nigerian Military: Disintegration or Integration?", in *Nigerian Politics and Military Rule: Prelude to the Civil War*, edited by S. K. Panter-Brick (London: Athlone Press, 1970).

5. Ibid., p. 75.

6. Ibid., pp. 76–77.

7. See Rebecca Schiff, "Civil-Military Relations Reconsidered: A Theory of Concordance", *Armed Forces & Society* 22, no. 1 (1995).

8. James Ockey, "Thailand: The Struggle to Redefine Civil-Military Relations", in *Coercion and Governance: The Declining Political Role of the Military in Asia*, edited by Muthiah Alagappa (Palo Alto, CA: Stanford University Press, 2001).

9. See Saiyud Kerdphol, *The Struggle for Thailand* (Bangkok: S. Research Centre, 1986).

10. For a critical examination of this shaping of parliamentary rule, see Connors (2003).

11. See Chai-anan Samudavanija, Kusuma Snitwongse and Suchit Bunbongkarn, *From Armed Suppression to Political Offensive* (Bangkok: Institute of Security and International Studies, 1990), Chapters 2 and 3.

12. I have written about this coup in detail in "Thailand's 'Professional Soldiers' and Coup-making: The Coup of 2006", *Crossroads* 19 (Fall 2007): 95–127. This section is in part a summary of the argument there.

13. Stockholm International Peace Research Institute Military Expenditure Database: Thailand <http://milexdata.sipri.org>.

14. Former Army Commander and future privy councillor Prem Tinsulanonda was succeeded by elected Prime Minister Chatichai Choonhawan in 1988.

15. While the close personal relationships that link some horizontal military factions develop in the Armed Forces Academies Preparatory School, so that understanding factional ties often requires looking at those classes, understanding the structural stresses and promotion blockages in the military can best be done by looking at the military academy class sizes, as they are a later and better indication of the sizes of cohorts in the different armed services.

16. See Chai-Anan Samudavanija, *The Thai Young Turks* (Singapore: Institute of Southeast Asian Studies, 1982).

17. See James Ockey, "Thailand's Professional Soldiers and Coup-making: The Coup of 2006", *Crossroads* 19 (Fall 2007).

18. See *The Nation*, 15 July 2006 and 1 September 2006.

19. Chairat Charoensin-o-larn, "Military Coup and Democracy in Thailand", *Divided over Thaksin: Thailand's Coup and Problematic Transition*, edited by John Funston (Chiang Mai: Silkworm, 2009), p. 70.

20. Ibid.
21. For more details, see *Bangkok Post*, 29 March 2011, and *The Nation*, 6 April 2011.
22. See *The Nation*, 5 April 2011.
23. See Chapter 5, Part 2, Article 77 of the 2007 Constitution <http://www.krisdika.go.th>.
24. Marc Askew, "Thailand's Intractable Southern War: Policy, Insurgency and Discourse", *Contemporary Southeast Asia* 30, no. 2 (2008): 198–99.
25. Chairat, "Military Coup and Democracy in Thailand", p. 66.
26. The U.S. Embassy reported on the re-creation of ISOC in a cable titled 07BANGKOK1754 THAILAND\'S NEW SECURITY STRUCTURE: BETTER LIVING THROUGH ISOC <http://thaicables.wordpress.com/2011/06/24/07bangkok1754-thailands-new-security-structure-better-living-through-isoc/>. The report was submitted before the scope and nature of the new ISOC had been clarified.
27. "Phrarachabanyat Kanraksa Khwammangkhon Phainai Rachaanajak" (Internal Security Act of 2551), in *Aekotmaikhwammangkhon* (*Security Act*) (Bangkok: Sutphaisan Law, 2008), p. 6.
28. Prayuth Chan-O-Cha, "Kanprap Botbat Khong Kongthap Thai Phua Rongrap Phaikhuk Khwamrupbaebmai" [Roles and Responsibilities Reform of the Royal Thai Armed Forced against the Non-traditional Threats [sic]] (Bangkok: National Defence College, 2007), pp. 56–58.
29. Prayuth's classmate from the Armed Forces Academies Preparatory School, Surasak Karnjanarat, joined him at the National Defence College in Class 20, where he wrote his thesis on improving military public relations efforts, recommending a more concerted and sophisticated system for engaging with the media. See Surasak Karnjanarat, *Botbat lae khwamsamphan kap thahan lae sue muanchon* (Roles and relationship: the Military and Mass Media), National Defence College 2007. He was appointed director of the army's Centre for Mass Relations and Information.
30. See *Bangkok Post*, 21 January 2010.
31. See *Bangkok Post*, 7 October 2011.
32. Also called the Queen's Musketeers.
33. Fablo Scarpelio, "Guarding the Guards: Fault Lines in Thailand's Military", *Jane's Intelligence Review* (November 2010), p. 26 <http://www.jir.janes.com> (accessed 10 September 2011).
34. *Bangkok Post*, 21 January 2010 and 26 August 2010.
35. The opposition to this "Wang Burapha" faction has been dubbed Wong Thewan. Wong Thewan appears to be only a very loose-knit group, united primarily in its opposition to the favouritism shown to Burapha Phayak in the promotion process. It does not have the close structural or personal ties exhibited by

Burapha Phayak. However, with the appointment of retired general Yutthasak Sasiprapa as Minister of Defence, Wong Thewan may have developed some structure by rallying around him. Yutthasak's replacement as minister of defence, Sukumpol Suwanatat, a Thaksin classmate, has been more effective, as he appoints advisors and fills positions in the ministry, although given his civilian and retired status, Wong Thewan will remain much less organized than Burapha Phayak. See *Bangkok Post*, 31 July 2010.

36. Chairat, "Military Coup and Democracy in Thailand", p. 71.
37. Ibid., p. 72.
38. Paul Chambers, "In the Shadows of the Soldier's Boot: Assessing Civil-Military Relations in Thailand", *Legitimacy Crisis in Thailand*, edited by Marc Askew (Bangkok: King Prajadipok's Institute, 2010), p. 207.
39. See *Prachatai*, 6 July 2010.
40. See *The Nation*, 24 December 2008.
41. *Bangkok Post*, 21 January 2010.
42. This focus on *lèse-majesté* is linked to the "intelligence" produced during the 2011 red-shirt demonstrations alleging the existence of an anti-monarchy conspiracy. Vulnerable to charges of being anti-democratic, the military, and the coalition government, have sought to shift the focus of their constituents and voters more generally to loyalty to the monarchy. See also *The Nation*, 20 April 2011.
43. See *Bangkok Post*, 15 June 2001.
44. See *The Nation*, 27 June 2011.
45. Ibid.
46. Chambers, "In the Shadows of the Soldier's Boot", p. 228.
47. See *The Nation*, 24 December 2008.
48. See *Bangkok Post*, 8 April 2010.
49. See *Bangkok Post*, 6 July 2011 and 7 July 2011.
50. See *Bangkok Post*, 8 April 2010.
51. Cole and Sciaccitano claim that, "according to military insiders and Western diplomats", three active-duty AFPS classmates of Thaksin "effectively ran and directed the pro-Thaksin red shirt protest operations in Bangkok during last year's street violence". Cole and Sciaccitano are characterized as retired U.S. military officers who graduated from the Thai army's Command and Staff College, see *Asia Times* 6 October 2011.
52. See *Bangkok Post*, 23 January 2010.
53. Rumours abound regarding the killing of Seh Daeng. For a good summary of the rumours, see the blog of photo journalist John Lefevre, "Who Killed Sae Daeng" <http://photo-journ.com/2011/who-killed-seh-daeng>. See also *Bangkok Post*, 13 May 2010.
54. Human Rights Watch, *Descent into Chaos: Thailand's 2010 Red Shirt Protests and*

the Government Crackdown, Group/NOOR (January 2011) <http://www.hrw. org/node/98416> (accessed 10 September 2011).

55. Ibid., p. 46.
56. See *Bangkok Post*, 15 June 2011 and 2 July 2011. See also *Bangkok Post*, 13 August 2011.
57. Cole and Sciaccitano claim that an explicit "secret accommodation" was negotiated to this effect behind the scenes. This secret accommodation also allegedly included allowing Prayuth to serve out his time as army commander, and no legal action to be taken against military officers for the violent crackdown on red-shirt protesters. Military leaders denied any secret accommodation had been reached, see *Asia Times*, 30 June 2011; *Bangkok Post*, 1 July 2011. See also *The Nation*, 30 June 2011.
58. See *Bangkok Post*, 9 July 2011.
59. See the leaked cable from the U.S. embassy, "Background on General Panlop Panmanee", 07BANGKOK3625 dated 29 June 2007, available at <http:// dazzlepod.com/cable/07BANGKOK3625/>; *The Nation*, 4 February 2010; *Asia Times*, 6 October 2011.
60. Cole and Sciaccitano, *Asia Times* 6 October 2011.
61. See *Bangkok Post*, 6 October 2011 and 7 October 2011.
62. *Asia Times*, 6 October 2011.
63. *Bangkok Post*, 27 September 2012.
64. *Asia Times*, 11 May 2012.
65. See *Bangkok Post*, 8 April 2010.

References

Askew, Marc. "Thailand's Intractable Southern War: Policy, Insurgency and Discourse". *Contemporary Southeast Asia* 30, no. 2 (2008): 186–214.

Chai-Anan Samudavanija. *The Thai Young Turks*. Singapore: Institute of Southeast Asian Studies, 1982.

————, Kusuma Snitwongse and Suchit Bunbongkarn. *From Armed Suppression to Political Offensive*. Bangkok: Institute of Security and International Studies, 1990.

Chairat Charoensin-o-larn. "Military Coup and Democracy in Thailand". In *Divided Over Thaksin: Thailand's Coup and Problematic Transition*, edited by John Funston, pp. 49–79. Chiang Mai: Silkworm, 2009.

Chambers, Paul. "In the Shadows of the Soldier's Boot: Assessing Civil-Military Relations in Thailand". In *Legitimacy Crisis in Thailand*, edited by Marc Askew, pp. 197–233. Bangkok: King Prajadipok Institute, 2010.

Cole, John, and Steve Sciacchitano. "Machinations Behind Thai Military Movements". *Asia Times*, 6 October 2011 <http://www.atimes.com/atimes/ Southeast_Asia/MJ06Ae01.html/>.

Connors, Michael Kelly. *Democracy and national identity in Thailand*. New York and London: RoutledgeCurzon, 2003.

Human Rights Watch. *Descent into Chaos: Thailand's 2010 Red Shirt Protests and the Government Crackdown*. Group/NOOR (January 2011) <http://www.hrw.org/node/98416>.

Ko Oh. Ro Mo No (Kong amnuaikan raksa khwammangkhong phainai racha anajak) [ISOC]. *Ruam botkhwam Sayamanusati* [2008] Bangkok: Aroon printing, 2008.

———. Ro Mo No (Kong amnuaikan raksa khwammangkhong phainai racha anajak) [ISOC]. *Ruam botkhwam Sayamanusati* [2009] Bangkok: Aroon printing, 2008.

Luckham, A. R. "The Nigerian Military: Disintegration or Integration?". In *Nigerian Politics and Military Rule: Prelude to the Civil War*, edited by S. K. Panter-Brick, pp. 58–77. London: Athlone Press, 1970.

Meyer, Stephen. "How the Threat (and the Coup) Collapsed". *International Security* 16 (Winter 1992): 5–38.

Ministry of Defence. *Defence of Thailand 2008*. Bangkok, Royal Thai Armed Forces Headquarters. Strategic Research Institute, National Defence Studies Institute, 2008.

Ockey, James. "Thailand's 'Professional Soldiers' and Coup-making: The Coup of 2006". *Crossroads* 19 (Fall 2007): 95–127.

———. "Thailand: The Struggle to Redefine Civil-Military Relations". In *Coercion and Governance: The Declining Political Role of the Military in Asia*, edited by Muthiah Alagappa, pp. 187–208. Palo Alto, CA: Stanford University Press, 2001.

"Phrarachabanyat kanraksa khwammangkhon phainai rachaanajak". In *Aekotmaikhwammangkhon*. Bangkok: Sutphaisan Law, n.d. [2008].

Prayuth Chan-O-Cha. "Kanprap botbat khong kongthap Thai phua rongrap phaikhuk khwamrupbaebmai" [Roles and Responsibilities Reform of the Royal Thai Armed Forced Against the Non-traditional Threats [sic]]. Bangkok: National Defence College, 2007.

Saiyud Kerdphol. *The Struggle for Thailand*. Bangkok: S. Research Centre, 1986.

Scarpelio, Fablo. "Guarding the Guards: Fault Lines in Thailand's Military". *Jane's Intelligence Review*, November 2010, pp. 34–37 <http://www.jir.janes.com>.

Schiff, Rebecca. "Civil-Military Relations Reconsidered: A Theory of Concordance". *Armed Forces & Society* 22, no. 1 (1995): 7–24.

———. *The Military and Domestic Politics: A Concordance Theory of Civil-Military Relations*. New York: Routledge, 2009.

Surachart Bamrungsuk. "Thahan kap kanmuang Thai lung 9/19" [Soldiers and Thai politics in the Post 9/19]. Bangkok: Julasan khwammangkhongsuksa no. 25, 2007.

Surasak Karnjanarat. *Botbat lae khwamsamphan kap thahan lae sue muanchon* [Roles and relationship: the Military and Mass Media]. Bangkok: National Defence College 2007.

Wassana Nanuam. "Looking Out for his Boss, Prayuth is the Man to Watch". *Bangkok Post*, 21 January 2010 <http://www.bangkokpost.com/opinion/opinion/31368/looking-out-for-his-boss-Prayuth-is-the-man-to-watch>.

4

THE MONARCHY AND ANTI-MONARCHY
Two Elephants in the Room of Thai Politics and the State of Denial[1]

Thongchai Winichakul

During the 2010 crackdown of the red-shirt demonstration in Bangkok, many observers wondered aloud why the King had not intervened to stop the killing as he did during the bloodshed of 1973 and 1992 that helped end the carnage. The absence of his intervention in 2010 became conspicuous. Why did these observers have such a false hope that the King might have intervened in political killings? He did not intervene to stop the killing in the 1976 massacre either. In fact, the roles of the palace in each of those bloodbaths remain a mystery.[2] It is naïve to assume that the King is the peace-maker amidst political polarization. In Thailand, sadly, such a naïve assumption is perpetuated widely.

Until recently the scholarship on Thai politics and the state rarely discusses the monarchy, taking for granted that the monarchy is non-political. Contrary to such view, this chapter offers a history of the active monarchy in Thai politics, creating the royalist democracy whose legitimacy is based on the monarch's moral authority and his popularity. King Bhumibol Adulyadej in particular has been a major political actor but observers usually do not see it. The monarchy is an elephant in the room of Thai politics, thanks not only to suppressive measures but probably due to the royalist ideology that puts the elephant under a cloak. On the other hand, criticism of the monarchy usually is non-existent in the country. Suppression of critics, this chapter will show, has been constant since the late 1970s with the rise of hyper-royalism. The royal-nationalist logic that a Thai must naturally be a royalist, therefore a non-royalist must not be a Thai, is not absurd in Thailand. As this ideology is widespread, it generates the climate of fear in which the non-conformist individuals must learn to live in silence and anonymity. Critics and sceptics of royalism are therefore the other elephant in the room of Thai politics. It is forced to disappear by the same ideology that cloaks the monarchy's political role. While the attention to the monarchist politics has increased in the past few years since the royalist coup in 2006, anti-monarchy has yet been a subject of any study. This chapter will offer a preliminary history of it with some observations on the differences between the current anti-monarchy and all previous ones.

Why are these two elephants important to the current situation in Thailand? Because they are integral and probably the most important factors that contribute to the current political crisis. Yet, Thais generally do not see the two elephants. To be more precise, they may see them but they are in the state of denial. The country is probably in the state of denial.

Five years after the coup, the denial of these two elephants is no longer wise if it is at all possible. Polarization has severely damaged the credibility and trust in the parliamentary system, the judiciary, media and academics, no matter which side one takes. But the most serious damage is to the public reverence to the monarchy. No matter how strong the state and the royalists' denial may be, there is little doubt among the observers of Thailand that the political force underlying the crises since 2006 has been the "network monarchy". As a reaction to this condition, disappointment with the palace rises while disillusion has spread. There is a seismic wave underneath the pretence of a royalist society. After a long and costly silence, at the expense of those hundred lives and severe damage to democratization, one elephant can no longer hide under a cloak while the other marches into the street in daylight.

Nevertheless, the official mantra of Thai politics remains the same, that those two elephants are not in the room, that the monarchy is above politics, and that anti-monarchy is a negligible discomforting deviant that is not Thai. The chapter points out that this denial and delusional politics exacerbates the political crisis as the end of King Bhumibol's era is approaching. In turn, the looming succession crisis intensifies the denial and delusion, hence the deeper political and succession crises. The Thai monarchy which has been lauded as the rock that provided stability to the country's democratization looks to become the cause of the worst instability in modern Thai history.

PART ONE: THE WHITE ELEPHANT

The Monarch/y and the Network Monarchy

It is necessary to begin with the clarifications of two confusions when we talk about Thai monarchy during the reign of King Bhumibol. First, does the monarchy mean the "institution" of which Bhumibol is an individual king, or do we consider King Bhumibol as an individual monarch in particular? Can the two notions be distinguished or in what ways have they been conflated? Second, as an institution, does the monarchy include the monarchists and other operators who serve the interests of the monarchy but who are not royals? Should or can we differentiate the actions by the King himself and by those associates who claim to act on behalf or in the name of the monarchy? As we shall see, for the first confusion, it is very difficult to distinguish the two. They are two sides of the same coin during the reign of King Bhumibol. For the second one, we need to understand the relationship between the King and other monarchist actors.

For the first one, as I shall argue later, the success of the monarchists in establishing their dominance over Thai politics relies heavily on the performances of King Bhumibol. He is a charismatic, accomplished, and memorable king. The longevity of his reign is an important factor for people's faith and veneration of the King. It is not an exaggeration to say that most living Thais today do not have an experiential imagination of any other monarchs but Bhumibol. He is *the* king to them. The monarchy as a public institution and King Bhumibol are currently inseparable in Thai imagination. This fused notion of the "monarch/y" is productive in peculiar ways. We may say that the rise to dominance of the monarchy in Thai democracy and the successes of the Thai monarchy during Bhumibol's reign are the outcome of the fused monarch/y.

For the second one, the answer is provided by Duncan McCargo in the concept of "network monarchy", proposed in 2005. McCargo warns us not to think about the monarchy as a one-person institution. The monarchy, he suggests, is a network of people who have vested interests in the longevity, strength, and dominance of the monarchy as a social and political institution. Their vested interests could be purely ideological such as political conviction, or tangible and material benefits, or anything in between such as one's reputation, dignity, or personal fulfillment. The network comprises of people who are political operators with agenda, purposes and assignments, and those who are not. Some are in the agencies formally linked to the palace. Most are not. Some may have access to or are in contact with the palace, the royals, or even to the King. But a larger number of them do not have such access. The network monarchy includes rival factions among the royals and kingmakers, rich and not so, and from different walks of life. The network monarchy is not a homogeneous entity under the command of the King. Nor are the interests and politics of those people. There are ultra-conservatives and royalist liberals, pro and anti-military, pro-capitalism and its opponents; all of whom serve the monarch/y in various ways according to their own views. As the epicentre of the network monarchy, the King, I believe, stays aloof from those differences, tensions, and conflicts among the key individuals and factions in the network, letting them operate under the broad interests of the monarch/y. A capable king would intervene only when necessary.

Legacies of the Absolute Monarchy in Democratization

The fact that Siam was not formally colonized contributed to the enduring political roles of the monarchy in two ways. First, unlike their colonized neighbours, the ruling royal elite in Siam survived and became stronger and more powerful, thanks to the modern technology of the state that allowed them to consolidate and centralize their power as never before. The modern Siamese state emerged as a royal absolutism. Secondly, the escape from colonization was attributed to the superior ability of the enlightened monarchs. They were regarded as the national saviours. This uncritical royalist history and the strong monarchy were parts of the foundations of modern Siam. Even long after the absolute monarchy had ended, its legacies have remained, for the monarchists have persistently tried to establish the dominance of the monarchy in the political system.

Under colonial pressure, the royal rulers embraced the colonial projects for modernity, nation-state and the colonial global economy.[3] They welcomed Western ideas and technologies that strengthened their rule, particularly modern bureaucracy, the budgetary and taxation system, the standing army, and the colonial administrative system to control Siamese provinces. Socially and culturally, they accommodated new ideas in order to, in their own views, be on par with the advanced civilizations and simultaneously reaffirm the superiority of the Bangkok's rule in the region.[4] The absolute monarchy in Siam expanded its power further and became much stronger than any previous rulers in the country's history.[5] As socio-economy changed and new social forces emerged, other social classes were brought into the bureaucracy and political process. The absolute monarchy from 1910 to 1932 found its legitimacy being challenged. The first attempt at a revolution was in 1912, but the plot was discovered before any action was taken, resulting in the arrests and severe punishment of all plotters. Challenges from the non-royal new elite for political changes continued.[6] Finally, the revolution in 1932 by the People's Party ended the absolute monarchy and opened up the opportunity for political participation by common (non-royal) people. It was regarded as the beginning of Thai democracy. Unfortunately, the focal issue of disputes that led to serious rifts and weakened the revolutionary regime was the place, role and power of the monarchy under the constitutional democracy.[7]

The governments of the People's Party lasted for only fifteen years, during which the monarchists tried to return to power by various means but failed.[8] In November 1947, the monarchists finally struck back, collaborating with the army in a coup that brought them back to power and forced the remaining leaders of the People's Party into exile. The monarchists' return to political prominence coincided with the beginning of King Bhumibol's reign (born 1927, reigning 1946), although the King remained in Switzerland most of the time until 1952. To return to political dominance under the post-absolutist condition, the monarchists articulated the constitutional monarchy in such a way that put the monarchy at the zenith of the political system. I call it the royalist democracy, even though it was not at all democratic.

Royalist Democracy[9]

During their brief ascendency in 1947–52, the monarchists articulated the position of the monarchy in the post-absolutist political system and called the regime, as appeared in the 1949 constitution, the "Democratic Regime with the Monarchy as the Head of the State". It was a euphemism for the royalist dominance over the regular government, be it a democracy or military rule. In the same constitution, the legal stipulation that no one could charge or bring a legal action against the King also appeared for the first time. Also in 1949, the legal foundation the Crown Property Bureau, the business arm of the palace to the present day, was also enacted.[10] In addition, many royal rituals — old, modified, and invented ones — were (re)introduced, many of which would serve to magnify the aura of King Bhumibol later.

In 1957, the monarchists helped bring a dictatorial regime to power. In return, for the first time since the end of the absolute monarchy, the regime helped promote royalism and King Bhumibol.[11] One of the most telling actions regarding the promotion of royalism was the change in 1960 of Thailand's National Day from 24 June, the day that marked the revolution in 1932, to 5 December, Bhumibol's birthday. The United States played a crucial role in this alliance and the rise of the monarchy as the national symbol since the latter was believed to be an effective apparatus against communism.[12] With the emphasis on civic actions and political counter-insurgency from the early 1960s, the monarchy played a leading role in civic action projects among the upland minorities along the borders and hundreds of royal projects for rural and social developments proliferated.[13] By early 1970s the royalist historiography that credited previous monarchs as champions of democracy became an educational staple while the image of Bhumibol as a democratic king grew among the urban bourgeoisie who began to challenge the military rule.[14] The breakthrough for royalist democracy came in the popular uprising against the military rule in 1973. On 14 October, as the demonstrators were under attack by police and soldiers, the royal family hurriedly came out in public to allow them to take refuge in the palace compound. By the evening, the palace struck a deal forcing the junta to leave the country and appointed the President of the Privy Council the new prime minister. The uprising was a historic beginning of popular democracy but it was a turning point for the royalist democracy as well. The King's act created a lasting impression of him as a democratic monarch who has been the highest moral authority above all political forces. It is popular democracy with the monarch/y on top of it.[15]

The royalist democracy was firmly established in the early 1990s following two more political atrocities. With the communist revolutions in Indochina in 1975 and as the Thai radical movement grew rapidly after 1973, the monarchy was active in the anti-communist efforts, supporting the right-wing and paramilitary groups, many of which were involved in the 1976 massacre.[16] Royalism was promoted intensively as the ideology to fight communism. During the 1980s, the moral authority of the monarch/y grew while the credibility and legitimacy of the military and elected governments suffered. The popular uprising in 1992 sent the military back to barracks (until 2006), whereas the King's intervention to end the clashes elevated the monarch/y to the supreme moral authority above the messy political system.

It is no secret that the monarchists despise elected politicians whom they perceive as selfish entrepreneurs who "buy" their ways to power because people are too ignorant to care about democracy.[17] The monarchists prefer "Thai-style democracy" that grants more power to the non-elected, "uncorrupt" professionals and technocrats, to guide and control the elected politicians.[18] The royalists have proposed in recent years, for example, the Upper House appointed by the King or his representatives such as the Privy Council or the high court. Since the 1980s, the parliaments were usually fractured and fragile, while governments were weak, none of which lasted full term until the arrival of the Thaksin Shinawatra government in 2001. The monarchy became more politically active. Many top positions in the bureaucracy need approval from the palace. Interventions by the palace were more frequent and in various forms including public comments on politics. The King's annual birthday speech, beginning in 1994, became an annual ritual of royal reprimands on politicians that the entire country waits eagerly to listen. Other royals and people close to the palace also interfered more often with the government's decision making and public policies. While democratic institutions, especially political parties and parliamentary system remain weak, the monarchy's prominence rose to strength.

Modern Monarchy

The success of royalist democracy is not simply the result of political and opportunistic manoeuvres. Rather, it rests more on social and cultural capital that no other political groups could match. The ideal type for the post-absolutist monarchy was articulated by royalist ideologues such as Prince Dhani Nivat in his seminal essay in 1947.[19] According to his interpretation of Buddhist concepts, the Siamese monarchy had always been democratic given the popular mandate based on moral righteousness and given the monarch's dedication to people. The age-old Buddhist concept of the righteous king, Dhammaracha, was rearticulated for the constitutional monarchy. Based on Dhani's framework, the success of the Thai monarchy during the reign of King Bhumibol can be characterized by four fundamental and intertwining elements: (1) the Dhammaracha occult, (2) royal populism, (3) royal capitalism, and (4) the above-politics politics. The cornerstone of all four — we may call the fifth element, is King Bhumibol himself, without which the modern monarchy project for royalist democracy might have been a failure.

Let us consider each element.

Dhammaracha Occult

Dhammaracha (lit. righteous/*dharma* king), a Hindu-Buddhist concept of kingship and power based on moral authority, had been the ideology of Theravada Buddhist polity in Southeast Asia for centuries. A great king is a combination (two sides of the same coin) of a great emperor who expanded and protected a Buddhist empire, and an exalted religious king whose moral superiority is second to none.[20] In this concept, a good rule is the one by moral authority. But the degree of power and that of righteousness go hand in hand, one reflecting and resulting in the other; that is to say, power does not corrupt and absolute power is absolutely virtuous. This concept of kingship and power was modified in at least two respects in the nineteenth century. First, the righteous king is "assumed by popular consent" thanks to his indisputable moral superiority.[21] Royalist scholars then assert that the king is "elected". Secondly, whereas the ancient Dhammaracha acquired moral authority by ritual and religious performances, modern Dhammaracha perform public services. The image of Bhumibol as a modern Dhammaracha was fashioned from the moment of his coronation in 1950 when he pledged that he would "reign with righteousness for the happiness of the Siamese people". Note the words righteousness (*dharma*) and people (*mahachon*, lit. people at large) in the same sentence here. This image has been intensified over the years.

But contrary to the Weberian idea that with modernity comes secularization, during his reign Bhumibol-the-Dhammaracha was increasingly sacralized. The attribution of the current magical religiosity of Thai king to the age-old tradition is disputable. At least for most of the first half of the twentieth century, the monarchy was not semi-deity. Peter

Jackson argues that the "virtual divinity" of Bhumibol is the "mythopraxis" of our time.[22] In similar vein as Christine Gray, he suggests that the scared monarchy is the product of modern capitalism and neo-liberalism in which magic is commodified and prosperity is superstitious.[23] Sacredness is also attributed to the visual mass media, public spectacles and the visual society. The age of television, which coincidentally became a household fixture around the same time as Bhumibol's reign, is part of hyper-royalism. Irene Stengs also demonstrates the reciprocal transaction of magic and aura between the cult of Bhumibol and the one of King Chulalongkorn in our modern condition. The current Thai god-kingship is a capitalist, neo-liberal occult that no traditional or previous reign could achieve.[24]

Royal Populism

Instead of the assumed consent, the new Dhammaracha engages the public for reverence. How a modern monarchy earned public reverence changed according to the changing public sphere in the country since the nineteenth century. King Chulalongkorn's popularity owed as much to his diplomatic success as to the images of him being down to earth and showing care for his subjects. In his time, the public participated in and was astounded by several grand royal rituals and public galas that amplified his eminence on par with other great European monarchs.[25]

King Bhumibol engaged and earned public reverence by his tireless public services, exemplified by his regular visits all over the country to oversee hundreds of royal projects. Starting in 1952, the number and locations of these projects expanded rapidly throughout the country under the military regime after 1958.[26] Bhumibol brought projects to people and visited them similarly to a politician would do to his constituents. The differences were that his constituencies were country-wide, that he has been doing this over the past sixty years — a much longer period than any politicians might, and people were informed of his services on a daily basis on television. Bhumibol has been a popular monarch. In return, a mark of Thai royalism since the 1970s has been the public participation and popular initiatives for royal pageantry. This is elaborated below.

Royal Capitalism

Since 2006, Forbes listed King Bhumibol as the richest monarch in the world.[27] The Crown Property Bureau (CPB), the corporate arms of the monarchy, is the major shareholder of the biggest cement-producing company, the third largest commercial bank in the country, and many others. Nonetheless, the highest valuable assets the monarchy owns are the huge swathes of land in Bangkok including much prime real estate. The King and his family as individuals and the CPB as a corporate also own or hold the majority stakes in many domestic and international businesses, including luxury hotels in Berlin, Chicago, Bangkok, a huge theme park in Spain, the largest insurance company in Thailand, and a few of the most extravagant shopping centers in the prime areas of Bangkok.[28]

The CPB's success is owed to special privileges that no other corporations can enjoy. It does not pay tax. Its books and operations are not subjected to audit by a public or private authority; it is not accountable to anyone except to the reigning monarch. Its profits and revenues do not go to the treasury, yet when it was hit by economic crisis in 1997, the rescue came from public funds. Meanwhile, the regular operations of the Royal Household and the expenses of the monarch and his extended family are taken care of by government budgets.[29] Even the royal projects, once funded by the CPB and royal purses, have been financed by the state budget since the 1980s. The Thai monarchy is no longer a remnant of the feudal society (known as "Sakdina" in Thai). Rather, as Gray explains based on her study in the 1970s, royalism was good for capitalism and vice versa.[30] The latter's development strengthens the former which plays a significant role in advancing capitalism in Thailand. The difference is that the non-royal capitalists do not have the huge "cultural capital" as their asset and do not enjoy privileges like the CPB does.

Above Politics

Like "above" in English, *nua* in Thai means beyond, at/in a higher place. The notion that the monarchy is "above" politics was a euphemism that the People's Party imposed on the royals after the 1932 revolution to exclude them from politics. The monarchists quietly twisted its meaning to serve their benefits. Like in English, "above" in Thai also means upstairs, on top of, superior, higher (authority or place) than, or not liable to. Being above politics, as the monarchists quietly asserted, means the monarch/y is superior to the ordinary politics of self interests, on top of it, or in the higher place over normal political system. The monarch/y is clean, incorruptible, and morally superior to those in ordinary politics — be they the military junta, interest groups, or elected politicians.

The Thai state and political system under the royal dominance comprises of two realms: the ordinary one and the extraordinary one or the "above". The former is the normal and formal political system, be it military rule or parliamentary democracy. The upper realm is exclusively for the monarchy, royals, and those royalists who claim to be cleaner, uncorrupt, and superior to the ordinary. It is therefore naïve and misleading to talk about the "Thai state" minus the upper realm of the official political system. In saying that the 1976 massacre was a state crime, for example, it does not simply mean a crime by the government. Ironically, the political credibility, legitimacy, and influence of the monarchy derive from its paradoxical place in politics, namely, being apolitical or "above" and outside politics. The more it is believed to be outside politics, the higher moral authority thus more influence it earns because, in the logic of Dhammaracha, non-partisan and disengagement means cleaner and more virtuous, hence more power, which does not corrupt. Over time, people look "up" to the royal authority when they are dissatisfied with the normal political system.

In this sense, the red-shirt movement hit the bull's eye when they criticized the Thai political system as a hierarchical one with the "invisible hand" or the "power beyond the constitution" interfering and trying to dictate the democratic system. The red shirts' use of certain terms from the old Thai feudal society to characterize the contentious political forces — one is *ammat* (aristocrats), the other is *phrai* (serf, plebian) — also reflects the current condition of the Thai political system very well. Those who rejected the *ammat versus phrai* characterization fail to see the white elephant in the room of Thai politics.[31]

Hyper-Royalism

In the wake of the October 1973 revolution, the student movement became rapidly radicalized, and this alarmed the military and the monarchists. The Indochina revolution in 1975 made the communist threat even more real to them. Seeing the radicals as the urban communists with a mission to push over another domino to, they employed royal-nationalism as an ideological weapon against the communists. Originated in the 1910s under King Rama VI, the mantra "Nation, Religion, Monarchy", or the three pillars of the Thai nation, was invoked intensively in public everyday. Royalism spearheaded the fight since, as they believed, the communists wanted to destroy the country by abolishing the monarchy. The 1976 massacre and the collapse of the communist movement in early 1980s meant that royalism prevailed. After that, however, it has never subsided. On the contrary, royalism has been intensified and more pervasive. Since the mid-1970s this "hyper-royalism" has engulfed Thailand's public life.

The characteristics of hyper-royalism are as follows. First, it is royalism with excessive intensity. The demand for expressive loyalty to the monarchy has increased enormously. The number and frequency of public events in which individuals and collectives are supposed (or obliged) to demonstrate their loyalty has grown endlessly. Old and invented royal ceremonies have added up. Special occasions and anniversaries become common every few years while the annual ones, especially the King's and Queen's birthdays, become annual specials. Here is a list of the special royal occasions since 1976, each of which included many grand events and activities nationwide throughout the years. (This list is incomplete as it does not include special occasions for the Queen.)

1976	The first celebration of the National Mother's Day on 12 August (Queen Sirikit's birthday)
1977	The 50th birthday anniversary for the King
1979–80	The (first) marriage of the Crown Prince Vajiralongkorn
1980	The first celebration of the National Father's Day on 5 December (King Bhumibol's birthday)
1982	The Bicentennial of Bangkok and the Chakri Dynasty
1987	The 60th birthday anniversary (the 5th twelve-year cycle) for the King
1988	The celebration of the longest reign in Thai history (beyond King Chulalongkorn's 42 years)
1996	The Golden Jubilee, 50th anniversary of the reign
1997	The 70th birthday anniversary for the King
1999	The 6th twelve-year cycle (72nd) birthday anniversary for the King
2006	The 60th anniversary of the reign; the grand celebration of royals from all over the world for Bhumibol as the world's longest-reigning living monarch
2007	The 80th birthday anniversary for the King
2010	The 60th anniversary of the royal marriage (Bhumibol and Sirikit)
2011	The 7th twelve-year cycle (84th) birthday anniversary for the King

Second, hyper-royalism indulges ridiculous exaggeration and exaltation. The Thai royal family, from the King to the third-generation prince and princesses, are bloated to be the best at everything, from sport, fashion, acting, singing, cooking, to the more serious endeavours in scientific research, academic studies, writing, music, painting and the arts, and to social services in poverty alleviation, narcotic eradication, health, irrigation and education. Most finished at the top of their respective classes from grade-schools to colleges and graduate schools. They have been conferred many honorary degrees and awards every year. A university once conferred more than two dozen honorary doctoral degrees to the King at one commencement. Hyperbole then becomes normative; eulogies become truths. Academics earned recognition and promotion by composing hagiography of the King and royals. Royals are pampered by absurd exaltations while people make themselves believe in such absurdity. As Viengrat shows, every virtue in the nation must be connected to the King — Love the King, say no to narcotics, drive safely, eliminate mosquito larvae, and more.[32]

Third, the excessive royalism has survived owing to the control of public discourse on the monarchy by meeting it with harsh punishment. Article 112 of the criminal code, commonly known as the *lèse-majesté* law, stipulates that "Whoever defames, insults or threatens the King, Queen, the Heir-apparent or the Regent..." will be punished by imprisonment for three to fifteen years. The law itself is problematic, but the procedure and enforcement of the law is far worse.[33] Problems with the law include the lack of clear definitions or precedents of what constitute "defames" or "insults". The fifteen-year penalty makes it the harshest *lèse-majesté* law in the world. Above all, it is a thought crime or crime against expression. The worst flaw of this law is the provision that anybody can bring the charge against anybody. Thus, the law has been abused to hurt or destroy one's opponent in politics and sometimes even in a personal conflict. Absurdly, the police, prosecutor and judge usually deny bail to the accused, no matter how serious or trivial the violation is, out of fear that they could themselves be charged for *lèse-majesté* too. *Lèse-majesté* also brings public censure to the accused and family without any proven guilt. As a consequence, the climate of fear is pervasive. One cannot know for sure what or why is or is not permissible to speak, think or act. For safety, hyperbolic royalism is common in public. Since 2006, according to Streckfuss (in Chapter 5 of this volume), political conflicts have led to the unprecedented number of *lèse-majesté* cases, from a few per year before 2006 to hundreds a year since then. In addition, the Computer Crime Act 2007 was enacted to suppress the critics of the monarchy in cyberspace. Since the coup, thousands of websites have been blocked by the government agencies each year, putting Thailand high on the list of countries with serious Internet suppression. An increasing number of *lèse-majesté* cases involve Internet providers, webmasters, and users.

Fourth, hyper-royalism is not simply the project and propaganda by the state or the palace. It involves popular participation and integrates into everyday life of the public. Many projects and celebrations are initiated and carried out by civil society. Hyperbolic royalism is not exclusive to the state and government agency but prevalent in mass media and academic discourse as well. It is a public culture. Civil society and the public are also actively involved in the suppression of criticism and scepticism of the monarch/y. Volunteers are recruited by the government in the project "cyber-scout" while many people by themselves seek to track, hunt and hack the critics of the monarchy on cyberspace. Arguably, hyper-royalism is probably not possible without popular participation or if it was not a public culture. Television plays an important role in mediating hyper-royalism. Royal benevolence is assured, repeated, and reassured everyday. Public space is saturated with the sanitized images and stories of the monarchy. Hyper-royalism is not simply a design or project totally manipulated by a super state like Orwell's Big Brother. It is public culture.

For decades, hyper-royalism has saturated the air and everyday life. The reverence is not limited to the royal family, but also to other royals, Privy Councillors, judges, and palace associates. On the other hand, like any totalitarian society, hyper-royalism is never absolute. The ridiculous exaltations and suppression push the unspeakable facts underground. Gossip about the royals is widespread under hyper-royalism, becoming part of public life parallel to the hyperbolic royalism. Critics and opponents of the monarchy emerge too. Hyper-royalism breeds anti-monarchy.

PART TWO: THE ORDINARY ELEPHANT

Disappointment with the Sky

At a rally of the red-shirt movement on 30 December 2008, Nattawut Saikua, one the movement leaders, delivered a historic speech. He spoke about the rights and voices of the lower class people that were robbed and the injustice they had received. The final six minutes were one of the best public speeches in recent Thai history. Improvised but beautiful, the speech played with two metaphors, *din* and *fa* – literally soil or earth and sky. Each of them signifies multiple meanings and nuances. In the particular moment of the speech, nevertheless, hundreds of thousands of people there and those who were watching it subsequently on YouTube understood both metaphors. Here is an excerpted translation of the final six minutes, minus its poetic elements which are beyond my abilities to translate.

> There is no justice left in this country.... We do not get fair treatment from (the state). There is no space for us in the media either. No opportunity for us to announce what we fight for or why. Definitely, we do not have "connections" (*sen*).[34] ...
>
> We were born on the soil, growing up on the soil, and walking on the soil. When we stand on the soil, the distance from the sky is so vast. (Roars, Cheers) Standing on the soil, looking up high above, we know that sky is so far away. Looking down, we know we are worthy like dirt. But with the increasing power of the red shirts ... even when we stand on earth, speaking from the earth, the sky will hear us. For sure (emphasized). (Roars and cheers) The cheers right now, from people who are on the soil, grew up on the soil, will be heard by the sky. For sure (emphasized). The red-shirt people will tell the soil and the sky that "we have hearts too" (emphasized). (Louder roars and cheers) ... The red-shirt people tell the soil and the sky that "we are Thai people too (emphasized).
>
> The red-shirt people want to ask the soil and the sky, if there is no place to stand, they want us to find our own place, don't they? (Louder roars and cheers) ... These cheers will be heard by the sky ....
>
> No matter what have happened, we already have the greatest thing in our life ... the democratic spirit. For this great spirit... for the greatness of all of you [the crowd], the only thing I could do is this.... [He then kneeled down to the floor, bent his body down, paying respect (*wai*) to the crowd; very loud and lengthy cheers from the crowd]. ... People's power is so great![35]

This rally took place two years after the coup in 2006. By then, it was known that General Prem Tinsulanonda, the President of the Privy Council, had engineered the coup. Thus, the palace was implicated too.[36] Since the coup, public gossip about the monarchy's political action was widespread because the palace had showed on many occasions its partisanship in the polarized politics. The alleged judicial "double standard" was also attributed to the monarch/y instruction. Widespread sarcasm among the red-shirt people had it that "the yellows (royalists) can take any action thanks to impunity; the reds are definitely guilty even if they take no action." They were extremely frustrated.

The speech was historic for its courage, empathy and beauty. It was an expression of strong disappointment at the sky, a complaint for being neglected, yet begging for benevolence from it. The loud and lengthy roars and cheers signalled the crowd's agreement and the sentiment they shared with him. Yet, the multiplicity and nuances of the words were up to anybody's interpretations. People cheered for Nattawut's speech according to their own interpretations.

Critics and Anti-Monarchy in the Past

In pre-modern polity, although a king was deified as a heavenly being on earth, critics and challenges were abundant. Folk stories, mythologies, and Buddhist Jataka of a bad king who deserved to be deposed are plenty. Even the top deities are not perfect and may commit wrongdoing. These tales do not inform the anti-monarchy ideology but constitute the normative views between the good and bad rulers. A bad king was part of living culture as much as a good one. People could find religious frameworks to justify a revolt against the bad ruler. Contenders within a court were also common. Despite its sacredness, a reigning monarch was not above challenges or contests, let alone a critic. The absolute monarchs were not exempt from criticism and discontent either. They were abundant. Of course, criticizing the monarch was hazardous. Two writers were punished; Thianwan was put in jail for years and Kulap was sent to a mental asylum for a month with tarnished his reputation to the end of his life.[37] In the 1920s, criticism of the monarchy was increasing inside the court and in public. The last two absolute monarchs were subjects of ridicule, satire, and nasty remarks even in newspapers, including the likening of them to beasts and lizards.[38] Despite the risks, sacredness did not make the monarchs free from criticism and overt discontent.

The first attempt at a revolution against the absolute monarchy, planned for April 1912, grew out of the anti-monarchy views in favour of a republic or at least a limited monarchy.[39] The Announcement #1 by the People's Party in 1932 was historic. It strongly condemned the monarchy, princes and royals for their oppression and exploitation of common people. The People's Party, however, wanted Siam to become a constitutional monarchy, not a republic. During the early years of the new regimes, criticism and rebuke of the monarchy were common. Many princes and high royals fell from their heavenly abodes, forced into exile or ended up on a prison island in the Andaman Sea near the Thai-Malaysian borders. As the monarchists briefly arose again after 1947, so did their critics and the anti-monarchy intellectuals who produced critique of the royalist literature, culture, and historiography. They were the Leftists who had been influenced by Marxism and Maoism. These radicals were severely suppressed after the anti-communist military coup in 1957. As the leftist ideology was revived in the radical period between 1973 and 1976, many writings from the 1950s generation that were critical to the monarchy were reprinted and widely circulated in public. An example of the most influential writings of the time is *The Real Face of Thai Feudalism Today* by Jit Phoumisak, a revolutionary intellectual who was arrested in 1957, went to join the communist guerillas after his release in 1965, and died in fighting in 1966.[40] But in the same period, anti-communism also reached its height to counter the rise of Thai radicalism and the perceived communist threat. While hyper-royalism as a political ideology to fight communism began to emerge, critique of the monarchy and anti-monarchy literature was also abundant in public. Anti-communism and anti-monarchy generated their adversaries.

After the 1976 massacre, the radicals went underground or into exile. They subsequently produced a large amount of highly damaging anti-monarchy literature, mostly for underground circulation. This literature included the damning analysis of the monarch/y role in the 1976 massacre, several coups and political events, studies of the royal monopolies and business, anti-monarchy history, poems, satires, and damaging gossips about the royals.[41] A few anti-monarchy historical writings, such as *Kao Ratchakan* [Nine Reigns], imitate the royal chronicle by focusing on each reign of the Chakri Dynasty. But instead of accomplishments, it is a history of wrongdoings, crimes, corruption, scandals, adultery, sexual predations and exploitation, and royal incest. Many are similar to the gossips and literature of later years produced by non-communists and by some royalist rivals. As the radical movement, including the Communist Party of Thailand (CPT), folded in the mid-1980s, these critics also faded away. By the 2000s a large number of these former radicals turned royalists, supporting the yellow-shirt movement and the royalist coup in 2006. Meanwhile, a new generation and new kind of critiques of the monarchy and anti-monarchy was born.

The Disillusioned and Awakened

The red-shirt movement originally comprises of those Thaksin supporters against the 2006 coup. Most had no backgrounds connecting to the radicals of the earlier generations. Quite the contrary, not so long ago they were non-political, non-ideological, common folks who typically were royalist and conservative. Before the coup in 2006, as Thaksin was under attacks by media and public intellectuals, they threw the communist allegations and *lèse-majesté* charges against some of those critics of Thaksin and called for the ban of a book that published critical comments against the monarchy.[42] They showed not a slight hint of criticism to the monarchy. They fought the opponents of Thaksin, not the monarchy, because they were royalists too. It was the 2006 coup and its ramifications that overhauled their views on the monarchy.

To these supporters of Thaksin, the palace's alleged involvement in the coup was shocking. Apart from the claim by the coup group that their action was approved by the palace, it was revealed later that the coup was engineered by the palace's inner circle, involving the President of the Privy Council and some Councillors, the Supreme Court President, the Administrative Court President, and His Majesty's long-time personal acquaintance. Thaksin once referred to these people as (literally translated) "the meritorious people outside the constitution", i.e. the unconstitutional powerful people. At first, the red-shirt movement pointed to Prem and other monarchists, but drew a line below the monarch. Many of them could defend the King but showed no mercy to Prem.[43] It was with this definition that the category of "*ammat*" was formulated by the red shirts. From there, it did not take a leap for the line under the monarch to blur or disappear. Among the red shirts, the realization of the role of the monarch/y is called *ta sawaang*, literally eyes cleared or eyes brightened up, i.e. awakened or disillusioned.

The last straw that opened up the eyes of many red shirts was the Queen's attendance of the funeral of a female member of the royalist yellow-shirt movement (the People's Alliance for Democracy) who died in a clash with the police in October 2007. Despite doubts by many experts and the public, it was officially concluded that she was killed by the explosion of a tear-gas canister near her body.[44] The Queen made the remark that the dead was a good person who was loyal to the monarchy. Not only did the Queen mark the death as a royalist martyr, but her presence and remark was an unambiguous statement of the palace's view of the incident, the demonstration, the PAD, Thaksin, and the whole political conflict that have engulfed the country from then up to now. Many red shirts later dubbed the incident as the "National Awakening Day" (*Wan ta sawaang haeng chat*).

Nattawut's speech represented the widespread collective disappointment with the sky. As the red shirts were insulted by their opponents through these years as "dirt", "water-buffalo", "idiots", "foot rags" and so on, his offer of a *wai* on his knees to these foot rags hinted at the Thai world being turned upside down, since such an act is normally reserved for a sacred object or a higher being such as a monk or royals. The widespread *ta sawaang* phenomenon was beyond anticipation by any political observer, whereas many found it difficult to let go of their life-long faith in the monarchy. We may never know the numbers, degree or nuances among the disillusioned ones because the subject is unspeakable. It is obvious, nonetheless, that after the killings of the red shirts in April–May 2010, the disillusionment has grown exponentially both in size and degree. They took their voices onto the main street, literally.

The Ta Sawaang in Public Sphere

Here are some observations of the "Awakened" in current Thai politics. They bear at least three important differences from previous critics of royalism and anti-monarchy. First of all, it is not an outgrowth of a leftist or anti-monarchy ideology or movement. The ideologues of the Awakened are mostly the pseudonymous of organic intellectuals among the red shirts, namely Choophong, Akhom Sydney, Banpot, Woodside, and Khathawut with a few exceptions who use real names such as Surachai Danwattananuson. None of them, except Surachai, are academics or the old leftists of the 1970s. Their critical discourse is not the radical leftist and without academic pretension.[45] Nonetheless, their Internet broadcasts are followed by thousands of loyal followers who redistribute the broadcasts further via cyber media. In fact, the intellectual foods that nourish their discontent with the establishment are from daily newspapers, ordinary comments in cyberspace, gossip and rumours, secret recordings and photos of the unholy lifestyles of the royals, and public discussions on current issues. More accounts of how one became *ta sawaang* appear in cyberspace (for example, Junya 2010 and 2011). There is not yet a treatise or manifesto of their views. The *ta sawaang* people are the anti-thesis, the counterpart of the monarchist, royal democracy and especially hyper-royalism. The monarch/y and hyper-royalism breed their own critics.

Secondly, the Awakened are massive in scale. Although we might say that the radicals of the 1970s were also a mass movement, they were not a huge political community. The Awakened this time, on the other hand, is widespread across the country and deep among the lower class population. It is fair to say that the scale of the anti-thesis to the monarchy this time is unprecedented and would dwarf all previous anti-monarchy. Thirdly, the Awakened survive by open politics, not a clandestine operation like the anti-monarchists of the past. The Internet is their home and refuge to vent their disappointment, disillusionment and anger, and to coordinate their activities. Public demonstrations are actual meeting places. The state, on the contrary, tries to silence them, putting them out of sight or pushing them underground by blocking and suppressing hundreds of websites, blogs and web boards, and by arrests. The suppression has so far has failed to stop the spread of the Awakened phenomenon. Criticism, nasty remarks, anti-monarchy expressions have found their audience by the use of metaphors, codes, metonymical insinuation, jokes, and a large number of allusions that are understood by the *ta sawaang* community but that do not cross the legal line of *lèse-majesté*. Like the users of social media, the *ta sawaang* community has produced its own language, forms of expressions, and literary genres for their communication and circulations of ideas, views and feelings — all in open space.

On 19 September 2010, at the first commemoration of the red shirts after the killings in May 2010, tens of thousands of people showed up at the site of the killings. The gathering was initiated via Internet by a small group of the red shirts to mourn their fellows. Even without a leader and no planned activity, so much took place spontaneously by the people themselves. The most striking thing was when people tied small strips of red cloth to form a giant net covering the entire intersection and the streets that witnessed the atrocity. Then, another act that the media could not report was thousands of small items of graffiti written onto any possible surface in the public space including walls, pavements, bus shelters, and on the street furniture. The authorities spent the entire night afterward cleaning everything off. The dangerous words and statements were clear in plain sight. Yet, this elephant is not supposed to be seen either.

Among words on the streets found that evening, many were straightforward and harsh, while some were comical, cute, clever and creative. A new literary practice of the *ta sawaang* people was born and has become common since that gathering. Instead of writing graffiti on a public surface, the creative words found another surface in public sphere — on T-shirts. An industry of *ta sawaang* T-shirts spread like wildfire at every gathering of the reds. "I don't know; I am sick", for example, is a plain seemingly irrelevant statement that in fact says a lot. "The Bitch ordered to shoot; the Bastard ordered to kill" is widespread among the Awakened who know what the two Bs mean. There are more popular and hilarious coded phrases in the streets and on T-shirts than I can report.

Witch-Hunt

The second elephant is a phantasm to the authorities. They deny the public discussion of it even though they are alarmed and frightened and react strongly. The notorious *lèse-majesté* law has been enforced and abused in recent years to the extent never seen before. In response to the uses of the new media among the Awakened, the Computer Crime Act 2007 is another tool to battle the growing cyber critique of the monarchy. In July 2010, the Democrat-led government launched a new programme called "Cyber Scout" to recruit young people to help the government watch out for the alleged dangerous activities on the Internet and report to the police. The name "Cyber Scout" is a reminiscence of the royalist right-wing movement, the "Village Scout", that was active in the 1976 massacre. Another group of Thai Facebook users who call themselves "Social Sanctions" or "SS" was set up for the same purpose. Many more cyber police were created to hunt down the cyber critics of the monarchy. In March 2009, dozens of international dignitaries and known scholars signed a letter to the Thai government calling for a reform of the *lèse-majesté* law, warning that the law and its abuse to suppress freedom of expression would likely backfire to hurt the monarchy. As one of the campaigners, I was slandered in the Thai media for being an anti-monarchist, traitor, and for being ignorant about Thai history and culture. A retired police general and a famous royalist, Vasit Dejkunchorn, alleged that there was a plot for a republic. While the Democrat government and some senior royalists said they would look into the abuses of the law, nothing was done but more arrests. The climate of fear and witch-hunts continue.

Many royalist Thais often say that one does not have to live in fear of the law if he loves the monarchy like most Thais do, and that the law is harmless to the true Thai people. If one does not like the monarchy, they often say too, he should not be Thai and should go to live elsewhere. These sayings make sense only in the cocoon of hyper-royalism, but nowhere else. Unfortunately, as hyper-royalism gets stronger and Bhumibol becomes a sacred cult, he cannot be mentioned with less than the superlative exaltations. Thailand at the end of King Bhumibol's era looks like a living Orwellian society. Hyper-royalism, royal democracy and the cult of Bhumibol fortify one another. Unfortunately, he is mortal and his mortality is coming soon. Given the likely mess during succession transition, the Orwellian conditions are likely to intensify unless Thailand can get out of its state of denial.

FINAL WORDS: TWO ELEPHANTS IN THE ROOM = STATE OF DENIAL

Nowadays, no one would disagree that the 2006 coup was one the most damaging political disasters in modern Thai history. Yet, the deep roots of the disaster remain unspeakable. Thanks to his popularity as evident in landslide victories in the five elections, Thaksin was seen as the challenger to the monarchy.[46] The latter also believed that Thaksin financed some high royals to pave the way for his highly ambitious position in the future.[47] The monarchists' paranoia was reflected in various allegations of Thaksin's disrespect to the monarchy and his desire for a republic. A crucial condition for such paranoia is their anxiety that the end of the reign is coming any time; thus, the monarchist kingmakers cannot tolerate a powerful political regime for it might jeopardize the interests of the entire network monarchy and the royal democracy that they have nurtured for decades. Hence, Thaksin had to be removed from power. This probably is the most important ulterior motive of the coup-makers. Had the succession not been an issue, the Thaksin-phobia among the monarchists might not have been hysterical. The political crisis since 2006 is the ramifications of this paranoid phobia.

Nonetheless, the crisis was also the result of several deep holes into which Thailand had long dug before the coup. First, had the monarchy been truly "above" politics, a succession would have been inconsequential. Instead of institutionalizing the democratic system without interference by the monarch/y, royal democracy has done the opposite, making the succession so crucial to the future of the country. Secondly, royal democracy is fundamentally flawed for two reasons. One, it requires a charismatic monarch which is an exception rather than a norm. Royal democracy is therefore unstable. Two, the cult of a sacred monarch in a democracy is oxymoronic because sacredness survives by hyperbole and unaccountability while accountability is indispensable for popular democracy. It is impossible to have both. Royal democracy is therefore anti-democratic. Both flaws are revealed in the condition described above.

Third, the success and otherwise of the monarchy in the past sixty years cannot be separable from King Bhumibol. But his virtues are not transferable to the next king. It is no secret in Thailand how extremely unpopular the Crown Prince has been. Some monarchists, like the PAD, have made it clear that their royalism is for Bhumibol only. This is probably the case for the military too. Wishful rumours and fantasies are widespread in Thailand today for an alternative scenario of the next monarch.[48] But they are merely wishful thinking. Moreover, most people do not realize that the father's shoes are too big for the next king anyway. Bhumibol's perceived success sets the next king for failure; probably similar to what King Chulalongkorn did to his son, Vajiravudh, a hundred years ago. The mountain is too steep for the successor to reach the top. Hyper-royalism digs a grave for the next king.

For the fourth and final hole, due to all of the uncertainties, the significance of the kingmakers increases. Politics within the network monarchy is not less deadly. The roles of the Privy Council and the judiciary in fighting Thaksin have been astonishingly naked because the stakes are very high. But the military certainly is important as well. However, their overt roles have resulted in the emergence of *ta sawaang* people who are not blindly obedient anymore. Suppression in the name of protecting the monarchy does not work but backfires. Hyper-royalism and suppression produce anti-monarchy.

In climbing out of these deep holes, the two elephants must be recognized in order to chart a proper course for a peaceful solution. But most people still refuse to see the elephants in the room, and for those who do, they are not allowed to acknowledge them but are supposed to deny seeing them. Instead of confronting the reality, the country celebrates the Emperor's magical clothes even when there are none. And when a boy says out loud that the king is naked, unlike in the well-known fable, he is thrown into jail. Both the state and the civil society are cooperatively in the state of denial and self-delusion. Since the Cold War, the Thai monarchy has been praised as the key to stability. It is time to admit that such stability hinges primarily on a deeply flawed and unstable system with extraordinary costs, such as four mass-bloodsheds in less than forty years. At the end of Bhumibol's era, it is time to admit that the dominance of the monarchy in the political system is at the heart of Thailand's current political instability and could remain the source of more serious instability for some years to come.

Notes

1. The first part of this chapter is based on two previous incarnations. The first one was a paper presented at the workshop on "Monarchies in Transition", Stanford University in June 2008. The revised version for publication was done shortly after the massacre in 2010. But it was never published due to concerns for several authors in the same project. In this paper, I have revised the earlier draft thoroughly. Then the section on the anti-monarchy is added. Thanks to Larry Diamond (CDDRL, Stanford University) for encouraging the author to finish the earlier draft even though the publication never materialized.

2. The 1976 massacre remains a sensitive subject in Thailand exactly because the roles of the palace in mobilizing the right-wing perpetrators, in the conspiracy that led to the bloodshed, and in the killing itself remaining mysterious, hence an unspeakable subject (Thongchai 2002). The usual acclaims of the king's roles in the 1973 and 1992 incidents are mostly without a critical investigation into the reasons or politics of the interventions, with Somsak (1996) a rare exception.

3. See Chaiyan Rajchagool, *The Absolute Monarchy in Siam* (Bangkok: White Lotus, 1994); Kullada Kesbunchoo, *The Rise and Fall of Absolute Monarchy in Siam* (London: Routledge Curzon, 2005); and Thongchai Winichakul, *Siam Mapped: A History of the Geo-Body of a Nation* (Honolulu: Hawaii University Press, 1994).

4. See Thongchai Winichakul, "The Quest for 'Siwilai': A geographical discourse of Civilizational Thinking in the Late 19th and early 20th Century Siam", *Journal of Asian Studies* 59, no. 3 (Aug 2000): 528–49.

5. See Chaiyan, *The Absolute Monarchy in Siam*; and Tamara Loos, *Subject Siam, Subject Siam: Family, Law and Colonial Modernity in Thailand* (Ithaca, NY: Cornell University Press, 2006), Ch. 2.

6. See Matthew Copeland, "Contested Nationalism and the 1932 Overthrow of the Absolute Monarchy in Siam", unpublished Ph.D. thesis, Australian National University, 1993.

7. See Thongchai Winichakul "Toppling Democracy", *Journal of Contemporary Asia* 38, no. 1 (Feb 2008): 14–15 and 19–21.

8. See Nattapoll Chaiching, "The Monarchy and the Royalist Movement in Modern Thai Politics 1932–1957", in *Saying the Unsayable*, edited by Søren Ivarsson and Lotte Isager (Copenhagen: NIAS Press, 2010), pp. 151–63.

9. For an extensive account, see Thongchai, "Toppling Democracy".

10. See Phorphant Ouyyanont, "Crown Property Bureau from Crisis to Opportunity", in *Thai Capital after the 1997 Crisis*, edited by Pasuk Phongpaichit and Chris Baker (Singapore: Institute of Southeast Asian Studies, 2008), pp. 155–86.

11. See Thak Chaloemtiarana, *Thailand: The Politics of Despotic Paternalism* (Bangkok: Social Science Association of Thailand, 1979).

12. See Nattapoll Chaiching, "Phra Barami Pokklao Tai Ngao Insi: Phaen Sonkkhram Chittawitthaya Amerikan Kap Kansang Sathaban Kasat Pen Sanyalak Haengchat [The royal benevolence under the eagle's shadow: American's psychological warfare and the making of the monarchy as the national symbol], *Fa Diew Kan* 9, no. 2 (Apr–Jun 2001): 94–166.

13. See Sinae Hyun, "Do Good by Stealth (*Pit Thong Lang Phra*): Cold War Thai Nation Building through the Border Patrol Police School Project, 1951–1980", paper presented at the AAS-ICAS Conference, Honolulu, Hawaii, 2011.

14. See Prajak Kongkirati, *Lae Laew Khwam Khluanwai Ko Prakot* [Thus, the Movement Emerges], (Bangkok: Thammasat University Press, 2005), pp. 464–85.

15. See Thongchai, "Toppling Democracy", pp. 15–17.

16. See Katherine Bowie, *Rituals of National Loyalty: the Village Scout Movement in Thailand* (New York: Columbia University Press, 1997); and David Morell and Chai-anan Samudavanich, *Political Conflicts in Thailand: Reform, Reaction and Revolution* (Cambridge: Oelschlager, Gunn & Hain, 1981).

17. See William Callahan, "The Discourse of Vote Buying and Political Reform in Thailand", *Pacific Affairs* (Spring 2005): 95–113.

18. See Kevin Hewison and Kengkij Kittirainglarp, "Thai-Style Democracy: the Royalist Struggle for Thailand's Politics", in *Saying the Unsayable: Monarchy and Democracy in Thailand*, edited by Søren Ivarsson and Lotte Isager (Copenhagen: NIAS Press, 2010), pp. 179–202.

19. The article was originally presented to the young King Anand, Rama VIII, in 1946. Prince Dhani Nivat was a key member of the royalist leadership during 1945–51, later a Privy Councillor, the Regent and personal teacher of King Bhumibol. The most important leader for the royalist revival after World War II was Prince Rangsit. Handley (2006) provides excellent accounts of the importance of both princes.

20. See Stanley J. Tambiah, *World Conqueror, World Renouncer* (Cambridge University Press, 1976).

21. The Pali phrase *mahasamarta* was usually translated as "the Great Elected". Murashima traces the idea to Prince Dhani (1947). In my opinion, "assumed" might be a better translation than elected or chosen, and the first claim to this

Buddhist concept was by King Mongkut (r. 1851–68). See also Eiji Murashima, "The Origin of Modern Official State Ideology in Thailand", *Journal of Southeast Asian Studies* 19, no. 1 (Mar 1988): 80–96.

22. See Peter Jackson, "Virtual Divinity: A 21st Century Discourse of Thai Royal Influence", in *Saying the Unsayable*, edited by Søren Ivarsson and Lotte Isager (Copenhagen, NIAS Press, 2010), pp. 29–60.

23. See Christine Gray, "Thailand: The Soteriological State in the 1970s", unpublished Ph.D. dissertation, University of Chicago, 1986.

24. See Irene Stengs, *Worshipping the Great Moderniser: King Chulalongkorn, Patron Saint of the Thai Middle Class* (Seattle: University of Washington Press, 2009).

25. See Maurizio Peleggi, *Lords of Things: the Fashioning of the Siamese Monarchy's Modern Image* (Honolulu: University of Hawaii Press, 2002).

26. See Chanida Chitbundit, *Khrongkan An-nuang Machak Phraratchadamri: Kan Satha-Pana Phraratcha Amnat-nam Nai Phrabatsomdet Phrachaoyuhua* [The Royal Projects: the Establishment of Royal Hegemony], (Bangkok: the Foundation for Textbooks in Social Science and the Humanities, 2007).

27. See, for example, "The World's Richest Royals", by Tatiana Serafin, in <http://www.forbes.com>, 17 June 2007. Similar rankings appear every year since then.

28. Information about the CPB here and below is from Phorphant 2008*a*, 2008*b*.

29. Each year the Royal Household receives budget from the government. In addition, expenses for the monarchy are allocated in various government agencies, for instance in the police and defence budgets for security expenses. See the annual budgets for the Bureau of the Thai Royal Household 1997–2008 (in baht) in *Fa Diew Kan* 6, no. 1 (Jan–Mar 2008), p. 21, which also refers to the comparison with the budgets of the British monarchy according to "World's Most Expensive Royal Family" <http://jotman.blogspot.com/2008/02/worlds-most-expensive-royal-family.html>.

30. See Gray, "Thailand: The Soteriological State in the 1970s".

31. The remarks mentioned in this paragraph can be easily found in the red-shirt movement. The "invisible hand" and the "power beyond the constitution" first appeared before the coup and became controversial as Thaksin's opponents charged that they meant the monarchy. They were even more widespread after the coup as codes to mean the royalists and, for some, the monarch. The *ammat-prai* characterization of hierarchy in Thai society became widespread as the red-shirt movement since 2008. At every gathering especially the one that ended up in bloodshed in 2010, the two words were written and uttered everywhere, in the street and literature, by the leaders and the grass root supporters, as they captured the fundamental grievance all in the movement shared.

32. Viengrat Nethipo, "Structural Context of the Thai Political Crisis: the Shift in Triangle of the Power Sphere", paper presented at the AAS-ICAS Conference, Honolulu, Hawaii, April 2011, pp. 7–8.

33. See David Streckfuss, *Truth on Trial in Thailand: Defamation, Treason and Lèse-majesté* (London: Routledge, 2011).

34. "Connection" here means access to privileges, favours and probably impunity. It is generally understood to be a property of the elite or people with either wealth or power.

35. See <http://www.youtube.com/watch?v=LDLIqdc4yro&feature=related>.

36. The photo of the coup leaders having an audience with Their Majesties on 19 September 2006 was publicized by the coup group itself to suggest the approval of the coup by the monarch. Anti-coup people read the same message from the photo.

37. See Chai-anan Samudavanich, *Chiwit Lae Ngan Khong Thianwan Lae Ko So Ro Kulap* [Lives and Works of Thianwan and K.S. R. Kulab] (Bangkok: Thiranan, 1979); and Mananya (pseudo), *K. R. R. Kulap* [K.S.R. Kulab] (Bangkok: Chulalongkorn University Press, 1982).

38. Copeland explains that harsh criticism to the absolute monarchy was possible thanks to the extraterritoriality, as they were published as the subjects of European powers. Semi-colonialism provided freedom of expression. See Copeland, "Contested Nationalism and the 1932 Overthrow of the Absolute Monarchy in Siam", unpublished Ph.D. thesis, Australian National University, 1993.

39. See Nattapoll, "Phra Barami Pokklao Tai Ngao Insi".

40. See Craig Reynolds, *Thai Radical Discourse, The Real Face of Thai Feudalism Today* (Ithaca: Cornell Southeast Asia Programme, 1987).

41. See microfilm Reel #6, A.1.6.2 of the collections "Thai Radicalism" at Thammasat University Archives or at University of Wisconsin Library.

42. In early 2006, Sulak Sivaraksa, a prominent social critic, and Thanapol Eawsakul, the editor of a radical journal were charged for *lèse-majesté* by these supporters of Thaksin for Sulak's article in the journal.

43. A demonstration outside Prem's residence in early 2007 was raucous, with harsh and nasty words, anger and hostility. It ended in a violent clash with the police. The demonstrators made clear to the public that their target were Prem and his royalist conspirators of the coup, not the monarch.

44. The counter account alleges that she carried a number of fragile explosive devices for the PAD's use when the chaos took place and people ran amok due to the tear gas. The bombs accidentally went off.

45. Some critics of the monarchists are academics and/or strongly ideological, such as Giles Ji Ungpakorn (2007) and Somsak Jeamteerasakul (1996). But they are not the ideologues of the Awakened.

46. Thaksin's party won the elections in 2000, 2004, 2005, 2007 and 2011. But the 2005 one was nullified by the court for the alleged illegal voting booths.

47. In 2002, the Thaksin government expelled a journalist for his report of a monetary transaction between Thaksin and a high royal. A well-known royalist said at a meeting I attended in mid-2009 that the king and royals were worried

that Thaksin was trying to, in his words, "privatize the royals". Thaksin's associates denied the allegations.

48. It is widely misunderstood that Princess Sirindhorn, who is more popular than her brother and is acceptable by the military, is eligible for the throne. Legally as of now, Prince Vajiralongkorn is the only legitimate heir to the throne. No one else is. The law of succession was established in 1886 to avoid turmoil within the courts and in the royal family as had occurred before. A sudden change of the heir would be like tearing down the succession law. Not only the country but also the royal family would be in turmoil.

References

Bowie, Katherine. *Rituals of National Loyalty: the Village Scout Movement in Thailand*. New York: Columbia University Press, 1997.

Callahan, William. "The Discourse of Vote Buying and Political Reform in Thailand". *Pacific Affairs* (Spring 2005): 95–113.

Chai-anan Samudavanich. *Chiwit Lae Ngan Khong Thianwan Lae Ko So Ro Kulap* [Lives and Works of Thianwan and K.S. R. Kulab]. Bangkok: Thiranan, 1979.

Chanida Chitbundit. *Khrongkan An-nuang Machak Phraratchadamri: Kan Satha-Pana Phraratcha Amnat-nam Nai Phrabatsomdet Phrachaoyuhua* [The Royal Projects: the Establishment of Royal Hegemony]. Bangkok: the Foundation for Textbooks in Social Science and the Humanities, 2007.

Chaiyan Rajchagool. *The Absolute Monarchy in Siam*. Bangkok: White Lotus, 1994.

Copeland, Matthew. "Contested Nationalism and the 1932 Overthrow of the Absolute Monarchy in Siam". Unpublished Ph.D. thesis, Australian National University, 1993.

Dhani Nivat, Prince. "The Old Conceptions of the Siamese Monarchy". *Journal of the Siam Society* 36 (1947), Pt. 2.

Giles Ji Ungpakorn. *A Coup for the Rich: Thailand's Political Crisis*. Bangkok: Workers Democracy Publishing, 2007.

Gray, Christine. "Thailand: The Soteriological State in the 1970s". Unpublished Ph.D. dissertation, University of Chicago, 1986.

Handley, Paul. *The King Never Smiles*. New Haven: Yale University Press, 2006.

Hewison, Kevin and Kengkij Kittirainglarp. "Thai-Style Democracy: the Royalist Struggle for Thailand's Politics". In *Saying the Unsayable: Monarchy and Democracy in Thailand*, edited by Søren Ivarsson and Lotte Isager. Copenhagen: NIAS Press, 2010.

Hyun, Sinae. " 'Do Good by Stealth (*Pit Thong Lang Phra*)': Cold War Thai Nation Building through the Border Patrol Police School Project, 1951–1980". Paper presented at the AAS-ICAS Conference, Honolulu, Hawaii, 2011.

Jackson, Peter. "Virtual Divinity: A 21st Century Discourse of Thai Royal Influence". In *Saying the Unsayable: Monarchy and Democracy in Thailand*, edited by Søren Ivarsson and Lotte Isager. Copenhagen: NIAS Press, 2010.

Junya Yimprasert. "Thammai Thung Mai Rak Nailuang" [Why don't I love the King?]. Posted on <http://hirvikatu10.net/timeupthailand/?page_id=88&lang=th> on 24 June 2010.

———. "Ao-chana Khwamklua Phraborom Dechanuphap" [Overcoming fear of monarchy in Thailand] <www.junyayimprasert.blogspot.com>, 2011.

Kullada Kesbunchoo. *The Rise and Fall of Absolute Monarchy in Siam*. London: RoutledgeCurzon, 2005.

Loos, Tamara. *Subject Siam, Subject Siam: Family, Law and Colonial Modernity in Thailand*. Ithaca, NY: Cornell University Press, 2006.

Mananya (pseudo). *K.s.r. kulap* [K.S.R. Kulab]. Bangkok: Chulalongkorn University Press, 1982.

McCargo, Duncan. "Network Monarchy and Legitimacy Crises in Thailand". *Pacific Review* 18, no. 4 (2005): 499–519.

Morell, David and Chai-anan Samudavanich. *Political Conflicts in Thailand: Reform, Reaction and Revolution*. Cambridge: Oelschlager, Gunn & Hain, 1981.

Murashima, Eiji. "The Origin of Modern Official State Ideology in Thailand". *Journal of Southeast Asian Studies* 19, no. 1 (March 1988): 80–96.

Nattapoll Chaiching. "The Monarchy and the Royalist Movement in Modern Thai Politics 1932-1957". In *Saying the Unsayable: Monarchy and Democracy in Thailand*, edited by Søren Ivarsson and Lotte Isager. Copenhagen: NIAS Press, 2010.

———. "Chak Khana R. S. 130 Thung Khana Ratsadon: Khwampenma Khong Khwamkit Prachathippatai Nai Prathetthai" [From the 1912 Group to the People's Party: Backgrounds of the ideas of 'democracy' in Thailand]. *Sinlapawatthanatham* [Arts and Culture] 32, no. 4 (February 2011a): 80–99.

———. "Phra Barami Pokklao Tai Ngao Insi: Phaen Sonkkhram Chittawitthaya Amerikan Kap Kansang Sathaban Kasat Pen Sanyalak Haengchat" [The royal benevolence under the eagle's shadow: American's psychological warfare and the making of the monarchy as the national symbol]. *Fa Diew Kan* 9, no. 2 (Apr–Jun 2011b): 94–166.

Peleggi, Maurizio. *Lords of Things: The Fashioning of the Siamese Monarchy's Modern Image*. Honolulu: University of Hawaii Press, 2002.

Phorphant Ouyyanont. "Crown Property Bureau from Crisis to Opportunity". In *Thai Capital after the 1997 Crisis*, edited by Pasuk Phongpaichit and Chris Baker, pp. 155–86. Singapore: Institute of Southeast Asian Studies, 2008a.

———. "Crown Property Bureau in Thailand and the Crisis of 1997". *Journal of Contemporary Asia* 38, no. 1 (2008b): 166–89.

Prajak Kongkirati. *Lae Laew Khwam Khluanwai Ko Prakot* [Thus, the Movement Emerges]. Bangkok: Thammasat University Press, 2005.

Reynolds, Craig. *Thai Radical Discourse, The Real Face of Thai Feudalism Today*. Ithaca: Cornell Southeast Asia Programme, 1987.

Somsak Jeamteerasakul. *Prawattisat Thi Pheung Sang* [History that was just constructed]. Bangkok: Tula Ramluk Publishing, 1996.

Stengs, Irene. *Worshipping the Great Moderniser: King Chulalongkorn, Patron Saint of the Thai Middle Class*. Seattle: University of Washington Press, 2009.

Streckfuss, David. *Truth on Trial in Thailand: Defamation, Treason and Lèse-majesté*. London: Routledge, 2011.

Tambiah, Stanley J. *World Conqueror, World Renouncer*. Cambridge: Cambridge University Press, 1976.

Thak Chaloemtiarana. *Thailand: The Politics of Despotic Paternalism*. Bangkok: Social Science Association of Thailand, 1979.

Thongchai Winichakul. "The Quest for 'Siwilai': A Geographical Discourse of Civilizational Thinking in the Late 19th and early 20th Century Siam". *Journal of Asian Studies* 59, no. 3 (Aug 2000): 528–49.

―――. "Remembering/Silencing the Traumatic Past: Ambivalent Memories of the October 1976 Massacre in Bangkok". In *Cultural Crisis and Social Memory*, edited by Charles Keyes and Shigeharu Tanabe, pp. 243–83. London: RoutledgeCurzon, 2002.

―――. "Toppling Democracy". *Journal of Contemporary Asia* 38, no. 1 (Feb 2008): 11–37.

Viengrat Nethipo. "Structural Context of the Thai Political Crisis: the Shift in Triangle of the Power Sphere". Ppaper presented at the AAS-ICAS Conference, Honolulu, Hawaii, April 2011.

5

FREEDOM AND SILENCING UNDER THE NEO-ABSOLUTIST MONARCHY REGIME IN THAILAND, 2006–2011

David Streckfuss

At first glance, one of the clearest indicators of the changes wrought by the 19 September 2006 coup in Thailand is the sharp decline in freedom of expression. In the five years since the coup, the number of *lèse-majesté* prosecutions has skyrocketed to heretofore unimaginable highs while the post-coup cyber control legislation — the Computer Crimes Act — has allowed the Thai government to erect a firewall almost as thick as that of China. By all international indices, freedom of expression and political freedom in general have declined in Thailand to such an extent that any claims by the Thai state of being democratic at all ring hollow indeed. While there is no question that the post-coup conditions in Thailand have further eroded constitutional or other legal protections of the right to freedom of expression, it might make more sense from a historical perspective to speak of the post-2006 Thai regimes as the culmination of a six-decade-long process that ironically has made Thailand into something more akin to absolute monarchies of the past or to the few more-or-less absolute monarchies of the present.

In this study, we will use "absolutism" as a jumping-off point for examining the results of the remarkable confluence of historical legacies stretching back the late 1940s with the partial restoration of the monarchy. This process was judicially legitimated by Supreme Court decisions of the 1950s, crystallized ideologically and resacralized under Sarit Thanarat in the early 1960s, and legally secured after 1976 with a toughened *lèse-majesté* law. For the next three decades, Thailand swayed to and fro, between democracy and authoritarianism, but lurching sharply towards the latter with the 2006 coup. Figure 5.1 gives some idea how the "normal" progression from absolute monarchy to democratic constitutional monarchy was arrested in 1958. In the last five years, this shift toward neo-absolutism culminated, transforming the appearance if not the essence of Thailand into a formation sharing more features with an absolute monarchy than with democratic constitutional monarchies.

More than any other feature that came to define absolutism in Europe and Thailand's neo-absolutism is the legal provision protecting the monarchy, the *lèse-majesté* law. Examining the pattern and frequency of its use, the political context in which it resides, and the way it comes to

FIGURE 5.1
"Typical" Historical Evolution vs. Thailand's Historical (D)evolution

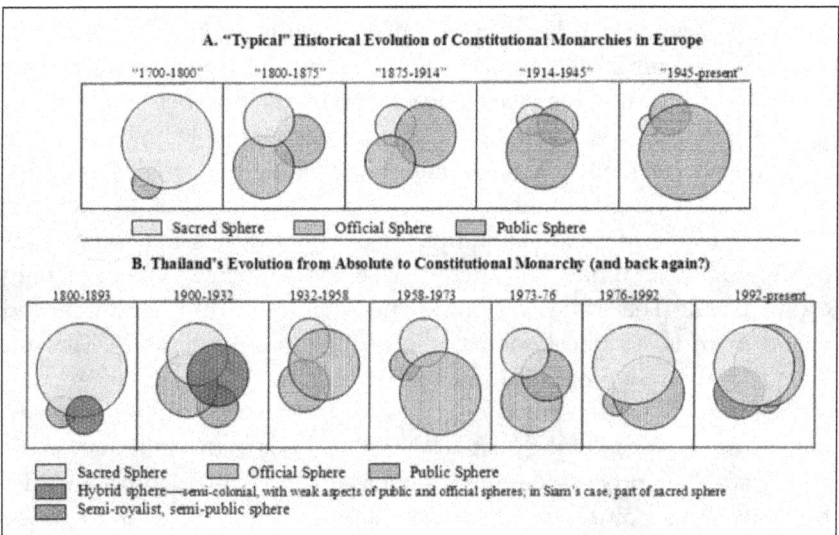

A. "Typical" Historical Evolution of Constitutional Monarchies in Europe

"1700-1800"   "1800-1875"   "1875-1914"   "1914-1945"   "1945-present"

☐ Sacred Sphere   ▨ Official Sphere   ▨ Public Sphere

B. Thailand's Evolution from Absolute to Constitutional Monarchy (and back again?)

1800-1893   1900-1932   1932-1958   1958-1973   1973-76   1976-1992   1992-present

☐ Sacred Sphere   ▨ Official Sphere   ▨ Public Sphere
▨ Hybrid sphere—semi-colonial, with weak aspects of public and official spheres; in Siam's case, part of sacred sphere
▨ Semi-royalist, semi-public sphere

Source: Streckfuss (2011), p. 31.

define the political regime itself show most clearly the essential structure of absolutism — what we would today call a form of authoritarianism. Like all types of authoritarianism, there is a tendency to justify the regime due to some "exceptionalism". In Thailand, this exceptionalism has been expressed through the propensity to use emergency laws defined semi-legally as "abnormal times", and in government claims that the *lèse-majesté* law is culturally unique. Because authoritarianism in Thailand has almost always been adept in masking itself underneath a veneer of political liberalness, post-2006 coup governments have only until very recently been able to argue that legal restraint has defined the government's use of the *lèse-majesté* law. While acknowledging some problems, the government in a July 2011 report said that it had struck a "balance between protecting the monarchy ... and the right of individuals to express their views".[1]

As this chapter will indicate, nothing could be further from the truth. Where rule of law has been shattered within an entrenched culture of impunity, the *lèse-majesté* law in Thailand has thrived as never before. As a surviving remnant of absolute monarchy and a living legacy of military dictatorship, *lèse-majesté* is an expression of "the state of the exception" under which rule of law and democratic accountability have no role. *Lèse-majesté* is, in other words, an expression of neo-absolutism.

ABSOLUTISM, DUAL STATE, NEO-ABSOLUTISM

The term "absolute monarchy" describes a specific historical stage of state development as European societies passed from feudalism to capitalism.[2] Absolutism was characterized by a consolidation of power of the monarch against the nobility and church, codification of laws and creation of a single justice system, administrative centralization, creation of a professional standing army, the sponsoring and propagation of an ideology justifying an absolutist model, and usually adorning the monarch in the "trappings of majesty", thus placing it in a position of "awe and reverence".[3] Contemporary theorists advocating absolutism differentiated it from arbitrary power, arguing that monarchical power was subject to the laws of God.[4] Absolutism was underpinned by a written constitution for the first time in Europe in 1665 as "King's Law" of Denmark-Norway which said that the monarch "shall from this day forth be revered and considered the most perfect and supreme person on the Earth by all his subjects, standing above all human laws and having no judge above his person, neither in spiritual nor temporal matters, except God alone."[5]

Absolutism was, and is, geographically and historically specific. When absolutist states in Eastern Europe emerged, for instance, they were quite different from their earlier Western counterparts. In the same way, Russia and the Holy German Empire had their own versions of absolutism, mixed with traditions particular to the area but also often adding more liberal elements imported from other contemporary constitutional monarchies. Similarly, "absolute" monarchies of the twentieth century emerged in a milieu quite different from that of the eighteenth century, mixing it with modern elements of totalitarianism, colonialism, socialism, and so on.[6] In some ways, then, it does not seem reasonable to use the phrase "absolute monarchy" to describe anything from this century. However (and perhaps unfortunately), using absolutism to frame what has happened in Thailand brings into relief similarities more akin and more salient with absolutism than with mere authoritarianism.

As absolute monarchies, with the courts as an extension of the Crown, were always subject to a certain level of arbitrariness and/or legal intervention, the term "rule of law" seems to better apply only after a "normal legal order" (i.e. "modern") has already been established.[7] Since the 1940s, Thailand has been caught in what I have termed persistent "abnormal times". Although the importance of "rule of law" is often heralded by Thai leaders, in practice much political action is carried out in opposition to rule of law. In Thai law, there is a state described as "abnormal times' in which the "normal" regime of law may be suspended. Originally conceived as a temporary measure, military and/or authoritarian rule extended temporary emergency law beyond weeks or months to year and decades.[8] As a whole, it was the military that cited abnormal times and consistently frustrated and undermined popular sovereignty. But civilian administrations have done similarly by declaring emergency law, and more recently, Thai courts have seemingly undermined rule of law by handing down decisions that have thwarted the popular will.

Robert Amsterdam has recently argued that modern Thai politics can best be understood through the work of German theorist Ernst Fraenkel's "Dual State" schema. On the one hand, there is the "Normative State" which is "a state governed according to clearly elaborated legal norms, adhering to some level of accountability and due process pursuant to the law". On the other hand, there co-exists the "Prerogative State" which "is a state defined by the arbitrary exercise of power, unchecked by law, subject to the discretion of more or less hidden powers". The Dual State "allows illiberal regimes to preserve the appearance of legalism". From the perspective of the Normative State, Thailand's formal political system can be "described as a parliamentary democracy that operates under the framework of constitutional monarchy". But in reality, it is the Prerogative State that actually governs in Thailand, "defined by the presence of political actors, informal networks, and institutions (including the bureaucracy, the armed forces, Privy Councillors, and their cronies in the business community) that exercise unchecked, unaccountable powers outside the formal rules of the Normative State".[9] Fraenkel notes that the Prerogative State "thrives by veiling its true face". In Thailand, this mechanism is described in Thailand as the "invisible hand".[10] The *lèse-majesté* law, argues Amsterdam, serves to "obscure the intricacies of the Prerogative State, shielding the army and other elites from public scrutiny so long as their actions are justified by the false pretence of 'protecting the monarchy'", and is maintained "by banishing discussion of the Prerogative State's workings to the margins of tolerated public discourse".[11]

A Dual State or a State in a State is not unique to Thailand: it could describe the governing system of any number of countries in the world today. The *lèse-majesté* law in particular has an important relationship to the Dual State theory. The *lèse-majesté* law is a remnant of military dictatorship — that is, of abnormal times and the arbitrary use of power reminiscent of absolutism — and its continued use in its present form undermines actual rule of law.[12] Although some other features of absolutism bear some resemblance to the present situation in Thailand, we restrict our comments only to the most obvious expression of absolutism — the *lèse-majesté* law.[13] *Lèse-majesté* laws in democratic constitutional monarchies are designed to protect the reputation of certain members of the royal family. *Lèse-majesté* laws in less democratic monarchies are used to protect more than just royal personages: they are intended to protect the system of power. To differentiate between the two types, we look back at the examples of pre-revolutionary France and late nineteenth-century Germany, as well as at other contemporary monarchies in the world today. We examine *lèse-majesté* according to the following metrics: (1) the punishment and its evolution, (2) its relationship to constitutional guarantees to freedom of speech, (3) its frequency of use, (4) the targets of charges, (5) the nature of charges, and (6) to what degree the *lèse-majesté* law comes to define the institution and the political order in general.

PUNISHMENT AND ITS EVOLUTION

At the height of absolutism in Europe, the punishment for *lèse-majesté* knew few limits: the penalty could range from relatively light sentences to horrific executions like that of Damiens who was tortured, quartered, and burned at the stake in 1757.[14] By the early twentieth century, *lèse-majesté* in most contexts had become clearly a crime of words, related to sedition. As such, some more conservative regimes still boasted long jail sentences for violators. The maximum punishment in the monarchy of Spain and Tsarist Russia was eight years. Although *lèse-majesté* could result in up to five years' imprisonment in Germany at the time, most sentences were around six months.

Siam was not that different from other monarchies in 1900, with a comparatively lighter maximum sentence of only three years in prison for those convicted of *lèse-majesté* (see Figure 5.2). In 1908, the maximum sentence was raised to seven years, but with no minimum sentence. It appears from anecdotal evidence that most of those found guilty of the crime

FIGURE 5.2
Increase of Punishment under Thai Monarchy, 1900–2011
(In maximum no. of years' imprisonment)

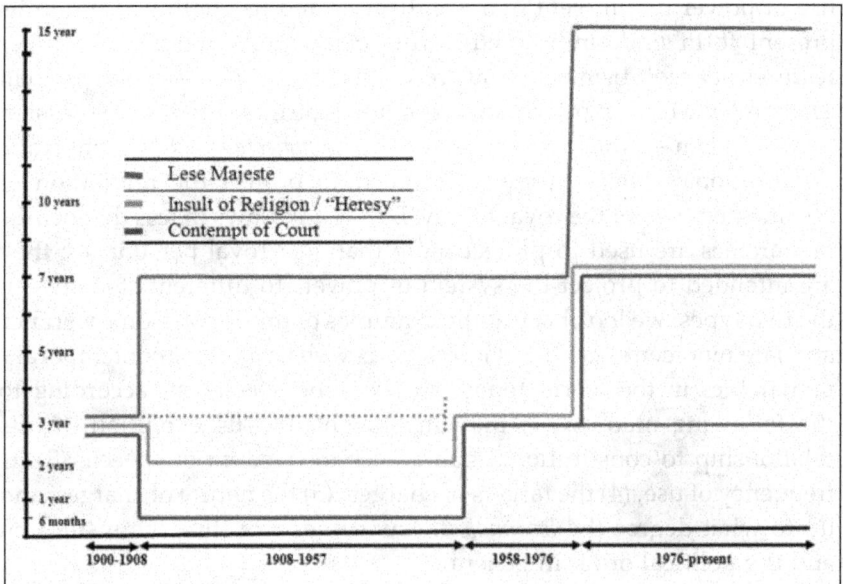

Source: Based on Streckfuss (2011), p. 109.

did not spend more than a few years in jail. As constitutional monarchies in Europe democratized, the punishment for *lèse-majesté* either remained constant or was reduced. Siam followed this trend at first. Although the penalty for *lèse-majesté* was not lessened after the absolute monarchy was overthrown in 1932, the law was relatively little used even up through the 1950s. However, after a coup in 1976, the pro-military coup group upped the maximum punishment to fifteen years and set the minimum sentence to three years. The result is quizzical. The constitutional monarchy in 2011 Thailand has a maximum sentence five times more severe than under the absolute monarchy of 1900; the 2011 minimum sentence is the maximum sentence of 1900. Moreover, the punishment for contempt of courts and insulting religion (more like "heresy") is given protection equal to that of the monarchy prior to 1932.

Comparatively, the maximum sentence in Thailand today is two and a half times higher than in the next closest democratic constitutional monarchy of Sweden, and three times higher than in the more or less "absolute monarchy" of Morocco (see Figure 5.3).[15] With the exception of

FIGURE 5.3
Punishment for *Lèse-majesté* Worldwide, 2011
(In maximum no. of years' imprisonment)

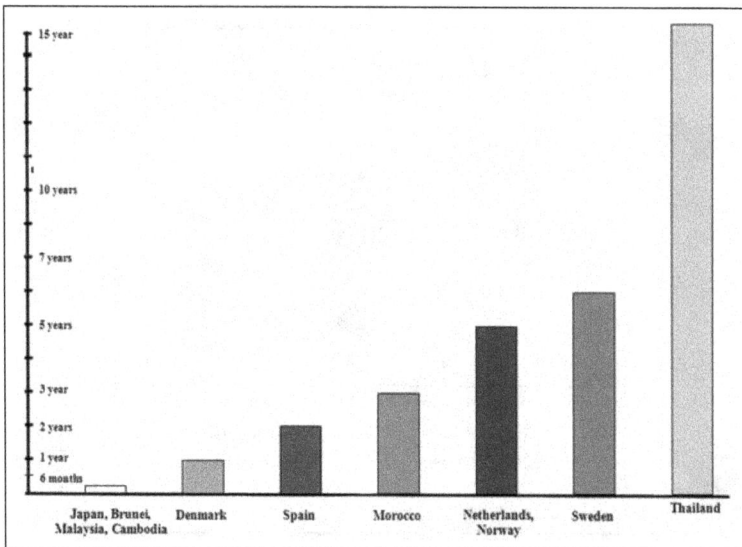

Source: Various law codes.

wartime Japan, Thailand is the only "constitutional monarchy" to have increased punishment for *lèse-majesté* in the last century.

RELATIONSHIP WITH "FREEDOM"/PRESS FREEDOM

The potency of a *lèse-majesté* law can be linked to the general freedom enjoyed by a country. As Figures 5.4 and 5.5 show, freedom in Thailand dropped considerably after the coup in 2006.

Although Thailand's ranking in terms of press freedom has generally dropped over the past decade, it at least had a rather commendable ranking in the top third of countries in 2004. By 2010, Thailand had plummeted to the bottom 16 per cent of countries worldwide. When considered against other constitutional monarchies, Thailand's ranking is more similar to more or less present absolute monarchies than it is to any democratic constitutional monarchy (Figure 5.6).[16] Although higher than Saudi Arabia (which makes little pretence of being democratic), Thailand is close to Jordan and Bahrain, considerably lower than Morocco, Qatar, and Oman, and much lower than the other Buddhist kingdom of Bhutan.

FIGURE 5.4
Freedom House's "Freedom in the World" Score of Thailand, 2002–11

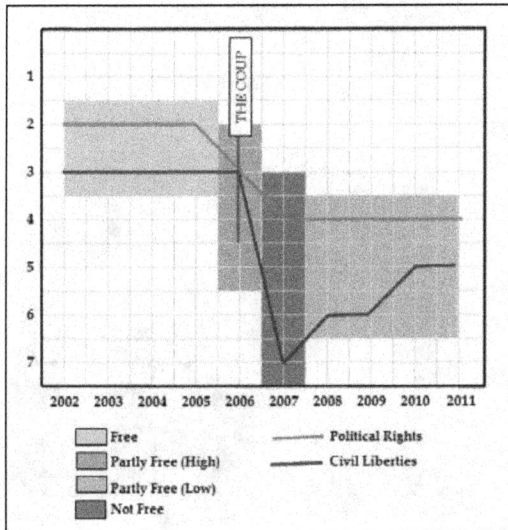

Source: Freedom House.

FIGURE 5.5
Ranking of Thailand, 2002–10 Worldwide Press Freedom Index

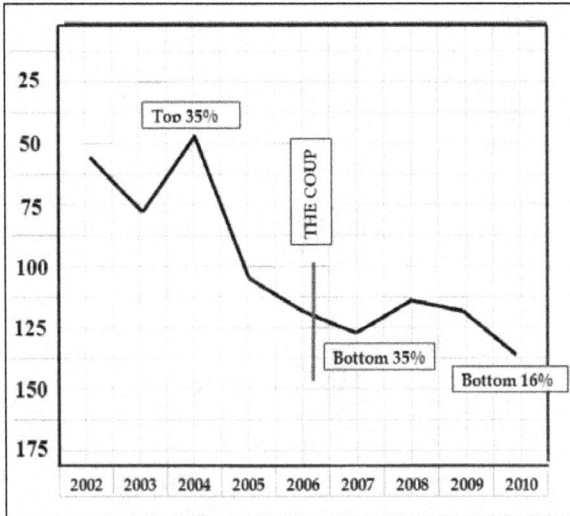

A *lèse-majesté* law copiously applied in a less than democratic country does not necessarily mean a cowered and craven press. In Germany of the 1890s when the *lèse-majesté* law was invoked with abandon, many newspaper editors, immediately upon being freed after a time in jail published new articles deemed as *lèse-majesté* and were tossed right back in again.[17] A political correspondent in Germany noted that when a "prominent academic" was accused of *lèse-majesté*, even conservative newspapers called the prosecution "a grave political faux pas".[18] Even during the absolute monarchy in Siam, the press had spirited commentary and cartoon.[19] But the mainstream press in Thailand has since been tamed. It "cannot or is not willing to risk discussing the perceived role of the palace in politics", thus leading to a "distorted" public view of politics. Rather than acting in the name of the public good and challenging laws like *lèse-majesté*, the Thai mainstream press has instead supported use of the law and has even avoided covering *lèse-majesté* cases. The president of the Thai Journalists Association demurely reported in 2009 that the press does not cover such cases because "we have been taught that way. It's a deep-rooted culture."[20] In Thailand when a prominent academic

FIGURE 5.6
Press Freedom Index Rankings, 2002–10

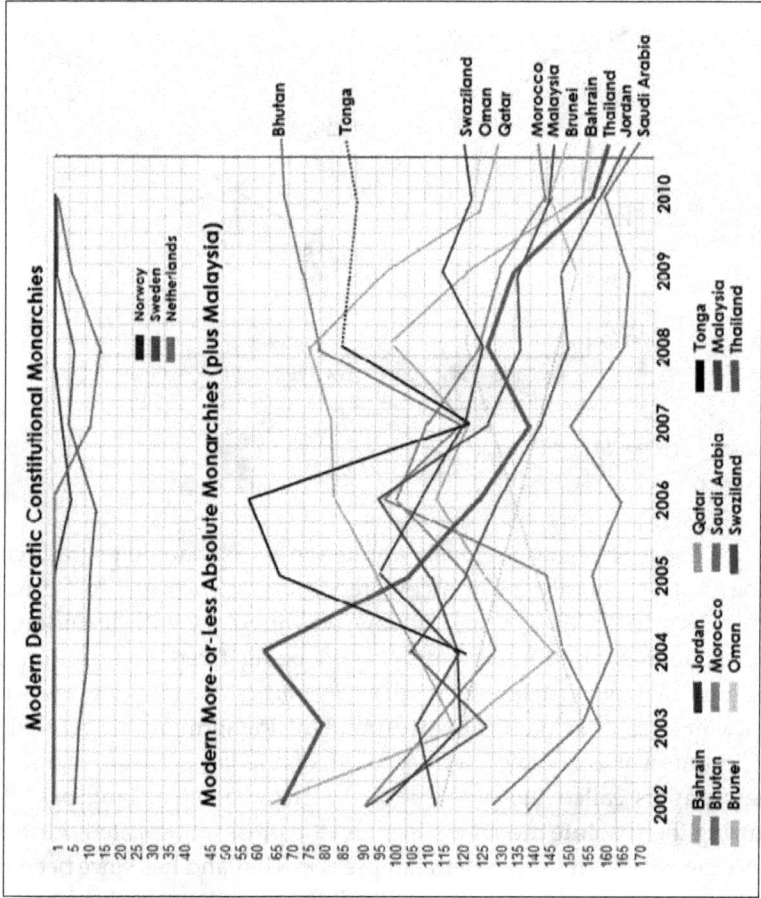

Source: Reporters Without Borders.

was accused of *lèse-majesté* in May 2011, the mainstream press made little mention of the case.[21]

USE OF *LÈSE-MAJESTÉ* CLIMBS, 2005–2011

In the last century and a half, there is little doubt that *lèse-majesté* was used most aggressively in the German Empire, where two forces contended with one another: "the utter persistence exercised by the German state in using the *lèse-majesté* law, and the remarkable tenacity of the German press in challenging it. It is truly history's finest example of the increasingly desperate attempts by a 'sacred' regime to preserve its prestige through the *lèse-majesté* law." Over about a twenty-five-year period (1882–1906), there was an average of more than 500 *lèse-majesté* cases per year. It was estimated that by the mid-1890s, 4,965 sentences for *lèse-majesté* had been handed down by German courts.[22]

The existence of a *lèse-majesté* law with a particularly heavy punishment does not necessarily become controversial if rarely used. Sweden, for instance, has a maximum punishment of six years' imprisonment for each count. However, the law is not the subject of public debate as it is rarely applied. Thailand is quite different in this respect. The punishment is extraordinarily heavy and it is applied at an alarming rate. Government statistics in Thailand on the number of *lèse-majesté* "items" over the last five years often appear divergent as each law agency collects different things. The Office of the Judiciary collects statistics on the number of charges going before the court. The Office of the Attorney General counts cases and number of persons. The police focus on the number of complaints. Regardless of which set of statistics is considered, though, they all indicate that the number of complaints, cases, and charges have all risen dramatically since 2006.

The statistics from the Office of the Judiciary track the number of *lèse-majesté* charges going before the courts, and the numbers are much more dramatic (see Figure 5.7).[23] In 2005, thirty-three charges came before the Court of First Instance and it handed down decisions on eighteen. In 2007, the number of charges had increased almost fourfold to 126. This number jumped to 164 in 2009, and then tripled to 478 cases by 2010. The most significant increases came under the Democrat Party-led government of Abhisit Vejjajiva of 2009 to 2011 when more than 300 counts of *lèse-majesté* were adjudicated by the lower court. If "counts" have any sort of

FIGURE 5.7
Number of *Lèse-majesté* Charges/Cases Sent to and Successfully Prosecuted by the Court of First Instance Appeals Court, and Supreme Court, 2005–11

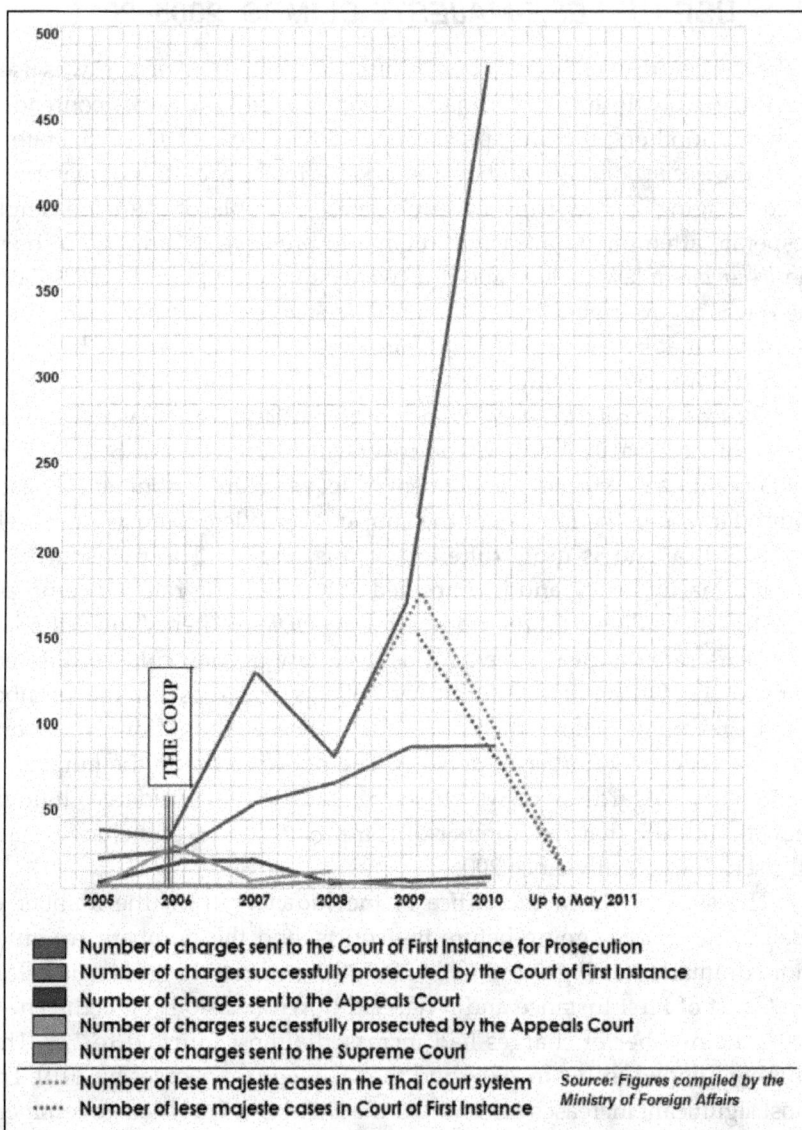

Source: Annual Statistics, Office of the Judiciary.

correspondence with "cases" and the 94 per cent conviction rate for *lèse-majesté* cases from 1993 to 2005 holds, it means that since the coup there may have been hundreds jailed for *lèse-majesté*. Equally interesting to note is that forty-six counts of *lèse-majesté* came before the Appeals Court since 2005, and the Appeals Court handed down decisions on forty-one counts from 2005 to 2008. Since 2005, the Thai Supreme Court has received eleven counts/cases, and handed down a decision on one of them.[24] However, in another rendering of statistics compiled by the Division of Information at the Ministry of Foreign Affairs, the Office of the Judiciary is counting the number of cases rather than counting counts. These statistics show that in 2008, Thai courts handled a total of seventy-seven *lèse-majesté* cases, a number that more than doubled in 2009 with 159 cases before the lower courts, four cases before the Appeals courts, and two before the Supreme Court. This number was halved in 2010 as seventy-eight cases were before the lower courts, seven were in the Appeal courts, and two were before the Supreme Court. Up until May 2011, there were only ten cases of *lèse-majesté* before the lower courts.

The Office of the Attorney General, police, and court statistics compiled by the Division of Information at the Ministry of Foreign Affairs indicate that the number of complaints, charges, or decisions on *lèse-majesté* cases peaked in 2009 and dropped off in 2010 and the first half of 2011. Statistics from the Office of the Attorney General show there were eighteen cases of *lèse-majesté* involving twenty-four persons before the court in 2005 in contrast with thirty-seven cases involving fifty-three persons in 2010 (see Figure 5.8).[25] The statistics collected by the Ministry of Foreign Affairs indicate that in 2008, the police received fifty-five *lèse-majesté* complaints and recommended either ending investigations or not forwarding the case to the Office of the Attorney General in twenty-one of them. In 2009, the number of complaints to the police peaked at 104, and more than half of these were apparently dropped. In 2010, sixty-two complaints were received, of which only five were dropped. Complaints dropped off dramatically in the first half of 2011. Another set of statistics show that state prosecutors considered seventy cases of *lèse-majesté* between 2007 and 2009, at an average of about twenty-three cases per year, which is well above the average annual number of *lèse-majesté* cases between 1993 and 2005 of 5.5. The same set of statistics show that for the seventeen-month period of 2010 to May 2011, the number of *lèse-majesté* cases dropped to a total of twenty-four.

FIGURE 5.8

Number of New *Lèse-majesté* Cases Received and Prosecuted 2000–10; *Lèse-majesté* Complaints Received and Disposed of by Police, 2008–11

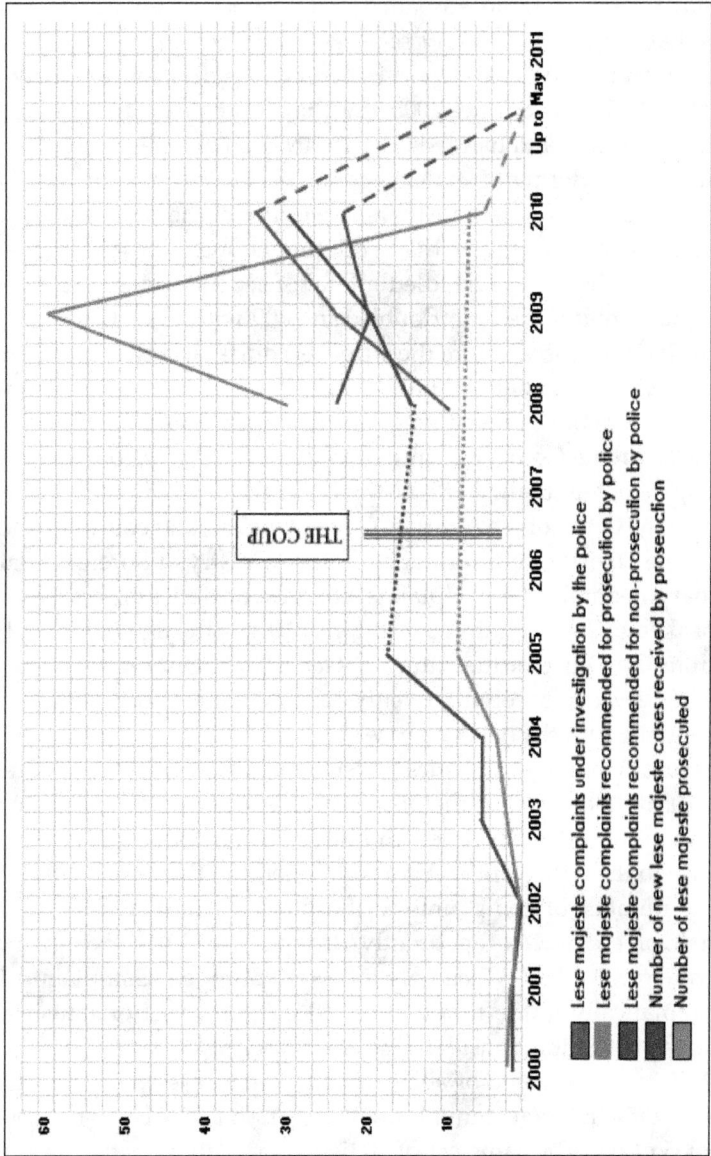

Lese majeste complaints under investigation by the police
Lese majeste complaints recommended for prosecution by police
Lese majeste complaints recommended for non-prosecution by police
Number of new lese majeste cases received by prosecution
Number of lese majeste prosecuted

Source: Office of the Attorney General, Department of Information, Ministry of Foreign Affairs.

None of the statistics above include violations of the Computer Crimes Act of 2007. The Office of the Judiciary shows that thirty-six counts of *lèse-majesté* came before the Court of First Instance from 2008 to the middle of 2011, during which the court handed down judgements on twenty-two charges.[26] According to a study released in December 2010, there had been up until the middle of 2010, thhrity-one *"lèse-majesté-content"* cases pursued under the Computer Crime Act. Of these, all four cases in which the court handed down a decision resulted in conviction, and in no case documented did public prosecutors drop or courts dismiss a case.[27] According to the Political Prisoners in Thailand website, some seventy-one people have been charged with *lèse-majesté* in Thailand since 2008, and charges dropped against at least fourteen (thirteen members of the board of the Foreign Correspondents Club of Thailand and Sulak Sivaraksa).[28] Many of those charged or waiting for trial are still in jail. According to the same website, eight persons have been jailed. Of those three have since been pardoned, one is out on bail while appealing the case, and the other four remain in jail. These numbers roughly approximate the sixty-nine *lèse-majesté* complaints that police forwarded to the Office of the Attorney General for either further investigation or prosecution between 2008 and 2011, but seems well below the 300 or so cases considered by the lower courts in statistics compiled by the Ministry of Foreign Affairs. In any case, the rather different sets of statistics and metrics make it difficult for anyone to know with any certainty how many people are presently in jail for *lèse-majesté* and the Computer Crimes Act.

TARGET OF CHARGES

Prior to the mid-eighteenth century in France, *lèse-majesté* was primarily an elite affair: most of those charging and those charged were members of the elite. But after the Damiens Affair of 1757, decidedly common folk became the primary target of *lèse-majesté* charges. Among those arrested were:

> a lawyer, a *huissier* [doorman; usher], a *greffier* [clerk of the court], a law student, a master locksmith, a master blacksmith, a journeyman and an apprentice hatter, a shoemaker and his wife, five or six domestic servants plus a jeweller's shop boy.

Moreover, French state officials recognized the "noisy, conspicuous character" of public trials would further desacralize the monarchy, and so preference was given to the "extrajudicial" method of imprisonment without charges.[29] In Germany, a similar trend could be seen. Those jailed for *lèse-majesté* were: a scoffer, a comedian, a singer, a drunk German-American, a librarian, a seventeen-year-old girl, a deaf man, a worker, a thirteen-year-old boy, a street porter, a worker, a farmer, and newspaper editors.[30]

Prior to the coup, those accusing and those accused of *lèse-majesté* were mostly politicians, leading bureaucrats, and extra-constitutional figures. *Lèse-majesté* was primarily an inter-elite weapon for ruining one's enemies. In the 2005 "sticker case", for instance, Thai Rak Thai political party leaders accused some members of the opposition Democrat Party of *lèse-majesté* for using the words of the King and Queen in campaign stickers. Later that year, there were the acrimonious accusations of *lèse-majesté* flung back and forth between then-prime minister Thaksin Shinawatra and opposition movement leader of the People's Alliance for Democracy (PAD), Sondhi Limthongkul. The accusers were politicians or political movement leaders, and the accused were politicians or political movement leaders. But beginning in 2007, there was a change in the target of *lèse-majesté* accusations. Now joining former prime ministers, foreign ministers, and politicians as those charged are a vast array of common people: a drunk foreigner, video compact disc sellers, lawyers, fiction writers, computer store owners in the United States, Internet publication editors, privy councillors, those who refuse to stand for the royal anthem prior to the showing of movies, a disgruntled foreign clothes seller, labour activists, academics, Internet users, journalists, red-shirt speechmakers, political theorists, securities traders, students, and so on.[31] Moreover, there have been many cases where the "noisy, conspicuous character" of public trials in Thailand has been avoided altogether with secret or endlessly delayed proceedings and suspects languishing in jail for months or years before trial.

NATURE OF CHARGES: THE LAW BECOMES THE INSTITUTION

As the target of *lèse-majesté* arrest and prosecutions shifted from elite to common folk in Germany, the content or nature of charges shifts as well. In Germany, for instance, people were jailed for scoffing at a song the

Emperor composed, criticizing a picture of the Emperor, tearing a picture of the Emperor off her own wall, calling the Emperor a sheep-head, making jokes about the Emperor, insulting the Empress, questioning the piety of the Emperor, and saying a recently deceased tramp was really the son of the Emperor. These comments were, if anything, insults. Those accused or found guilty of insulting the monarch were not necessarily assumed to be disloyal to the institution. Interestingly, the existence and frequent use of the *lèse-majesté* law in Germany did not outlaw political expression favouring republicanism over monarchism. In the Reichstag in 1903, the leader of the Social Democratic Party laid out the Socialists' position on monarchy:

> ...we are against the monarchy, but not opponents of rulers. It is with them as with our position to the bourgeois society, for which we do not hold every single member responsible. A Prince is born as a Prince. Is it his fault? By chance he has become a ruler, and if a Prince is human, is not personal toward us in his opposition, we shall never personally oppose him. Monarchy is an institution, not a question of person.[32]

Although the constitutional monarchy was established in 1932 in Siam, even two decades later the country's primary legal body, the Council of State, opined that expression of republican sentiment was illegal.[33] *Lèse-majesté* charges of the late 1950s through mid-1970s stemmed from what would be best termed as insults (for example, naming one's dogs after the king and queen). But since 1976 at least, the conflation of the person of the king with the institution of the monarchy, with national security and treason charges, has blurred any of the law's precision. In the past thirty-five years, complaints have been filed against individuals for comments made in regard to a great-great grandfather of Queen Sirikit, a daughter of the King, the institution of the monarchy itself, and to symbols or symbolic references that could be equated with the King. Charges for the crime show the law has come to cover a widening number of associations, whether it is other members of the royal family, Thai history, the institution of the monarchy, development strategies the King supports, implying that the King has (or does not have) power, the privy council, the royal anthem, and the status of the Crown Property Bureau. Although it appears from the law that the institution of the monarchy is not protected by the *lèse-majesté* law, in practice it seems it is. And anything like the critique that the German lawmaker made above has been deemed illegal. Even suggestions of reform of the institution are interpreted as a call for the overthrow of the monarchy.[34]

As the core of public discussion on legitimacy, politics, and law more and more centres directly or indirectly on the role of the monarchy in Thailand, as the result of these myriad justification and the mobilizations and government mechanisms dedicated to seeking out disloyalty, the *lèse-majesté* law itself no longer simply protects the institution of the monarchy. In many ways, it has come to define the institution of the monarchy in Thailand, much like towards the end of absolutism in various regimes in Europe where the suppressive mechanism connected to the monarchy became its most prominent feature.

LÈSE-MAJESTÉ AND TREASON

Under absolute monarchy, *lèse-majesté* and treason were perfectly synonymous. But as the idea of the citizen and nation expanded, treason became increasingly distinct from *lèse-majesté* in constitutional monarchies. Treason charges stemmed no longer from showing disloyalty to a monarch and began instead to mean aiding foreign enemies or conspiring against the constitutional order. In Thailand, there were indications up through the 1970s that the country would follow the trend of other constitutional monarchies. This trend then rather quickly reversed after 1976, and the reversal continues to the present. The 1908 criminal code still retained a "treason" provision. Section 104 said that anyone who appeared in public in order to "create disloyalty or to insult the King, the government, or the country" could be punished with a maximum of three years' imprisonment. When the criminal code was revised in 1956, "treason" was for the most part relegated to those providing material comfort to the external enemies of Thailand. What remained was section 113 which punishes those who use violence to "overthrow or change the Constitution" with "death or imprisonment for life". Section 116 forbids anyone appearing before the public "to bring about a change in the Laws of the Country or the Government by the use of force or violence" with up to seven years' imprisonment, with the exception for those who "act within the purpose of the Constitution or for expressing an honest opinion or criticism".[35]

From the 1960s up through the late 1980s, *lèse-majesté* played second fiddle to the more encompassing enemy of "the communist". Even though the student leaders after the 6 October 1976 massacre were charged with both *lèse-majesté* and being communists, communism still provided the framework for defining the ultimate traitor. With the decline of communism, though, *lèse-majesté* began to define a new kind of traitor. I argued in the mid-1990s that *lèse-majesté* was becoming "a kind of cultural crime perpetrated against Thainess", "the quintessential crime of cultural betrayal".[36] As a national security offence, *lèse-majesté* became perfectly suited to serve as a weapon against political opponents. For the past five years, and most recently during the protests in Bangkok in April–May of 2010, the military, the PAD, and much of the Democrat Party have attempted to portray the movement of the United Front for Democracy against Dictatorship (UDD) as part of an anti-monarchist conspiracy. The vast majority of those charged or sentenced with *lèse-majesté* are connected in some way to the UDD.[37] The insinuation — and quite often a direct accusation about Thaksin, the red shirts, and those who opposed the coup — is that they are somehow involved in a conspiracy to overthrow the monarchy. Discussions of reforming the monarchy or even analyses of the power structure in Thailand have typically been depicted as acts of treason. For certain acts unrelated to the throne, treason occasionally appears in Thai political discourse. But generally recent Thai politics have always been competitions of loud and ostentatious displays of loyalty to the monarchy in attempts to impugn the opposing side's lack thereof.

The idea that every single Thai may not be enthralled with the throne or that a Thai might be against the monarchy is nearly unimaginable. A display of a single Thai allegedly acting contrary to the institution has the power to affect "the mind of the entire people" even if there was not a single Thai to witness it. Thai loyalty to the throne is so powerful and all-consuming it would seem that even the collective mind of the nation is affected when such a dastardly act is carried out in secret.[38] *Lèse-majesté* suspect Joe Gordon has been accused of translating parts of, and providing links to, *The King Never Smiles*, a 2006 unauthorized biography of the King that was banned even before it was published. In denying Gordon bail, the Appeals Court in its 6 September 2011 ruling said the "behaviour of this case and the nature of the action has brought dishonour to the institution of the monarchy which is revered and held in high esteem, affecting the mind of the entire people of those who are loyal."[39] That Gordon's alleged offence was committed in another country makes the case even more intriguing: the fact that an alleged offence against the monarchy does not have to even be witnessed by Thai eyes to offend the entire nation is geographically universalized.[40]

As the call for all true Thais to show absolute and unwavering loyalty to the monarchy has intensified in the past several years, treason (and traitors) seems to be everywhere. Such might be in the case of Jakrapob Penkair, a former Minister of the Prime Minister's Office in a pro-Thaksin government of 2008. In reference to a 2007 speech he gave in front of foreign journalists, the climax of a linguistic analysis is when the antagonist shows his true colours. It centres on one particular passage in the transcript. After Jakrapob finished his talk, he was asked whether he had claimed that Thaksin's loyalty to the monarchy was 100 per cent. Jakrapob said, no, he had not said that. When asked to clarify, Jakrapob said that Thaksin had "some" loyalty to the throne. Here was the proof of Thaksin's treachery, and, by association, Jakrapob's. The linguist explains, "Only one sentence can explain it; all his intentions in saying other things were excuses" obscuring his real crime:

> People who have studied English or foreigners, even ordinary Thai children who study English in primary school can tell you that "some loyalty" means "partial loyalty" not 100 per cent. In considering what Jakrapob said, you have to think about his attitude, and the attitude of the people behind him, towards the institution.

What constitutes treason and an offence against the monarchy has narrowed considerably, thus alienating those with a different view. All Thais must be monarchists. Not being a monarchist is to be against the throne, and to be against the throne is not to be Thai. This phenomenon is much more reminiscent of an absolute monarchy than a constitutional monarchy where right to political speech and expression are protected by the constitution.

Listening to the pronouncements of Thai governments since the coup, it would seem that the state's very *raisons d'être* is to shore up the loyalty of the people. After the bloody crackdown in May last year, for instance, it was reported that the Ministry of Interior "have intensified royalist campaigning" in rural provinces. In one programme, village leaders were to secure signed oaths of villagers that read: "This person wants to show their willingness to worship the monarchy ... and to protect the monarchy with his or her life." Village heads who failed to secure a certain percentage of the village's population were put under pressure. In such cases, village heads were to "organize" teams of twenty people, in what appeared to be "a type of royalist village militia", to "implement" the royalist oath.[41] Meanwhile, cyber-scouts/spies scoured the Internet to find traces of subversion and *lèse-majesté* linked to hotlines maintained by government agencies. Substantial security budgets were given to various agencies to root out those deemed as having committed *lèse-majesté*. These agencies include but may not be limited to the Department of Special Investigations, the Internal Security Operations Command, and the Ministry of Information and Communications Technology.

In 2010, the Special Branch police initiated a programme that encourages citizens to help protect the monarchy. The programme, "Raising Consciousness about the Institution of the Monarchy", recently released a citizen's manual that points out that, in "the general situation", there is an increasing number of *lèse-majesté* violations connected to attempts to undermine the security of the monarchy. Those joining the training learn the ways to show loyalty to the monarchy include: flying the royal flag, putting a picture of the King on the walls of home and office, standing at attention when hearing the royal anthem, learning about the sufficiency economy, telling family members about how important royal activities have been to the nation and so on. They also learn how to recognize treasonous activities and how to apply to be a spy for the special branch.[42]

Just as under absolutism, neo-absolutism in Thailand has seen the emergence of its apologists who justify not just Thai-style monarchy, but the *lèse-majesté* law itself as a unique cultural expression of Thainess. A leading Thai legal mind, Borwornsak Uwanno, felt compelled to write a defence of the *lèse-majesté* law in 2009. The core of his argument is that countries place certain limitations on free speech due to their specific cultural-legal circumstances.[43] The Thai people's relationship to the monarchy is unique and an expression of its particular ethical and cultural character. The *lèse-majesté* law exists as the result of a "societal consensus" and therefore Thailand should be allowed to use the *lèse-majesté* law without being judged by other countries. The Thai monarchy's relationship to society is different from other constitutional monarchies, Borwornsak argues, for it not only "has a long history dating back to ancient times, [it] has an exalted religious and social status ... but has close bonds with the people, who love and respect [it] for the monarch's contributions to their wellbeing."[44] Thus, the *lèse-majesté* law itself is a unique cultural expression of Thailand.[45]

The result of these justifications, expansions, and mobilizations is that the *lèse-majesté* law itself no longer simply protects the institution of the monarchy. In many ways, it has come to define the institution of the monarchy in Thailand, much like towards the end of absolutism in various regimes in Europe where the suppressive mechanism connected to the monarchy became its most prominent feature.[46]

LESSONS FROM THE END OF ABSOLUTE MONARCHIES

The historical record clearly shows what happens to regimes that abuse the *lèse-majesté* law. In the France of the mid to late eighteenth century, it was only a matter of three decades that the intensification of the use of the law played a part in the French Revolution. In the Germany of the late nineteenth century, massive use and abuse of the law did nothing to endear the institution to its citizenry. In the end, it was the emperor himself who intervened in the early 1900s and ordered *lèse-majesté* prosecutions to end and a release of all those held for the crime from prison. Nonetheless, the damage was already done. Within less than two decades, the German monarchy was abolished.[47] In Thailand, no one can claim any longer to be unaware of the precarious situation created by the law. Both in word and practice, the Thai *lèse-majesté* law is extremely problematic, as Leyland explains:

> From the standpoint of the basic human rights of the defendant, this offence displays alarming features. First, it can be committed entirely without criminal intent. There is no need for the prosecuting authorities to bring any evidence to bear relating to foresight on the part of the defendant with regard to the effect of the statement or conduct. This failure to introduce a subjective element removes the vital link for establishing serious criminality resulting in deprivation of liberty.... Secondly, the insidiousness of the process is compounded by the lack of any prospect of "independent" justice in Thailand in relation to this offence. The police, prosecuting authorities and judges not only act in the name of the King, but there is an expectation that their loyalty to the Crown will be reflected in an outcome that confirms the dignity of the King at the expense of the accused.[48]

But the law is also counterproductive. Recognizing the danger the abuse of the law might have on the long-term interests of the monarchy has not been lost to observers. The U.S. Ambassador to Thailand in 2009, Eric G. John, discerned the obvious problem:

> Ironically, the heightened pace of arrests and charges, especially those involving prominent figures, may cause liberal-minded Thais to resent restrictions on speech and to associate the monarchy with acts of repression, weakening domestic support for the institution the legal actions seek to protect.[49]

Long-time American residents of Thailand told the U.S. embassy that "the increased application of *lèse-majesté*, without distinction between those who mean ill towards the monarchy and those who otherwise would be ignored, ran the risk of undermining the very institution the law seeks to protect, and which they feel has served Thailand well through the decades."[50]

When it has gotten to this point, a far more serious threat to the monarchy in Thailand than the purported republican movement(s) is the law itself. If the *lèse-majesté* law's purpose is to protect the institution, then it stands to reason that if the law is creating the primary threat, the law itself should be charged with *lèse-majesté*. All the warning signs are acutely present: Beware when the number of cases shoot up. Beware when the targets are no longer competing elite but just common folk. Beware when reasonable, well-intentioned suggestions are twisted into perceived threats to the institution. But mostly, beware turning citizens into spies and thugs, and Thai society into a battle of the loyalists versus the evil ones, traitors. Nonetheless, despite evidence to the contrary, the Thai elite, labouring under it "alternative reality" have contentiously slapped down any attempts to even discuss reforming the institution or modifying the law, locking Thailand into a future of further jailing, divisiveness, and bloodshed.

A small snippet from the case of Germany reflects much of the caustic atmosphere of present-day Thailand:[51]

> *Dec. 7, 1894* — In first sitting of the Reichstag, President von Levetzow "delivered a brief address ... concluding his remarks with a call for cheers for the Emperor. All the members present, with the exception of the Socialists, responded, rising from their seats and cheering heartily. Upon seeing that the Socialists retained their seats, the other members were greatly excited, howling and shouting at the Socialists to get out.... The Socialists, during the disorder, retorted, calling the other members rowdies and making use of many other invectives.... Herr von Levetzow

sternly censured the Socialists for not responding to the call for cheers for the Emperor. He said he was sorry he did not possess the means of punishing the members of who had remained seated ... and declared that their action was unworthy of Germans. His remarks were received with vociferous applause from all but the Social Democrats. Herr Singer, the Socialist leader, in reply ... said that he would never unite in cheering for a man who told his soldiers that at his command they must fire upon their fellow-citizens.

This declaration, which was drowned out by cries of "Turn him out!" was applauded by Singer's followers.

President von Levetzow then declared that he would not allow his Majesty's name to be dragged into the debate ... Herr von Manteufiel was heartily cheered when he declared that Herr Singer's scandalous words and the revolting actions of the Social Democrats would result in the House making inquiries into the charges of *lèse-majesté* more strict than ever.

The conservatives kept their word and let loose on German society the greatest concentration of *lèse-majesté* cases in recent world history. Maybe what will make the difference will not be Thai society making the "right" or "wrong" choice about the *lèse-majesté* law. It might depend instead on how that decision is made, how careful people are not to arouse passions, and how they can develop greater tolerance.

It is important, for the way that the conservatives held on to power, and how their opponents chose to respond, as we can see in this German case where both sides contributed to inflaming the situation, said a lot about what was to come. Germany was to enter World War I where its eventual loss was humiliating, leading to the end of the German monarch, and perhaps laying the foundations for the violent and horrific regime that was to come under the Nazis.

Notes

1. Peter Leyland, "The Struggle for Freedom of Expression in Thailand: Media Moguls, The King, Citizen Politics and the Law", *Journal of Media Law* 2, no. 1 (2010): 118–22; "National Report Submitted in Accordance with Paragraph 15(A) of the Annex to the Human Rights Council Resolution 5/1* Thailand" <http://www.ecoi.net/file_upload/1930_1314628672_a-hrc-wg-6-12-tha-1-thailand-e.pdf> (accessed 11 September 2011).
2. Jackson J. Spielvogel, *Western Civilization* (London: St. Paul, 1991), p. 506.

3. <http://www2.sunysuffolk.edu/westn/absolutism.html> (accessed 11 September 2011).
4. <http://www2.stetson.edu/~psteeves/classes/louisxiv.html> (accessed 11 September 2011).
5. <http://www.enotes.com/topic/Absolute_monarchy> (accessed 11 September 2011).
6. This reality provides for many different kinds of hybrid regimes. Absolute monarchies in Europe never approached anything like twentieth-century totalitarian regimes. A modern neo-absolutist regime in its purest form could come much closer <http://www2.sunysuffolk.edu/westn/absolutism.html> (accessed 11 September 2011).
7. David Streckfuss, *Truth on Trial in Thailand: Defamation, Treason and Lèse-majesté* (London: Routledge, 2011), pp. 294–97.
8. See, in particular, Chapter 5 in, Streckfuss, *Truth on Trial in Thailand*.
9. Amsterdam writes that in the past five years, "The judiciary has played an increasingly political role, often acting as the linchpin in the Prerogative State's effort to carry out its agenda through the procedures of the Normative State.... the power of the courts to remove governments and dissolve popular political parties at the behest of forces in the Prerogative State has been increased and formalized in the (2007) constitution. Written by the military junta in 2007, the primary goal of the new constitution was to curtail the ability of institutions within the Normative State to check the activities of actors in the Prerogative State. Robert Amsterdam, "Thailand through the prism of the dual state" <http://asiapacific.anu.edu.au/newmandala/2011/08/29/amsterdam-on-thailands-dual-state/> (accessed 11 September 2011).
10. Critiquing the way "culture" is defined, Ferrara approached this by arguing that political institutions are not so much about culture as "they are about power". More often than not, "hierarchy makes culture — or better still, the ideologies habitually camouflaged as culture that are disseminated through the methodical application of state power". The military in Thailand has traditionally claimed itself the protector of the throne "in an attempt to legitimize their extra-constitutional, corrupt, violent rule — Thailand's elites have in lèse majesté a powerful instrument to defend their own hold on power." Federico Ferrara, *Thailand Unhinged: Unraveling the Myth of a Thai-Style Democracy* (Singapore: Equinox, 2010), pp. 136–37.
11. Amsterdam, "Thailand through the prism of the dual state". A similar argument for Thailand has been made by Jakrapob Penkair who has argued that Thailand is actually governed by a "State within the state" <http://asiapacific.anu.edu.au/newmandala/2009/09/25/jakrapob-on-the-state-within-the-state/> (accessed 11 September 2011).
12. Somchai Preechasilpakul and David Streckfuss, "Ramification and Re-

Sacralisation of the Lèse-majesté Law in Thailand", paper presented at the 10th International Conference on Thai Studies (Bangkok: The Thai Khadi Research Institute/Thammasat University), 9–11 January 2008; Streckfuss, *Truth on Trial in Thailand*, pp. 309–10.

13. For instance, like a possible configuration within an absolutist monarchy, there has been a remarkable collaboration of "progressives" with what we might call "the royalist project". Coming together with sizeable factions of the aristocracy, clergy, bourgeoisie, and even select groups of commoners/peasants, the urban intelligentsia cemented a collaboration under the auspices of the monarchy in 2006 that has repelled the incursions of competing bourgeoisie and notions of popular sovereignty. This has made Thailand's political evolution quite distinct from other constitutional monarchies, and representing a neo-absolutist development (see Figure 5.1). Another attribute of the neo-absolutist state is a carefully produced and orchestrated image of royalty in Thailand that invokes creation of the full blown "trappings of majesty" intended to foster the kind of "awe and reverence" more common to absolutist regimes (Leyland, "The Struggle for Freedom of Expression in Thailand", p. 124). Although not quite the same, the secular or republican version of this phenomenon is the sort of personality cults surrounding Stalin or Kim Il-sung. It is the same carefully constructed and maintained aura that blocks public access or scrutiny to the monarchy writ large in a neo-absolutist polity as opposed to a democratic constitutional monarchy.

14. Michel Foucault, *Discipline and Punish* (New York: Vintage Books, 1979), pp. 3–5.

15. Morocco would seem, for instance, to be much more conservative than Thailand, given that the king has only recently flirted with the idea of reducing the power of the absolute monarchy with a constitution and so on. However, its *lèse-majesté* law provides for a minimum of one year for unpublicized sentiments, and a minimum of three and maximum of five years for public statements. In a recent case, an eighteen-year-old male was sentenced to one year in prison for distorting the national creed of "God, Country, King" when writing on a school blackboard he replaced "King" with his favourite Spanish football team: "God, Country, Barca". <http://www.barcelonareporter.com/index. php?/news/comments/barcelona_fans_plead_for_jailed_supporter_caught_ offside_by_king/> (accessed 11 September 2011).

16. To be fair, absolute monarchies are not necessarily less free than repressive republics. In 2010, for instance, of the bottom ten countries in ranking, none were a monarchy.

17. David Streckfuss, "Intricacies of Lese-Majesty: A Comparative Study of Imperial Germany and Modern Thailand", in *Saying the Unsayable: Monarchy and Democracy Thailand*, edited by Søren Ivarsson and Lotte Isager (Copenhagen: NIAS Press, 2010), pp. 118–19.

18. *New York Times*, 8 January 1899. A recently discovered apparently fictional story about a *lèse-majesté* case in Imperial Germany has been attributed to Breck. See "Crimes against the State" [Verbrechen Gegen Den Staat] in New Mandala's website <http://asiapacific.anu.edu.au/newmandala/2009/11/03/crimes-against-the-state-a-long-lost-manuscript/> (accessed 11 September 2011).

19. Matthew Copeland, "Political Journalism", in "Contested Nationalism and the 1932 Overthrow of the Absolute Monarchy in Siam", Ph.D. dissertation, Australia National University, 1993, Ch. 4.

20. Pravit Rojanaphruk and Jiranan Hanthamrongwit, "Distorted Mirror and Lamp: The Politicization of the Thai Media in the Post-Thaksin Era", in *Legitimacy Crisis in Thailand*, edited by Marc Askew (Chiang Mai: Prajadhipok Institute/Silkworm Books, 2010), p. 185.

21. <http://thaipoliticalprisoners.wordpress.com/pendingcases/somsak-jeamteerasakul/> (accessed 18 September 2011).

22. Streckfuss, "Intricacies of Lese-Majesty", pp. 110–11.

23. Office of the Judiciary [Samnak-ngan san yuttitham], *Annual Judicial Statistics, Thailand 2010* [Rai-ngan statiti khadi san thua ratcha-anajak prajam pi 2553].

24. Ibid. Using a different metric, statistics from the Office of the Attorney General seem to indicate a much lower number. In 2010 state prosecutors were working on thirty-seven cases of *lèse-majesté* in 2010 as compared with eighteen in 2005. Office of the Attorney General [Samnakngan Aiyakan Songsut], *Rai-ngan prajam pi 2553* [Annual Report of the Office of the Attorney General, 2010] [Samnakngan aiyakan phiset fai sarasonthet, samnakngan wichakan] [electronic excel file]. The Advisory Committee on the Security of the Kingdom reports that numbers peaked in 2009 with 165 cases before dropping off to 87 and 10 cases in 2010 and the first half of 2011 respectively. It also indicates that the number of *lèse-majesté* complaints filed with the police shows a similar trend, peaking in 2009 with 104 cases before decreasing to 62 and 10 cases in 2010 and the first half of 2011 respectively.

25. Office of the Attorney General [Samnakngan Aiyakan Songsut], *Rai-ngam Prajam Pi 2553* [Annual Report of the Office of the Attorney General, 2010] [Samnakngan Aiyakan Phiset Fai Sarasonthet, Samnakngan Wichakan] [electronic excel file].

26. Samnak-ngan san yuthitham [Office of the Judiciary], "Rai-ngan Jamnuan Kho Ha Thi khun Su Kanphitjarana Nai Khadi Aya [Kho Ha Un Noknua Jak Banchi Khong San Chan Ton Thua Ratcha-Anajak" ["Report of number of charges sent for consideration as criminal case (other charges beyond those listed) of the Court of First Instance throughout the kingdom"].

27. Research Team on "The Effect of the Computer Crime Act (2007) and State Policy on the Right to Freedom of Expression", *Situational Report on Control and Censorship of Online Media, through the Use of Laws and the Imposition of Thai State Policies*, released 8 December 2010, Thammasart University, Bangkok.

28. <http://thaipoliticalprisoners.wordpress.com/pendingcases/> (accessed 11 September 2011).
29. Streckfuss, *Truth on Trial in Thailand*, p. 17.
30. Streckfuss, "Intricacies of Lese-Majesty", p. 112.
31. <http://www.universityworldnews.com/article.php?story=201108130847126 38> (accessed 11 September 2011)
32. *New York Times*, 8 February 1903.
33. Streckfuss, *Truth on Trial in Thailand*, pp. 118–19.
34. Nicholas Grossman and Dominic Faulder, eds, *King Bhumibol Adulyadej: A Life's Work* (Singapore: Editions Didier Millet, 2012).
35. Streckfuss, *Truth on Trial in Thailand*, pp. 418–19.
36. Streckfuss, "Kings in the Age of Nations", p. 466.
37. For instance, in November 2009, Thai Foreign Minister Kasit Piromya claimed Thaksin "is using a helping hand from a neighbouring country as a tool to overthrow the monarchy and the Thai government" <http://asiancorrespondent.com/bangkok-pundit-blog/kasit-:-thaksin-wants-to-overthrow-.htm?utm_source=feedburner&utm_medium=feed&utm_campaign=Feed%3A+BangkokPundit+%28Bangkok+Pundit%29> (accessed 11 September 2011).
38. The possibility of this happening has been confirmed legally in some rather remarkable moments of Thai jurisprudence. See Streckfuss, *Truth on Trial in Thailand*, p. 208.
39. <http://www.prachatai.com/journal/2011/09/36839> (accessed 11 September 2011).
40. An unnamed senior foreign diplomat was incredulous that a Thai treason charge of this type can occur in another country and still prosecuted in Thailand.
41 < http://www.greenleft.org.au/node/44743> (accessed 11 September 2011).
42. <http://www.sbpolice.go.th/upload/pb/2011060700010001.pdf> (accessed 18 September 2011]; Tyrell Haberkorn, "Special Branch Police", in Craig J. Reynolds and Team, "Time's Arrow and the Burden of the Past: A Primer on the Thai Un-state" <http://anu.academia.edu/CraigReynolds/Papers/924979/Times_Arrow_and_the_Burden_of_the_Past_A_Primer_on_the_Thai_Un-state> (accessed 18 September 2011).
43. Borwornsak Uwanno, "The Law of Inviolability in Thailand", *Bangkok Post*, 7 April 2009 <http://www.bangkokpost.com/opinion/opinion/14660/the-law-of-inviolability-in-thailand> (accessed 4 June 2009).
44. Borwornsak Uwanno, "Thai Culture and the Law on Lèse-majesté", *Bangkok Post*, 8 April 2009 <http://www.bangkokpost.com/opinion/opinion/14766/lese-majeste-abuse-and-benevolence> (accessed 4 June 2009). He counters the contention that there are no legal limits to the law, by stating that the courts can focus on the intent of a defendant in determining a suitable punishment,

and the king has asked that the law not be applied "too liberally" as he "allows fair criticism".

45. This point has also been made by Ferrara, *Thailand Unhinged*, p. 125.
46. A recent online publication has examined the effects of the *lèse-majesté* law on society. See Andrew MacGregor Marshall, *Thailand's Moment of Truth: A Secret History of 21st Century Siam* (Part 1 of 4, Version 1.1, 23 June 2011), p. 9.
47. Streckfuss, "Intricacies of Lese-Majesty", p. 119.
48. Leyland, "The Struggle for Freedom of Expression in Thailand", pp. 130–31.
49. 09BANGKOK610, "Lèse-majesté Debate Enters Public Domain; Website Moderator Arrested under Computer Crime Act <http://www.zenjournalist. com/2011/06/09bangkok610/> (accessed 11 September 2011); also in Andrew MacGregor Marshall, *Thailand's Moment of Truth: A Secret History of 21st Century Siam* (Part 2 of 4, Version 1.2, 24 June 2011), pp. 5–6.
50. 09BANGKOK325, "Lèse-majesté Arrests and Actions against Web Content on the Rise, but Risk Backlash" <http://www.zenjournalist.com/2011/06/ 09bangkok325/> (accessed 11 September 2011); also in Marshall, *Thailand's Moment of Truth*, p. 34.
51. *New York Times*, 8 December 1894.

References

Amsterdam, Robert. "Thailand through the prism of the dual state". <http:// asiapacific.anu.edu.au/newmandala/2011/08/29/amsterdam-on-thailands-dual-state/> (accessed 11 September 2011).

Borwornsak, Uwanno. "The Law of Inviolability in Thailand". *Bangkok Post*, 7 April 2009 <http://www.bangkokpost.com/opinion/opinion/14660/the-law-of-inviolability-in-thailand> (accessed 4 June 2009).

———. "Thai Culture and the Law on Lèse-majesté". *Bangkok Post*, 8 April 2009. <http://www.bangkokpost.com/opinion/opinion/14766/lese-majeste-abuse-and-benevolence> (accessed 4 June 2009).

Copeland, Matthew. "Political Journalis". In "Contested Nationalism and the 1932 Overthrow of the Absolute Monarchy in Siam". Ph.D. dissertation, Australia National University, 1993.

Ferrara, Federico. *Thailand Unhinged: Unraveling the Myth of a Thai-Style Democracy.* Singapore: Equinox, 2010.

Foucault, Michel. *Discipline and Punish.* New York: Vintage Books, 1979.

Grossman, Nicholas and Dominic Faulder, eds. *King Bhumibol Adulyadej: A Life's Work* Singapore: Editions Didier Millet, 2012.

Haberkorn, Tyrell. "Special Branch Police". In "Time's Arrow and the Burden of the Past: A Primer on the Thai Un-state", by Craig J. Reynolds and Team <http://anu.academia.edu/CraigReynolds/Papers/924979/Times_Arrow_

and_the_Burden_of_the_Past_A_Primer_on_the_Thai_Un-state> (accessed 18 September 2011).

Leyland, Peter. "The Struggle for Freedom of Expression in Thailand: Media Moguls, The King, Citizen Politics and the Law". *Journal of Media Law* 2, no. 1 (2010): 115–37.

Marshall, Andrew MacGregor. *Thailand's Moment of Truth: A Secret History of 21st Century Siam*. Part 1 of 4, Version 1.1, 23 June 2011.

———. *Thailand's Moment of Truth: A Secret History of 21st Century Siam*. Part 2 of 4, Version 1.2, 24 June 2011, pp. 5–6.

Office of the Attorney General [Samnakngan Aiyakan Songsut]. *Rai-ngan prajam pi 2548-2553* [Annual Report of the Office of General]. [Samnakngan aiyakan phiset fai sarasonthet, samnakngan wichakan] (separate annual reports). (2005–2010).

Office of the Judiciary [Samnak-ngan san yuttitham]. *Annual Judicial Statistics, Thailand 2010* [Rai-ngan statiti khadi san thua ratcha-anajak prajam pi 2548-2553] (separate annual reports). (2005–2010).

Pravit Rojanaphruk. and Jiranan Hanthamrongwit. "Distorted Mirror and Lamp: The Politicization of the Thai Media in the Post-Thaksin Era". In *Legitimacy Crisis in Thailand*, edited by Marc Askew. Chiang Mai: Prajadhipok Institute/ Silkworm Books, 2010.

Samnak-ngan san yuthitham [Office of the Judiciary]. "Rai-ngan Jamnuan Kho Ha Thi khun Su Kanphitjarana Nai Khadi Aya [Kho Ha Un Noknua Jak Banchi Khong San Chan Ton Thua Ratcha-Anajak" [Report of number of charges sent for consideration as criminal case (other charges beyond those listed) of the Court of First Instance throughout the kingdom] (no year).

Spielvogel, Jackson J. *Western Civilization*. London: St. Paul, 1991.

Streckfuss. David. "Intricacies of Lese-Majesty: A Comparative Study of Imperial Germany and Modern Thailand". In *Saying the Unsayable: Monarchy and Democracy Thailand*, edited by Søren Ivarsson and Lotte Isager. Copenhagen: NIAS Press, 2010.

———. *Truth on Trial in Thailand: Defamation, Treason and Lèse-majesté*. London: Routledge. 2011.

——— and Somchai Preechasilpakul. "Ramification and Re-Sacralisation of the Lèse-majesté Law in Thailand". Paper presented at the 10th International Conference on Thai Studies. Bangkok: The Thai Khadi Research Institute/ Thammasat University, 9–11 January 2008.

Section III

New Political Discourses and the Emergence of Yellows and Reds

6

"VOTE NO!"
The PAD's Decline from Powerful Movement to Political Sect?

Michael H. Nelson

Since the elections of 6 January 2001 that brought Thaksin Shinawatra into power, conflicting assessments of his actions and goals have shaped much of Thai politics. The establishment's (*aphichon*) key concern with Thaksin (later complemented by supporting issues such as corruption, doubtful loyalty to the monarchy, and human rights violations) was put forward as early as October 2001 when a most respected *aphichon* member, former Prime Minister Anand Panyarachun warned, "Danger caused by people with dictatorial inclinations has not disappeared from Thailand".[1] One decade later, after the electoral triumph of Thaksin's youngest sister, Yingluck Shinawatra, *The Nation* reported a very similar statement, again by Anand. He had "called on all Thais to fight against any move to bring the government, court and legislature under the control of one person or group" since this might lead to "tyranny".[2] Both statements aimed at awakening the public to the assumed (not without reason) dangers posed by Thaksin, and spurring concomitant counter-measures.

Seen from this angle, the political struggles of the years 2001 to 2011 were largely about averting a potential "tyrant" Thaksin. In order to destroy its arch-enemy, various components of the establishment made use of political, military, and judicial (but significantly not electoral) opportunities that opened up at certain times. Measures taken included the protests by the People's Alliance for Democracy (PAD) in 2006 and 2008, the election boycott by the Democrat and Chart Thai Parties in April 2006, the military coup in September 2006 (which came after a royal decree had announced fresh elections for October 2006), the dissolution of two Thaksin parties (Thai Rak Thai in 2007 and People's Power in 2008), the drafting of the supposedly anti-Thaksin constitution of 2007, the sentencing of Thaksin to two years in prison without probation in October 2008, Democrat Abhisit Vejjajiva becoming prime minister in December 2008, the court-ordered confiscation of the bigger part of Thaksin's assets in February 2010, and the appointment of seventy-three senators in April 2011.

In this series of anti-Thaksin actions,[3] or battles in a "political war",[4] first Sondhi Limthongkul and then the PAD (it was established only on 9 February 2006) were important actors by organizing mass protests before and especially after Thaksin had sold his company to Singapore's Temasek in January 2006. The PAD's second round of protests started on 25 May 2008, and lasted for 193 days. It included the occupation of the Government House compound, and Don Muang and Suvarnabhumi Airports. Thus, the PAD's reputation as a powerful movement capable of putting tremendous pressure on governments was well earned. When they started their third round of protests in January 2011, however, Thaksin was not the enemy any longer. Instead, the PAD had turned against an erstwhile ally, the Democrat Party and its chairperson, Prime Minister Abhisit. Unlike the two earlier rounds, this one was largely ignored by the people, the mass media, and even the government.

This chapter will shed light on this change in protest fortunes in four sections. First, it will distinguish between the PAD and the movement in dealing with a failed attempt at street politics. Second, it will outline how the PAD viewed the problems of Thai politics. Third, the chapter will describe what happened to the PAD's very own New Politics Party (NPP), which had been established with great fanfare in May 2009. Fourth, I will turn to the PAD's failed attempt to use a means of the formal political system — the elections of 3 July 2011 — fundamentally to undermine the legitimacy of this very same system. This attempt was made possible by the election system, which allowed voters to mark a special "Vote No" box on their ballot papers for constituency and party-list candidates in order to express that they did not want to vote for any constituency candidate, and neither for the proportional list of any political party. The PAD leaders abandoned their New Politics Party, and instead ran a "Vote No" campaign.[5]

THE PAD IS NOT IDENTICAL WITH THE MOVEMENT

Not long after Abhisit had assumed the premiership on 15 December 2008, the PAD turned against him and his government. On 25 January 2011, the PAD and the Santi Asoke Buddhist sect (also referred to as Dhamma Army), led by Samana Photirak, and mobilized by one of the PAD's core leaders, Chamlong Srimuang, joined the Thai Patriots Network (or Committee for the Protection of the Thai Kingdom, known in Thai as *khanakammakan pongkan ratcha-anachak thai*) in blocking the area around Government House. Santi Asoke occupied most of Phitsanulok Road passing Government House; they also had erected their own stage there.[6] Before the left-turn into Ratchadamnoen Nok Avenue, there was a small contingent of the Thai Patriots Network, while the PAD covered this road up to the Makkawan Rangsan Bridge, where it had also erected their stage. Thus, the overall protest setting was similar to the one in 2008. Chamlong even felt confident enough to threaten, "We won't lay siege to Government House or parliament today or tomorrow, but we're not sure if we won't do so in the future."[7]

Certainly, the organizational strength of the PAD and Santi Asoke had remained the same. It was their infrastructure, resources, material, and personnel that could in no time establish a huge protest site, including the installation of sixty toilets and sixty bathrooms.[8] Thus, the first two rounds of menacing PAD protests in 2006 and 2008 came to mind as the benchmarks against which the success of this third round had to be measured. Two months later, however, the protesters were said to have become "disheartened by a poor response". They were called a "once-powerful alliance" (and later, "a one-time popular movement"[9]) that had "failed to capture the attention of the larger public or powerful political figures".[10]

This reference to a larger public is especially important, because it is not the leaders of a small group, or alliances of such groups, and their core followers that make social movements successful. Rather, a protest movement becomes successful when calls for collective action are based on communicatively generated and widely shared grievances that members of the public are prepared to express, if the occasion arises. Clearly, this had been the case in 2006 and 2008 with the high-profile public discourse against the "Thaksin regime". This discourse had started as early as late 2001, and gained strength during the following years (fuelled by Thaksin's own actions). Thus, when Sondhi reacted on losing his TV show "Thailand Weekly" in September 2005 by going public, first at Thammasat University, and then at Lumpini Park, individuals sharing his critical perspective on Thaksin experienced that they were not alone, and that coming together as collective gave them motivational and political power.

Nothing even remotely similar had preceded the protests of 2011. Rather, the tiny and obscure Thai Patriots Network, which Thitinan Pongsudhirak called "the extremist ultra-nationalist wing of the PAD,"[11] in its campaign centred on the Preah Vihear temple, had provoked the Cambodian authorities by trespassing on the country's territory on 29 December 2010. Network coordinator Veera Somkwamkid, Democrat Member of Parliament Panich Vikitsreth, and some other members were arrested. While most of them were freed soon afterwards, Veera and his secretary were sentenced to many years in prison. The key protest issues concerned merely a small band of ludicrous ultranationalists, their circle of political friends, amongst them Sondhi and Chamlong, and the narrow PAD "fan club".[12]

According to Sondhi, Chamlong had initiated this round of protests. He had told him that he could not stand that Thailand would lose territory to Cambodia. Chamlong would come out and protest, but added that Sondhi did not have to join him. Nevertheless, he did, because it was the right thing to do. Sondhi said that he believed Chamlong 100 per cent. Moreover, he himself was clever enough to analyse things for himself. After he had done this, he found that Chamlong had been right in every respect.[13] Thus, a small group of right-wing political activists with no support in public opinion turned against their erstwhile supporter, Abhisit. Sondhi had certainly not forgotten the roses that Abhisit had given him to show his gratefulness for the role that the PAD protests had played in paving his path to the premiership. Sondhi also admitted that he had initially liked him.[14] But now he sounded dejected: "I've never found a prime minister who tells as many lies as Abhisit Vejjajiva. Thaksin Shinawatra was the slyest prime minister but Abhisit is the biggest liar."[15] Later, Sondhi added, "A moment ago, I listened to Abhisit declaring the dissolution of parliament. I wanted to vomit. He said he had already worked to the best of his ability although, in fact, he cannot work."[16] In addition, the PAD's mass media mouthpiece, *ASTV Phuchadkan*, published a book the cover of which was dominated by a picture of Abhisit's head, while the title accused him of losing Thai territory to Cambodia.[17]

This approach could not but antagonize all those potential participants in the PAD protests, who were in fact followers of the Democrat Party, voted for it in elections, and admired Abhisit. Two interviewers of *Matichon* newspaper asked Chamlong about the relatively small number of protest participants. When his response was aggressively defensive, they were bold enough to follow up with the question: "Has the number of people turning out for the protests decreased because in the past it was the Democrat Party that had mobilized them?"[18] Chamlong did not take the bait about the role of the Democrats in the PAD's previous rallies of 2006 and 2008. Rather, he asked back, "What criterion do you use to say that there are not as many participants as on previous occasions? (Talking in a loud voice) Look, especially on Saturdays and Sundays, there is no space to walk. It is only some periods, how can you compare them?"[19] Sondhi provided a more nuanced perspective on the comparative dynamics of past and present PAD protests. He said,

> At the beginning, it was about building a united front by those who hated Thaksin. But there were swingers among those who joined, namely those of the Democrat Party, those who "loved" the Democrats, for example the *mom chao*, or the *mom ratchawong* (ranks of the old aristocracy), HiSo (high society). When Abhisit became prime minister, they were satisfied, and started to cheer Abhisit.[20]

In the same issue of the paper, an attack against the PAD's New Politics Party (NPP) went into a similar direction. It said that the insubordination of the NPP against the PAD's wishes showed that during the PAD's rallies to topple the Thaksin regime, many groups of "electocrats" (*naklueaktang*)[21] had hung around in the PAD movement, such as *sakdina* (aristocrats) groups, Democrat Party members, local electocrats, and new-face electocrats (supposedly those in the NPP who wanted to field candidates in the 2011 elections).[22] Suriyasai Katasila, PAD coordinator and secretary-general of the NPP, added to this perspective when interviewers asked him how many kinds of "yellow shirts" existed these days. He responded by saying that there were many varieties of yellow shirts. For example, some of them had thought that the Abhisit government already tended to the country's problems, and was less corrupt than the Thaksin government. He said, "When the Abhisit government was given the opportunity (to assume power), their mood to join the PAD had decreased. Thus, this (variety of yellow) shirt has withdrawn".[23] Suriyasai also added a key point regarding the dynamics of mass protests. He noted that the PAD had taken a more long-term view after the Abhisit government had come to power. Yet, the "masses" might not have caught up with them (*muanchon arj-cha tam mai tan*). This had led to a gap between the PAD and potential protest participants.

> Some people might think that the PAD's protest issue (*praden kankhlueanwai*) is rather remote.... They only wanted to topple a corrupt government. When the government is not good, they would come out and topple it again.... If the theme responds to the majority, then we will get the majority as our allies. If (it) responds to the minority or to the elite, then we will lose the majority.[24]

In their protests of 2006 and 2008, the PAD had drawn in those who rejected Thaksin. Consequently, those two rounds saw considerable participation. By comparison, the "protest issues" of the third round obviously did not resonate with greater numbers of people. Those issues were minority themes that did not appeal to the public. In other words, there was no market for the protest that the PAD, the Thai Patriots Network, and Santi Asoke had produced. For this reason, the consumers of previous protests simply stayed at home, and left the organizers alone at their protest site. Almost two months after the protest had started, the headline of an editorial said, "Time for PAD to head home." It rightly pointed out, "The rally had little meaning when it began in January."[25]

Suriyasai noted that those who the PAD in the past four to five years had thought of as allies did not support them any longer. Whom they had thought of as their *phuak* (clique) had become doubtful. He said, "This is a problem that challenges the PAD core leaders".[26] Niklas Luhmann once noted about social movements that had lost their identity-building and participant-generating protest issue (that would provide a homogeneous motivational resource), "In the case of failure, the movement fizzles out until a more opportune time arises."[27] Whether the Yingluck government would create such an opportune time remained to be seen. Both Chamlong[28] and Panthep Puangpongpan,[29] the PAD's main propagandist, confirmed that they were ready to fight against any attempt of this government to pass an amnesty that would bring Thaksin back to Thailand. A few months later, Panthep reiterated the readiness of the PAD to start another round of street protests in case the government tried to get a royal pardon for Thaksin.[30] Earlier, Suriyasai had thought that it was worth pondering whether the Democrat Party could return as the PAD's ally if Thaksin returned to the country.[31] Certainly, it would also help if the PAD could heal the internal and personal rifts that had occurred since this third round of protests started.

DETERMINING THE PROBLEMS OF THAI POLITICS

The Thai political system is in many respects structurally and culturally rather unsettled. Calling it a "hybrid" system indicates some of the tensions, contestations, and struggles in this political formation.[32] Therefore, it was not surprising to find not merely routine statements about everyday political processes and policy debates, but rather discourse that asked whether the system and its personnel should not be fundamentally changed, because it was seen as having too many defects (the PAD was merely the most extreme proponent of such changes). Suthichai Yoon, an influential political commentator with yellow leanings, mentioned people (he probably included), who were "desperately seeking an alternative to the current brand of politics".[33] His statement indicated a high level of emotional anguish that must have been pushed to new heights with the arrival of the Yingluck government. Suvit Maesincee, a director in the country's most elitist business school (Sasin of Chulalongkorn University), called Thai politics "dysfunctional". He went on to suggest that, "Thailand might need to consider whether the system of one man, one vote is best for us or not".[34] Apparently, Suvit thought that the electoral votes of people such as himself and Suthichai should carry much more weight than those of red-shirt voters, or anybody who had voted for the Pheu Thai party, and happened to reside upcountry. Suthichai and Suvit were typical members of the Bangkok-based establishment, and thus their statements needed to be taken seriously as representing important currents in the political culture of this elite social stratum. During the run-up to the latest election, Sondhi said, "I do not agree with the characteristics of electing representatives that imitates the West.... Should those having the right to vote not have knowledge about politics? ... If you are a doctor, you must have knowledge about medicine. Some people are ready, some are not."[35]

The above remarks fit into the PAD's conception of "New Politics" as proposed during their occupation of the Government House compound in 2008. Its signature proposal was that only 30 per cent of the members of parliament (MPs) should be elected, while 70 per cent should be appointed or selected. Thai-style politics, according to a later remark by Sondhi, had to be based on selection, election, and appointment, including people from many occupations. Western democracy could not work in Thailand.[36] There is no need to recapitulate the key elements of the PAD's "New Politics" ideas from the protest in 2009.[37] Instead, I will offer some additional statements made during the election campaign in 2011 in order to justify the PAD's "Vote No" stance.

Understandably, the PAD's view of Thai politics had not become any more charitable since the group had tried to impose a debate about "New Politics" on the Thai public. At that time, at least, they could still hope that a government led by Abhisit would come closer to their requirements for an ethical and competent political performance. As mentioned above, that hope had been badly squashed. Sondhi now included the Democrat Party in his condemnation of Thai political parties saying that Thailand had "a system of political party companies". They hired the MPs to vote for the prime minister and his policies. Members of Parliament did not act as lawmakers at all. They only raised their hands for the owner of those companies, whether it were the "Pheu Thai company or the Democrat company".[38] Thailand's "foul-water political system" (*rabop kanmueang namnao*) now included the Democrats among all the other political "beasts from hell" (*sat narok*) that, without exception, "cheated the nation and sold the land" (*kong chat khai phaendin*).[39]

Ahead of the elections, the "political investors" (*naklongthun thang kanmueang*) had moved to assess the prices for the buying and selling of MPs. Ad hoc alliances had been formed to bargain for positions in a future coalition government. All this was about "political business" (*thurakit kanmueang*). Most agreements had been made in advance. What remained was the "price bargaining" (*torrong raka*) regarding leaving or joining parties by grade B and C MPs. This was their "golden minute" (*nathee thong*) to make a profit.[40] Well-known PAD leader Praphan Khunmi put it this way:

The MPs are merely tools of the political parties, not independent representatives of the entire Thai people in order to protect the power of the people. The MPs are subject to dictatorial resolutions of their parties, because they have to use the party financiers' money to protect their power. The cabinet comprises representative of groups and political parties that share in the spoils. If many parties join the government, they will share them according to their quotas. They do not divide the work to further the benefit of the country and the people.[41]

This situation, according to Praphan, demonstrated that Thailand had "a dictatorial system by political parties, not a system of democracy."[42] An anonymous author made a much stronger assessment saying that Thai parties were "not at all different from Chinese underworld gangs (*kaeng angyi*) or Yakuza gangs (*kaeng yakusa*)".[43] In other words, "political parties have become mafia gangs".[44] Sondhi assisted with the allegation that Thai politics were not only an affair of different cliques within the capitalist oligarchy, but that this form of politics had to "end in banditcracy (*chon-athipatai*), that is, the politics of the bandits".[45] In this system, the people became similar to "debt slaves" (*that nai rueanbia*), who were controlled by the *hua khanaen* (vote canvassers), who would bring money for vote buying. The people only thought about the money that the politicians would give them.[46] Another PAD author, who had helped formulate its "New Politics" proposals, labelled Thailand's political system "concessionocracy" (*sampattanathipatai*). Capitalists and their relatives monopolized politics, and governed to advance their class interests. They did not even shrink back from stirring up the masses to cause terrorism if it benefited the capitalists (a reference to the red shirts and Thaksin).[47]

Social movements in general "are satisfied with a strongly schematized description of the problem ... and they portray their initiatives as reactions on intolerable conditions".[48] When key PAD activists defined Thai politics as a criminal enterprise that endangered the very existence of their beloved motherland (in particular its "revered highest institution"), they could certainly not tolerate this grave danger, even though this view might have looked like a bizarrely sectarian distortion to less emotionally involved observers. Yet, "One cannot expect from protest movements that they understand why a situation is as it is and that they can explain to themselves what the consequences would be if society gave in to their protest".[49] Rather, they operate based on the "apportioning of blame",[50]

here to the "beasts from hell". Moralistic approaches to societal problems
(such as that of the PAD) suggest that:

> Instead of analysing system structures, the guilty should be found out,
> restrained and, if necessary, opposed and punished. Moral right, then, is
> on the side of those who intervene against the self-destruction of society.
> In this way the theoretical discussion surreptitiously becomes a moral
> question and any of its possible theoretical shortcomings are offset by
> moral zeal. In other words, the intention to demonstrate good intentions
> determines the formulation of the problem.[51]

Alarmist messages and terrifying problem portrayals are thus necessary
for convincing the leaders themselves of the urgency and justification
of their mission, and to mobilize their key support groups, as well as
recruiting a broader audience ready to take to the streets in order to avert
the imminent danger. Chatchawal Chartsuthichai noted that the "evil
politicians or political businessmen are the cause of the severe calamity
of the system of democracy".[52] Phichai Rattanadilok Na Phuket noted that
political revolutions occurred because the old political system could not
solve the problems of a country. The problems therefore accumulated, and
eventually led to disaster, which caused revolutions. "Present Thai society
clearly is in this situation.... If this [political] system continues to exist,
very soon Thai society will experience catastrophe." A political revolution
was necessary to create "real democracy".[53]

Views such as those listed here cannot but lead to strong feelings
of disgust, contempt, condemnation, and despair. Combined with the
PAD members' heightened sense of the national good and their peculiar
version of self-righteousness, this kind of problem definitions must have
led to enormous pressure for action in order to save the nation from the
claws of all these evil political criminals that prevented the country from
progressing, and the people from gaining happiness. It probably also led
to great frustration with their fellow Thais, who did not seem to share the
PAD's opinions. The "refractoriness of society (*Renitenz der Gesellschaft*)",[54]
therefore, is a most important motivational force of social movements
such as the PAD (or the United Front for Democracy against Dictatorship
"UDD") in choosing the form of protest.

When the protests do not seem to succeed, measures that are more
drastic might be proposed. For example, the PAD had suggested "closing
down" the country for a few years by "pushing for a national government

headed by an outsider as prime minister",[55] who could then proceed to reform Thai politics for the better. Anchalee Paireerak demanded the creation of a "New Thailand Order" by way of an "orchid revolution" (*patiwat dok kluaimai*).

> Otherwise, we topple Thaksin and get Abhisit. We topple Abhisit and get Thaksin. We will move in circles without end.... The time has come to stop fighting, to put things in order, and create order in Thailand — before a Zapatista movement occurs in Thailand.[56]

Praphan also used the word *"kanchad rabiap prathet thai mai"* (by Anchalee translated as "creating a New Thailand Order"). He appealed to "all people who love the nation to have unity, and stop the parliamentary session that sold the country, and support the creation of a New Thailand Order. This will enable them to protect their country".[57] However, the time had not yet come for such radical measures to deal with a political system that the PAD activists found repulsive. At this point of their struggle, they were satisfied with starting their "Vote No" campaign for the election of 3 July 2011. Yet, this set them on a collision course with a formal political organization that they themselves had created — the New Politics Party.

THE NEW POLITICS PARTY

The PAD's protests in 2008 mainly aimed to topple Thaksin's "nominee" governments. But they had also pushed for "new politics", meaning a fundamental restructuring of Thailand's polity, especially concerning the electoral process. To carry on with this issue after the protests had ended, the PAD founded the NPP on 24–25 May 2009.[58] In an interview given two years later, Sondhi related that he had wanted to continue his work with ASTV, the newspaper, and the website. "Those who wanted to establish a political party were Suriyasai Katasila and Somsak Kosaisuk. I had opposed that, opposed it all the time. However, in the end, there was the resolution to call a PAD meeting."[59] Nevertheless, Sondhi ended up as the party's first chairperson, elected on 6 October 2009. There had been many candidates, and in order to avoid quarrelling, it was finally suggested that he should be the party leader, and everybody agreed. Khun Praphan (Khunmi) had started this talk. Deep inside, Sondhi said, he was still somewhat angry with Praphan that he had pulled him into this thing. Pinyo Traisuriyatham, the interviewer, followed up with the question whether Khun Sondhi never really wanted to be party leader, on which Sondhi said, "Never, never." However, there were two reasons that he had to do it. First, he told them that it would be temporary. Second, if the party was established, he would not stand in elections, and he would leave (the party). He had overseen the setting up of the structures, and after not even one year, he had resigned. Sondhi was followed by Somsak Kosaisuk, seeing him as "the representative of the PAD's core leaders".[60]

Specifically founded as the "second leg" of the PAD, the latter did not see the NPP as an independent political organization. Consequently, when the PAD leaders decided that the NPP should not field any candidates in the elections but join their "Vote No" campaign, a struggle between both units ensued. In a speech at the PAD's stage at Makkawan Bridge on 23 March 2011, Sondhi, in front of a few hundred (mostly female) die-hard fans first pointed out that he was quite at peace these days, because he used the *dhamma* (Buddhist teachings) for the consideration of all issues. He confirmed that he did not want to see elections, and that the country would surely be ruined (*chib-hai*) if politicians came to power again while the world was in crisis. Sondhi went on to attack Abhisit, accusing him of being a big liar, and of not being any better than Thaksin was. Finally, he came to the main point saying that the PAD's core leaders had decided that they would ask the people in the entire country to do a "No Vote".[61] The PAD, as the creator of the NPP, had officially informed Somsak and Suriyasai of their decision that the NPP should not field any candidates while Thai politics was still "rotten" (*nao*) and "evil" (*leo*). This statement was greeted with much applause. If people in the NPP still insisted on fielding candidates, it would have to be considered whether it still belonged to the PAD, or whether they had to sever their ties entirely, Sondhi thundered to great approval. All this was about ideals (*udomkan*), and not about the concerns of some people who wanted to run in elections. Somsak and Suriyasai had to make it clear whether they were with the NPP or with the PAD. If they were still with the PAD, they had to leave the NPP (in case the party insisted on fielding candidates in the elections). After all, Sondhi made clear, the NPP had been established as a tool of the PAD. How could it elevate itself above the PAD (that is, above the resolution of the PAD's core leaders)?[62]

In an interview about the infighting between the PAD and the NPP, Suriyasai at one point expressed his frustration saying, "I have asked myself whether our endpoint has come already.... This situation is no fun. I have no happiness."[63] Though PAD and NPP still shared the same objective, creating "new politics", their methods differed. People in the party thought that since they had established the NPP already, they could not reject the elections. The NPP had many branches, and it had long prepared for contesting this election.[64] Yet, Suriyasai accepted that — under the prevailing political circumstances — one could not expect the NPP to be a major driving force for political reform. If the party merely gained ten to twenty MPs, it could not do much in parliament. The NPP MPs could only be a limited voice of protest and investigation.[65]

Obviously, it was not to the PAD's liking to start small and then grow slowly. They wanted immediately to play a top-level role in the political system's formal structures. Patient development work was not their strong point — the country was in immediate danger, after all. They did not seem to have considered that, in a democracy, they needed to gain acceptance for their ideas in the population. Organizing protests and acting as a pressure group was so much easier. One might see this as a rather arrogant position by a group that was but a marginal player in the polity. Yet, from the PAD's perspective, there had been no democracy in Thailand, no "true democracy" anyway. Depending on merely ten to twenty MPs did not agree with their view that, "large-scale reform of Thailand is the destination of this round of the PAD's struggle".[66] Sondhi was more pessimistic regarding the NPP's electoral prospects and said, "We rather look at the overall picture. We rather look at political reform than at four to five party-list MPs showing themselves off in the House, being in the whirlpool of foul water (politics) just as before".[67] However, Suriyasai also saw the danger that the conflict between the NPP and the PAD may well make both entities tumble, while acknowledging that Thailand still needed an institutionalized "mass party" (English in the original). Neither the Pheu Thai nor the Democrat Parties were institutionalized and open to the masses. But for creating such a mass party, they needed twenty to thirty years time.[68]

Despite being under high pressure from Sondhi and the pro-PAD executive board members in the NPP, the party's chairperson Somsak still tried to defend the separate roles of the NPP and PAD.

> I believe there was interference in the party by the people on the (PAD) stage. I wanted to ask if this was appropriate. Certainly, the PAD and the party are allies. The PAD must respect party affairs. (It cannot be)

that the PAD wants no vote and mobilizes people to disrupt the party's activities and pressures the party to follow their decision. I wanted to know then — why set up this party? We set up this party so that people could decide if our policies should be supported.[69]

Defiantly, Somsak added,[70]

If the PAD wants no-vote, they should just campaign for no-vote and respect the party's decision to field candidates. Then there will not be any problem.... The party should be independent and should not come under the influence of any particular group or be used as a tool by some people. I have been accused of being politically lustful. I believe that is the old way of thinking. I have never thought of how many seats the party will win. The New Politics Party must not think like that. We must think of public interest. The party must contest the election to solve people's problems. I cannot see any option for helping the country — if we do not join the election.[71]

His show of defiance did not help Somsak. The split between PAD and NPP was confirmed when Suriyasai and Samran Rotphet, another member of the ten-person PAD faction on the NPP's executive board, issued a press release on 3 May 2011 accusing him of non-democratic behaviour, and asking why Somsak had to be stubborn (*danthurang*). They also insinuated that he was only interested in becoming MP via the NPP's party list. This was not different from "old politics".[72] Somsak was branded as the leader of "the electocrats in the New Politics Party". People of his ilk had merely hidden in the PAD "in order to make a name for themselves before they would run in elections".[73] PAD-oriented members on NPP's executive board also approached the Election Commission, telling them that any candidate list submitted by Somsak was invalid, because he had ignored an overwhelming vote against fielding candidates at the NPP's ordinary meeting on 24 April 2011. Part of the subheading reporting this step read, "If you love the NPP dismiss the traitors".[74] Meanwhile, Somsak accused Suriyasai of not having handed over 600,000 baht of donations to the NPP.[75] Suriyasai, in response, accused Somsak of "trying to smear his reputation by making false charges. He said Somsak, in a conspiracy with the party's treasurer, had tampered with the financial records to frame him."[76]

Thus, no love was lost between these two camps that were supposed to share the same goal, namely new and clean politics. Yet, strategic, tactical, and personal incompatibilities undermined what should have been an identity and cooperation-building set of shared political ideas, which had been nurtured since the first big anti-Thaksin protests in early 2006. Eventually, the NPP registered twenty-four party-list and sixteen constituency candidates.[77] The NPP's only newspaper advertisement that I saw asked the voters to "elect true people, elect daring people, elect people that have ideals".[78] Besides listing ten policies, the advertisement mentioned that Somsak had received the Human Rights Award from the German Friedrich Ebert Foundation. It did not help. The NPP, with number twenty for its party list (and consequently for its constituency candidates), received a paltry 34,883 votes, a mere 0.11 per cent of all party-list votes.[79] For gaining at least one single party-list MP, the NPP would have needed 125,754 votes, or 0.39 per cent of the vote total. It is a moot question whether a determined countrywide party-list campaign jointly performed by PAD and NPP would have produced those four to five seats Sondhi had expected; Suriyasai's projection of ten to twenty seats had certainly been unrealistic.

After the election, the NPP seemed to be finished. Separated from the PAD, it had lost whatever limited socio-political basis it could once claim to represent. Somsak entirely disappeared from the pages of the newspapers. As for former NPP secretary general Suriyasai and ten former members of the NPP's executive board (who were said to have run the "Vote No" campaign), they proceeded to establish a "Green Politics group". Suriyasai stated, "His new group would not let the Pheu Thai-led government help Thaksin return to the country without serving a prison sentence." They would also oppose an amnesty for Thaksin. According to Suriyasai, Sondhi and Chamlong backed this new initiative to pursue "clean, effective, and fair politics". Importantly, "The first principles of the group are to strengthen people politics, and develop a quality political party", though no deadline had been set when this step should be achieved. The major target groups of this new informal political organization were PAD supporters, environmental activists, and farmers' groups.[80]

Phiphob Thongchai, one of the PAD core leaders (now reduced to four by the withdrawal of Somsak), added that the new group's approach used to be the political direction of the NPP (the signature colours of its logo were yellow and green, the latter symbolizing environmentalism). "However, in the end, it failed because it was not strict about its (political) ideals." If the green politics group developed into a party, it would not be a big one, but based on a strong social movement, similar to the "Green

Party" in other countries.[81] Interestingly, Rat Bamrungrat connected this
new outfit to Suriyasai's earlier studies of the green movements in Europe,
especially Germany. At that time, he was still the secretary general of the
Campaign for Popular Democracy, and helped alternative political forces
think about the creation of a new-choice or third-way political party, when
Thai Rak Thai and the Democrats dominated the lead-up to the 2005
elections. Somsak, on the other hand, originated from the state-enterprise
labour unions, making his approach more traditionally oriented towards
welfare state policies. The author concluded that Suriyasai and Somsak
had returned to their basic political outlooks in acting within the New
Politics Party, and in creating the "Green Politics group".[82]

Critical observers of the Thai political party system, who normally
hope to see the emergence of horizontally integrated and nationalized
membership parties with countrywide distributed branches, and clearly
different policy platforms, will probably have to wait a while longer until
their normative hopes will be realized. I will now turn my attention to the
PAD's "Vote No" campaign.

THE PAD'S "VOTE NO" APPROACH

Abhisit dissolved the House of Representatives on 9 May 2011, thereby
making new elections necessary. He thereby also cruelly opened the door
for the "return of the Thaksin regime" without having done anything
about the suppression of corruption or political reform.[83] In late January,
the agenda of the most extremist part of the yellow-shirt organizations, the
Thai Patriots Network, had already included the proposal to campaign "for
five million no-vote ballots in the next election".[84] The first April issue of
ASTV Phuchadkan Sutsapda then included an article headlined, "Vote No:
Resolution of the great people. Reform the character of the breed of evil
politicians." After the elections, "society" could already imagine the next
government's "reality of evil ruthlessness" (*khwampenching an hodrai*) in this
"political theatre".[85] The article claimed that there was a strong "current"
(*krasae*) wanting to inflict some feeling of loss on the politicians. Some
people even rejected elections altogether as long as Thailand had the current
breed of politicians. "In short, elections are not the solution for Thailand".[86]
However, another (supposedly strong) *krasae* was, "to go and cast one's
vote, but use one's right in the box Vote No [English and capitalized in
the original] in order to make the electocrats know that they are no longer

what the people want". Voting "No" was thus intended as a protest vote against Thailand's politicians, the Democrats included, "because they have never done anything good for the country".[87] Voting "No" was, "like a protest against the politicians, and the rejection of the surrender to a political system that has failed, without having to rally".[88]

Therefore, in this election, the voters were asked to make a "historic decision" (*tatsinchai khrang prawattisat*) by taking part in the election but marking the "Vote No" (*mai prasong long khanaen*, or "do not wish to cast my vote") box on the ballot paper in order to "protect nation, religion, monarchy, and the people".[89] This goal included the reform of the system of democracy that had the King as head of state, "to make it a system that really works for the people". It had to be "the biggest ever political reform in Thailand".[90] The logic of this approach was that if the number of "Vote No" (or abstentions), together with the number of those who did not turn out to vote, were more than half, then this would mean that the entire political system was only based on a minority of the country's population. Consequently, the legitimacy of the politicians in governing the country would be reduced. At the same time, the legitimacy for substantial reform of the country would increase.[91]

Obviously, this logic depended on a large turnout of voters who would mark the "Vote No" box. Surawit Wirawan suggested that 5 to 10 million of such votes would be good enough to push for political reform. "If the Vote No is low, nothing will happen, because the Democrat Party will have no chance whatsoever to win (the election)".[92] Their goal was five million, which was the same number that the Thai Patriots Network had originally determined in January.[93] Similarly, Sondhi suggested that, "Assuming that at least 5 million people will 'vote no', this will have great political effect. It will have an effect in the sense that it will create political ethics."[94] Sondhi added,

> Regarding "Vote No", I still believe that if the entire country agrees and understands political activity, understands political mechanisms, they will create an unprecedented number of "Vote No". And this "Vote No" will be like a weight that will compel society, compel civil servants, compel politicians that it is necessary to reform themselves.[95]

Since the PAD had placed so much emphasis on achieving a high number of abstentions for creating "bargaining power for the people's sector outside parliament"[96] as the basis for their demands for fundamental political reform, the reverse logic was also clear enough, as Surawit acknowledged:

> (If there were a high number of abstentions) Society would be legitimized to stand up and demand that the currently existing evil political system changes itself. However, we must accept that if there are few "no" votes, then we can for sure not change the currently existing evil political system by taking part in elections for merely four seconds.[97]

Of course, there were voices that warned the PAD that its logic was flawed and its hopes groundless. An author not without sympathy for the yellow-shirt movement, Withayakorn Chiengkul of Rangsit University, noted that the political reality was that the PAD's current protest had attracted much smaller numbers of participants than when it protested against Thaksin. It would thus not be able to convince many people to tick the "vote no" box. Moreover, the majority of voters still thought that the means of elections was all right, and certainly better than military coups. Withayakorn left no doubts about his view of the PAD's "Vote No" campaign when calling it an unsubstantiated idea, illusionary, and romantic.[98] Yet, two days before the election, illusion prevailed as the following statement by Praphan Khunmi indicates.

> That the politicians and electocrats have come out heavily to counter, oppose, and attack "Vote No" (English in the original) on the home bend (of the election campaign) demonstrates that the people's "Vote No" campaign has achieved its ends. It has achieved a great political victory that will make politicians and political parties writhe in agony.... However, they will not be able to stop this current, because today the country needs to be freed from the old political system. The people need change. "Vote No" therefore is the political victory of the people with legal consequences that nobody can destroy.[99]

If Praphan's words were aimed at creating a miracle, it did not happen. The abstentions (note that blank ballots were counted as invalid votes) on the party-list ballot were a mere 958,213 (2.72 per cent) of the vote total.[100] Though the number of abstentions had increased slightly from the 935,306 of the elections in 2007, the percentage share of the total vote was slightly lower, down from 2.85 per cent in 2007. Regarding the constituency ballot, both the absolute figures and the percentages declined, from 1,499,707 (4.58 per cent) in 2007 to 1,419,148 (4.03 per cent) in 2011.[101] Obviously, the PAD's "Vote No" campaign was a dismal failure.[102]

Understandably, the PAD camp did not enter into a public self-searching discourse about what went wrong. However, some members did express dismay at the people's indifference towards three groups that had seen themselves as heroic warriors on the path towards a brighter political future in Thailand. Chatchawal Chartsuthichai put it this way,

> In current Thai society, although there are Thais who love the nation and make sacrifices in opposing alone and continuously the politicians who buy votes in elections and capture state power by using money, it is regrettable and sad that the majority of society still allows this small number of evil politicians to lead the entire nation into disaster.[103]

Surawit Wirawan added,

> Carrying the burden of the nation on its shoulders, and fighting on the streets, the PAD paid with their lives and a great many charges leading to imprisonment by state authorities and those who have captured state power. Rising up to fight for protecting the interests of the country and the people has come to be seen as the struggle of a street gang for creating turmoil in the country.[104]

Perhaps, the feelings expressed by Chatchawal and Surawit are the price that has to be paid for a moralistic and sectarian approach to interpreting how the Thai political system operates.

CONCLUSION

It is probably not an exaggeration when we conclude that the year 2011 was politically disastrous for the once-mighty PAD, the Thai Patriots Network, and Santi Asoke. They challenged the state with a long-term protest around Government House using a protest issue for which there was no demand in society. The Abhisit government did well mainly just to ignore the gathering until it had found a reason to pack up and go home. Speakers on the PAD stage, Sondhi included, insulted many of their erstwhile allies, supporters, and friends. They will not easily forget what had been said about them in public. One of them is Somsak, a previous core leader of the PAD and chairperson of the NPP. The PAD had created this party with great hopes in 2009, and it destroyed it in 2011. Finally, the PAD set out to teach the hated Thai politicians a lesson of such a weight with its "Vote No" campaign that they would be forced into accepting a fundamental restructuring of the Thai political system, initiated by the "people's sector". Yet, the "people", in their capacity as voters, ignored the PAD campaign. Almost three months before the elections, Suriyasai said in an interview, "I believe that after the 'vote no' campaign is behind us, the PAD must learn a big lesson about how and in which way we can move forward".[105] The need for the PAD to learn lessons had only become more urgent by what had happened between January and July 2011. It was an open question whether these lessons would lead into a politically constructive future for the PAD and the groups that were allied with it. Nevertheless, the societal infrastructure and its political culture out of which the PAD arose in interaction with their perception of the "Thaksin regime" were still there. They could well produce another round of political opposition — with or without the PAD — if their relationship with the Yingluck government seriously deteriorated.

Notes

1. *Matichon*, 8 October 2001.
2. *The Nation*, 3 October 2011.
3. Prime Minister Yingluck Shinawatra partly was an unintended consequence of the establishment's efforts to destroy her elder brother.
4. *The Nation*, 10 February 2006.
5. The present paper follows up on Nelson (2010). Reports on the first round of PAD protests in 2006 include Nelson (2007), Pye and Schaffar (2008), and Supalak (2006). A sympathetic journalistic account of the PAD protests is Kongbannathikan (2008).
6. The backdrop of their stage showed the word "Neo Protest" in big letters. Fortunately, a stall had leaflets on this "Whole New Kind of Demonstration" for distribution. In short, the "Philosophy of the Neo-Protest (was): Peace, Non-violence, Integrity, Purity, Profundity and Straightness" (Neo Protest n.d.).
7. *Bangkok Post*, 26 January 2011.
8. Ibid.
9. *Bangkok Post*, 3 May 2011.
10. Nattaya Chetchotiros and Anucha Charoenpo, "Poor Support could Spell Death Knell for the PAD", *Bangkok Post*, 8 March 2011.
11. Thitinan Pongsudhirak, "Where is the PAD Going This Time with its Protests?", *Bangkok Post*, 8 February 2011.
12. They included that the government must revoke the memorandum of understanding signed by Thailand and Cambodia in 2000, cancel the country's membership in the World Heritage Committee, and expel Cambodian

villagers from the disputed area at the Preah Vihear temple. The PAD also demanded that Abhisit and his government resign for what the group saw as his mishandling of the Thai-Cambodian border conflict (see Wassayos and Nattaya 2011, and Lamphai and Pradit 2011).

13. *ASTV Phuchadkan Sutsapda*, 7–13 May 2011.

14. Ibid.

15. *Bangkok Post*, 6 January 2011.

16. *ASTV Phuchadkan Sutsapda*, 14–20 May 2011.

17. Kongbannathikan ASTV Phuchadkan, *Duetasai Tham Thai Sia Dindaeng* (Bangkok: ASTV Phuchadkan 2011).

18. Sumet Thongphan and Sakda Samoephop, "Mahachamlong No Kantosu Thi 9.5 Pharakit Phothomo Nai Krasae Patiwat" [The Great Chamlong in the 9th-and-a-half Struggle. The PAD's Mission during the Current of Revolution (military coup)], *Matichon*, 8 February 2011.

19. Ibid.

20. *ASTV Phuchadkan Sutsapda*, 7–13 May 2011.

21. This usage of "electocrats" is different from the meaning that Kasian Tejapira had given the word. Kasian referred to locally based politicians who had turned themselves into experts at winning general elections (Kasian 2005). The ASTV source uses the word "electocrats" against all those who thought that elections were the democratic way to go in Thai politics.

22. *ASTV Phuchadkan Sutsapda*, 7–13 May 2011.

23. Sakda Samoephop and Sumet Thongphan, "Suriyasai Khayai Pom Sueknai PAD — NPP Thueng Thang Phraeng" [Suriyasai Reveals the Infighting between the PAD and the NPP — at the Crossroads], *Matichon Raiwan*, 11 April 2011.

24. Ibid.

25. *Bangkok Post*, 15 March 2011.

26. Sakda and Sumet, "Suriyasai Khayai Pom Sueknai PAD — NPP Thueng Thang Phraeng".

27. Niklas Luhmann, *Die Gesellschaft der Gesellschaft*, 2 vols (Frankfurt am Main: Suhrkamp, 1997), p. 863.

28. *ASTV Phuchadkan*, 15 June 2011.

29. *Bangkok Post*, 4 July 2011.

30. *The Nation*, 8 October 2011.

31. Sumet and Sakda, "Suriyasai Khayai Pom Sueknai PAD — NPP Thueng Thang Phraeng".

32. For some analysis with many references, see Nelson (2011).

33. Suthichai Yoon, "Only Major Overhaul Can Save Democrat Party", *Suthichaiyoon* <Blogspot.com/2011/08/democrat-party-cannot-afford-to-loose.html>, 7 August 2011.

34. *Bangkok Post*, 15 August 2011.

35. *ASTV Phuchadkan Sutsapda*, 7–13 May 2011.

36. Ibid.

37. See Nelson (2010), pp. 128–42. For a "Theory of New Politics", see the collection of newspaper articles from *ASTV Phuchadkan* written by Santi (2010), and published by the NPP as "required reading" for party members.

38. *ASTV Phuchadkan Sutsapda*, 14–20 May 2011.

39. *ASTV Phuchadkan Sutsapda*, 7–13 May 2011.

40. *ASTV Phuchadkan Sutsapda*, 14–20 May 2011.

41. This statement comes from an interview with Praphan (*Post Today*, 13 June 2011), who was a regular columnist in *ASTV Phuchadkan* daily newspaper. Praphan (2008) outlines his political views. This book is preceded by a poem of yellow-shirt poet Naowarat Phongphaibun, and forewords by Prasong Sunsiri (a supporter of Sondhi from the beginning of the protests in late 2005, and chairperson of the coup-appointed Constitution Drafting Committee), Sondhi Limthongkul, and Kalaya Sophonpanich, a leading member of the Democrat Party. Praphan used to be a student activist, and went into the jungle after the massacre at Thammasat University on 6 October 1976 (see the portrait in Thoettham 2008, pp. 193–207).

42. *Post Today*, 13 June 2011.

43. *ASTV Phuchadkan Sutsapda*, 2–8 April 2011.

44. Prasat Mitaem, "Langchak Vote No Laew Tham Arai To?" [After we have Voted No, What will We Do?], *ASTV Phuchadkan*, 20 June 2011.

45. As quoted in *ASTV Phuchadkan Sutsapda*, 2–8 April 2011.

46. *ASTV Phuchadkan Sutsapda*, 16–22 April 2011.

47. Phichai Rattanadilog Na Phuket, "Patiwat Duay Batlueaktang" [Revolution through the Ballot Paper], *ASTV Phuchadkan Sutsapda*, 2–8 July 2011.

48. Niklas Luhmann, *Die Gesellschaft der Gesellschaft*, 2 vols (Frankfurt am Main: Suhrkamp, 1997), p. 854.

49. Ibid., p. 857.

50. Ibid., p. 848.

51. Niklas Luhmann, *Ecological Communication*, translated by John Bednarz, Jr. (Chicago: University of Chicago Press; Cambridge: Polity Press, 1989), p. 5.

52. Chatchawan Chartsuthichai, "Krai Kamlang Thamhai Mueang Thai Lomchom???" [Who is Ruining Thailand???], *ASTV Phuchadkan*, 20 July 2011.

53. Phichai was a lecturer at the National Institute of Development Administration (NIDA). He regularly contributed a column to *ASTV Phuchadkan Sutsapda*. The Abhisit government appointed Phichai to the committee that was tasked with changing the election system of the 2007 constitution. Then NIDA president Sombat Thamrongthanyawong, who was himself well known for

his strongly yellow leanings, chaired that committee. See Phichai, "Patiwat Duay Batlueaktang".

54. Luhmann, *Die Gesellschaft der Gesellschaft*, p. 856.

55. Pradit Ruangdit, "PAD Calls for an Outsider to Run Country", *Bangkok Post*, 7 February 2011.

56. Anchalee Paireerak, "Patiwat Dok Kluaimai [The Orchid Revolution]", *ASTV Phuchadkan Sutsapda*, Vol. 2, No. 70 (5–11 February 2011). Anchalee was a propagandistic hawk in the PAD protests of 2008. After the column from which the quote is taken was published, she disappeared from the paper, and the PAD stage, reportedly because of conflicting loyalties with a Democrat minister.

57. Praphan Khunmi, "Yut!!! Ratthasapha Khai Chart Chatrabiap Prathet Thai Mai" [Stop!!! the National Assembly that Sells the Country, Create a New Thailand Order], *ASTV Phuchadkan*, 25 March 2011), p. 12.

58. For details, see Nelson (2010), pp. 142–52. Sondhi's printing house also published a book on the "PAD Party" (*phak phanthamit*) (Suwinai 2010).

59. *ASTV Phuchadkan Sutsapda*, 7–13 May 2011.

60. Ibid.

61. Sondhi indeed put it this way. The title of the VCD with the speech of Sondhi also still says, "*no wot*" (Ruam Phalang 2011).

62. The preceding account is based on watching the VCD "Ruam Phalang" (2011).

63. Sakda and Sumet, "Suriyasai Khayai Pom Sueknai PAD — NPP Thueng Thang Phraeng".

64. Ibid. According to the NPP's document for its annual assembly on 24 April 2011, the party had ten branches and fifteen so-called "coordination centres" countrywide. The number of party members stood at 13,180 (Phak Kanmueang Mai 2011, p. 4; thanks to Nicola Glass for sending me this document). The total expenses of the NPP in 2010 were given as 16.5 million baht, 14.4 million of which were spent for the NPP's headquarters (ibid., appendix). Given these less than impressive figures, the targets contained in the NPP's action plan, which was presented at the first general meeting of the NPP on 6 October 2009, seemed to be overly ambitious. They envisaged 500,000 party members, 40 party branches by the end of 2010, and a budget of 117.9 million baht for 2010 (Nelson 2010, p. 151). It seemed that Thailand's first self-proclaimed "mass party" (Suriyasai in an interview [Sakda and Sumet 2011], he used the English word) did not attract the masses.

65. Ibid.

66. Suriyasai, as quoted in Sakda and Sumet, "Suriyasai Khayai Pom Sueknai PAD — NPP Thueng Thang Phraeng".

67. *ASTV Phuchadkan Sutsapda*, 30 April–6 May 2011.

68. Sakda and Sumet, "Suriyasai Khayai Pom Sueknai PAD — NPP Thueng Thang Phraeng".
69. *The Nation*, 2 May 2011.
70. Challenging Sondhi's favourite claim of superior morality based on the Buddhist teachings, Somsak asked whether it was "true that they (those attacking him over the NPP issue) are led by the Dharma and morality" (*The Nation*, 2 May 2011).
71. Ibid.
72. *Thai Post*, 4 May 2011.
73. *ASTV Phuchadkan*, 7–13 May 2011.
74. *ASTV Phuchadkan*, 13 May 2011.
75. Ibid.
76. *The Nation*, 3 June 2011.
77. *Thai Rath*, 4 June 2011.
78. *Khom Chat Luek*, 1 July 2011.
79. For the data, see Samnakngan Khanakammakan Kanlueaktang, *Khomun sathiti kanlueaktang samachik saphaphuthaenratsaton pho.so. 2554* [Data and Statistics of the Election of Members of the House of Representatives 2011] (Bangkok: Office of the Election Commission of Thailand, 2012), p. 228.
80. Aekarach Sattaburuth, "Green Politics Airs 'People Party' Hopes: Government Charter Rewrite, Reds Early Target", *Bangkok Post*, 28 August 2011.
81. Khunsi Samyaek, "Hualiewhuato Pochopo — Phothomo?" [A Turning Point for the Democrats — PAD?], *Lokwanni Wansuk*, 3–9 September 2011, p. 14.
82. Rat Bamrungrat, "Yonroi Fan Phak Krin Chak 2554 Ritoen Pi 2547" [Returning to the Dream of a Green Party from 2011 Return to 2004], *Nation Sutsapda*, 2 September 2011, p. 22.
83. *ASTV Phuchadkan*, 11 June 2011.
84. Wassayos Ngamkham and Nattaya Chetchotiros, "Police Thwart Protest Bomb Bid: Suspects Say They Were Hired to Instigate Unrest", *Bangkok Post*, 25 January 2011.
85. *ASTV Phuchadkan Sutsapda*, 2–8 April 2011.
86. Ibid.
87. Ibid.
88. Panthep Phuaphongphan, "Lueak Phak Nai Ko Phae Phuea Thai: Ruam Ka 'Vote No' Yut Sang Kwamchotham Hai Thaksin" [Whichever Party you Chose, It will Lose to Pheu Thai: Join 'Vote No,' and Stop Creating Legitimacy for Thaksin]", *ASTV Phuchadkan*, 1 June 2011, p. 1.
89. Note that the usual trinity of the long-standing official state ideology — "Nation, Religion, Monarchy" — was complemented by "the people".
90. *ASTV Phuchadkan Sutsapda*, 16–22 April 2011.
91. Ibid.

92. Surawit Wirawan, "Thammai Vote No Di Kwa Lueak Thuk Phak" [Why is the Vote No Better than Electing any Party?], *ASTV Phuchadkan*, 22 April 2011, p. 12.

93. Surawit Wirawan, "Wot No Laew Dai Aria" [What will we Get from Voting No?], *ASTV Phuchadkan*, 13 May 2011, p. 12.

94. *ASTV Phuchadkan Sutsapda*, 7–13 May 2011.

95. Ibid.

96. Panthep, "Lueak Phak Nai Ko Phae Phuea Thai".

97. Surawit, "Wot No Laew Dai Arai".

98. Withayakorn Chiengkul, "Wiphak Rueang Kanronnarong Wot No" [Critiquing the Vote No Campaign], *Post Today*, 25 April 2011, p. 2. On the other hand, a full professor of political science, who served in the coup government, praised the Vote No campaign as having great value for democracy. It would lead to comprehensive political reform to solve the problem of "rotten politics". If they did not urgently act, politics would lead the country into "turbulent days" (*kaliyuk*). Solving the problems would necessarily use violent means. In Thiraphat Serirangsan, "Wot No ... Laew Dai Arai" [What will we Get from Voting No?], *Matichon*, 28 June 2011, p. 6.

99. Praphan Khunmi, "Vote No Chaichana Thangkanmueang Khong Prachachon Lae Phon Thangkotmai Thi Khrai Mi At Thamlai Dai" [Vote No – the Political Victory of the People with Legal Consequences that Nobody can Destroy], *ASTV Phuchadkan*, 1 July 2011.

100. "Analysis of the 2011 Thai Election — Part 1: Nationwide", *Bangkok Pundit Blog*.

101. "Analysis of the 2011 Thai Election — Part 4: Constituency Vote", *Bangkok Pundit Blog*. The figures for 2007 are taken from Samnakngan Khanakammakan Kanlueaktang, *Khomun Sathiti Lae Phonkanlueaktang Samachik Sapha Phuthaenratsadorn Pho So 2550* [Data, Statistics and the Election Result of the Members of the House of Representatives 2007] (Bangkok: Office of the Election Commission of Thailand, 2008), p. 42.

102. The "Vote No" posters seen on Bangkok streets, depicting politicians as animals, were technically election posters of Santi Asoke's inactive "For Heaven and Earth Party". It had registered one party-list candidate, received the number 18, and gained 12,823 votes (0.04 per cent) (*Bangkok Pundit Blog*, 2011). The PAD also published a leaflet explaining their stance to the voters (Khanakammakan 2011). It was repeatedly printed in *ASTV Phuchadkan*.

103. Chatchawan, "Krai Kamlang Thamhai Mueang Thai Lomchom???".

104. Surawit Wirawan, "Prathet Tai Rabop Chinawatra" [The Country under the Shinawatra System], *ASTV Phuchadkan*, 22 July 2011, p. 12.

105. Sakda and Sumet, "Mahachamlong No Kantosu Thi 9.5 Pharakit Phothomo Nai Krasae Patiwat".

References

Aekarach Sattaburuth. "Green Politics Airs People Party Hopes: Government Charter Rewrite, Reds Early Target". *Bangkok Post*, 28 August 2011.

Anchalee Paireerak. "New Thailand Order: Patiwat Dok Kluaimai [The Orchid Revolution]". *ASTV Phuchadkan Sutsapda* 2, no. 70 (5–11 February 2011).

ASTV Phuchadkan Sutsapda, various issues.

Bangkok Post, various issues.

Bangkok Pundit Blog. "Analysis of the 2011 Thai Election — Part 1: Nationwide". 4 October 2011.

———. "Analysis of the 2011 Thai Election — Part 4: Constituency Vote". 6 October 2011.

Chatchawan Chartsuthichai. "Krai Kamlang Thamhai Mueang Thai Lomchom???" [Who is Ruining Thailand?]. *ASTV Phuchadkan*, 20 July 2011.

Kasian Tejapira. "Reform and Counter-Reform: Democratization and its Discontents in Post-May 1992 Thai Politics". In *Towards Good Society: Civil Society Actors, the State, and the Business Class in Southeast Asia: Facilitators of or Impediments to a Strong, Democratic, and Fair Society?*, pp. 125–46. Berlin: Heinrich Böll Foundation, 2005.

Khanakammakan Ronnarong Pai Chai Sit Kakbat Mai Prasong Cha Lueak Khrai Phuea Kanpattirup Kanmueang. *Wot No Ya Ploi Hai Nakkanmueang Duthuk Prachachon*. [Committee for the Campaign to Use One's Voting Right to Mark that One does not Wish to Elect Anybody for Political Reform. "Vote No, do not Allow the Politicians to Look down on the People."]. 8pp. 2011.

Khom Chat Luek newspaper (1 July 2011).

Khunsi Samyaek. "Hualiewhuato 'Pochopo — Phothomo'?" [A Turning Point for the Democrats — PAD?]. *Lokwanni Wansuk*, 3–9 September 2011.

Kongbannathikan ASTV Phuchadkan. *Duetasai Tham Thai Sia Dindaeng*. Bangkok: ASTV Phuchadkan, 2011.

Kongbannathikan Matichon. *Lap Luang Luek: Panthamit Prachachon Phuea Prachathipattai* [Secret, Eliciting, Penetrating: The People's Alliance for Democracy]. Bangkok: Samnakphim Matichon, 2008.

Lamphai Intathep and Pradit Ruangdit. "Yellow Shirts Target Key City Locations: Fury over Cambodian issue Sparks more Rallies". *Bangkok Post*, 7 February 2011.

Luhmann, Niklas. *Ecological Communication*. Translated by John Bednarz, Jr. Chicago: University of Chicago Press; Cambridge: Polity Press, 1989.

———. *Die Gesellschaft der Gesellschaft*. 2 vols. Frankfurt am Main: Suhrkamp, 1997.

Nattaya Chetchotiros and Anucha Charoenpo. "Poor Support could Spell Death Knell for the PAD". *Bangkok Post*, 28 March 2011.

Nelson, Michael H. "People's Sector Politics (*Kanmueang Phak Prachachon*) in Thailand: Problems of Democracy in Ousting Prime Minister Thaksin Shinawatra". Working Paper Series No. 87. Hong Kong: Southeast Asia Research Centre, City University of Hong Kong, 2007.

————. "Thailand's People's Alliance for Democracy: From 'New Politics' to a 'Real' Political Party?". In *Legitimacy Crisis and Political Conflict in Thailand*, edited by Marc Askew, pp. 119–59. Chiang Mai: Silkworm Books, 2010.

————. "Some Observations on Democracy in Thailand". Working Paper Series No. 125. Hong Kong: Southeast Asia Research Centre, City University of Hong Kong, 2011.

"Neo Protest: A Whole New Kind of Demonstration" (leaflet). Bangkok: Fah-Apai Co. Ltd, n.d.

Panthep Phuaphongphan. "Lueak Phak Nai Ko Phae Phuea Thai: Ruam Ka 'Vote No' Yut Sang Kwamchobtham Hai Thaksin" [Whichever Party You Chose, It Will Lose to Phue Thai: Join 'Vote No', and Stop Creating Legitimacy for Thaksin]. *ASTV Phuchadkan*, 1 June 2011.

Phak Kanmueang Mai. "Rabiap Wara Kanprachum Yai Saman, Khrang Thi 1/2554". Wan Thi 24 Mesayon Pho. So. 2554 No Samakhom Chin Phaoleng Haeng Prathet Thai [New Politics Party: Agenda of the First Ordinary General Assembly on 24 April 2011]. (Document distributed at the event.)

Phichai Rattanadilog Na Phuket. "Patiwat Duay Batlueaktang" [Revolution through the Ballot Paper]. *ASTV Phuchadkan Sutsapda*, 2–8 July 2011.

Post Today, 13 June 2011.

Pradit Ruangdit. "PAD Calls for an Outsider to Run Country". *Bangkok Post*, 7 February 2011.

Praphan Khunmi. *Chiwit Ni Kho Pen Kha Phrabat ThatPprachachon* [This Life Wants to be the Servant of the Royal Feet, and the Slave of the People]. Klairung Thiphana Riapriang. Bangkok: Samnakphim Krin-Panyachon, 2008.

————. "Yut!!! Ratthasapha Khai Chart Chatrabiap Prathet Thai Mai" [Stop!!! the National Assembly that Sells the Country, Create a New Thailand Order]. *ASTV Phuchadkan*, 25 March 2011.

————. "Vote No Chaichana Thangkanmueang Khong Prachachon Lae Phon Thangkotmai Thi Khrai Mi At Thamlai Dai" [Vote No — The Political Victory of the People with Legal Consequences that Nobody can Destroy]. *ASTV Phuchadkan*, 1 July 2011.

Prasat Mitaem. "*Langchak Vote No Laew Tham Arai To?*" [After we have Voted No, What will We Do?]. *ASTV Phuchadkan*, 20 June 2011.

Pye, Oliver and Wolfram Schaffar. "The Anti-Thaksin Movement in Thailand: An Analysis". *Journal of Contemporary Asia* 38, no. 1 (2008): 38–61.

Rat Bamrungrat. "Yonroi Fan 'Phak Krin' Chak 2554 Ritoen Pi 2547" [Returning to the Dream of a 'Green Party'. From 2011 Return to 2004]. *Nation Sutsapda*, 2 September 2011.

"Ruam Phalang Pokpong Phaendin". Mati Kaennam Phothomo No Wot; Yam Thuk Phak Kanmueang Luan Tham Phuea Ngoen-Amnat Kongkin Banmueang. Wan Thi 23 Minakhom 2554 No Saphan Makkawan ["Uniting the Forces to Protect the Nation". Resolution of the PAD Core Leaders to Vote No: Confirming that all Political Parties Work for Money and Power, and Corrupt the Country, 2 March 2011, at the Makkawan Bridge]. VCD.

Sakda Samoephop and Sumet Thongphan. "Suriyasai Khayai Pom Sueknai PAD — NPP Thueng Thang Phraeng" [Suriyasai Reveals the Infighting between the PAD and the NPP — at the Crossroads]. *Matichon Raiwan*, April 2011.

Samnakngan Khanakammakan Kanlueaktang. *Khomun Sathiti Lae Phonkanlueaktang Samachik Sapha Phuthaenratsadorn Pho. So. 2550* [Data, Statistics and the Election Result of the Members of the House of Representatives 2007]. Bangkok: Office of the Election Commission of Thailand, 2008.

Samnakngan Khanakammakan Kanlueaktang. *Khomun Sathiti Kanlueaktang samachik saphaphuthaenratsaton pho.so. 2554* [Data and Statistics of the Election of Members of the House of Representatives 2011]. Bangkok: Office of the Election Commission of Thailand, 2012.

Santi Tangraphiphakon. *Tritsadi Kanmueang Mai (2551–2553)* [Theory of New Politics, 2008–2010]. Bangkok: New Politics Party, 2010.

Sumet Thongphan and Sakda Samoephop. "'Mahachamlong' No Kantosu Thi 9.5 Pharakit Phothomo Nai Krasae Patiwat" [The Great Chamlong in the 9th-and-a-half Struggle. The PAD's Mission during the Current of Revolution (military coup)]. *Matichon*, 8 February 2011.

Supalak Ganjanakhundee. 'Khabuankanprachachon Kueng Samretrup Kap Kantosu Phuea Prachathipattai Baep Phuengphing (Botpramoen Khabuanhae Khong Phuprakopkan) [The Semi-instant People's Movement and the Struggle for a Dependent Democracy (An Assessment of the Entrepreneurs' Parade)]. *Fa Diewgan* 4, no. 2 (2006): 166–86.

Surawit Wirawan. "Thammai Vote No Di Kwa Lueak Thuk Phak" [Why is the Vote No Better than Electing any Party?]. *ASTV Phuchadkan*, 22 April 2011.

———. "Wot No Laew Dai Aria" [What will we Get from Voting No?]. *ASTV Phuchadkan*, 13 May 2011.

———. "Prathet Tai Rabop Chinawatra" [The Country under the Shinawatra System]. *ASTV Phuchadkan*, 22 July 2011.

Suthichai Yoon. "Only Major Overhaul Can Save Democrat Party". *Suthichaiyoon.* <Blogspot.com/2011/08/democrat-party-cannot-afford-to-loose.html>, 7 August 2011 (accessed 5 November 2012).

Suwinai Pharanawalai. *Phak Phanthamit: Nakrop Haeng Thamm Kap Kansang Phak Kanmueang Mai Khong Phanthamit Prachachon Phuea Prachathipattai* [The PAD

Party: The Fighters for Virtue and the Creation of the New Politics Party of the People's Alliance for Democracy]. Bangkok: Samnakphim Ban Phraathit, 2010.

Thai Post, 4 May 2011.

Thai Rath, 4 June 2011.

The Nation, various issues.

Thiraphat Serirangsan. "Wot no … Laew Dai Arai" [What will we Get from Voting No?]. *Matichon*, 28 June 2011, p. 6.

Thitinan Pongsudhirak. "Where is the PAD Going this Time with its Protests?". *Bangkok Post*, 8 February 2011.

Thoettham Thongthai. *Kha Khue Nakrop Prachachon Ku Chat*. Nonthaburi: Samnakphim Krin-Panyayan, 2008.

Wassayos Ngamkham and Nattaya Chetchotiros. "Police Thwart Protest Bomb Bid: Suspects Say they were Hired to Instigate Unrest". *Bangkok Post*, 25 January 2011.

Withayakorn Chiengkul. "Wiphak Rueang Kanronnarong Wot No" [Critiquing the Vote No Campaign]. *Post Today*, 25 April 2011, p. 2 (*wikhro* section).

7

THE RED SHIRTS
From Anti-Coup Protesters
to Social Mass Movement

Nick Nostitz

The continuing political conflict between forces in favour and against then Prime Minister Thaksin Shinawatra that became visible in late 2005 has led to fundamental changes in Thai politics and society. When Sondhi Limthongkul started his protests against the Thaksin government, which were followed by the founding of the ultra-royalist People's Alliance for Democracy (PAD) in early 2006, and their mass protests over the following months,[1] very few observers could have imagined that the supporters of Thaksin would transform themselves from passive voters into possibly the biggest social mass movement Thailand has ever seen — the red-shirt movement, born out of the 19 September 2006 military coup. This transformation took place in four distinct phases of development, which were closely connected to developments at the street level. While most commentators view the turmoil as an elite conflict, especially between Thaksin/new money and the military/bureaucracy/palace conglomerate, this article argues that the driving force of the socio-political turmoil is indeed at the street level. Even though the elite level conflict may have initiated this crisis, it had over time become more reactive to ground level developments, based on the collective experience of ordinary protesters and the increase in their political awareness. This also means that the ongoing conflict is not just a power conflict between two opposing elite factions, but has developed into a historical identity crisis over two opposing philosophies represented by the colour codes of yellow — the old style Thai system of semi- or managed democracy with the role of ordinary people as subjects, and red — the demand to be citizens in a modern democratic system.

While unsolved political conflicts of the past — the 1932 abolition of the absolute monarchy and in particular the turmoil of the 1970s — can be seen as the root causes of the present conflict, also as many leading figures of the different sides then in the 1970s still play large roles today, the focus of this article is primarily on the effects of the 2006 military coup, and especially on how it altered the perceptions of the red shirts and their view of society. For the first time in Thai history, critical views of the state are now held not just by university educated sectors of society or elite factions, but also by large sectors of common Thais — villagers, urban labourers, and the middle class.

The precursor of what the red shirts are today emerged after Thaksin Shinawatra's election rally speech at Sanam Luang on 3 March 2006, as a counter protest against the "yellow shirts" of the PAD. The so-called "Caravan of the Poor", which consisted of villagers from the north and the northeast, was mobilized by Newin Chidchob's networks. These villagers travelled in their anti-PAD march on *rot e-tan* — small agricultural vehicles — to Bangkok. While these pro-Thaksin protesters were an organized political mob, they were politically aware and diversified in their opinions.[2] Their support for Thaksin was based mostly on his populist programmes, such as the 30-baht health scheme and the different microloan programmes, which they viewed as a substantial improvement in their standard of living. Yet, they also criticized him, and some of his policies sullied by corruption. There was also a strong sense of empowerment in their position, stemming from voting for Thaksin's Thai Rak Thai (TRT) — the party that they felt best represented their interests. On their final leg into Bangkok along the multilane Vibhavadi Rangsit highway, their caravan was cheered on by many motorcycle taxi drivers, factory workers and residents. They joined pro-Thaksin groups at Chatuchak Park where they camped out until the Constitution Court, on 8 May 2006, nullified the election of 2 April 2006 that had been boycotted by the Democrat and Chart Thai Parties. After initially not moving from their campsite, the government supporters carried out different protest activities, such as the seven-hour blockade of The Nation building on 30 March 2006 by about 2000 pro-Thaksin protesters who rallied against *Kom Chad Luek*, a Thai-language newspaper belonging to the strongly anti-Thaksin Nation Group, over the newspaper's interview with Sondhi Limthongkul and his comments made on the PAD stage on 23 March 2006, which they viewed as *lèse-majesté*.[3] Two days later, on 1 April 2006, about 200 motorcycle taxi drivers protested at Sondhi's Manager Media Group office over the same issue where insults and an exchange of bottles throwing between the protesters and staff of the office occurred.[4]

In late June 2006, Thaksin accused a "charismatic figure" to be working against him, generally understood to be Privy Council President General Prem Tinsulanonda. Prem subsequently, in his lecture on 14 July 2006 at the Chulachomklao Royal Military Academy, reminded the cadets of their loyalties. He said, "Soldiers are like horses, and governments are like jockeys but not owners. Soldiers belong to the nation and His Majesty the King";[5] this was widely seen as an answer to Thaksin's accusation. On that occasion, Prem, dressed in combat uniform, was surrounded by several senior military figures, retired and active, including Army Chief General Sonthi Boonyaratglin and Privy Councillor General Surayud Chulanont. Two days later, on 17 July, in a surprise reshuffle,[6] General Sonthi transferred 129 mid-ranked officers under the command of Generals of Class 10 of the Armed Forces Preparatory School who were seen as close to Thaksin.[7] Prem continued to hold similar speeches at the academies of the Navy and the Air Force that were harshly critical of Thaksin and the government.[8] Other senior figures in Thai society followed suit, such as Prawase Wasi[9] and former Prime Minister and palace insider Anand Panyarachun.[10]

More minor incidents of violence occurred after the PAD initiated "guerrilla" style protest tactics in August 2006, accosting Thaksin with small groups of protesters at public appearances. The most notorious one was the fight between PAD protesters and Thaksin supporters, which occurred on 21 August 2006, after Thaksin opened a digital learning centre at Central World Plaza where Thaksin's supporters attacked the PAD protesters.[11] Another often cited incident took place on 16 August 2006 when 100 forestry officials and rangers, organized by chief of Tak provincial forestry office Saneh Thipburi, who had also previously supported the "Caravan of the Poor", attempted to break up a PAD protest in Tak province during Thaksin's tour through the north. The police had to step in to prevent violence.[12]

New elections were underway, and the PAD threatened further protests against Thaksin on 20 September 2006.[13] While Thaksin was in New York preparing a speech at the UN General Assembly, and just before the annual military reshuffle, the military led by General Sonthi staged a coup on 19 September 2006.[14] Tanks appeared on the streets of Bangkok. Soldiers wearing royal yellow ribbons on their uniforms took control. The night of the takeover, the coup leaders were granted an audience with the King.[15] Three days later, on 22 September 2006, the "Council for Democratic Reform under Constitutional Monarchy", as the coup makers called themselves, received the official royal endorsement with General Sonthi as its leader, who kneeled during the reading of the order in front of a portrait of the King.[16] In their first announcement, the coup makers justified their action by saying that society had never experienced a conflict like this before, which was caused by the government, widespread corruption, political domination over independent agencies and the danger of the occurrence of violations against the King.[17] Martial law was declared, the 1997 constitution repealed, and parliament, senate, cabinet and the constitutional court dissolved. The announcement also pointed out that Privy Councillors were to remain in their duty, that the coup leaders had no intention to rule and that they were "to return the power to the people as soon as possible, to preserve peace and honour the King who is the most revered to all Thais". Initially the coup group's official English moniker was "Council for Democratic Reform under Constitutional Monarchy". But after speculation in foreign media appeared over royal involvement, the coup group shortened the English name to "Council for Democratic Reform" (CDR).[18] But the Thai name of the council "*Khana patiroop kanpokkhrong nai rabop prachathipatai an mi phramahakasat song pen pramook*" (Committee for the reform of government in the system of democracy that has the King as head of the state) remained unchanged. When the interim constitution was endorsed on 1 October 2006, and the new governing bodies, such as the appointed National Legislative Assembly (NLA) and the Constitution Drafting Assembly (CDA), were set up, and a referendum on the new constitution was ruled, the CDR transformed itself into the Council for National Security (CNS).[19] With Prem's blessing,[20] General Surayud Chulanont was confirmed as new prime minister on 1 October 2006.

PHASE 1: THE SANAM LUANG ERA

The military and their supporters, including the PAD and the Democrat
Party, thought that they had overthrown an authoritarian prime minister
who in their view had merely bought his voters' support, and thus did
not command any real loyalty. Initially, the coup seemed to be successful.
The coup group's analysis also seemed to be confirmed by the numerically
tiny protests and the looming collapse of the TRT Party which saw, in
the aftermath of Thaksin's resignation as party leader from his exile
in London on 2 October 2006,[21] many important former members of
parliament, following the CNS's announcement stipulating a possible
five-year ban from politics in case of a court ordering dissolution of a
political party, resigning from their party membership in an attempt to
evade the ban.[22] The attempts of agitating against the coup were easily
stifled by the closure of critical websites, including the website of the
popular Midnight University,[23] or the repeated blocking of the website of
the Anti-19 September Coup Network, 19sep.org.[24] The majority of news
coverage was about coup supporters who visited the Royal Plaza on a
daily basis to congratulate the soldiers and to pose for photos in front of
the tanks stationed there. Two weeks after the coup, the army drastically
reduced its presence on the streets.

Various protest groups mostly gathered at Sanam Luang, and organized
for the most part peaceful protest marches to the nearby Democracy
Monument and the Army headquarters. In this phase, one could still
see a more traditional form of the Thai protest game. There were small
groups of highly motivated activists. For the larger rallies, protesters were
mobilized by canvassers linked to TRT Party politicians. By then, there
were the first tacit indications for an imminent change in the socio-political
landscape of Thailand, in which, for the common Thai people, loyalty to
policies, designed to empower them and symbolized by Thaksin, increased
in importance over loyalty to political networks. Groups with traditional
protest backgrounds and the capability to mobilize protesters mostly
refrained from joining the anti-coup protests as many of them, such as
the majority of NGOs and labour unions, either supported the military
coup or remained silent because of their alliance with the PAD. Therefore,
the anti-coup protest groups had to start from scratch. In this period, the
number of protesters remained relatively low, both because provincial
protesters were regularly discouraged from joining the rallies and because

they mostly came from sectors new to street politics.[25] Nevertheless, the coup era was a seminal period of ideological building amongst those who later became the red shirts.

Soon after the coup, a large number of small anti-coup groups were formed. Following a small protest on 2 September 2006 led by Giles Ungpakorn, a leftist academic who is now in exile in the United Kingdom because of a *lèse-majesté* case filed against him over his book *A Coup for the Rich*,[26] the first was the Anti 19 September Coup Network, led by NGO activist Sombat Boon-ngamanong and several students. Other groups then began to form, such as Nok Pilap Khao (White Dove) and Saturday People against Dictatorship. The latter is now defunct after its leader, Suchart Nakbangsai, has been charged and arrested, after two years on the run, and subsequently sentenced to two years in prison for *lèse-majesté* (he was released in August 2012). The Saturday People against Dictatorship group mostly comprised of members of the middle class who discussed politics on the Internet. Their first protest took place on 1 November 2006 at Sanam Luang, then under the initial name of the group D-Code.[27] During their first protest, it was evident that they lacked organization. Their "stage" consisted of just a chair and a handheld megaphone. During their following protest, on 11 November 2006, they had a small stage of approximately two metres by two metres, including a small speaker system, and only drew a crowd of around 200 to 300 protesters. From then on, they held rallies every Saturday at Sanam Luang, drawing several hundred participants. Saturday People against Dictatorship staged perhaps the most innovative and creative protest of this era on the day of the TRT dissolution verdict, on 30 May 2007. At the time, a new, unprecedented amulet craze gripped Thai society. Previously, obscure Brahmanistic amulets from the southern city of Nakhorn Sri Thammarat — the Jatukham Ramathep amulets — became immensely popular all over the country. The members of Saturday People against Dictatorship decided to issue their own Jatukham Ramathep amulet. As opposed to the very expensive editions, they distributed their Jatukham Ramathep 1 Baht edition under their name that day at Sanam Luang.[28] In the following months, many anti-coup protesters wore these amulets around their neck as a sign of their struggle.

The anti-coup groups had their first martyr with the taxi driver Nuamthong Praiwan, who committed suicide by hanging himself from a pedestrian bridge in front of *Thai Rath* newspaper office on Vibhavadi Rangsit Road on 31 October 2006,[29] a month after he drove his taxi, painted with anti-coup slogans, into the army tanks parked at the Royal Plaza in protest against the coup.[30] The funeral at Bua Kwan Temple in Nonthaburi was very significant. Displayed next to a picture of Nuamthong's portrait was his farewell letter, which was reproduced in countless flyers for months. Numerous representatives of the TRT Party attended the daily funeral ceremony and took turns in presiding over the rites, such as then Thaksin's spokesman Pongthep Thepkanjana and many of the later red-shirt leaders including Veera Musikapong, Jatuporn Prompan, Prateep Ungsongtham Hata, Human Rights Commissioner Jaran Dithapichai, Chairman of the Foundation of Democracy Heroes Sant Hatirat, and Dr Weng Tojirakarn who was briefly allied with the pre-coup PAD but later left because he would not accept the PAD's demand of a royally appointed prime minister. On 9 November 2006, the cremation day, a taped farewell message by Nuamthong was played over loudspeakers, in which he argued against the military coup and stated his reasons for his protest suicide. The commemoration of Nuamthong's suicide is still organized yearly. His bust moulded in plaster in March 2010, mixed with a portion of blood left over from the rites and the red shirts' donated blood, was displayed behind the Rachaprasong stage during the 2010 protests, and was adorned with flower garlands.[31]

In the summer of 2007, amidst increasing conflicts within the coup group and the Surayud government, constant rumours of another military coup, as well as ongoing investigations into Thaksin's alleged corruption, the anti-coup groups began to gain momentum and their protests intensified. People's Television (PTV) appeared on the scene on 24 February 2007.[32] The new TV station, fashioned after Sondhi Limthongkul's ASTV as a vehicle for political activism, was organized by former TRT politicians — Veera Musikapong, Jatuporn Promphan, Jakrapob Penkair and Nattawut Saikua. PTV was not allowed to go on air. Instead, it held regular public protests at Sanam Luang, drawing larger crowds through their networks.

Six days after the constitutional court ordered the dissolution of TRT Party, the government lifted the ban on political party activities, paving the way for the elections scheduled for December 2007.[33] During ongoing protests at Sanam Luang with thousands of attendants, the twenty-two anti-coup groups, including about sixty former TRT members, held a meeting on 6 June 2007 at Thammasat University and formalized their earlier formed alliance[34] under one umbrella,[35] with a seven-member leadership council.[36] The United Front of Democracy against Dictatorship

(UDD) was born, and Sanam Luang became a permanent protest base with 6,000 to 8,000 protesters turning up on an average day, and between 10,000 and more than 20,000 during marches.[37] On 22 July 2007, the rallies culminated in the only protest of this phase with substantial violence. About 20,000 anti-coup protesters rallied at Si Sao Thewet, Prem's residence.[38] Protesters retreated after three failed attempts by the police to disperse them, injuring about 100 police officers and protesters. The protest leaders were arrested and jailed for twelve days. Prime Minister Surayud, after a meeting with Prem, accused the UDD of having demonstrated "their intention of undermining the highest institution on which the country and people rely". Surayud argued that as Privy Councillors were appointed by the King; they are to be seen as a crucial component of the monarchy.[39] It is interesting to note that, particularly for this protest, the protesters were asked by their leaders to wear royal yellow T-shirts to make clear that their protest was limited to Prem and was not directed against the monarchy.

In the coup period, while the military may have been relatively soft to its opponents, its actions of constant intimidation and occasional arrests and harassment built a strong feeling among the protesters of them being victims of a paternalistic system. In the period leading up to the constitution referendum, two very significant cases created a climate of fear among the protesters based on an ill-defined law that was passed by the National Legislative Aseembly — the referendum bill — which saw harsh penalties of up to ten years in jail for violations against the referendum.[40] On 6 July 2007, NGO activist and one of the first anti-coup protest leaders Sombat Boonngamanong was arrested, questioned and detained for twenty-four hours in Chiang Rai while holding a protest speech in a campaign against the new draft charter.[41] Sombat was the founder of the "Thais Say No" group, which campaigned against the military-sponsored new constitution. The members of the group dressed in red-coloured T-shirts; this was the initial spark of the use of the colour red as the identification colour for the UDD protesters.[42] A few weeks later, the police, by order of the military, raided the offices of UDD leader Prateep Ungsongtham Hata's Duang Prateep Foundation in Klong Toey slum and confiscated 4,000 posters.[43] CNS spokesman Colonel Sansern Kaewkamnerd and ISOC spokesman Colonel Thanathip Sawangsaeng reasoned that they conducted the raid because they suspected that weapons may have been hidden in the premises.[44]

But constant claims of royal legitimacy by the coup group and accusations against the anti-coup protesters of being anti-monarchists produced serious long-term effects. Protesters felt increasingly alienated from the state. Thaksin was accused of having agitated against the monarchy.[45] Meanwhile, the anti-coup protesters were labelled with the catchphrase of *khluean tai din* ("underground wave" or usually called in English "undercurrents").[46] Against those unspecified political "undercurrents", Thailand's mantra of "unity" was set. And against the "CEO style politics" of Thaksin, the relentless propagation of the King's sufficiency economy philosophy was launched.[47] When Saturday People against Dictatorship campaigned to remove Prem from the Privy Council, it was investigated for violations against the *lèse-majesté* law.[48] In the meantime, CNS member General Saprang Kalayanamitr commented that as they now began to "shift target to the highest institution", "sometimes it may be necessary to use a machine gun to shoot (kill) a dog".[49] Accusations against Prem were viewed by ultra-royalists as *lèse-majesté* because of the King's prerogative to appoint members of the Privy Council. During the constitution referendum campaign, the propaganda intensified. In the northeast, the TRT Party heartland, billboards were placed with the message "Love the King. Care about the King. Vote in a referendum. Accept the 2007 draft charter".[50] One of the most bewildering comments was by a former judge and charter drafter Wicha Mahakhun who answered a criticism regarding the first draft of the constitution, which gave the judges the power over the selection of members of the senate and independent organizations. Wicha said, "We all know elections are evil, but (why do) many people still want to see history repeated? Even His Majesty the King places trust in the judges. Would you condemn them?". Wicha was referring to the King's speech on 9 April 2006.[51] While the coup makers may have believed that this ultra-royalist strategy may persuade the TRT voters to turn their back to Thaksin, the opposite happened. The first cracks began to appear in the previously almost universal support for the monarchy among the common Thai population. Under Thaksin's rule, the strong conviction of Thaksin's supporters was that Thaksin and the King would together stand for the development of Thailand, and still, most anti-coup protesters were staunch royalists who often wore royal yellow T-shirts to show their allegiance to the royal institution and the King. But gradually over time, a transformation never witnessed before in Thailand began to take shape, for the first time in recent Thai history. Increasingly, large sectors of the common population started to question the monarchical system. Critical information regarding the monarchy was distributed underground; foremost was the Thai translation of a critical biography of King Bhumibol, *The King Never Smiles* by Paul M. Handley.[52]

The referendum on 19 August 2007 approved the new constitution with a much lower margin than the coup makers hoped for and expected,[53] with 56.61 per cent "Yes" votes, and 41.36 per cent "No" votes,[54] leaving Thai society even more divided than before the coup. The following national elections resulted in a clear defeat of the coup makers when politicians of the dissolved TRT Party who contested the elections under the Palang Prachachon Party (People's Power Party, or PPP) won and formed the next coalition government under Prime Minister Samak Sundaravej. The UDD, after the election, ceased the protest and only held occasional political seminars.

PHASE 2: THE TRANSFORMATION INTO RED SHIRTS

The PAD leadership decided on 25 February 2008 to regroup and continue their protests.[55] The PAD held its first public meeting on 28 March 2008 in a packed auditorium inside Thammasat University to renew its agenda to rid Thailand of Thaksin's influence. The UDD, as a reaction, also decided to resume their protests. This second phase highlighted a transformation for the red shirts, from a rather disorganized protest group without ideological fundaments to becoming a movement with a more firm position on supporting a one-man one-vote system against the PAD's proposed changes in the electoral system towards a semi-appointed parliament. Moreover, the goal here is not just to defend the PPP government. Eventually, the red shirts have formed a highly diversified movement with increasingly sophisticated ideologies and strategic approaches, and lasted until the end of 2008. This era witnessed numerous incidents of major violence by all sides. The first was an attack by pro-Thaksin "Udon Lovers" against PAD protesters in Udon Thani on 24 July 2008, injuring many. On 26 August 2008, the PAD supporters occupied Government House, with much covert support from the Democrat Party and parts of the military for their protests, ranging from supplementing both guards and protesters with personnel, to institutional support by independent organizations consisting of Thaksin's opponents, such as the National Anti-Corruption

Commission. For the UDD protesters, this was a continuation of the interference in electoral politics by the same extra-constitutional powers which had orchestrated and supported the 2006 coup. On 29 August, the police tried to disperse the PAD protesters, but the action had to be halted after interference on the ground by a group of senators, then active General Pathumpong Kesornsuk, and opposition leader and later Prime Minister Abhisit Vejjajiva; this interference gave the PAD the necessary time to regroup and chase the police off the streets.[56] A few days later, on 2 September 2008, Newin Chidchob, who then still controlled the budgets of the UDD, came up with a failed plan to surround the PAD and starve them out, instead resulting in an uncoordinated attack against the PAD and the first recorded death in the conflict — of Narongsak Krobtaisong, a fifty-two-year-old UDD protester who was beaten to death by PAD guards in the chaotic battle.[57] The UDD had experienced a major internal crisis after such a failed attack as most leaders were not informed of Newin's plan. They finally changed their strategy to organize large-scale mass events in which tens of thousands of their supporters, now dressed in red, gathered at concert halls and stadiums.[58] The protesters have been known as "red shirts" ever since.

The Government House occupation, the inability of the government and the police to disperse the PAD protesters, and especially the bloodshed of the night of 2 September 2008, all caused the beginning of armed militant factions under the red shirts. For militant red shirts, the situation became a warlike scenario in which, from their perspective, the elected government and the democratic system needed to be protected against extra-constitutional powers and their forces on the street. For the remainder of the year, M79 grenades were regularly launched into the PAD encampments, wounding and killing many of its members. It is generally believed that the outspoken renegade Major General Khattiya "Sae Deang" Sawasdipol may have been the organizer of these attacks. At the time, Sae Daeng trained the "Nakrop Prachao Taksin" (King Taksin warriors), a counterforce of the elitist PAD bodyguard unit of the "Naklop Srivijaya" (Srivichai Warriors). In this context, it has to be pointed out that armed militants under the PAD had already existed as well, since the PAD confiscated eleven automatic rifles from a Special Branch police station during the first night of the Government House occupation, only one of which, a Uzi, was returned when Din Daeng police arrested a member of the "Naklop Srivijaya" in possession of weapons during a sting operation on 25 November 2008. PAD guards killed and injured several people as well, both at Government House and at the occupied airports.

During this period, a day of enormous historical significance occurred; that is, the funeral of Angkhana "Nong Bo" Radappanyawut, one of the two PAD protesters who died during the 7 October 2008 clashes between the PAD and the police. Several protesters lost limbs from tear-gas canisters with explosive charges used by the police in that tragic incident. The funeral, on 13 October 2008, was presided over by the Queen, accompanied by Princess Chulabhorn. Also present were Abhisit and then Army Chief Anupong Paochinda. The Queen reportedly described Angkhana to her father as "a good girl who had helped to protect the country and the monarchy".[59] Such a royal visit to the funeral led to the perception among the UDD protesters that they were up against overwhelming forces that did not accept their electoral vote. More significantly, from their previous tacit support, many, if not most, police officers now began to openly support the red shirts against the military and other powerful sections of Thai society.

The airport occupation of the PAD in late 2008 saw more violence by both the reds and yellows. The violence lasted until the PPP was dissolved by the court and the Abhisit-led government was installed. The rather open military involvement in the formation of the new government coalition, and especially the change of allegiance by Newin Chidchob, convinced the red shirts that another legitimate government was again ousted in another coup. They, and other observers, labelled it a "silent coup".[60]

PHASE 3: BUILDING A SOCIAL MASS MOVEMENT

The next era of the red shirts arrived, with the formation of a social mass movement buttressed by increasingly diversified ideological beliefs. This period had lasted from early 2009 up to the Rachaprasong dispersal on 19 May 2010. Two prolonged protests with several incidents of major violence followed by harsh crackdowns accelerated the red-shirt ideological development, improvements of organizational structures and the founding of several splinter groups with differences in ideology, strategy and tactics. These groups were not part of the UDD, but remained under the larger umbrella of the red shirts. The red shirt's communication networks and especially their mass media — in print, radio, Internet and television

— became highly sophisticated tools of political indoctrination. And for red-shirt protesters, these had replaced state-owned and traditional media as their prime source of information.

The first prolonged protest resulted in the Songkran riots in April 2009, or *Sonkgran Leuad* (Bloody Songkran) as called by the red shirts, which was the first open military crackdown against the red shirts. In March 2009, after several preceding protests against the Abhisit government, the red shirts embarked on a protest with an aim to oust the government by permanently occupying the streets surrounding Government House. In April, the situation began to heat up with the red shirts blocking several important roads and intersections in Bangkok. From 10 to 11 April 2009, there were clashes in Pattaya between the red shirts and a state-organized militia, called the "Blue Shirts" whose members were soldiers, police officers beholden to Newin Chidchob, and a few PAD guards. These led to the collapse of the ASEAN Summit when red shirts stormed the venue of the meeting.[61] On the following day in Bangkok, Prime Minister Abhisit was attacked in the grounds of the Ministry of Interior by enraged red shirts after he had declared a state of emergency. Finally, in the early morning hours of 13 April 2009, soldiers from the 2nd Infantry Division, Queen's Guard, began the dispersal at Samliem Dindaeng where they fired directly at protesters, injuring several (and possibly killing a few as well).[62] Consequently, over the next twenty-four hours, the red-shirt protest was dissolved. Several clashes between red shirts and fighters affiliated with the PAD occurred in the late afternoon, leaving two anti-red fighters and two red-shirt guards dead. The latter's corpses were fished out of the river with bound hands a day after the dispersal.

The violent crackdown was a seminal moment for the red shirts. Realizing that the leaders' loss of control over the protesters contributed to the clashes and the dispersal, their strategists set up UDD schools in which ideology and protest strategies were taught so as to avoid the same mistakes in future protests.[63] The first major split in the red shirts occurred in the aftermath of the 2009 crackdown. Jakrapob Penkair, a first generation UDD leader, former spokesman during the Thaksin administration and former Minister of the Prime Minister's Office, fled during the crackdown into exile, evading imprisonment for a *lèse-majesté* charge filed against him after he delivered a speech at the Foreign Correspondents' Club of Thailand in August 2007 (the charges were finally dropped by prosecutors in 2012). Over the following months, differences between him and the other UDD leaders developed. For example, Jakrapob favoured a more ideologically radical course. Together with Surachai Saedan, Jakrapob founded the group "Daeng Siam" (Red Siam).[64] However, there are overlaps between the UDD and "Daeng Siam", particularly regarding the level of common protesters who often attend rallies of both groups. Daeng Siam, as a group, was dissolved not long after its leader Surachai was arrested for *lèse-majesté* on 22 February 2011. Today, the members of Deang Siam are still active in smaller splinter groups.

Also for the militant factions, the use of the blue shirts by the state, which until today has not been investigated, and the early morning crackdown by the military meant that the red shirts had to build wider forces than their precursors in 2008 to repel the military in case of future dispersals. Some of their organizers told me in interviews that this happened in secrecy as they distrusted the UDD leadership. In the months leading to the next big rally, the red shirts staged many preparation protests. Probably the most spectacular rally was when the red shirts protested at the Khao Yai Thieng forest reserve in front of Privy Councillor Surayud's illegally built holiday home, acquired after a series of murky transactions,[65] on a large prime plot of land at a mountain cliff overlooking the surrounding countryside.[66] Failing to achieve their aim of winning a court case against Surayud and his dismissal from the Privy Council, the red shirts managed to deeply embarrass him by exposing the issues of both the encroachment and the lack of legal consequences as examples of double standards. Surayud was forced to dismantle his beloved retreat and hand the land back to the state.[67]

After several delays, the big rally started off on 12 March 2010 with a religious ceremony at Laksi Monument and lasted until the dispersal on 19 May 2010. This protest can be separated into two periods: the peaceful Phan Fa period until early April, and the Rachaprasong period which saw the occupation of Bangkok's commercial centre that soon disintegrated into several incidents of terrible violence. It ended with six days of urban warfare in which soldiers shot protesters during the daytime, and the red-shirt militants, soldiers and pro-government militants battled each other on several frontlines at night, with a final official body count of 91 or 92 dead, and approximately 2,000 injured. During the Phan Fa period the red shirts camped out in Bangkok's traditional centre for political protest, at Rachadamnern Avenue where the UDD had their main stage at Phan Fa bridge, and in some distance several smaller stages of splinter groups.

The red shirts moved from there around Bangkok in large convoys for different protest activities, the most successful being caravans with tens of thousands of cars and motorcycles roaming Bangkok's neighbourhoods with supporters lining the route and cheering on the red shirts. While the UDD protests were peaceful, militants regularly launched M79 grenades into selected targets, such as military installations and the Bangkok Bank which was rumoured to have supported the PAD and the Democrat Party. The red shirts' main demand was an immediate dissolution of parliament, and new elections. While this could be seen as an offer for compromise, since their earlier demand for the dissolution of the Privy Council under Prem was no longer at the forefront, this change of target contributed to the distrust between more ideologically radical groups among the red shirts and the mainstream UDD. On 17 March 2010, the UDD publicly distanced itself from Daeng Siam, the 24th of June Group, and Sae Daeng.[68] Nonetheless, these groups still kept their presence at the rally sites, and guards commanded by Sae Daeng continued their duties.

Soon after the red shirts increased their pressure and occupied Bangkok's commercial centre near Rachaprasong intersection, the government declared the emergency decree following an invasion of red shirts led by Arisman Pongruangrong into the parliament grounds on 7 April 2010. After a brief clash on 9 April 2010, at the Thaicom satellite relay station between the army and red shirts, brutal violence took place on 10 April when the army attempted to disperse the protesters at the Phan Fa protest camp which then only hosted their secondary stage (the primary stage was at the Rachaprasong intersection). In the afternoon and at sunset, during which several red-shirt protesters were shot dead by the military, militants within the red-shirt movement revealed their identity for the first time, openly engaged in the clash and finally defeated the army. As a result of continued battles, twenty of the red shirts and five of the Thai soldiers were killed. One of the killed soldiers was Colonel Romklao Thuwatham, deputy chief of staff and a rising star of the 2nd Infantry Division, Queen's Guards, who also led the crackdown at Samliem Dindaeng the previous year. On 28 April, the next incident of violence occurred; this was the last time a red-shirt caravan left the Rachaprasong fortification which was stopped at the outskirts of Bangkok at the National Memorial. During this incident, which revealed an enormous incompetence on the part of the military, several red shirts were injured, and one young soldier died in a "friendly fire incident" in front of me and a few other foreign photographers.

The internal differences and conflicts within the red-shirt movement increased, and culminated when the last negotiated compromise, through Abhisit's roadmap for political reconciliation, was rejected by the red shirts. UDD chairman Veera Musikapong, a strong proponent for accepting the compromise and part of the negotiation team with the government, vacated his position and left the camp. Hardliners dominated the stage, with the support of the protesters. Sae Daeng, who by then had taken control over most of the barricades, was openly agitating against the leadership of the UDD, advocating replacing Veera Musikapong, Nattawut Saikua and Jatuporn Prompan with the "hardcore" factions under Arisman Pongruangrong and Suporn "Rambo Isan" Atthawong. A few days later, in the evening of 13 May 2010, Sae Deang was assassinated by a sniper while giving an interview to foreign journalists.[69] The state began the crackdown against the red-shirt protesters. These were six terrible days of brutal urban warfare. My most vivid memory was in the afternoon of 15 May, when I was caught up in a gas station, and a few metres from me, a small group of unarmed red-shirt protesters hiding behind a flimsy tire barricade, were fired at continuously by the military for over 16 minutes with their automatic rifles.[70] One of them, Channarong Ponsrila, died, and two were injured, with more casualties in other locations on that same road. On 19 May, the red shirts were finally dispersed. With the main leaders either incarcerated, or in exile, the movement seemed in complete disarray and defeated.

Symbolic of the ideological development during this era were the terms *"ammat"* — a definition of their enemy — the traditional elite; *"song matratan"* — double standards in the treatment of the red shirts and their opponents, and; probably the most powerful term popularized just before and during the mass protests in 2010, *"phrai"* — a term from Thailand's feudal past meaning "serf". *Phrai* has now been mostly used as a derogative term and adopted by the red shirts as a self description to identify themselves in relation to the *ammat*. Using this term thus expressed a sense of pride and empowerment. It also reflected in the red shirt's analysis of the conflict as a class struggle in which *phrai* tried to free themselves from the oppression by the *amart*. This hit a raw nerve in their opponents, as it invalidated the fundamentals of the official Thai state ideology based on the concept of unity of all Thais under the overall structure of the three pillars: nation, religion and monarchy.

After the 2010 events, in which the red-shirt armed militants fought against the military on the street, this issue became, and still is, highly politicized, yet shrouded by a cloak of both myth and obfuscation. Red-shirt opponents and especially the Democrat Party propagate the view that these armed militants — dubbed as *Chai Chood Dam* or, in its English moniker "Men in Black", were simply Thaksin's and the UDD leaders' hired gunmen to create chaos in order to bring Thaksin back to power, and that, as part of this propaganda, the men in black did not just attack soldiers, but also killed unarmed red-shirt supporters during the 2010 events. Many red-shirt supporters have not just disputed this view, but also denied any connection between the red shirts and these armed militants, or even their existence. Interviewing several of their organizers and also individual armed militants, I can state that they were indeed acting on ideological motivations. There is no indication, based not only on what they have stated, but also what I myself and other sources witnessed in the frontlines of the 2010 conflict, that they have killed red-shirt protesters. They viewed themselves as a protection force for the protesters against the military, and as a militant force in a warlike scenario against their political opponents. While it cannot be excluded that one or the other individual UDD leader may have had links kept secret from other leaders with these armed militants, I have found no indication that there was any official or secret UDD policy to employ these armed militants. The armed militants themselves have insisted that they are outside UDD control, but see themselves as red shirts. Nevertheless, more research into the issue of the armed militants is necessary.

PHASE 4: THE LEADERLESS ERA

The current fourth phase can be defined as the leaderless phase, characterized by accelerated ideological radicalization and empowerment of the grassroots levels, as well as a decreased role of the leadership. After the initial shock in the wake of crackdown brutality, sadness and fear began to subside and the red shirts regrouped quickly by first gathering in temples to circumvent the emergency decree. At the beginning, there were substantial fears that militant elements within the red shirts would initiate a guerrilla campaign. A few bombs went off in Bangkok, most likely planted by militants. But soon this subsided, and it became evident that the bombs were merely a post-crackdown phenomenon.[71]

Seriously lacking their main leadership, a few remaining leaders propagated the motto of *tuk khon pen phunam tua eng* or "everybody is his/her own leader", a philosophy that was first introduced by Sombat Boonngamanong. Suddenly, a myriad of events took place, initially just in the provinces adjacent to Bangkok, or the areas outside of the operation of the emergency decree. Later, several events were organized all over Thailand's heartland provinces. There were fund-raising concerts, seminars, rallying stages, and flash mobs — all of them were organized at the grassroots level, with leading figures invited to participate. The main leaders were released on 22 February 2011 from their nine-month imprisonment, and most exiled leaders began to return home. This trend has continued. Nowadays, it is almost impossible to keep up with the developments of the different red-shirt groups. While the UDD is still the majority red-shirt group, many of the so-called "free" red-shirt groups grew in ideological influence, such as the groups under the dissolved Daeng Siam and the 24th of June Group whose leader Somyos Prueksakasemsuk, the editor of *Red Power* magazine, is awaiting trial in prison for *lèse-majesté*. Many grassroots-level organizations, often centred around increasingly independent and evolving community radio stations and/or part of the new phenomenon of the "Red-shirt Village Movement" (semi-independent of the UDD) now with more than 10,000 affiliated villages, have successfully developed lateral communication lines nationwide, and no longer rely solely on hierarchical communication from the top.[72] Another important ongoing development is an increased questioning of the monarchy by ordinary people, in villages of the north and northeast regions and urban labour class districts in the red heartlands. It is impossible to quantify these developments, but it can be stated that sizeable and significant sectors of Thai society are now rejecting the traditional system.

These developments were unveiled on 19 September 2010, in the first of a series of unauthorized and leaderless though peaceful red-shirt mass protests in Bangkok in which hundreds of anti-monarchy graffiti and flyers suddenly appeared. Sombat Boonngamanong posted on his Facebook account that he would be tying red ribbons at Rachaprasong on 19 September again in his ongoing flash mob protest style, and invited red shirts to take part. Between 10,000 and 20,000 red shirts followed the call. When the protesters occupied the intersection, police lent a truck with loudspeakers to Sombat (any sophisticated loudspeaker system was at the time forbidden to be used by political groups under the emergency decree). Sombat tried to convince the red shirts to move their protest to the nearby Wat Pratum, but was ignored by the mass of protesters. He finally left after being unable to control the angry crowd. The majority of remaining protesters began chanting *"ku ma eng"* (I came by myself), and suddenly a chant continued and was taken up by the crowd — *"ai hia sang ka"* ("the bastard ordered the killings"). Many interpreted this as a thinly veiled accusation against the monarch. On the Internet, and even on T-shirts, coded insults against members of the royal family became very common. This initiated a surge of arrests and charges filed against many red shirts that became much bolder in expressing their political views. On 1 December 2010, when the new acting red-shirt leadership council was formed, their first and very difficult task was to persuade the grassroots leaders to try to convince the common red shirts to abstain from voicing critical views vis-à-vis the monarchy and to not give the state another reason to further crackdown on the red shirts. Today, this is an ongoing effort.[73] This has led to several conflicts between the UDD and Daeng Siam affiliated groups which have shown the trend of stalwartly agitating against the restrictive *lèse-majesté* law and using very strong language on their stage.[74] At the time, Daeng Siam erected their stage right next to the UDD protests. Meanwhile, the UDD did not allow red-shirt protesters who wore the Daeng Siam's favoured T-shirts with the print of Article 112 crossed out into their protest area.

Undoubtedly, the red shirts supported the Pheu Thai Party which won the July 2011 elections. Thaksin's sister, Yingluck, is now Thailand's first female prime minister. The UDD is presently not holding any mass protests, other than commemorative events for landmark incidents. Both UDD and the many splinter groups constantly hold small rallies, seminars and concerts. Many new community radio stations are founded. By mid-2012, frictions between the red-shirt movement and the government developed over Thaksin's and Pheu Thai politicians' sponsor of the reconciliation bill which was also supported by the military. Not just the Democrat Party and the PAD opposed the reconciliation bill, but also some red shirts who however could not openly protest against the government they supported. While the Democrat Party and the PAD viewed the proposed reconciliation bill as an attempt to whitewash Thaksin, the red shirts opposed the included amnesties for the military over the 2010 deadly crackdowns against the people. Another source of conflict within the red-shirt movement is a split between groups that regard the UDD and the Pheu Thai Party as reformists while they see their ideology as revolutionary. While initially mostly Daeng Siam and the 24th of June Group were the more ideologically radical groups, after the 2010 crackdown, many independent community radio stations have adopted similar positions. The reconciliation bill and the government's proposed constitution changes continue to fuel the conflict. Both the Democrat Party and the PAD are trying to ignite street mobs in opposition to the government. Despite their fallout in 2011, when the PAD protested for several months against the Democrat Party-led government, they now seem to some degree to tacitly collaborate. This regrouping of the forces that led to the removal of their governments twice is naturally strongly opposed by the red shirts and becomes an issue that unifies all red-shirt factions, although it has to be noted that conflicts among them remain over counter-strategies. A continuation of the conflict is to be expected.

CONCLUSION

It is quite difficult to describe exactly the red shirts' ideology, as it is still in a period of transformation and development. Apart from the UDD, the red-shirt movement contains a large variety of independent and splinter groups. None has come under absolute control of any leader or leadership circle, with organically developing ideologies, strategies and tactics. Nevertheless, one could describe their overall views on the future Thai state which could be characterized as a social liberal, pro-capitalist entity, with clear positions on respecting the outcome of elections, and a clearly defined role of the Thai military to be subservient to civilian control. On top of this, the red shirts have aspired to be united in their fight against what they define as *ammat*. There is of course a minority that espouses more radical socialist ideas. But even most of the former communists, especially in the UDD, do not propose socialism/communism anymore because ordinary Thais would not accept such radical views. Certainly, a number of red shirts still admire the more authoritarian CEO approach of Thaksin. Yet, the movement as a whole has outgrown their singular support of Thaksin who continues to play a major role as a symbol of the fight, and possibly as a financier playing a part in the decision-making process. The movement's demands are now considerably structural rather than merely for Thaksin's return to power. However, a form of pluralism has already been established among different red-shirt groups. And there exist difficulties to develop the idea of pluralism further under the current atmosphere of high political polarization. The different political discourses still take place within each side and do not cross over in any significant attempt of dialogue between the opposing sides.

A greater difficulty is the fact that while the UDD itself is upholding a constitutional monarchy, the views of many of the ordinary protesters have gone more radical and some splinter groups are almost openly agitating against the monarchy. Due to restrictions of Article 112, anti-monarchy rhetoric goes much further in the underground and in closed circles.[75] On stages, the Japanese or European examples are often cited, in which the monarchies are mostly restricted to playing ceremonial and symbolic roles. Already, this view reaches the limits of what the legal space permits, and is viewed by ultra-conservatives as an unbearable insult, almost sacrilege as many see the King as a semi-divine being, close to enlightenment.[76] These demands of the red shirts stand in stark contrast to the ultra-royalist view of Thailand as an idealized system ruled by the almost divine Dhammaracha King, protected by the military and supported by the civil service, which work on behalf of the King for the benefits of his loyal subjects.[77] The constant appeals for "unity" in Thai society are rooted in the ideal of such an ideologically homogeneous state. Publicly stated opinions of high-ranking members within this system are very revealing of the view on the ideal Thai society, as reflected for example in a speech by Privy Councillor Ampol Senanarong which was given at the opening of a museum at Kasetsart University. Ampol urged Thais to emulate ants in their work together to build unity.[78] On the contrary, the red shirts demand to be citizens of a modern nation, with popular elections as the ultimate decision-making process of the formation of the government.

The conflict has now turned from a political conflict into an identity conflict, touching the core of "Thainess", or what it means to be Thai. However, it is almost impossible to address these issues in the public sphere through vigorous discussion and debate, thus forcing the shift of topics of primary importance to go further underground. Any criticism of the state dogma can still not be voiced in the open in Thailand, as this can be seen as a violation of the *lèse-majesté* law.[79] In early 2012, a group known in the name "Khana Nitirat" or in English "Enlightened Jurists", comprising of several law lecturers, held symposiums in which they proposed amendments to the *lèse-majesté* law and also proposed a new constitution with redefined roles of the head of state, the judiciary and the military. While many more radical red-shirt intellectuals criticized the group for not advocating abolishment of the *lèse-majesté* law, Nitirat's proposals could be seen as a compromise, a way out of the stalemate. Nevertheless, their opponents in the yellow-shirt camp accused Nitirat of trying to overthrow the monarchy, and its leader, Worachet Pakeerat, was beaten up in the parking lot of Thammasat University.

Opponents of the red shirts accused Thaksin and the red-shirt leadership and intellectuals of having fed red-shirt protesters with what they deemed as false information about the monarchy and saw this as the reason behind the rise of anti-monarchy attitude among the red-shirt protesters. However, it must be noted that the groups that transformed themselves into the red shirts were initially strongly pro-monarchy, as seen, for example, when the "Caravan of the Poor" protested against a publication of the left leanings *Fah Diew Kan* and demanded *lèse-majesté* charges to be filed against its editor.[80] The gradual steps of the development into anti-monarchy position and the acceptance of critical information concerning the monarchy can be clearly rationalized through key events at the street level. The most important incidents which concretized such anti-monarchy perception were the 2006 coup, the funeral of Angkhana "Nong Bo" Radappanyawut, and the 2010 crackdown at Rachaprasong. Given the sensitive nature of the subject, quantitative data is not available. But I have noticed the changes of perception through discussions with common red-shirt protesters over the years, and especially when they analysed the aforementioned key events. From the perspective of the red shirts, the coup is not yet over. The power grab in 2006 is still on their minds. The recent election triumph of the Pheu Thai Party is only one step in a continuing and yet undecided conflict over the future of Thailand.

Opponents of the red shirts often analyse the conflict along the lines of the competing elite with the role of ordinary red-shirt protesters playing a supporting part in the patronage networks with their loyalty ultimately tied to Thaksin. However, this is an oversimplification of reducing the complex nature of the red-shirt social mass movement, therefore denying the developments that have taken place over the past years in Thai society through this conflict, especially now that the conflict is primarily driven by an increasingly empowered grassroots population. The emergence of the red shirts is a consequence of decades of development in Thai society, in which Thaksin was a catalyst who brought long-standing divisions of Thai society into the political sphere.[81] The red shirts may be portrayed by their opponents as terrorists, and in the media often as the poor fighting against the rich. In reality, their leaders are people with different political and economic backgrounds; many of whom have served the state as politicians, police officers and academics. Some are just ordinary protesters from all walks of life, be they farmers, teachers, office workers, and business people. Many of them have participated in the movement nationwide at different levels of groups and grassroots organizations. The total numbers of red-shirt sympathizers and supporters may range up to two-digit millions, a major percentage of the Thai population.

As long as the Thai state continues to refuse to engage with the red shirts as a partner in the political development, a logical consequence could be that the red shirts may one day evolve into a revolutionary phase of armed struggle, a danger which most of the moderate leaders are aware of and try to avoid. Two crackdowns with increasingly violent resistance by the red shirts and the nature of the subsequent rapid ideological, structural and organizational developments have already proven that the red shirts are not going to disappear anytime soon.

POSTSCRIPT

Since the article was written in 2012, the red-yellow conflict has developed further. While after the elections there was a period of relative calm, in later 2013 the yellow alliance formed again, this time under the main leadership of politicians of the Democrat Party, foremost Suthep Thaugsuban, former deputy prime minister in the Abhisit government, and the leaders of the now dissolved PAD playing a side role. Mass street protests against the Yingluck government took place, resulting in several incidents of violence, during which more than twenty people of all sides were killed. Another military or judicial coup may force the red-shirt movement to return to the streets. The outcome of this present round of conflict is unpredictable and fears of a possible civil war are regularly voiced.

Notes

1. See Michael H. Nelson, "People Sector Politics (Kanmueang Phak Prachachon) in Thailand: Problems of Democracy in Ousting Prime Minister Thaksin Shinawatra", Working Papers Series, No. 87, May 2007.
2. I have driven out to Navanakorn where the Caravan of the Poor's final campsite was, and spent several hours talking with the villagers while accompanying them on their march to Bangkok.

3. "Protests Shuts Newspaper", *Bangkok Post*, 31 March 2006.
4. "Tempers Flare at Sondhi's Manager Office", *The Nation*, 1 April 2006.
5. "Military Must Back King", *The Nation*, 15 July 2006.
6. "Sonthi Stuns by Shifting PM's Allies", *The Nation*, 20 July 2006.
7. Control of battalion and regimental commanders is essential in the success of a military coup, as they directly command the troops. General Sonthi, through this control, ensured the loyalty of these mostly Bangkok-based key regiments and battalions.
8. Panya Thiewsangwan, "Prem: Bad Leaders are Doomed to Failure", *The Nation*, 1 September 2006.
9. "Thaksin must Quit to Avoid Bloodshed, says Prawase", *Bangkok Post*, 29 August 2006.
10. "Thailand at Risk of Becoming Failed State", *Bangkok Post*, 31 August 2006.
11. "Supporters, Protesters of Thaksin Clash at Central World", *The Nation*, 21 August 2006.
12. "Tak Forestry Chief Sent to Inactive Post", *Bangkok Post*, 2 September 2006.
13. "Divided Kingdom, Political Battle to Resume", *The Nation*, 19 September 2006.
14. "Coup as it Unfolds", *The Nation*, 20 September 2006.
15. "Thailand's King Gives Blessing to Coup", CNN, 20 September 2006.
16. "Coup Leaders Get 'Official' Royal Endorsement", *Bangkok Post*, 22 September 2006.
17. "Text: Thai Coup-Leaders' Statements", BBC, 19 September 2006.
18. "Clarification on the English Translation of the Title of the Council for Democratic Reform", Ministry of Foreign Affairs, No. 428/2549, 26 September 2006.
19. "Unofficial Translation, Constitution of the Kingdom of Thailand (Interim Edition) of B.E. 2549", *The Nation*, 2 October 2006.
20. "Supachai to Discuss Terms' for PM's Post", *The Nation*, 26 September 2006.
21. "Unofficial Translation of Thaksin's Letter — Thaksin: I'll quit", *The Nation*, 3 October 2006.
22. "Members Exodus at Thai Rak Thai Party", TNA, 3 October 2006.
23. "Popular Political Website Shut Down after Holding Anti-coup Protest", Southeast Asian Press Alliance, 3 October 2006.
24. "19sep.org Shut Down", *The Nation*, 22 September 2006.
25. "Third Army Chief Orders Phitsanulok Police to Block Protesters from Reaching Bangkok", *The Nation*, 8 December 2006.
26. See Giles Ungpakorn, *A Coup For The Rich* (Bangkok: Workers Publishing Company, 2007).
27. "Anti-coup protesters test waters of dissent", *Bangkok Post*, 2 November 2006.

28. "Mass Rally Planned at Sanam Luang on Judgement Day", *The Nation*, 26 May 2007.
29. "Thai Cabby Hangs Himself in Coup Protest", Reuters, 1 November 2006.
30. "Protesting Driver Rams Taxi into Army Tank", *The Nation*, 1 October 2006.
31. The original bust was taken by the military the day after the 19 May 2010 dispersal of the Rachaprasong protest. The last time the author saw it was on the back of a military truck at Rachaprasong on 20 May 2010. The bust of Nuamthong Praiwan was used at a later death anniversary at the 14th October Memorial in which red shirts handed over donations to Nuamthong's family. But the author believed it was a replacement and not the original.
32. "PTV to Go on Air Wednesday", *The Nation*, 24 February 2007.
33. "The Cabinet Gives Green Light for Political Parties to Resume Activities", *Thai National News Bureau Public Relations Department*, 6 June 2007.
34. Pravit Rojanaphruk, "Groups Rally against CNS", *The Nation*, 20 May 2007.
35. "Group Aims to Topple Junta", *The Nation*, 7 June 2007.
36. Veteran politician and former member of TRT executive committee Veera Musikapong, former Supreme Court Judge Manit Jitjanklab, Viphutalaeng Pattanaphumthai of the "Saturday People Against Dictatorship", student activist of the October generation and former member of the Communist Party of Thailand (CPT) Dr Weng Tojirakan, former senator and Magsaysay Award recipient Prateep Ungsongtham Hata, Taxi Drivers Protection Association President Shinawat Habunphad, and community radio station DJ Chupon Teetuan.
37. There was, and still is, much confusion over the English language name of the group. While some called the group "Democratic Alliance against Dictatorship" (DAAD), others called it United Front of Democracy against Dictatorship (UDD). In Thai, the name of this alliance was "Nor Por Ko", short for "naewruam prachathipattai khaplai phadetkan" (Democratic United Front/United Front of Democracy to Oust Dictatorship), which was changed on 23 August 2007 after the constitution referendum into "No Po Cho", short for "naewruam prachathipattai totan phadetkan haeng chat" (National United Front of Democracy against Dictatorship).
38. Nick Nostitz, "Revisiting the Prem Compound Clashes", *New Mandala*, 12 August 2008.
39. "Surayud: UDD Aims to Damage Monarchy", *Bangkok Post*, 25 July 2007.
40. Somroutai Sapsomboon and Supalak Ganjanakhundee, "Referendum Law or Penalty Law?", *The Nation*, 6 July 2007.
41. Theerawat Khamthita and Kultida Samabuddhi, "Activist's Arrest Fuels Protests", *Bangkok Post*, 8 July 2007.
42. Tunya Sukpanich, "Raising a Red Flag", *Bangkok Post*, 12 August 2007.

43. Pravit Rojanaphruk and Jumpol Nopthip, "No-vote Raid Illegal, Says Election Official", *The Nation*, 29 July 2007.

44. "The Search for WMD", *Bangkok Pundit*, 30 July 2007.

45. General Sonthi, for example, in an interview with *Time* magazine stated, "There are many cases in which the previous government was impolite to the royal family and to the King himself. The Thai people cannot and will not tolerate anybody who shows even slight disrespect to the King or his family." In Hannah Beach, "The Military Will Withdraw from Politics", *Time*, 1 March 2007. Thus, several *lèse-majesté* cases were filed against Thaksin. In "Police Probe Six Cases of Lèse-majesté against Ousted Premier", *The Nation*, 20 March 2007.

46. "Secret Cells Discovered in Thailand's Pro-Thaksin North", AFP, 6 November 2006.

47. "Surayud Stands Firm on Reform, Charter — Cites South, Justice as his Main Priorities", *The Nation*, 1 January 2007.

48. "RTP Chief Investigates Website Alleged to have Committed Lèse-majesté", Thai National News Bureau Public Relations Department, 2 April 2007.

49. "Boonrod Cha Kloom PTV Khaichat Khoochai Por Ror Kor Chukchuen" ["Boonrod Criticizes PTV Group, Threatens to Arrest it under Emergency Decree"], *Thai Rath*, 8 April 2007.

50. See *Bangkok Post*, 12 July 2007.

51. Subhatra Bhumiprabhas, "Charter Drafter Pans 'Evil' Elections", *The Nation*, 27 April 2007.

52. See Paul Handley, *The King Never Smiles: A Biography of Thailand's Bhumibol Adulyadej* (New Haven: Yale University Press, 2006).

53. General Sonthi stated during an interview with Channel 9, "I previously expected a majority vote of 60 to 65 per cent but, in a democracy, a majority of one vote indicates a passage of the charter." In "Sonthi Satisfied with Outcome", *The Nation*, 21 August 2007.

54. "National Referendum: Official Results", *The Nation*, 20 August 2007.

55. "Activists Reverse, Oppose Return of Thaksin", *Bangkok Post*, 25 February 2008.

56. Nick Nostitz, *Red vs. Yellow, Volume 1: Thailand's Crisis of Identity* (Bangkok: White Lotus, 2009), p. 25.

57. Ibid., p. 29.

58. "Over 10,000 Government Supporters Gather at Muang Thong Thani", *The Nation*, 11 October 2008.

59. "Queen Attends Slain Protester's Cremation", *The Nation*, 14 October 2008.

60. Pravit Rojanaphruk, "Questions Loom over New Prime Minister's Legitimacy", *The Nation*, 17 December 2008.

61. Nick Nostitz, *Red vs. Yellow, Volume 2: Thailand's Political Awakening* (Bangkok: White Lotus, 2011), p. 15.

62. Ibid., p. 21.

63. Marwaan Macan-Markar, "Anti-Government Movement Opens Rural Minds through Schools", *IPS*, 10 February 2010.

64. During the years of the communist insurgency, Surachai, a high-ranking CPT Cadet was sentenced to death in 1981, but released from prison in 1996. It is noteworthy that the name "Red Siam" was inspired by the title of Giles Ungpakorn's "Red Siam Manifesto", which he wrote while on the plane on his way to exile in the United Kingdom. However, Surachai emphasized that his group did not support the manifesto, as it was too radical for Thailand's present situation.

65. "Khao Yai Land was Sold to Cash Buyer", *Bangkok Post*, 10 January 2010.

66. Nick Nostitz, "Red Shirts at Surayud's Holiday Paradise", *New Mandala*, 13 January 2010.

67. Publicly, Surayud always emphasized his readiness to comply with the law and would be "pleased to return" the land if ordered so. But sources in the military explained to the author that General Surayud was furious as he deeply loved his house in Khao Yai Thieng, and that in times of stress he meditated and relaxed at a veranda looking over the cliff where nobody was allowed to disturb him.

68. "Red Leaders Vow Class War will be Peaceful", *The Nation*, 18 March 2010.

69. Thomas Fuller, "In Bangkok, Gunfire Outside a Reporter's Window", *New York Times*, 15 May 2010.

70. Nick Nostitz, "Nick Nostitz in the Killing Zone", *New Mandala*, 16 May 2010.

71. Nick Nostitz, "The Red shirts in Ayutthaya", *New Mandala*, 21 October 2010. Also see Nick Nostitz, "A Small Stage, a Ping Pong Bomb and a Burning Spirit House", *New Mandala*, 1 December 2010.

72. Tida Tawornset, the acting chairwoman of the UDD, explained to the author that while she and many other red-shirt leaders support the Red Shirt Village movement, and attend the opening ceremonies, the movement is not controlled by the UDD. Also, one of the movement's founders and chairman retired Police Sub-Lieutenant Kamolsilp Singhasuriya insisted on the movement's independence when the author interviewed him. Clearly, there are factional problems. For example, the leader of the "Udon Lovers" Kwanchai Praipana has engaged in conflicts with the "Red shirt Village Movement".

73. This was based on interviews with leaders at both national and grassroots levels.

74. "Red Shirt Seized by UDD Guards for Handing out Leaflets during Rally", *Prachatai*, 14 March 2011.

75. "Achieving the Goal of Establishing a Genuine Democracy that has the King as our Head of State, with Political Power Bonging Exclusively to the People.

We Reject any Attempt, Past or Future, at Using the Monarchy to Silence Dissent or Advance a Particular Agenda", *UDD, Red in the Land*, 16 February 2010. See also "The Obligations and Directions for UDD Red in the Land at this Moment have not Changed: To Fight with Peaceful Methods without Weapons for Democracy under the King as Head of State, and with Sovereignty Belonging to the People", UDD's Statement, 1 December 2010.

76. Thanong Khanthong, "Lord of Suvaranabhumi", *The Nation*, 5 December 2009.

77. Sumet Tantivejakul, "Buddhist Virtues in Socio-Economic Development in the Footsteps of His Majesty the King", speech delivered at the 8th Conference of the United Nations Day of Visak, 14 May 2011. The author's own copy.

78. "Privy Councilor Advises Nation to Emulate Ants", *Thai National News Bureau Public Relations Department*, 4 June 2007.

79. Marwaan Macan-Markar, "Lèse-majesté Cases Rise, But Public in the Dark", *IPS*, 14 May 2010.

80. "Magazine Banned for Articles on Monarchy", *Bangkok Post*, 31 March 2006.

81. Pasuk Phongpaichit, "Thai Politics beyond the 2006 Coup", *Bangkok Post*, 31 July 2006.

References

Beach, Hannah. "The Military Will Withdraw from Politics". *Time*, 1 March 2007.

"Clarification on the English Translation of the Title of the Council for Democratic Reform". Ministry of Foreign Affairs, No. 428/2549, 26 September 2006.

Fuller, Thomas. "In Bangkok, Gunfire Outside a Reporter's Window". *New York Times*, 15 May 2010.

Giles Ungpakorn. *A Coup For The Rich*. Bangkok: Workers Publishing Company, 2007.

Handley, Paul. *The King Never Smiles: A Biography of Thailand's Bhumibol Adulyade*. New Haven: Yale University Press, 2006.

Macan-Markar, Marwaan. "Anti-Government Movement Opens Rural Minds through Schools". *IPS*, 10 February 2010.

———. "Lèse-majesté Cases Rise, But Public in the Dark". *IPS*, 14 May 2010.

Nelson, Michael H. "People Sector Politics (Kanmueang Phak Prachachon) in Thailand: Problems of Democracy in Ousting Prime Minister Thaksin Shinawatra". Working Papers Series, No. 87, May 2007.

Nostitz, Nick. "Revisiting the Prem Compound Clashes". *New Mandala*, 12 August 2008.

———. *Red vs. Yellow, Volume 1: Thailand's Crisis of Identity*. Bangkok: White Lotus, 2009.

————. "Red Shirts at Surayud's Holiday Paradise". *New Mandala*, 13 January 2010.

————. "Nick Nostitz in the Killing Zone". *New Mandala*, 16 May 2010.

————. "The Red shirts in Ayutthaya". *New Mandala*, 21 October 2010.

————. "A Small Stage, a Ping Pong Bomb and a Burning Spirit House". *New Mandala*, 1 December 2010.

————. *Red vs. Yellow, Volume 2: Thailand's Political Awakening*. Bangkok, White Lotus, 2011.

Panya Thiewsangwan. "Prem: Bad Leaders are Doomed to Failure". *The Nation*, 1 September 2006.

Pasuk Phongpaichit. "Thai Politics beyond the 2006 Coup". *Bangkok Post*, 31 July 2006.

Pravit Rojanaphruk. "Groups Rally against CNS". *The Nation*, 20 May 2007.

———— and Jumpol Nopthip. "No-vote Raid Illegal, Says Election Official". *The Nation*, 29 July 2007.

————. "Questions Loom over New Prime Minister's Legitimacy". *The Nation*, 17 December 2008.

Somroutai Sapsomboon and Supalak Ganjanakhundee. "Referendum Law or Penalty Law?". *The Nation*, 6 July 2007.

Subhatra Bhumiprabhas. "Charter Drafter Pans 'Evil' Elections". *The Nation*, 27 April 2007.

Sumet Tantivejakul. "Buddhist Virtues in Socio-Economic Development in the Footsteps of His Majesty the King". Speech delivered at the 8th Conference of the United Nations Day of Visak, 14 May 2011.

Thanong Khanthong. "Lord of Suvaranabhumi". *The Nation*, 5 December 2009.

Theerawat Khamthita and Kultida Samabuddhi. "Activist's Arrest Fuels Protests". *Bangkok Post*, 8 July 2007.

Tunya Sukpanich. "Raising a Red Flag". *Bangkok Post*, 12 August 2007.

8

IS PEASANT POLITICS IN THAILAND CIVIL?

Andrew Walker

This chapter asks a simple question: Is peasant politics in Thailand civil? The answer is straightforward: No. Peasant politics in Thailand is not civil if it is judged by many of the established standards which define contemporary civil society, especially its institutionalization and relative autonomy from the state. Rather, I prefer to describe Thailand's modern peasantry as being involved in an active "political society" in which the primary desire is to draw state power into local circuits of exchange by means of diverse, informal and pragmatic relationships. The coup of September 2006 attempted to negate the influence of this non-civil rural politics. It was a failed attempt because it was impossible to reverse powerful economic, social and political developments that have been unfolding over the past fifty years. In order to understand Thailand's tumultuous politics over the past five years, it is necessary to understand the new politics of Thailand's new peasantry.

A BRIEF SKETCH OF RURAL CIVIL SOCIETY AND DEMOCRACY IN THAILAND

Observers of modern political systems often emphasize the role of civil society in supporting democratic consolidation. Civil society is regarded as a "realm of organized social life" that is located between the private sphere and the state.[1] Civil society's organized associations draw citizens out of their individual preoccupations and focus their attention on public undertakings, including policy advocacy, welfare improvement, education and environmental protection. This network of associations limits the power of the state, subjecting it to scrutiny, holding it accountable and sometimes providing an organizational framework for opposition to the illegitimate exercise of power. As citizens become involved in civil society organizations, they learn many of the skills that are essential for the smooth functioning of democracy: the ability to engage in debate, to respect the views of others and to develop organizational rules. Associations can also play a practical role in delivering services, disseminating information about rights and responsibilities, exposing corruption and assisting with the conduct or elections. Civil society citizens learn to consider their own views alongside the views of others, gradually "aggregating" their interests and feeding them into the political system in a coherent manner, thus contributing to the "stability, predictability, and governability of a democratic regime".[2]

Early observers of political behaviour in rural Thailand commented on the lack of civil society infrastructure that could provide a basis for political development. There was, of course, a rich associational life surrounding temples and irrigation systems, but these were portrayed as being unconcerned with matters of national politics. By and large, the peasantry was regarded as being politically disengaged and preoccupied with highly localized issues of livelihood security. Engagement in matters of the state existed only at the level of rural leaders: village headmen, businessmen, local officials and sometimes monks. To the extent that the peasantry was connected to the political process, it was not through their own direct involvement in independent associations, but via a hierarchy of patron-client ties that extended vertically from the village to the national capital. By providing protection and other benefits to their clients, competing patrons within the elite could readily mobilize political support, and votes, whenever it was required. This was not a promising picture for the development of a modern citizenry, but the imagery of benign patron-client relationships and an apolitical peasantry was a reassuring one in the regionally troubled times of the 1960s.

This portrayal of Thai peasant politics had to be rethought in the early 1970s, as farmers' groups became actively involved in the national contention that erupted from 1973 to 1976. The Peasants Federation of Thailand emerged as an important player on the national scene, performing many of the typical functions attributed to modern civil society: mobilizing disparate interests into a coherent group; lobbying for changes to government policy; and educating farmers about the rights they were granted under new legislation. As a result of peasant agitation, agrarian issues were central in the 1975 election campaign. This was a period in which civil society in Thailand flourished, with organizations formed among students and workers as well as peasants, and a proliferation of alternative literature. During this era, Thailand's outbreak of civil society took on a radical hue, generating fears and fantasies about class struggle and even revolution.

Of course, this phase of civil society mobilization was short-lived. Thailand's institutions in the 1970s were not yet ready for democratic consolidation, and the Peasants Federation of Thailand was brutally repressed, with many of its leaders assassinated. The state stepped in to stamp out opposition and to secure rural hearts and minds, employing both heavy-handed ideological repression and wide-ranging agricultural development programmes. The radicalism of the 1970s was defeated, but new spaces for civil society were created in the NGO-friendly space of rural development. The state's development efforts both necessitated and facilitated the establishment of local, provincial and national groups that could play a role in implementing its ambitious schemes of rural improvement. This new organizational infrastructure contributed to a "new round of political mobilization"[3] as farmer assertiveness emerged about low crop prices, high fertilizer costs, the failure of government-promoted agricultural schemes, indebtedness, the favourable treatment of agribusinesses, and, most spectacularly of all, army-led plans to relocate millions of farmers out of forest areas. According to Chris Baker's historical overview, this rural activism gradually divided into two streams.[4] Commercially oriented and secure farmers pursued market-based concerns about pricing, subsidies and credit. They negotiated with state agencies and political parties to provide financial relief to farmers who were hurt by climatic fluctuations, market instability and government mismanagement. A less collaborative approach was adopted by marginal farmers — many of whom lacked tenure security — who faced displacement as a result of dam building, forest conservation schemes and resource concessions provided to investors. They were much more cautious in their dealings with state agencies and politicians. Groups representing these poorer farmers eventually coalesced into the famous Assembly of the Poor which staged a high-profile ninety-nine-day rally in Bangkok in 1997 and succeeded in extracting important concessions from the government.[5] Supporters of this new phase of civil society mobilization argued that it had a democratizing force that was absent in the money politics and rampant patronage of the electoral system:

> The masses, especially in the countryside, have no chance to engage in other democratic activities. However, when they join grassroots organizations, they are able to learn how the democratic system works, and how to act democratically.[6]

DOUBTS ABOUT CIVIL SOCIETY

Over the past decade doubts have emerged over the contribution civil society can make to the empowerment and democratic engagement of rural people in Thailand. These doubts came to a head with the role played by civil society organizations in laying some of the ideological groundwork for the anti-Thaksin coup of September 2006, in their support for the coup after it occurred, and in their active role in bringing about the downfall of the pro-Thaksin government elected in late 2007.[7] The People's Alliance for Democracy (PAD) was a dramatic crystallization of the emerging doubts about the democratizing force of civil society.

These doubts cluster around two main issues: civil society's antipathy to the state and civil society's antipathy to the market. The oppositional stance taken by many civil society organizations to the state is understandable given the memories of violent repression in the 1970s and the heavy-handed implementation of some rural development schemes. However it is also often informed by a localized ideological standpoint that situates appropriate forms of development and empowerment in community-based organizations rather than in an engagement with the modern state. As in "new social movements" in other parts of the world, many Thai civil society organizations have preferred to pursue "direct democracy" rather than "representative democracy," seeking to limit the power of the state by creating semi-autonomous domains of local organization.[8] This localism informs a position that explicitly turns away from the formal political process, regarding it as a corrupted domain of vote-buying power brokers. Elections are seen as mechanisms for mobilizing voters merely to serve the interest of provincial and national elites. This negative view of elections brings some civil society advocates uncomfortably close to long-standing elite dismissal of the peasant voters as legitimate members of a democratic citizenry.

Secondly, many rural civil society organizations have adopted an anti-market and anti-capitalist standpoint. While some branches of rural civil society have pursued mainstream commercial matters — crop price support in particular — many of the most vocal organizations have been diverted by a nostalgic desire for a more subsistence-oriented rural economy. No doubt there has been vigorous debate within civil society organizations on appropriate development strategy, but the most influential campaigns have emphasized local capabilities, local knowledge and locally oriented production systems. As Katherine Bowie pointed out in the early 1990s, there is often an uncanny resemblance between leftist and royalist prescriptions for rural society, with both drawn to images of an authentically Thai village in which local production systems and local culture are mutually reinforcing.[9] There is no better illustration of civil society's subsistence cul-de-sac than its high-profile campaign for community forest legislation, a "reform" that would deliver no substantial livelihood benefit to the vast majority of rural people living in forested areas who are striving to improve their livelihoods by combining commercial agriculture with off-farm labour.[10] Substantial parts of civil society have also been distracted by the royalist sufficiency economy vision.

A MODERN, MIDDLE-INCOME PEASANTRY

Civil society's antipathy to both the state and the market is a reflection of its struggle to adequately address the transformations — and dramatic socioeconomic improvements — that have taken place in rural Thailand since the foundational phase of mobilization in the 1970s. The national-level conflict that has convulsed Thailand over the past decade owes much to the emergence of a new peasantry in rural Thailand. This is not the old-style Southeast Asian peasantry of rebellion, revolution or resistance. Contemporary rural politics is driven by a middle-income peasantry with a thoroughly modern political logic. Their strategy is to engage with sources of power, not to oppose them.

In the 1960s more than 90 per cent of rural people in Thailand were living in poverty. This was a predominantly subsistence-oriented peasantry, not unlike that described by James Scott in his "Moral Economy of the Peasant" when he wrote that "taxes and rents, together or individually, form the twin issues around which peasant anger in Southeast Asia has classically coalesced".[11] For subsistence-oriented peasants who are living on the margin of livelihood failure, state extraction and commercial disruption can be disastrous. In Thailand in the 1960s and 1970s, the state extracted a significant portion of value produced in rural areas via the rice premium. In some places tenancy was common and rents were very high indeed. Informal money lending was common, often with interest rates ranging between 25 per cent and 100 per cent per year.

In such a situation of vulnerability, it can make good political sense to pursue opposition and disengagement and to seek to strengthen community-based institutions that can provide for basic levels of social insurance. This is the template for political action that was adopted by many civil society organizations following the failure of the mobilization in the mid-1970s. The problem is that rural Thailand has changed dramatically in the decades that followed. Thailand is one of only thirteen developing countries that have maintained average growth rates over 7 per cent for at least twenty-five years.[12] The economy is now more than nine times bigger than it was in the 1970s and national income per capita is five times higher in real terms. Table 8.1 shows a few indicators of the social impacts of that change.

These transformations have produced what I call a "middle-income peasantry" among which subsistence rice farming, commercial agriculture and extensive off-farm employment is combined to produce levels of household income and consumption unthinkable a few decades ago. Rural poverty is still present, especially in the northeast, but it is continuing to decline rapidly. Between 2000 and 2009 poverty incidence in the northeast was cut by almost two-thirds, pushing more than 4 million people above the

TABLE 8.1
Social Impacts and Economic Change

	1960s	2000s
Rural poverty	96%	13%
Infant mortality	15%	<1%
Primary school completion	36%	100%

poverty line. Across Thailand, the average income of land-owning farmers is 280 per cent of the rural poverty line; tenant farmers are only slightly worse off at 270 per cent; and even agricultural workers have average incomes more than double the poverty line. In Thailand's modern rural economy, fear of outright subsistence failure is no longer a core driver of political activity. The majority of rural dwellers are no longer poor.

However, while Thailand has been very successful in managing absolute poverty it has a less impressive record on relative poverty. In the mid-1970s the richest 20 per cent of the population earned about eight times as much as the poorest 20 per cent, whereas in the 2000s this ratio has climbed to between twelve and fourteen.[13] The recent Human Development Report for Thailand highlights the regional dimensions of this inequality.[14] According to a range of human development indicators of income, health, education and housing, Bangkok and its hinterland performs very strongly whereas the worst performers are predominantly rural provinces in the northeast, north and far south. Average household income in Bangkok is about three times higher than in the rural north and northeast. One important reason for this inequality is that Thailand has maintained a relatively large agricultural workforce that is much less productive than its industrial workforce. The Thai peasantry has been remarkably persistent. There has been productivity growth in the agricultural sector, and this has made an important contribution to Thailand's dramatic reduction in rural poverty, but productivity in industry has increased much more rapidly, and from a much higher base. A worker in industry contributes 8.5 times as much to GDP as a worker in agriculture. Non-agricultural employment has certainly helped to increase the incomes of a great many peasant households but due to the low level of rural industrialization, jobs are most often available in the less productive parts of the non-farming economy.

Thailand's governments have been only too aware of the disparity problem and the political hazards of rural disadvantage. For the past half century, attempts to promote rural development have been the central feature of the relationship between the Thai state and the peasantry. These attempts certainly did not start with Thaksin Shinawatra's populism. His policy initiatives were consistent with a long-term trend that has gathered pace since the communist threat emerged in the 1950s and since newly-assertive farmer's organizations moved onto the national stage in the 1970s. In simple terms, the Thai government, like governments in many other developing countries, has moved from taxing the rural economy to subsidizing it. Government funding in the form of infrastructure, price support, subsidized credit, economic development, health, welfare and education has become an integral part of the complex livelihood mix pursued by peasant households throughout rural Thailand. Irrigation infrastructure, community-based projects, agricultural subsidy schemes and ever-active construction sites are local manifestations of the Thai state's high-profile presence in the rural economy.

The origins of Thailand's current political tension lie in the dilemmas of this transformed fiscal relationship. State investment, combined with wide-ranging support for the tenure of small-holders, has enhanced agricultural incomes and has created numerous sources of non-farm employment in the construction sector, local development projects and government agencies. However, the overall impact of this state support for rural Thailand has been to help develop and maintain a middle-income peasantry rather than fundamentally transform it. The government's performance on agricultural productivity has been lacklustre by the standards of many of its regional neighbours and, more importantly, it has had limited success in developing non-farm rural enterprise. As a result, the government's massive investment in the rural economy has helped to maintain a large rural population that, despite significant livelihood improvements, is insufficiently productive to fully meet the aspirations that economic growth has aroused. Political activity in rural Thailand is not driven by an impoverished peasantry that is staging a rearguard action against dissolution, but by a middle-income peasantry that is assertively negotiating the terms of its persistence. Political society, rather than civil society, is the primary site of mobilization for this middle-income peasantry.

WHAT IS POLITICAL SOCIETY?

I borrow the term "political society" from Partha Chatterjee in his writings about contemporary India and rural transformation in Asia more generally.[15] For Chatterjee, political society is quite distinct from civil society which, he argues, is confined to a predominantly urban and middle-class sphere. Political society refers to a much more subaltern domain where there is a productive interplay between local socioeconomic identity and external power, especially the power of the state. It is an informal arena of negotiation, compromise, deals and interpersonal transactions. Whereas civil society often promotes universal rights and clearly established principles, political society is much more concerned with what can be obtained from quite specific transactions.

In adapting this concept to use in rural Thailand, I focus on four basic features. First, political society is relatively non-institutionalized; it is not principally made up of formally constituted and enduring associations. Of course formal and informal groups are present — they certainly play an important role, especially in mediating relations with the state — but they are not a central feature of rural political society. Only a very small minority of Thailand's rural population is actively involved with NGOs. Most of the groups and networks that operate in political society's pursuit of livelihood, security and prosperity are unstable, highly personalized and have very situational specific goals. To pick up some rather old sociological terminology, many of the clusters of enterprise that form in political society are best regarded as "action sets" or "quasi groups" that coalesce around specific, and often time-limited, objectives.[16] Action sets in rural Thailand's political society are fragile and flexible; they are based on pragmatic connections rather than formal rights of association. A great deal of the action of rural political society takes place in a vast substratum of informal interaction, debate, discussion and gossip. Civil society advocates who see democratic consolidation as relying on formal associations simply overlook what is going on in this web of day-to-day interactions.

Second, political society has a strong focus on establishing connections with sources of power. Unlike civil society, which often seeks to constrain or limit the reach of power by establishing relatively autonomous domains of activity, political society is based on logic of drawing external power into local circuits of exchange. Within this orientation the modern community takes on a particular character. Whereas civil society organizations regularly view the community as a bulwark against external power, political society refashions the rural community to provide a framework for drawing external power into local circuits of livelihood and aspiration. The rural community is now only peripherally concerned with subsistence security. The central concern of communal practice is now to ensure that the village is favourably positioned as an appropriate site for subsidy and investment. This political logic of connection, rather than localism, is what energizes both the state's and rural society's preoccupation with community development, community organizations and community culture. Community is a powerful lure that can draw external sources of power into local circuits of exchange.

Third, these sources of power are highly diverse. They certainly include formal entities such as the state and private companies, but these relationships are domesticated and disaggregated into interpersonal dealings with members of parliament, local government officials, village committee members, company brokers and extension agents. The proliferation of officialdom in rural Thailand means that there are many nodes of power that can be tapped into. It also means that the demographic boundary between state, corporation and community is increasingly blurred. The economic diversification of the countryside has reconfigured old patron-client ties. The spatially and economically dispersed livelihood strategies pursued by most peasant households mean that multi-stranded ties with a single patron are much less common. Connections with economically influential figures remain important but the modern proliferation of economic and administrative power means that such linkages are now components in a much more dispersed network of livelihood security. Political society's relations with power also extend into unexpected domains, especially into the spirit world. In fact, the relationship with the unruly spirit world is an excellent starting point for understanding the power dynamics of rural political society. Spirits — like government officials — can be sources of prosperity, protection and retribution. Regular inducements need to be provided in order to channel their power in desired directions.

Fourth, notwithstanding the diversity of power, the state has come to assume a fundamentally important position in rural political society. The reason for this is straightforward: the relatively unproductive character of the rural economy, and the widespread lack of private capital, means that it is heavily dependent on state support. As such, the central element in the political strategy of the middle-income peasantry is to weave the power and resources of the state into the economic and social fabric of village life. The productive intersection between the welfare and subsidy programmes of the state and the aspirations of the middle-income peasantry is a central component of rural Thailand's political society. As the state has expanded its administrative reach and shifted its orientation from taxing the rural economy to supporting it, these productive nodes of intersection have proliferated. Unlike civil society, political society places no particular moral value on autonomy. Quite the opposite: political action, in the broadest sense of the word, is valued precisely when it draws the state — and other nodes of power — into systems of reciprocal exchange.

A DEFENCE OF POLITICAL SOCIETY

Thaksin cleverly capitalized on the dilemmas that have emerged in Thailand's modernization. His unprecedented political success owes much to the fact that he shaped his policies around rural political society's aspirations for productive connections with sources of power. He recognized that decades of rural economic growth and diversification had produced a very different type of peasantry. It was a peasantry for whom the most important challenges were not maintaining an adequate level of subsistence production but diversifying livelihoods, increasing productivity, mobilizing capital and maintaining the flow of government support for the rural economy. There was nothing particularly new about Thaksin's emphasis on rural modernization, but he packaged it in a way that was very attractive for an economically sophisticated electorate: rural households can turn their assets into capital; villagers can manage agricultural credit; farmers can implement infrastructure projects; local hospitals can provide universal health cover. He cashed in on the new social contract that embodied the notion that the state should play a direct and active role in supporting the rural economy. This social contract has been developing since the 1970s, but it took Thaksin to turn it into a core political asset.

The coup of September 2006 severed Thaksin's electorally successful engagement with rural Thailand's sprawling political society. Thaksin's rural support base had elected him three times: in 2001, 2005 and 2006. Defenders of the coup — including a good number who had been active in rural civil society — argued that electoral endorsement had been devalued by money politics. Many commentators resorted to old ideas about the moral pre-eminence of virtuous power embodied in the King and in his military, judicial and bureaucratic network. They refused to acknowledge that a vigorous electoral culture had developed in rural Thailand through which voters evaluate, applaud and critique the government's implementation of its new social contract. It was no accident that the post-coup government made the King's sufficiency economy philosophy the centrepiece of its political platform. Sufficiency economy is the antithesis of political society. Its heavily moralistic emphasis on the virtues of local knowledge, subsistence production and limited exchange forms a stark contrast with political society's pragmatic judgements about non-local connections, commercial engagement, development projects and state subsidy. Of course, there was no real economic substance to the coup-makers' sufficiency economy pitch: their economic agenda was business as usual, apart from a sharp increase in military spending. Their intention was to ideologically undercut Thaksin's cultivation of rural political society by arguing that his policies had eroded the authentic morality of rural culture by promoting immoderate economic expectations. This resonated with the anti-capitalist and anti-globalization agenda of some civil society organizations that had emerged from the social movements of the 1990s, and it is no surprise that some of their leaders took up the anti-Thaksin cause with such passion. Political society was under concerted attack.

Rural political society's defence of its relationship with the state has been an important factor energizing the violent confrontations on the streets of Bangkok and the strong support shown for Yingluck Shinawatra in the election of July 2011. Rural people are demanding an active role in the political process. They are rejecting a system in which their votes can be overruled when they elect governments that are unpalatable to powerful forces in Thailand's palace network, the military or the political elite. Rural Thailand cares about election results because elections have become an important mechanism for people to evaluate and domesticate the power of political leaders. During the red-shirt protests of 2010, some commentators complained that the red-shirt protesters had no clear policy agenda; the 1970s grievances about landlessness, indebtedness and onerous rents hardly featured. Others sought to discredit the red-shirt protests by pointing to vastly improved standards of living in rural areas, as if it is only the abjectly poor who have a right to political mobilization. These are out-dated assessments based on old-fashioned stereotypes of peasant protest. For Thailand's middle-income peasantry, specific policies are less important than a secure relationship with the state. Thaksin's clever promotion and timely implementation of specific policy initiatives was certainly important in galvanizing rural support but even more important was the strong sense that electoral force had shifted the nation's most important power bargains away from Bangkok and towards the rural electorates of north and northeast Thailand. The red-shirt protests have been defending political society's direct transactions with power in all its regular and irregular forms and rejecting the view that economic development and other matters of state should be guided by the elite embodiments of virtuous power located in the nation's capital.

POLITICAL SOCIETY AND DEMOCRACY

Of course, Thaksin's anti-democratic tendencies are well known and well documented. But does this failing extend to the forces of political society that played such an important role in bringing him to power? Can political society contribute to ongoing rural empowerment and democratic consolidation?

Many, especially the vocal critics of money politics, would suggest that it cannot. It is clear that political society has a dark side. Chatterjee, who writes about political society in India, acknowledges that "political society will bring into the hallways and corridors of power some of the squalor, ugliness and violence of popular life".[17] In Thailand, concerns about the squalor of local political culture coalesce around the image of the local strongman who uses coercion and financial inducement to consolidate political power. These provincial businessmen-cum-politicians enrich themselves by capturing government contracts and corruptly appropriating funds destined for local development. One of the enduring themes of modern Thai political commentary has been that democratic values are undermined by electors who are willing to go along with the abuses of strongmen in order to avoid recriminations and to obtain a paltry share of the benefits. In the political culture I have observed in northern Thailand there is no shortage of petty corruption, favouritism, factionalism, character assassination, illegality, and, at times, downright thuggery. The nationwide campaign of extrajudicial killings that the Thaksin government used to deal with alleged drug dealers won widespread local support, with firm and protective government action trumping due legal process. The practices and values of political society are sometimes far from edifying, and this gives plenty of ammunition for those who argue that Thailand's balance of power needs to be shifted in a more civil and virtuous direction.

Nevertheless, a realistic view of political society's shortcomings does not justify rejection of its democratic potential, as Chatterjee argues "If one truly values the freedom and equality that democracy promises, then one cannot imprison it within the sanitized fortress of civil society."[18] In the Thai context, I propose three reasons why this incarceration would be unjustified. First, political society is very diverse as a result of the economic, administrative and supernatural diversity of rural society. While some relations within political society may be corrupt or abusive, they exist within a wide network of relationships, some of which can provide a basis for critique and for promoting alternative styles of political behaviour. A diverse political culture certainly contains some very unattractive elements but, as in the natural world, diversity is also a basis for political resilience and adaptation.

Second, despite some of the stereotypes of rural people's acceptance of corrupt practice, actions in political society are subject to judgement and evaluation. Local political society is pragmatic and flexible but it is also experimental and evaluative. The rural constitution contains a range of informal precepts against which political action is assessed and there is good evidence that civil society's concerns with transparency and sound administration are steadily being drawn into local networks of appraisal. Values matter in political society. Finally, and most importantly, political society may well provide a more realistic basis for dealing with the realities of contemporary politics. In Thailand there is a powerful elite discourse, drawing on carefully cultivated royal imagery, about the need for "good men" to guide the political process. Some of the most prominent civil society figureheads are among the royal network of good men who are regularly called upon in times of crisis to provide wise and ethical counsel. Political society lacks this elite preoccupation with goodness, and its political values are not based on the assumption that good government can only be provided by good men. Evaluations of power within political society are more multi-dimensional and realistic; they are concerned with channelling power in desired directions, negotiating deals and striking a reasonable balance between private and public benefit. This template is certainly a lot more ragged than the purist appeal to absolute goodness but it is more likely to be able to deal with the warts-and-all realities of political life.

Some survey research in Thailand suggests that political society may not be all that bad at promoting democratic values. A recent survey of 1,500 voters in twenty-seven provinces conducted by the Asia Foundation found a high level of interest in politics, widespread experience of free speech and very considerable political tolerance.[19] Importantly, 83 per cent of respondents disagreed with the statement that "it makes sense to follow the recommendations of local leaders when deciding who to vote for"; 90 per cent felt that family members should make their own choice about voting (rather than follow the advice of the household head); and 91 per cent said that religious leaders have little or no influence on their voting. There was concern about vote buying, with 58 per cent saying that voters in the area could be influenced by it, but 84 per cent thought that it was reasonable to take money from a party and then vote for whoever you like. Other surveys, undertaken as part of the ongoing Asian Barometer project, have also found that satisfaction with democratic processes is very high in Thailand, in fact considerably higher than in other democratic countries in the region.[20] These surveys have also found that support for democracy is higher in rural Thailand than it is among the Bangkok middle class, contrary to the common view that the civil-society-oriented middle class is a strong defender of democratic values.

Rural political society is certainly not perfect, but its everyday role in the democratic life of the nation warrants much more respectful attention. Discussions of options for democratic strengthening, in Thailand and elsewhere, will be enriched when they are able to recognize the diversity of commonplace political practice that legitimately informs democratic decision-making. Without this respectful engagement with informal — and sometimes unattractive — political culture, there is a real risk that those who write about democracy's contemporary crisis of participation will unwittingly encourage the view that votes cast in elections can be discounted because they represent only fleeting and superficial engagements with the political process. In fact, elections are just one of the ways in which rural people in Thailand seek to marshal power in the pursuit of security and prosperity. The visit to the ballot box is just one moment in an ongoing process of culturally-informed judgement about the nature of power, in its many forms. Genuine democratic consolidation needs to take this rural political judgement seriously, even when, in fact especially when, it does not fit within the familiar templates of patron-client relations, class struggle or civil society mobilization.

Notes

1. Larry Diamond, "Toward Democratic Consolidation: Rethinking Civil Society", *Journal of Democracy* 5, no. 3 (1994).
2. Ibid.
3. Somchai Phatharathananunth, *Civil Society and Democratization: Social Movements in Northeast Thailand* (Copenhagen: NIAS Press, 2006).
4. Chris Baker, "Thailand's Assembly of the Poor: Background, Drama, Reaction", *South East Asia Research* 8, no. 1 (2000).
5. Bruce D. Missingham, *The Assembly of the Poor in Thailand: From Local Struggles to National Protest Movement* (Chiang Mai: Silkworm Books, 2003).

6. Somchai, *Civil Society and Democratization*, p. 16.
7. Kengkit Kitirianglarp and Kevin Hewison, "Social Movements and Political Opposition in Contemporary Thailand", *Pacific Review* 22, no. 4 (2009).
8. Ibid.
9. Katherine A. Bowie, "Unravelling the Myth of the Subsistence Economy: Textile Production in Nineteenth-Century Northern Thailand", *Journal of Asian Studies* 51, no. 4 (1992).
10. Andrew Walker, "Seeing Farmers for the Trees: Community Forestry and the Arborealisation of Agriculture in Northern Thailand", *Asia Pacific Viewpoint* 45, no. 3 (2004).
11. James C. Scott, *The Moral Economy of the Peasant: Rebellion and Subsistence in Southeast Asia* (New Haven: Yale University Press, 1976).
12. Michael Spence, *The Next Convergence: The Future of Economic Growth in a Multi-speed World* (Crawley, W.A: UWA Publishing, 2011).
13. Borwornsak Uwanno, "Thai Political Situation: Wherefrom and Whereto?", panel discussion on "Thai Political Situation: Wherefrom and Whereto?", co-hosted by the Royal Thai Embassy and the School of Oriental and African Studies, 29 January 2010.
14. UNDP, *Human Security, Today and Tomorrow: Thailand Human Development Report 2009* (Bangkok: UNDP, 2010).
15. Partha Chatterjee, *The Politics of the Governed: Reflections on Popular Politics in Most of the World* (New York: Columbia University Press, 2004). See also Partha Chatterjee, "Peasant Cultures of the Twenty-first Century", *Inter-Asia Cultural Studies* 9, no. 1 (2008).
16. Adrian C. Mayer, "The Significance of Quasi-groups in the Study of Complex Societies", in *The Social Anthropology of Complex Societies*, edited by Michael Banton, pp. 97–121 (London: Tavistock Publications, 1966).
17. Chatterjee, *The Politic of the Governed*, p. 74.
18. Ibid.
19. Tim Meisburger, *Constitutional Reform and Democracy in Thailand: A National Survey of the Thai People* (Bangkok: The Asia Foundation, 2009).
20. Robert Albritton and Bureekul Thawilwadee, "The State of Democracy in Thailand" <http://asiapacific.anu.edu.au/newmandala/wp-content/uploads/2008/09/state-of-democracy.pdf> (accessed 2 May 2012).

References

Albritton, Robert and Bureekul Thawilwadee. "The State of Democracy in Thailand", *New Mandala* <http://asiapacific.anu.edu.au/newmandala/wp-content/uploads/2008/09/state-of-democracy.pdf> (accessed 2 May 2012).
Baker, Chris. "Thailand's Assembly of the Poor: Background, Drama, Reaction". *South East Asia Research* 8, no. 1 (2000).

Borwornsak Uwanno. "Thai Political Situation: Wherefrom and Whereto?". Panel discussion on "Thai Political Situation: Wherefrom and Whereto?", co-hosted by the Royal Thai Embassy and the School of Oriental and African Studies, 29 January 2010.

Bowie, Katherine A. "Unravelling the Myth of the Subsistence Economy: Textile Production in Nineteenth-Century Northern Thailand". *Journal of Asian Studies* 51, no. 4 (1992).

Chatterjee, Partha. *The Politics of the Governed: Reflections on Popular Politics in Most of the World*. New York: Columbia University Press, 2004.

———. "Peasant Cultures of the Twenty-first Century". *Inter-Asia Cultural Studies* 9, no. 1 (2008).

Diamond, Larry. "Toward Democratic Consolidation: Rethinking Civil Society". *Journal of Democracy* 5, no. 3 (2004).

Kengkit Kitirianglarp and Kevin Hewison. "Social Movements and Political Opposition in Contemporary Thailand". *Pacific Review* 22, no. 4 (2009).

Mayer, Adrian C. "The Significance of Quasi-groups in the Study of Complex Societies". In *The Social Anthropology of Complex Societies*, edited by Michael Banton. London: Tavistock Publications, 1996.

Meisburger, Tim. *Constitutional Reform and Democracy in Thailand: A National Survey of the Thai People*. Bangkok: The Asia Foundation, 2009.

Missingham, Bruce D. *The Assembly of the Poor in Thailand: From Local Struggles to National Protest Movement*. Chiang Mai: Silkworm Books, 2003.

Scott, James C. *The Moral Economy of the Peasant: Rebellion and Subsistence in Southeast Asia*. New Haven: Yale University Press, 1976.

Somchai Phatharathananunth. *Civil Society and Democratization: Social Movements in Northeast Thailand*. Copenhagen: NIAS Press, 2006.

Spence, Michael. *The Next Convergence: The Future of Economic Growth in a Multi-speed World*. Crawley, W.A: UWA Publishing, 2011.

UNDP. *Human Security, Today and Tomorrow: Thailand Human Development Report 2009*. Bangkok: UNDP, 2010.

Walker, Andrew. "Seeing Farmers for the Trees: Community Forestry and the Arborealisation of Agriculture in Northern Thailand". *Asia Pacific Viewpoint* 45, no. 3 (2004).

Section IV

Crises of Legitimacy

9

REAPING THE WHIRLWIND
Thailand's Coup and the
Southern Problem

Marc Askew

In early November 2006, some six weeks after Thailand's coup, the junta-appointed interim Prime Minister, Surayud Chulanont, travelled to the embattled southern border provinces to address officials and community leaders. His speech on 8 November in Pattani Province was made famous by his so-called "apology" to southern Muslims for the State's previous mistakes in combating the violence. Surayud's presentation is notable for another reason. He began by speaking of two crises that faced his administration, namely: the national crisis of discord that had purportedly justified the coup against former Prime Minister Thaksin Shinawatra (though he was not named in the speech), and the southern strife. But Surayud made no attempt to link these national problems in "causal" terms. Was there any relationship between Thailand's coup of September 2006 and the southern unrest, whether in terms of cause or effects? Though by 2006 the insurgent-driven violence in Thailand's southern border provinces had become a serious national issue demanding a comprehensive government-led resolution, the "Southern Fire" actually played no role in provoking the military coup. The coup was an act staged by leading military factions supported by a conservative power elite and an urban middle class dedicated to removing Thaksin from power and eliminating his party's control over the Thai state apparatus. It was an issue of the "centre", and the south was conspicuously "marginal" to the key motivations and legitimating claims of the coup makers. The anti-Thaksin coup saw a reconfiguration in (and a reassertion of) the balance of power between key centres of conservative political influence in the country. It elevated to leadership the military elite and unelected representatives of the monarchy, who from 2006 to 2007 proceeded to sponsor a range of allied anti-Thaksin groups in an effort to re-engineer the country's legal framework to ensure the election of an anti-Thaksin post-coup parliament (a project which failed). Tackling the escalating violence in the south was not the motivation for their seizure of power, even though it was of major concern to the coup makers and their appointed interim government. That being the case, the question becomes one about the coup's consequences.

Did Thailand's coup make any difference to the situation prevailing in the strife-torn border provinces? Cast in such a broad manner, this question, which I recently posed to military officers, journalists and bureaucrats who were working in the border provinces in the period during the coup, elicited a uniformly negative response, partly because the question was taken to mean "was there was any fundamental advance in policy effectiveness?". To be sure, a year-and-a-half after the coup (by early 2008) the number of violent events and casualties had fallen by around 30 per cent, a statistic hailed by officials at the time as a sign of "improvement". Yet the negative tone of responses to the question "Did the coup make a difference?" draws attention to the gloomy vantage point of mid-2011, when continuing low-level violence and persistent insecurity in the border region defied optimistic proclamations based on incremental numerical drops in the body count or more qualitative upbeat statements delivered to visiting journalists in guided tours by the army and government public relations department.

This paper examines the question of the 2006 coup's effects on policy towards the south by comparing the pre- and post-coup periods with regard to four major areas, namely: the organization of security efforts; operational effectiveness in connection to the violence in the border provinces; official discourse surrounding policy; and the characteristics of dominant critiques of state policy. To what extent did the measures put in place for the south by the coup makers and their allies represent a departure from the Thaksin period? I argue that a number of continuities with the Thaksin period mark the post-coup years. Some changes, in particular the formal centralization of security operations under the military, were already in train prior to the September coup. Despite the embellishment of official rhetoric under Surayud with the global buzzword "reconciliation", key elements of official discourse underpinning state efforts and security arrangements before and after the coup — the definition of the "problem" and means to solve it — were marked by close similarities. In addition, the themes of most critiques of policy in the post-coup period (by academics, the press and by human rights and other advocacy groups) represent an obvious continuity with the pre-coup years. The conspicuous difference was that the object of blame for flawed policy and inadequate results shifted from the hubristic figure of Thaksin to that of Thailand's post-coup governments and the military.

The years of the coup government actually coincided with a worsening of the southern situation. If measured by the zero sum statistical criteria of the number of casualties and violent events, the coup makers and their allies clearly failed to meet the challenge, with insurgent violence increasing in intensity and brutality during the two years of the Surayud government. Despite the newly empowered army's security and development-focused operations implemented from 2007, the aim of minimizing "daily killings" by 2009 fell well short of their target.

The Democrat Party, which led a coalition government from late 2008 till its defeat at the polls in July 2011, can be counted as a key beneficiary of the anti-Thaksin coup. However, it also fell short of stated aims and achievements when it came to the test, and its leaders were just as prone as Thaksin had been to blame others for their shortcomings in solving the southern crisis. In the short term at least, the army clearly benefited the most from the coup in terms of power, prestige and resources, but subsequent developments showed that the coup was a mixed blessing for the army and its operations in the south. The elevation of the Democrat Party with army support in late 2008 (to act as a buttress against pro-Thaksin forces), actually undermined the army's control of affairs in the south to the benefit of civilian bureaucrats. After the coup, and with Thaksin out of the picture (certainly with regard to southern policy), the public blame game accompanying the southern violence shifted to focus directly on the military and the post-coup governments.

Political turbulence and polarization in the country escalated as a direct result of the coup. It climaxed in the downfall of pro-Thaksin governments in 2008 at the behest of judicial fiat, crowd politics and military collusion; it was followed during 2009–10 by a retaliatory extra-parliamentary assault on the anti-Thaksin coalition government. This persistent turbulence has been cited as a factor that compromised the government's efforts to grapple with the southern problem in the post-coup period. However, the logic of arguments about the "distracting" effects of the national conflict on government effort towards the south is flawed and based on simplistic assumptions. As during the Thaksin period, the southern "problem" in the post-coup years became part of the general "political noise" of the public blame game, whether played by opponents of governments or by single-issue groups. A key point can be drawn from the fact of the coup's minimal connection to the southern conundrum and its consequently minor status as a factor in Thailand's contemporary political struggles: that is, that the "southern problem" as a national issue has never reached a scale where it could, alone, threaten the survival of Thailand's national governments.

BEFORE THE COUP

The approach of Thaksin's administration (2001–06) to the southern crisis has been summarized *ad nauseam* as one marked by blunders stemming from policy short-sightedness and "hardline" security measures that alienated the southern Muslim population. Among the litany of other errors attributed to him are his disapproval of initiatives to seek a negotiated solution to the conflict and his poor record of relations with Malaysia.[1] Commonly, such criticism is centred on Thaksin himself as a fatally flawed administrator, bedevilled by his businessman's "results orientated" leadership, his background as a police officer (apparently suppression-orientated) and his habitual impatience, which revealed itself in rash public comments as well as the setting of impossible deadlines to his subordinates for the solving of problems.[2] This was early revealed in officials' frenetic and unsuccessful attempts to locate the culprits of the attack on and thefts of weapons from the Ratchanakarin army camp in Narathiwat, on 4 January 2004, which marked the escalation of insurgent violence. For Thailand's critical academics and prominent civil society wise men, the controversial events in the Deep South during 2004 (the military's killing of militants at Pattani's Krue Se mosque and the tragic blunder of Tak Bai) and other happenings (the abduction of Muslim rights lawyer Somchai Neelapaichit in March) were part of an expanding catalogue of flaws in Thaksin-style governance.[3] According to the opposition Democrat Party — desperately seeking to regain political clout since its comprehensive electoral defeat by Thaksin's Thai Rak Thai (TRT) Party in 2001 — Thaksin had caused the problems in the south. For Thailand's academics and other critics, Thaksin's culpability was expressed in terms of him having "reignited", or at the very least, "exacerbated" the southern violence.[4]

Such a simple portrayal of Thaksin's [mis]management of the southern crisis would make it easy to contrast the pre-coup period, marked by apparent insensitivity and harshness, with the post-coup government of the avuncular Surayud and his administration's peacemaking rhetoric. Yet this would be an exaggeration of the differences, notwithstanding the impact of Thaksin and his subordinates' evident mistakes during the first year of the violence. A more measured view would depict the period of 2004–06 as one when Thaksin and his administration were groping towards solutions to a novel situation. Notwithstanding the Democrat opposition's simplistic arguments that Thaksin's dissolution of the Southern Border Province's Administrative Centre in 2002 opened the door for insurgents to run riot, this insurgency had been long in the making and its structure, tactics and targets were new. Thaksin's unsuccessful efforts to manage the exploding crisis need to be viewed in the context of this novel and ambiguous violence. So too, his efforts took place in the environment of a security community, government subordinates and advisors who were divided in their views of the crisis.[5]

By 2005, the southern violence showed no sign of abating. Though his TRT Party's unprecedented victory at the national polls in February of that year apparently vindicated Thaksin's popularity in terms of economic policy, the persisting southern violence stood out as a constant taunt to his claims to policy success.

Delegating and Reshuffling

Finding a workable system of leadership to manage the southern crisis proved to be a major challenge to Thaksin. This was reflected in the high turnover among senior officials assigned to address the southern unrest. Over the period 2004–05 the south proved to be a career graveyard.

Beginning in early March 2004, the first casualties were the Minister for Defence General (retired) Thamarak Isarangura Na Ayutthaya and Minister for the Interior Wan Muhamad Nor Matha, who were removed from their responsibilities for southern affairs in a cabinet reshuffle. Thamarak's replacement by General (retired) Chettha Thanajaro was viewed by some as a move towards a "softer" approach in the wake of the declaration of Martial Law and vigorous search efforts by the army and police that were alienating the borderland Malay Muslim population.[6] Later in the month, following an emergency meeting of the National Security Council, Police Chief General Sant Sarutanont, and 4th (Southern Region) Army Commander Lt. General Pongsak Ekbannasingh were removed from their positions.

By late 2004, General (retired) Chavalit Yongchaiyudh, deputy prime minister in charge of security affairs, also became a casualty of the crisis. As a former army commander with extensive experience and strong ties to Muslim leaders in the border provinces, Chavalit was, in theory at least, an appropriate figure to deal with the challenge. After all, nearly two decades earlier he had been prominent in devising the army's civil action programmes to combat communist and separatist insurgency. He had promoted the village-orientated development project for the southern border provinces known as "Hariban Bahru (New Hope/Aspiration), later renamed "Taksin Pattana" (Developing the South). "New Aspiration" (*khwamwang mai*) became the name for his own political party (founded in 1990), which became the home of the Muslim Wadha political faction of the Malay Muslim provinces. Chavalit's New Aspiration Party joined Thaksin's TRT governing coalition in 2001 (fully merging with TRT in 2005), but its southern Malay Muslim parliamentarians were put in a difficult position by the violence, and suspected as insurgent organizers by the authorities.

During early 2004, Chavalit's efforts extended from meeting with borderland Muslim leaders to coordinating security measures. But he was put in a difficult position by the controversial storming of the Krue Se mosque on 28 April 2004, ordered by General Panlop Pinmanee. Though Chavalit had urged Panlop to end the Krue Se face-off by negotiation, Panlop ordered a decisive attack, which led to the killing of all the militants, including an innocent Muslim villager. Panlop was head of the Southern Border Provinces Peace Promotion Command (SBPPPC). This organizational unit was formed by Chavalit as a forward command of the Internal Security Operations Command (ISOC), to direct southern security operations in concert with the civilian administration (see discussion below). However, just days after the 28 April events this unit was consigned to administrative limbo by Thaksin, who passed control of security operations to Defence Minister Gen Chettha Thanajaro, arguing that the SBPPPC had confused the military chain of command. Panlop was reassigned to other duties, though Thaksin denied that this represented a punishment.[7] This debacle signalled the beginning of Chavalit's demise. In October (prior to the Tak Bai events late that month), he resigned after being sidelined by Thaksin in a cabinet reshuffle.

Security Operations, Rivalry and Confusion

In 2002, the army was formally relieved of security responsibilities for the southern border provinces and the police force took charge. This was in accordance with the official diagnosis that southern violence at that time was the work of drug rings and influential criminal figures. From that year, violent attacks (notably on police posts) had increased and the police were ill-equipped to cope with the menacing situation. Following the 4 January 2004 raid, the army quickly returned to the border provinces, though it did not displace the police. At the time of the raid, the regular army in the four southern provinces could boast little more than regimental strength (or three battalions). As a result of the government's directive of 2002, the army's fourth region units were sequestered in their main camps, only venturing forth to undertake development activities under the Taksin Pattana programme. Ranger units, formerly central to operations that monitored separatist groups, had been pulled out of the border provinces entirely or restricted to posts on the Malaysian-Thai Border. Though the army quickly assumed a critical security role in responding to the evolving insurgent violence, and steadily increased its troop strength in the region — particularly after the 28 April attacks — the command and control environment of their operations was very different to former times.

Traditionally, southern military operations were the responsibility of the fourth army region and its commanding general. However, this simple command structure did not apply in the context of the new insurgency, despite the urgings of former generals that the old system should be reinstated to enhance efficiency. Due to the host of agencies and security units that flooded the region, and to the volatility of government decision-making over the years 2004–05, the formal authority of the fourth army region chiefs fluctuated. Thus, though the fourth region commander was given full authority for the application of Martial Law after its declaration on 4 January 2004, by March, security operations were placed in the hands of General Panlop's Southern Border Provinces Peace Promotion Command (SBPPPC). Then, in October 2004, the fourth army region command was subsumed by the multi-agency Southern Border Provinces Peace-Building Command under the control of the army's deputy Supreme Commander. A year later, the SBPPPC was restructured, with the fourth region commander doubling as the director of the SBPPPC. The fourth army region chiefs were prime victims for punishment in the bureaucratic blame game. The two years 2004 to 2005 saw the position of fourth region commander change hands five times, though the standard tenure for an army commander was at least two years.

A competitive operational environment was a major challenge for the army, even as its troop numbers increased. The police, whose numbers also increased, did not come under the army's control, except for Border Patrol Police units. There were continued complaints of lack of cooperation between these two bodies as well as civilian bureaucrats. Critics complained that there were literally too many chiefs to which key groups were answerable.[8] In fact, such critiques exposed the central characteristic of Thailand's internally competitive bureaucracy. The southern insurgency simply exposed this generic flaw more clearly.[9] Nonetheless, from late-2005, when General Sonthi Boonyaratglin was elevated to army commander-in-chief, the army began gradually to claw its way back to dominance over security efforts in the south. This would take over a year, with escalating violence in the region being the key factor impelling Thaksin's frustrated administration to fully delegate the task.

DOUSING THE SOUTHERN FIRE: POLICY FORMULAS AND DISCOURSE

A consideration of the formulation of policy and administrative structures to deal with the southern strife during the Thaksin period helps bring into relief differences and similarities between the pre- and post-coup years. The periodic re-jigging of the security apparatus has been viewed and criticized largely in political and structural terms by academics and journalists alike,[10] but attention to the policy language and declarations that accompanied these measures is equally illuminating. Formal declarations about security and the aims of policy towards the south can be treated as discursive exercises in constructing policy "texts". In their content they highlight how key "problems" were classified and institutionalized as authorized knowledge, and incorporated into an ideal representation of the challenge facing the Thai state. Certainly these declarations are symbolic artefacts which mask differences of opinion that prevailed among officials, yet they also take on a life of their own as official representations of reality. They also highlight the political context of their production and the agendas of their framers. Several things are quite striking about these declarations during 2004 and after: firstly, the declarations reiterate earlier language about the southern "problem" which reaches back several decades; secondly, they show that most of the key official diagnostic categories of the southern violence employed by the post-coup government were articulated in the Thaksin period.

Chavalit's Decree

The first major formal declaration concerning the southern "problem" and its special administrative requirements was embodied in Prime Minister's Office Order 68/2547. Entitled "Policy for Promoting Peace in the 3 Border Provinces", this order was released on 1 March and enforced from 25 March 2004. Curiously, this order was formally approved by cabinet only in the first week of May, after the controversial 28 April events had provoked critics into branding security efforts under Thaksin's administration as "hardline." The declaration itself is far from being a hardline document advocating force. Much more notable are its clichés and truisms. Devised by Chavalit, the Prime Minister's Office Order designated a special structure to meet the escalating southern challenge, though this largely involved the harnessing of existing national agencies in the effort. The structure incorporated the National Security Council as the broad policy formulation agency, together with the National Economic and Social Development Board (NESBD) as the body responsible for framing an integrated strategy for economic and social development in the border provinces. Coordinated efforts were to be run by Chavalit under his authority as deputy prime minister and head of ISOC at the national level. A linked order (69/2547) authorized an ISOC forward command to be established in the three border provinces under the title of the Southern Border Provinces Peace

Promotion Command (SBPPPC), which was to operate under the national ISOC umbrella under Chavalit's authority. As with most Thai government policy documents, it tone and rhetoric was impressive and solemn, especially its call for "unity" (*ekkaphap*) and "integration" (*buranakan*) of government agency efforts. As always, such habitual rhetorical injunctions belied the reality of disunity and competition that is the perennial feature of the Thai bureaucratic apparatus.

The first section of Prime Minister's Office Order 68/2547 ("The Situation" — *Sathanakan*) sets out the background to the emerging unrest, incorporating the gamut of factors that had been proclaimed throughout the pre- and post-coup period about the causes of the "Southern Fire" and the responses required. It first describes the characteristics of post-Cold War conflict in the world; conflict which draws force from perceptions of differences in ethnicity and religion and contestation of the power of the United States, a clear reference to the post 9/11 world environment and jihadist terrorism. This is a trend that has impacted on Thailand's border provinces (section 1.1). It then highlights the border region as "special" in terms of the way of life, culture, religion and language of its majority Malay Muslim population. These characteristics are "conditions" (*ngeun khai*) that have been exploited by the insurgent movement to justify opposition to authority through various violent and disruptive acts (section 1.2). These internal characteristics are weak points within the region together with external influences (militant Islam) which have affected the consciousness of the region's youth (section 1.2.1–2). State authority has been weakened by an insurgent movement as well as by local influential groups and criminals. As a result, state officials have not received cooperation. Lack of cooperation and clear leadership among officials is a major obstacle to the work of addressing the problem of disturbances (section 1.2.3). Currently, the document emphasizes, there is no unity in the work between government officials, and agencies are not taking the initiative which is essential to revive the confidence of officials, business people and the population of the region (section 1.2.4).

The first section then goes on to stress that the government wants all people in the region to coexist in happiness according to their identities, religious faiths and cultures, that official agencies aim to promote civil society, self-reliance and strong communities without bias towards any particular group. The government urges all officials to adhere to the principle of peoples' happiness and peace as the central focus of all action, together with equality and dignity for all. The people have the opportunity and role of cooperating together to solve the problem and to protect their lives from the impact of the changes stemming from internal and external pressures. The gamut of key words, injunctions, truisms and "problems" enunciated in this document persisted as themes of pronouncements into the post-Thaksin years. Conspicuously, they included identification of the key challenge for the Thai state as being the weakness of its authority due to violent contestation, lack of cooperation and confidence.

The second brief section on objectives stresses that the policy aims to end the disturbances "urgently", in order "to transform the environment in the borderland to one that will bring about internal security at a level that will facilitate economic and social development". This goal is to be achieved within three years, an aim that clearly reflected the influence of Thaksin's deadline-fixated mode of governance. However, timetables have not been unique to the Thaksin period alone, as evidenced by the operational timetable of General Anupong Paochinda (introduced in late 2007) to reduce "daily killings" and "control the area" by 2010 (for which see discussion below). The third section on "Policy" repeats the aim to "integrate" government agencies in opposing the violence, facilitating "economic and social development" and "understanding and reaching" the population (invoking here the King's royal speech on "Understanding, Reaching out and Development" the previous February). "Taking the initiative" is also repeated, together with the aim to achieve "sustainable peace".

The fourth section on "Action" (*kanpatibat*) details a number of principles and aims that are remarkably similar to those enunciated in official pronouncements (both civil and military) in the post-Thaksin years. They also reflect Chavalit's conviction that the formula of "Politics Leading the Military", which he had developed during his years under General Prem Tinsulanonda in the counter-insurgency campaign against the communists, was the answer to the southern violence.[11] The key to this approach was "[we] have to reclaim the political initiative to gain victory over thought". This would be achieved by working to reduce violent thinking among insurgents as well as government officials whose behaviour was inappropriate. A key goal was to encourage people of the region to be conscious of themselves as Thais in all their cultural diversity and to consider themselves as all "owners of the country". Psychological operations were a key to the work of encouraging people to join together and exchange ideas in order to collectively develop the country. As Chavalit himself admitted, this was an elaboration of Prem's famous Prime Minister's Office Order 66/2523, which had become the army's established doctrine for combating insurgency. Though this key section lacks some of the fashionable normative keywords of post-coup proclamations — notably *santhiwithi* (peaceful means) and *samannachan* (reconciliation) — the model is very similar to post-coup objectives and ideals, e.g.: "participation"; "exchange of ideas between religious leaders"; "use lawful means in solving the problems"; and "develop the economy in a sustainable way consistent with the needs of local people".[12]

Prime Minister's Office Order 68/2547 was the first major policy statement of the Thaksin government that attempted to set out a rationale, strategy and methods for tackling the southern crisis. As mentioned, there are key similarities between this document and normative pronouncements that came later. To be sure, some elements of the document reflect the power of prevailing diagnoses of the southern problem at the time, such as the strong emphasis on the role of "influential figures" in the southern unrest, which match Thaksin's statements even up to 28 April that criminal groups were manipulating separatist ideology for pragmatic ends. As a text, the order projects a seamless diagnosis linked with organizational prescriptions for the realization of goals; but it was clear at the time that even in higher government circles there was no consensus in thinking. Notable among government mavericks was Deputy Prime Minister and Minister for Education Chaturon Chaisaeng, who in March had travelled to the south and returned with a body of proposals, including the selective lifting of martial law, an amnesty for the culprits of attacks, and the removal of non-southern police from the region. Ironically, Chaturon's proposals, which had been sidelined by Thaksin, were receiving renewed attention from academics just at the time when Prime Minister's Office Order 68/2547 was being considered by cabinet.[13] In common with policy documents on controversial issues, the Order obscures underlying differences within official circles and in the public sphere with its utterance of key words and phrases expressing general truisms and normative ideals. Though at the highest level, such words represented a type of consensus, their meanings have been continually contested. Scholars of policy discourse argue that certain keywords express "strategic ambiguity" which is central to the process of generating policy texts in fields characterized by conflicting views.[14] Such is the case with recurring key terms utilized in security policy texts from 2004 through to the period well beyond the coup. Key terms and phrases that stand out in Order 68/2547 include "participation"; "lawful means"; and notably the King's sacrosanct royal formula of "Understanding, Reaching out, and Development", which has been central to every key policy pronouncement since 2004, including the policy statement of the new government of Yingluck Shinawatra. Though obligatory, all such key words have been subject to different interpretations. Notwithstanding the hegemony of high-flown words, the solution to the southern "problems" remained highly contentious.

There are some obvious points to be made about the pronouncement in its guise as both a discursive text and organizing instruction. First, the government needed to be seen to be doing something decisive after the spike in violence following the 4 January arms raid. The Order represented a decisive stance. Notably, too, the formulation of this Order came hard on the heels of Thaksin's visit to the King in February, when the monarch had proffered the ambiguous triad of "Understanding, Reaching out, and Development" as the guide to solving the crisis. Just as striking was the contradiction between official practice and lofty principled rhetoric. The security structure mandated by the Order was in force from late March (significantly, before approval by cabinet in May), but within a month its ideals were blown out of the water by the security crackdown of 28 April. Within a few days of that event Chavalit's role was eclipsed by the defence minister, and his SBPPC as the coordinating agency for implementing policy in the border provinces appeared to be moribund.

Experiments and Policy Principles 2004–05

From the second half of 2004 to late 2005 more reorganization took place in the civilian-military apparatus as the Thaksin administration struggled to find an administratively efficient formula for alleviating the continuing violence and addressing its proximate causes. This period saw the reaffirmation of the prevailing policy emphasis on "peace-building" and "participation", with an increasing emphasis on economic development. The main initiative came in early October 2004 with the formation of the so-called Southern Border Provinces Peace-Building Command (SBPPC) (with the same name as Chavalit's ill-fated organization). Proclaimed in Prime Minister's Office Order 260/2547, it superseded a number of previous measures adopted since the 28 April events, including the "Prime Minister's Task Force" for the economic development of the three southern provinces (Prime Minister's Office Order 106/2547, 10 May). The remarkable feature of Prime Minister's Office Order 260 was its overall similarity to PMO 68, including its statement of "The Situation", and key principles and objectives (in particular increasing popular participation in programmes).[15] Aside from the conspicuous absence of a results deadline (present in Chavalit's Order 68), the main differences were in the details outlining the structural features of the organization and its authority. Also noticeable was the fact that, like its predecessor's proclamation, this Order was soon followed by an embarrassing public relations disaster for the government in the guise of the bungled operation at Tak Bai (25 October), where seventy-nine Malay Muslim protestors were suffocated while being transported to a military camp. Again, events on the ground mocked the publicly proclaimed ideals of policy.

Established at the Sirinthorn army base in Pattani Province, the SBPPC was given the same inter-agency coordinating responsibilities as its predecessor in relation to province administrations, ministries and the military. But its chain of command was different. It was a "special-purpose agency" (rather than a "forward command" under ISOC as previously) directly accountable to the prime minister, with its own director appointed by the prime minister. Its duties were to follow the policy aims of the Prime Minister's Office Order, the prime minister's instructions and the directives of the National Security Council. The SBPPC was also given the power (at least on paper) to recommend or punish civilian, police and military officials (section 3.1). Among its listed duties were to enhance "integration" in the work of agencies, review their performance, monitor violent events, propose and undertake projects, and promote efficiency and the lawful behaviour of officials.

In its role, the SBPPC appeared similar to the civilian-dominated SBPAC, which had been dissolved by Thaksin in 2002. The SBPPC even included an advisory committee, like the SBPAC. Its key staff, however, including its new director, General Sirichai Tanyasiri (formerly deputy Supreme Commander of the Armed Forces), were army officers. In his memoir *The Last War*, Chavalit defended the formation of the new agency (largely because it vindicated his original idea for the SBPPPC), emphasizing that it was likely to be more effective than the defunct SBPAC because it was answerable directly to the prime minister, whereas the SBPAC had been under the Ministry of the Interior with a less direct connection to the prime minister.[16] However, the powers of the SBPPC were limited. The Prime Minister's Office Order did not formally subordinate civilian bureaucratic departments and ministries to the SBPPC's authority; it simply enjoined civilian officials to "support" its work. The agency's power to command cooperation from the civilian bureaucracy was weak, a point made in critical press columns shortly after its establishment.[17]

The SBPPC under General Sirichai was active. During 2005 it undertook a range of population-focused activities. One of the first was a scheme for providing temporary employment in the border provinces. This scheme was a directive from Prime Minister Thaksin, who devised the scheme according to the logic that unemployment and underemployment were underlying factors in the insurgency. This became known as the "4,500 baht" project, after the monthly salary allowance that it provided. Another initiative, involving a budget outlay of over 20 million baht, was the "Tambon San Samphan" project ("Building Relationships in Sub-districts"), which involved the staging of meetings among villagers for the airing of local problems. Another project dealt with promoting morality through religious teaching. Some of these programmes, for example the 4,500 baht project, remained in place after the fall of Thaksin, and were managed by the new ISOC Region 4 Forward Command (which was essentially a mutation of the SBPPC with greater powers and budget). Others were echoed in projects implemented in the post-coup period by other agencies. Virtually all of them were founded on an established military counter-insurgency "winning hearts and minds" civil action approach.[18] This was the identical doctrine of General Sonthi Boonyaratglin, the coup leader. Six months after the formation of the SBPPC, Sirichai reported that SBPPC projects were achieving results, though he refused to commit to any prediction about when they might help reduce the prevailing violence.

PRE-COUP CHANGES: THE ARMY AND GENERAL SONTHI BOONYARATGLIN

The anti-Thaksin coup of 2006 brought the army into a position of dominance in both national security affairs and southern operations and can be identified as a "coup-effect" in relation to the handling of the southern crisis. However, the extent of this change is exaggerated when seen in the context of the gradual increase in the army's control prior to the coup. Though the army leadership was buffeted by transfers made in the wake of controversial events in the south during 2004, by late 2005 it was gradually regaining leadership over other agencies in the region following the appointment of General Sonthi Boonyaratglin as Army Commander-in-Chief.

Heads continued to roll in the second half of 2004 as army commanders at national and regional levels proved to be inept, or otherwise incapable of making decisive progress in security operations. In October 2004, at the same time as the proclamation of Prime Minister's Office Order 240/2547, General Chaiyasith Shinawatra (Thaksin's cousin) was moved from his position as army chief. His place was taken by General Prawit Wongsuwan. Announced earlier in August, Thaksin explicitly linked this change to the southern crisis, noting: "the long-standing problem in the south needs fresh and proactive people to tackle it."[19] This was also an admission that Thaksin's political appointments to police and army commands were not up to facing the southern challenge. Another political appointee, fourth army region commander Lt-Gen Pisarn Wattanawongkeeree, was transferred from his post after Tak Bai.[20] Thereafter, army officers with less intimate connections with Thaksin assumed key roles, beginning with Sonthi.

General Sonthi's elevation to Thailand's top army post (from October 2005) was announced in August 2005. The announcement was greeted positively by Muslim leaders in the border provinces, due to Sonthi's credentials as a Muslim, the first to occupy this powerful army post. In other quarters, it was hoped that Sonthi's Muslim background would be an asset in forging more trustful relations with southern Muslims as well as easing pressures mounting on Thailand's government from Muslim countries in the wake of the Tak Bai disaster. Sonthi was a Vietnam veteran and former commander of Thailand's elite Special Forces. In that capacity he had close ties to Surayud Chulanont, under whom he had served. During 2005 Sonthi had been a deputy director of the SBPPC under General Sirichai Thanyasiri. Deputy army chief since 2004, Sonthi was not part of Thaksin's clique and neither was he Thaksin's first choice. Critical of the government's approach to the southern violence, he was actually rumoured to be in line for transfer to an inactive post prior to the 2005 army reshuffle. Nonetheless, his promotion was reportedly strongly backed by the influential palace-aligned former generals, Privy Councillor (and former army commander) Surayud, and Privy Council President General Prem.[21]

Following his assumption to command, Sonthi announced a "restructuring" of leadership arrangements, appointing a new fourth army commander (Major-General Ongkorn Thongphasom) at the end of 2005 who shared his own background in the Special Forces. Earlier, in mid-2005, positions in the SBPPC had been reshuffled, and the directorship was passed to the fourth army commander, ostensibly for ensuring greater efficiency, though civilian bureaucrats and the police complained at the time.[22] Under Sonthi, the fourth army commander retained leadership of the SBPPC.

From the time of taking his post, Sonthi had made a variety of comments to the press suggesting that his approach to the south was distinctive, and perhaps even "dovish". For example, he openly expressed disapproval of "blacklists" of insurgent suspects maintained by security forces. He was upbeat about his capacity to reduce the insurgent violence, though shortly before the 2006 coup, major coordinated attacks by insurgents occurred, such as the simultaneous bombing of commercial banks in Yala Province in August 2006 and bombings in Hat Yai City. After this, and facing criticism from Thaksin for not preventing these attacks, Sonthi signalled a departure from stated government policy by announcing that he would attempt to negotiate with insurgent leaders, though admitting that "We still don't know who the real head of the militants is."[23] He also publicly criticized what he described as political interference, appealing for the army to be allowed to do its job. Coming just two weeks before the coup, Sonthi's announcements may well be viewed as opportunistic, casting the army in a role as a victim and deflecting responsibility for security mistakes in the south.

Most significant was Sonthi's eventual success in pushing for full army control over security efforts in the south. Thaksin yielded to his request in June, though it was not immediately formalized. Less than a fortnight before the coup, Thailand's deputy caretaker Prime Minister Chitchai Vanasatidya announced that the army's executive power in the south over other agencies (together with budget allocations) would shortly be formally declared by authority of a government decree.[24]

THE COUP GOVERNMENT: "RECONCILIATION" AND SECURITY CRACKDOWN

Within weeks after the coup, south-watchers voiced opinions about the significance of the event for the violence-plagued border provinces. Francesca Lawe-Davies of the highly-publicized International Crisis Group (ICG) suggested that the coup may well signal an advance in "conflict resolution" for the Muslim south. She pinned this hopeful prediction on the figure of General Sonthi, who after his rise to army leadership the previous October had voiced commitment to a "hearts and minds" approach. Fundamentally, her evaluation was based on three assumptions, namely: (1) that Thaksin had been a major part of the "southern problem"; (2) that the recommendations of the National Reconciliation Commission (the NRC, founded in early 2005 in the wake of the Tak Bai disaster) represented appropriate and workable policy; and (3) that the coup leadership and its appointed government under Surayud Chulanont would implement key NRC recommendations. Lawe-Davies suggested that there was now a greater possibility for initiatives towards opening negotiations with insurgent groups, measures that had been highly compromised during the Thaksin years.[25] Zachary Abuza's analysis, written days after the coup, was more cautious than the ICG. He argued that the coup would bring about an end to the constant flux in military leadership and political interference with security matters that had marked the Thaksin years. Implementation of the NRC's recommendations, though not sufficient to quell the insurgency, would "have an important impact in regaining the trust of the Muslim community", he predicted. With generals now having a freer hand to confront the insurgency, the critical matter was the improvement of intelligence on the shadowy insurgent networks. Realistically, Abuza pointed out that the insurgent violence had its own dynamic, unconnected to Thailand's national political situation, and that their aggressive offensive signalled in their major August–September attacks would likely continue.[26]

The ICG's judgement about the changes that the coup might make to southern policy and the situation in general, were arguably based on a misreading of Sonthi's position and an idealistic rendering of the solutions to the southern "problem" itself. To be sure, Sonthi had expressed some agreement with the NRC's assessments, including the negative effect of "blacklists" and the importance of engaging closely with the southern populace. Prior to the coup, Sonthi's various statements made him appear to be the "good guy" who was being stymied by the "bad guys", such as Thaksin and his ministers. Sonthi had made much of his Muslim credentials as a key to reaching out to the southern Muslim populace and boosting the trust that was so often cited as the factor limiting security efforts against insurgent networks. But this impression was, in fact, illusory. Sonthi and Surayud's statements about southern policy prior to the coup were part of the campaign against Thaksin, and they were lapped up by the news media in the maelstrom of criticism against the administration that surged from early 2006. Secondly, though the Surayud government incorporated the rhetoric of the academics and intellectuals who shaped the final NRC report, delivered in June 2006, none of the NRC's key proposals were in fact ever implemented by the coup-installed government.

It should be emphasized that, on their own admission, the NRC's leading figures did not aim to address the short-term challenge to reduce insurgent attacks. In fact, its report downplayed the significant of ethno-nationalist insurgents as a key agent in the violence, implying by this that state violence (such as extrajudicial killings) was a key driving force of the turbulence. Its self-appointed goal was to address what it described as "root causes", including matters of cultural identity and perceptions of injustice. The most publicized recommendations of the NRC included: designating the local Malay dialect as an additional working language for government offices in the south; introducing bilingual primary education in the border provinces, and setting up a regional development council and a policy coordination body with considerable popular input and with power to remove misbehaving officials. Though the latter recommendation suggested a revival of the defunct SBPAC, the level of popular input proposed for this agency was far more extensive than the bureaucrat-dominated SBPAC (both in its earlier and its post-coup incarnations). The short-term measures recommended by the NRC were particularly idealistic, notably the establishment of unarmed "peace units" to mediate disputes. Prior to the coup, nothing was done by the government to deliberate on the NRC's recommendations, which were presented in June. Whether or not Thaksin would have taken the NRC's recommendations on board if the coup had not been staged is a moot question. However, it is notable that open opposition to the NRC's recommendations, particularly the matter of language policy, was led not by Thaksin, but by the key palace-aligned figure of Prem Tinsulanonda. It was Prem who had warned the NRC chairman Anand Panyarachun not to formulate any recommendations that smacked of alternative governance models for the Muslim south. Given the ultimately conservative nature of the coup and its key supporters, it is therefore hardly surprising that the NRC's most distinctive recommendations were not implemented. On an ideological level, the solution to the southern violence would continue to be framed in terms of the King's moral triad of "Understanding, Reaching out, and Development."

The rhetoric informing the coup government's stated policy towards the south highlighted the imperative to affirm the state's goodwill towards the people of the south as equal (though different) citizens of Thailand. Much of this reflected earlier pronouncements of good intentions proclaimed during the Thaksin years, though it was now infused with a more thoroughgoing peacemaking jargon. Military-led security operations also reflected much the same as earlier, such as to identify insurgents, dismantle their networks, and protect officials and innocent civilians. To be sure, these efforts would become better coordinated (and funded) than earlier, but to ignore their pre-coup beginnings would be to overstate the differences between coup and post-coup periods.

The Post-Coup Conciliatory State Text: Defining Problems and Solutions

Surayud's government from late 2006 generated an official text of the southern problem and solutions aimed at re-establishing state legitimacy. Elements of this text drew on a previous oppositional discourse among peacemaking advocates during the Thaksin administration (who dominated the NRC and shaped its recommendations).[27] The conciliatory state text was embodied in Surayud's Prime Minister's Office Order 206, of October 2006. This pronouncement located the origins of the southern turbulence in the manipulation of ethnic and religious identity by ill-intentioned groups, insensitive and unjust treatment of local people by officials, as well as deficits in education and development. Solutions were proclaimed in categorical affirmations of "justice", "participation", "peace", and "peaceful means". Policy based on these normative imperatives was designed to reaffirm a nation where all citizens were "Thais" regardless of their ethno-linguistic differences; a nation that embraced the ideals of harmonious coexistence among people united by common birthplace, committed to equal rights, and united by a shared loyalty to and veneration of the King. Like the key pronouncements of the Thaksin administration, Prime Minister's Office Order 206 declared a commitment to follow the King's royal injunction to enact policy through "Understanding", "Reaching out", and "Development", with the addition of a commitment to the royal formula of the "Sufficiency Economy".[28] All governments after the Surayud administration have maintained this official text. Conscious of the impact of the controversial military suppression of insurgents at Pattani's Krue Se Mosque in April 2004 and the highly publicized Tak Bai events of that October, Surayud signalled a new start in the state's "reconciliation" effort by publicly apologizing to the borderland Muslims in November 2006. As goodwill gestures, cases were dismissed against those still incarcerated following their arrests in the Tak Bai protest of 2004, and a "blacklist" of some local Islamic leaders and separatist suspects was reportedly expunged.

The Post-Coup Security Structure

Prime Minister's Office Order 206 set the policy framework for Order 207, which established a new army-based ISOC Region 4 Forward Command (CPMC) and re-established the civilian-bureaucrat Southern Border Provinces Administrative Centre (SBPAC). Both were under the umbrella of a so-called Civilian-Police-Military Command (which had been dissolved by the Thaksin administration in 2002). The CPMC was intended to function as a coordinating body, with its own intelligence gathering unit, though it was effectively controlled by the military (its directors were army generals).[29] The police were now subordinate to the army.

Prime Minister's Office Orders 206 and 207 established the organizational framework and direction for policies that have remained largely in place until today, despite the Democrat Party's change in the balance of civilian-military oversight following the establishment of the SBPAC under its own legislation in late 2010. This framework was an effort to meet both the short and longer term challenge of simultaneously ensuring physical security to officials and ordinary civilians and winning hearts and minds to generate goodwill for cooperation in reducing militant groups' freedom of action. Though the Order apparently mandated a division of labour between the SBPAC (focusing on development) and the army-based ISOC Region 4 Forward Command (dealing with security), the army dealt as much with development projects and public relations as it did with security and military interdiction. Though staffed and headed by bureaucrats (with a staff of around 300), the new SBPAC differed from its predecessor by being subordinated to the security apparatus of ISOC Region 4, which authorized its budget. This soon generated complaints from SBPAC officials.

Security Operations after the Coup: Separating the Fish from the Water

The 2006 coup enabled the military to reclaim its dominance over southern operations and the police, which it had lost in 2002 after Thaksin restructured security responsibilities in the south. The army could now no longer use "lack of unity" or "interference" from politicians as reasons for lack of performance. Also, considerably more budget resources were forthcoming. Under Sonthi, troop numbers in the south increased, from around 20,000 to 30,000 (including regular troops and volunteer rangers).

The primary challenge was to reduce violent events, provide security for officials and the population at large, and make inroads into insurgent networks. Army Commander General Sonthi was an advocate of the Cold War counter-insurgency doctrine of "separating the fish from the water" by winning the hearts and minds of ordinary people so they would side with the state and shun insurgents. This task immediately gave the military a claim on development projects, with the aim of refashioning its public persona as the people's "protector" so as to undermine insurgent propaganda that the Thai military was the enemy of local Muslims.

Winning hearts and minds remained a tough challenge because troops were simultaneously undertaking cordon-sweep operations and rounding up insurgent suspects under Sonthi's "Operation Defend the Southern Border", launched in the second half of 2007. This major operation was approved by the Surayud government in early 2007, with the aim of dramatically reducing the southern violence by the end of the year, when the interim government was due to step down prior to elections under a new constitution. In October of that year, General Anupong Paochinda assumed command of the army. He refined Sonthi's operational plan: he increased checkpoints to limit insurgent mobility and moved small "peace-and-development" troop units into insurgent-influenced villages to enhance relations with the populace and gather intelligence. He devised an operational strategy with a phased timetable and targets. The aim was to end the turbulence within four years (by 2011), with the first main stage "to control the area and end daily killings" by late 2009.[30] By 2009, though total violent events in the borderland had dropped to 1,464 (from a high of 2,766 in 2007),[31] the military could hardly claim to have achieved its operational goal.

Notwithstanding the army command's stated "hearts and minds" ideals, incidents involving breaches of human rights (both real and rumoured) compromised the public relations goals of the military in the south. Human rights groups kept up a continued barrage of complaints against security officials' practice of summary questioning under martial law and the apparent immunity accorded to officials by the Emergency Decree of 2005.

After the coup, during General Sonthi's remaining tenure as army commander, (September 2006 to October 2007) violent events and killings in the south increased (respectively, from 2,194 to 2,766, and 760 to 1,118) and criticisms of the army for "catching goats" (apprehending innocent people) in its efforts to locate insurgents were frequent. Though Sonthi had spoken softly in public, he carried a big stick against insurgents. Regardless of his Muslim background, Sonthi was frequently denounced as an arch-enemy in insurgent leaflets during 2006–07. Under Sonthi and his successor General Anupong Paochinda (2007–10) the army made great efforts to affirm that they acted to uphold the law and protect citizens. Nonetheless, it is hard to find a difference between the critiques of security forces before and after the coup, despite the documented fact that violent events and casualties dropped by about 30 per cent by 2008. There was now no chance to pass the buck to politicians, or to Thaksin, as the cause of security officers' mistakes. To be sure, the striking blunders of the Thaksin years were avoided, but in the years following the 2006 coup there was no shortage of controversy facing the military regarding cases of torture (the case of the death-in-custody of Imam Yapa Kaseng, for example) or other problematic events (the mass shooting of worshippers at the Al Fuqan mosque in Cho-Airong, Narathiwat).[32]

THE ARMY AND THE DEMOCRATS

In late 2008 the Democrat Party assumed government following the collapse of Thailand's pro-Thaksin administration at the behest of powerful state and non-state actors and with the collusion of the army. As such, the Democrat-led coalition government and its policies may be deemed an "effect" (albeit unexpected) of the 2006 coup. Much of its time in government over the years 2009–10 was spent trying to ward off the assaults of an increasingly strident pro-Thaksin movement (the red shirts). A popular argument to explain the persistence of the violence over this period of profound national conflict has been that governments have been "distracted" from attending fully to the southern crisis.[33] This would appear to be fallacious and simplistic. After all, the most significant fall in the number of violent events (presumably reflecting effectiveness of security forces) had occurred during 2008, when the Samak Sundaravej and Somchai Wongsawat governments were battling the People's Alliance for Democracy (the "yellow shirts") and apparently "distracted". The budgets, policy, and personnel for the south were minimally affected by the national turmoil. At this time the military in the south was still following the operational guidelines set by General Anupong, who visited his regional commanders regularly.

If measured by the continuing impact of insurgent-driven and other violence in the south over its period in government (despite a slight decline in violent events and in the body count of casualties, both civilians and officials), the Democrats must be deemed to have done no better in their efforts to manage the southern turbulence than their pro-Thaksin predecessor administrations. In their diagnosis of the southern turbulence, the Democrats under Abhisit echoed previous administrations going all the way back to Thaksin in proposing solutions to the "problem" of the south in terms of "development". Abhisit's equally important stress on the rule of law and the uniform application of justice followed previous governments since 2006. In January, Suthep Thaugsuban, Democrat power broker and deputy prime minister for security affairs emphasized that the government was following two parallel approaches: protecting the security of people and restricting the attacks of insurgents, together with developing the region. He predicted that "the sound of guns will gradually reduce before the end of 2553 (2010)".[34]

At the same time as making the above statement, Suthep announced a "special panel of ministers for the far South". The foundation of this panel was accompanied by the usual Democrat Party self-promotion as the party that "knew the south".[35] But the subcommittee of cabinet turned out to be far more prosaic than the press reports implied, being a body dealing with the "special development zone of five southern provinces". The same idea of a special economic zone had been floated three years earlier by the Surayud government and the task of producing specific plans was passed to the National Economic and Social Development Board, where it languished.[36] It was revived in early 2008 under Prime Minister Samak, who chaired a committee with an identical name and purpose, but little happened.[37] The main role of the Democrat's special cabinet committee was to devise investment projects. Why this "special economic zone" should comprise five, rather than the three provinces primarily affected by the turbulence, was not explained. At the end of May, the Democrat-led government announced that its cabinet subcommittee was planning to channel 63 billion baht over three years into the five provinces as part of its *Thai Khem Khaeng* (Strength to Strength) programme, drawn from budget allocations and overseas loans.[38]

The Democrat's flagship measure for the south, as announced in its formal policy statement, was to convert the SBPAC into an independent, legislatively based agency, to allegedly bring about "unity" in policy delivery "to solve the problem of the south".[39] The SBPAC bureaucrats had complained about having their budget yoked to the army under the terms of Prime Minister's Office Order 207. Furthermore, the director of the SBPAC did not have the same powers as its earlier incarnation, in that he did not have formal authorizing power over projects directed through province governors, as before.[40] Legislation creating the SBPAC as an independent agency, free of policy and budget dependence on the army under ISOC, was finally passed late in 2010. The new SBPAC's jurisdiction covered five provinces of the south, not just the three provinces affected by the violence. During 2010, local community and business elites in the border provinces had opposed the five-province model, claiming that groups not affected by the violence would reap economic benefits. However, the key reason for the victory of the five-province model for the SBPAC was the fear among conservative groups (including the Democrat Party) that a three province jurisdiction would make the SBPAC vulnerable to a future takeover by separatist sympathizers, by providing an administrative core for a separate state. The two additional provinces of Satun and Songkhla (in the original SBPAC's jurisdiction) were essential buffers against this possibility (the former is a Thai-speaking Muslim province with no recent history of insurgency, and the latter is a large Thai Buddhist majority province).

Democrat politicians paraded their policy for the SBPAC under the evocative but ambiguous rubric of *Kanmueang Nam Kanthahan*. It was a clear effort at rhetorical entrepreneurship. The expression was not original, but had been purloined from the name of a well-established Thai military doctrine coined during the Cold War to affirm the importance of civil operations in combating communist insurgents. Military officers were unhappy with these developments, but they did not openly criticize the government.

It was clear that the Democrats were using their slogan to signal a shift in responsibility for southern policy away from the military to civilian administrators and, literally, to civilian government. This was certainly how it was understood by press commentators and concerned newspaper readers.[41] The question was, however, just how far the Democrats were prepared to follow through on their rhetoric, given that the party was beholden to military support for attaining and retaining government after the collapse of the Somchai administration. The Democrat's slogan had the effect of promoting a flurry of debate and discussion among academics and southern watchdog groups because it seemed to validate their existing criticisms of the military's hold on the lion's share of budget resources for the south. Military control of the bulk of budget resources for the south had attracted concerns over corruption and vested interests soon after ISOC took control over southern security and development operations. This suspicion persisted. To this were added observations on high military expenditure, which contrasted with its apparent failure to further reduce the number of violent events occurring in the borderland.[42] For its part, the military actively advertised the apparent achievements of its development projects in the south.

Though the Democrat-led government was dependent on the military both for its genesis and its survival against the Red Shirt movements assaults in 2009 and 2010, it distanced itself from the army when the latter came in for public criticism on a number of controversial matters, notably the issue of the ineffectiveness of the army's CT 200 bomb scanners. Over the period 2008–11, the army attracted the bulk of criticism for shortcomings in the south. The Democrat leadership was happy to offload the blame to the army, as evidenced in the matter of an embarrassing raid on an army base in Narathiwat in January 2011, which came only a few days after Prime Minister Abhisit had proclaimed the lifting of the Emergency Decree in the first district of the three provinces — this was staged to highlight the achievements of the government in peace-building. Unfortunately for Abhisit, this self-congratulatory official ceremony was a prelude to an upturn in insurgent attacks and the killing of school teachers.

At various times Abhisit had hinted to the press that his government might consider some special administrative status for the border provinces,[43] but in late October 2009 he opposed the idea when pressured by journalists after the visiting Malaysian prime minister, Najib Razak had made comments on "autonomy" in interviews.[44] This did not end the pressure on the issue of a possible "political solution" to the southern strife. In early November, Chavalit, now a member of the opposition Pheu Thai Party, visited the three provinces to propose a form of local self-government under the constitution, based on the city administrations of Pattaya and Bangkok. He labelled this proposal *Nakhon Pattani* (Pattani City). Abhisit disapproved of Chavalit's idea, and other Democrats derided it as a political stunt of the Pheu Thai Party, which was riding the tide of the pro-Thaksin red-shirt movement against the government. Though Chavalit's idea was well received in Pattani, critics warned that it was tantamount to a first step to independence for the border provinces.[45] Despite high-flown rhetoric about "politics leading the military", the Democrats revealed the limits of their definition by affirming that their model of the bureaucrat-run five-province SBPAC was the best available for the southern provinces, and that elective local government (sub-district and province councils) was already in place, as elsewhere in the country. The Democrats under Abhisit reaffirmed "justice" and "development" as the twin answers to southern unrest.[46]

The Democrat-led government came to power with a fanfare of self-promotion, claiming that it was dedicated to tackling the southern "problem" with the borrowed slogan of "Politics Leading the Military". Yet this government found itself facing the same intractable obstacles that confronted previous administrations, with an ever-bubbling violence that undermined its claims of steady progress. Throughout the year, when the Democrats were pressured with charges of lack of progress — as they were in no-confidence debates by the Pheu Thai Party opposition — a standard polemical fall-back defence was to blame the previous Thaksin administration for generating the violence. But the press did not fall for this deflection. Though constrained by the government in reporting on the red shirts during 2009–10 (both by their own superiors and by government pressure), media reporters vigorously covered the southern violence, and press opinion pieces blatantly critiqued government shortcomings.

CONCLUSION: AN ENDLESS WAR, THE COUP AS A "NON-EVENT"?

How much difference did Thailand's 2006 coup make to the situation in Thailand's south? In relation to policy, it ushered in a more emollient and politically correct state rhetoric than the Thaksin period, though the similarities between the key policy principles enunciated in the proclamations of pre- and post-coup administrations are as striking as the apparent differences. Did the coup-appointed government make any difference? Measured by the conditions on the ground, Surayud's government failed miserably during the sixteen-month term of its administration, when violence and deaths in the border provinces rose to an all time peak. Critics judged this failure to reduce violence in the south to be just one of the coup makers' many shortcomings.[47] Did the coup allow military specialists to "get on with the job", free of political interference, and devise workable measures to diminish the potency of insurgent networks? As argued, given the trends in train before the coup to vest authority in General Sonthi and the military, it is likely that something akin to the ISOC Region 4 Forward Command arrangement would have been put in place anyway. Indeed it is worth noting that the ISOC configuration that was mandated in Surayud's Prime Minister's Office Order 207 was simply an adjustment to the existing SBPPC anyway, and many of its leading military personnel simply changed titles (though not offices, since the new ISOC Region 4 was located in the same building in the Sirinthorn army base camp that housed the former SBPPC). The continued cries to "integrate" official efforts (*buranakan*) have always been a symptom of generic competition within the bureaucracy and a justification for rearranging administrative turf in a conflict-ridden state apparatus. The restoration of the SBPAC might be seen as a restoration of administrative territory to dissatisfied civilian bureaucrats. Security measures put in place in the south in 2007 had the effect of reducing insurgent violence, though not controlling it. By 2011, security forces were essentially maintaining a holding operation against a resilient core of insurgents. Civilian officials (particularly teachers) and ordinary villagers are still vulnerable. In short, the south is still an insecure place.

Seven years following the ousting of Thaksin by military coup, the "Southern Fire" continues to bedevil the country, its governments and security forces. If the south represented Thaksin's "Achilles' heel" — a problem he could never solve — then for the subsequent national administrations since Thaksin's political demise it might well be called the millstone around their necks.

Notes

1. See, for example, John Funston, *Southern Thailand: The Dynamics of Conflict* (Washington D.C. and Singapore: East-West Center and Institute of Southeast Asian Studies, 2008), pp. 23–24.

2. Ukrist Pathmanand, "Thaksin's Achilles' Heel: The Failure of Hawkish Approaches in the Thai South.", in *Rethinking Thailand's Southern Violence*, edited by Duncan McCargo (Singapore: National University of Singapore Press, 2007), pp. 69–71.

3. See Churairat Saenchairat, ed., *Chamlae Thaksimomik* [Dissecting Thaksinomics] (Bangkok: Witthithat Foundation, 2004).

4. See Kasian Tejapira, "Toppling Thaksin", *New Left Review* 39 (May–June 2006), pp. 30–31.

5. See Marc Askew, *Conspiracy, Politics and a Disorderly Border: The Struggle to Comprehend Insurgency in Thailand's Deep South* (Washington D.C. and Singapore: East-West Center and Institute of Southeast Asian Studies, 2007).

6. Anthony Davis, "Thailand's Southern Predicament", *Jane's Islamic Affairs Analyst*, 1 April 2004, and "Unrest in the South: Outrage over Claims of Torture", *The Nation*, 5 March 2004.

7. Yuwadee Tunyasiri and Sermsuk Kasitipradit, "Chettha Taking over Security: Forward Command Scrapped in Revamp", *Bangkok Post*, 1 May 2004.

8. See "Hamstrung by the Politicians", *The Nation*, 2 September 2006.

9. See Ora-orn Poocharoen, "The Bureaucracy: Problem or Solution to Thailand's Far South flames?", *Contemporary Southeast Asia* 32, no. 2 (2010): 186–93.

10. Ibid. See also "Pert Wiwatthanakan Ongkon Dap Fai Tai — Chak Sor Or Bor Tor Theung Ko Or Sor Sor Sor Ko Or Ro Mor Nor Laew Cha Pai Thang Nnai?" [Revealing the Development of Organizations to Quench the Southern Fire — From SBPAC to SBPPC to ISOC, Then to Where?], *Issara News Centre*, 24 November 2009 <http://www.isranews.org/south-news/scoop/item/1601-2009-11-24-07-33-52.html> (accessed 2 May 2012).

11. Bunkrom Donbangsattan, *Kandorsu Khrang Sut Thai khong Phon Ek Chavalit Yongchaiyudh* [The Last War of General Chavalit Yongchaiyudh] (Bangkok: Offset Press, 2005), pp. 193–94.

12. Prime Minister's Office Order 68/2547, "Nayobai Srang Santusuk Nai Pheunthi 3 Changwat Chaidaen Tai" [Policy for Building Peace in the Region of the Three Southern Border provinces], 4 May 2004, section 5.

13. "Government Told to Find Alternatives to Violence", *The Nation*, 2 May 2004.

14. See S.R. Leach and S. Davenport, "Strategic Ambiguity as a Discourse Practice: The Role of Keywords in the Discourse on Sustainable Biotechnology", *Discourse Studies* 9, no. 1 (2007): 43–61.

15. Prime Minister's Office Order 206/2547, Nayobai lae Neaothang Kanborihan-chatkan Pheu Serm Srang Santisuk nai Changwat Chaidaen Phak Tai [Policy and Directions for the organization of Peace-Building in the Southern Border Provinces], 5 October 2004.

16. Bunkrom, *Kandorsu Khrang Sut Thai*, pp. 193–95.

17. See Khubon Khanaiyao, opinion column untitled, ASTV Manager Online, 5 January 2005 <http://www.thaiday.com/Politics/viewnews.aspx?Newsid= 9480000001733> (accessed 2 May 2012).

18. See "Se Yak Chi Yuttasat Dap Fai Tai 'Khrai Khrongchai Muanchon Kheu Phu Channa'" [The Giant General Points to the Strategy to Quench the Southern Fire: "Whoever Controls the Hearts of the Masses is the Winner"], ASTV Manager Online, 10 March 2005 <http://www.manager.co.th/Politics/viewnews. aspx?Newsid=9480000034343> (accessed 2 May 2012).

19. "Thai Prime Minister Replaces Army Chief", *Voice of America*, 24 August 2004.

20. Ukrist, "Thaksin's Achilles Heel", p. 78.

21. "Sonthi's Meteoric Ascent to Power", *The Star Online*, 21 September 2006.

22. Prayuth Sivayaviroj, "Army Change Not a Problem", *The Nation*, 8 December 2005.

23. "Sonthi Calls for Talks", *The Nation*, 2 September 2006.

24. "Sonthi's Powers to be Beefed up", *Bangkok Post*, 7 September 2006.

25. Francesca Lawe-Davies, "Coups are Bad, but for Thailand, this Takeover may be Good", International Crisis Group, 28 September 2006 <http://www. crisisgroup.org/en/regions/asia/south-east-asia/thailand/coups-are-bad- but-for-thailand-this-takeover-may-be-good.aspx> (accessed 2 May 2012). This report was expanded, with similar conclusions, in a later report *Southern Thailand: The Impact of The Coup*, Asia Report No. 129 (15 March 2007).

26. Zachary Abuza, "Thailand's Coup and the Insurgency in the South", 20 September 2006 <http://counterterrorismblog.org/2006/09/thailands_ coup_and_the_insurge.php> (accessed 2 May 2012). Abuza produced a more expanded analysis two months later, for which see Zachary Abuza, "The Effects of Thailand's Coup on the Southern Insurgency", *Terrorism Monitor* 4, Issue 20 (20 October 2006) <http://www.jamestown.org/programs/gta/single/?Tx_ ttnews%5Btt_news%5D=940&tx_ttnews%5bbackpid%5D=181&no_cache=1> (accessed 2 May 2012).

27. For an expanded discussion of the emergence of this text and various oppositional texts, see Marc Askew, "Fighting with Ghosts: Querying Thailand's Southern Fire", *Contemporary Southeast Asia* 32, no. 2 (August 2010): 117–55.

28. Prime Minister's Office Order 206/2549, "Nayobai Serm Srang Santisuk Nai Peunthi Changwat Chaidaen Phak Tai" [Policy to Promote Peace in the Southern Border Provinces], 30 October 2006.

29. Prime Minister's Office Order 207/2549, "Kanborihan Ratchakan Nai Changwat Chaidaen Phak Tai" [Government Administration in the Southern Border Provinces], 30 October 2006.

30. "Neaothang Kanbatibat Yutthakan" [Guidelines for Operationalizing the Strategic Plan], Soon Patibatkan [Army Operations Centre] Memorandum, 30 November 2007.

31. These and subsequent figures referred to in the text are taken from *Khu Mue Sattiti Hetkan Lae Kansoonsia Nai 3 Chor Chor Tor Lae 4 Amphoe Khong Chor Sor Khor Tang Tae Mor Kho 47 – Mi 53* [Handbook of Events and Casualties in the 3 border provinces and 4 districts of Songkhla, from January 2004 to March 2010], ISOC Region 4 Forward Command, 2010.

32. See *Thailand: Torture in the Southern Counter-Insurgency* (ASA 39/001/2009) (London: Amnesty International, 2009).

33. See ICG (International Crisis Group), *Thailand: Political Turmoil and the Southern Insurgency*, Policy Briefing, Asia Briefing No. 80 (Brussels: International Crisis Group, 28 August 2008). Also Srisompob Jitpiromsri, "Updated Statistics: Thailand's Southern Violence from January 2004 through March 2009", Deep Southwatch Website, 20 April 2009 <http://www.deepsouthwatch.org/node/287> (accessed 2 May 2012).

34. Suthep Lan Korn Sin Pi 53 Siang Peun Tai Bao" [Suthep States that before the End of 2010 the Sound of Guns Will Lessen], *Matichon Raiwan*, 18 January 2009.

35. Anucha Charoenpo, "A New Government, a Fresh Effort to Restore Peace", *Bangkok Post*, 17 January 2009.

36. Don Pathan, "No Progress in Checking Unrest", *The Nation*, 29 December 2007.

37. "Military Will Lead Investment Bids to Spur Region's Economy", *Bangkok Post*, 22 March 2008.

38 "Government to Spend B63Bn to Develop Southern Region", *Bangkok Post*, 29 May 2009.

39. Council of Ministers, *Kham Thalaeng Nayobai khong Khanna Ratamontri* [Policy announcement of the Cabinet], 29 December 2008, p. 5

40. In 2008, the Democrats had called for a fully independent organization with its own legal mandate, since the current organization was authorized by decree only, and could be easily dissolved again (as it had been by Thaksin in 2002). Though mooted in the early months of the Samak administration, legislation for such an organization did not emerge.

41. See Burin Kantabutra, "Southern Peace a Civil Matter", Post Bag, *Bangkok Post*, 23 August 2009.

42. Mat Lek, "Arai Kheu Banha" [What is the Problem?], *Thai Rath*, 20 February 2009.

43. Wassana Nanuam and Waedao Harai, "PM Favours Admin Zone for South", *Bangkok Post*, 15 June 2009.

44. Suthichai Yoon, "What does Najib Razak Mean by 'Autonomy' for the South?", *The Nation*, 29 October 2009.

45. Aekarach Sattaburuth, Pradit Ruangdit and Muhammad Ayub Pathan, "Chavalit defends 'Pattani City' Proposal", *Bangkok Post*, 4 November 2010.

46. Achara Ashayagachat, "Government Defends its Performance", *Bangkok Post*, 30 November 2009.

47. Thitinan Pongsudhirak, "Thailand since the Coup", *Journal of Democracy* 19, No. 4 (October 2008), p. 145.

References

Abuza, Zachary. "Thailand's Coup and the Insurgency in the South". Counterterrorism blog, 20 September 2006 <http://counterterrorismblog.org/2006/09/thailands_coup_and_the_insurge.php (accessed 20 November 2007).

———. "The Effects of Thailand's Coup on the Southern Insurgency". *Terrorism Monitor* 4, Issue 20 (20 October 2006) <http://www.jamestown.org/programs/gta/single/?tx_ttnews%5Btt_news%5D=940&tx_ttnews%5BbackPid%5D=181&no_cache=1> (accessed 20 November 2007).

Achara Ashayagachat. "Government Defends its Performance". *Bangkok Post*, 30 November 2009.

Aekarach Sattaburuth, Pradit Ruangdit and Muhammad Ayub Pathan. "Chavalit Defends 'Pattani City' Proposal". *Bangkok Post*, 4 November 2010.

Amnesty International. *Thailand: Torture in the Southern Counter-Insurgency* (ASA 39/001/2009). London: Amnesty International, 2009.

Anucha Charoenpo. "A New Government, a Fresh Effort to Restore Peace". *Bangkok Post*, 17 January 2009.

Askew, Marc. *Conspiracy, Politics and a Disorderly Border: The Struggle to Comprehend Insurgency in Thailand's Deep South*. Washington D.C. and Singapore: East-West Center and Institute of Southeast Asian Studies, 2007.

———. "Fighting with Ghosts: Querying Thailand's 'Southern Fire'". *Contemporary Southeast Asia* 32, no. 2 (August 2010).

ASTV Manager Online. "Se Yak Chi Yuttasat Dap Fai Tai 'Khrai Khrongchai Muanchon Kheu Phu Channa'" [The Giant General points to the Strategy to Quench the Southern Fire: "Whoever controls the hearts of the masses is the winner"], 10 March 2005 <http://www.manager.co.th/Politics/ViewNews.aspx?NewsID=9480000034343> (accessed 30 August 2010).

Bangkok Post. "Sonthi's Powers to be Beefed up", 7 September 2006.

———. "Military Will Lead Investment Bids to Spur Region's Economy", 22 March 2008.

———. "Government to Spend B63Bn to Develop Southern Region", 29 May 2009.

Bunkrom Donbangsattan. *Kandorsu Khrang Sut Thai Khong Phon Ek Chavalit Yongchaiyudh* [The Last War of General Chavalit Yongchaiyudh]. Bangkok: Offset Press, 2005.

Burin Kantabutra. "Southern peace a civil matter". Post Bag, *Bangkok Post*, 23 August 2009.

Churairat Saenchairat, ed. *Chamlae Thaksimomik* [Dissecting Thaksinomics]. Bangkok: Witthithat Foundation, 2004.

Council of Ministers. "Kham Thalaeng Nayobai Khong Khana Ratamontri" [Policy Announcement of the Cabinet], 29 December 2008.

Davis, Anthony. "Thailand's Southern Predicament". *Jane's Islamic Affairs Analyst*, 1 April 2004.

Don Pathan. "No Progress in Checking Unrest". *The Nation*, 29 December 2007.

Funston, John. *Southern Thailand: The Dynamics of Conflict*. Washington, D.C. and Singapore: East-West Centre and Institute of Southeast Asian Studies, 2008.

ICG (International Crisis Group). *Southern Thailand: The Impact of the Coup*. Asia Report No. 129. Jakarta/Brussels: International Crisis Group, 15 March 2007.

———. *Thailand: Political Turmoil and the Southern Insurgency*. Policy Briefing. Asia Briefing No. 80. Brussels: International Crisis Group, 28 August 2008.

Issara News Centre. *"Pert Wiwatthanakan Ongkon Dap Fai Tai — Chak Sor Or Bor Tor Theung Ko Or Sor Sor Sor Ko Or Ro Mor Nor Laew Cha Pai Thang Nai?"* [Revealing the Development of Organizations to Quench the Southern Fire — From SBPAC to SBPPC to ISOC, Then to Where?], 24 November 2009 <http://www.isranews.org/south-news/scoop/item/1601-2009-11-24-07-33-52.html> (accessed 30 August 2010).

Kasian Tejapira. "Toppling Thaksin". *New Left Review* 39 (May–June 2006).

Khu Mue Sattiti Hetkan lae Kansoonsia Nai 3 Chor Chor Tor Lae 4 Amphoe Khong Chor Sor Khor Tang Tae Mor Kho 47 – Mi 53 [Handbook of Events and Casualties in the 3 border provinces and 4 districts of Songkhla, from January 2004 to March 2010]. ISOC Region 4 Forward Command 2010.

Khubon Khanaiyao. *ASTV Manager Online*, 5 January 2005 <http://www.thaiday.com/Politics/ViewNews.aspx?NewsID=9480000001733> (accessed 13 September 2007).

Lawe-Davies, Francesca. "Coups are Bad, but for Thailand, this Takeover may be Good". International Crisis Group, 28 September 2006 <http://www.crisisgroup.org/en/regions/asia/south-east-asia/thailand/coups-are-bad-but-for-thailand-this-takeover-may-be-good.aspx> (accessed 12 October 2006).

Leach S.R. and S. Davenport. "Strategic Ambiguity as a Discourse Practice: The Role of Keywords in the Discourse on 'Sustainable' Biotechnology". *Discourse Studies* 9, no. 1. (2007).

Mat Lek. "Arai Kheu Banha" [What is the Problem?]. *Thai Rath*, 20 February 2009.

Matichon Raiwan. "Suthep Lan Korn Sin Pi '53 Siang Peun Tai Bao" [Suthep States that before the End of 2010 the Sound of Guns will Lessen], 18 January 2009.

Nation, The. "Unrest in the South: Outrage over Claims of Torture", 5 March 2004.

———. "Government Told to Find Alternatives to Violence", 2 May 2004.

———. "Hamstrung by the Politicians", 2 September 2006.

————. "Sonthi Calls for Talks", 2 September 2006.

"Neaothang Kanbatibat Yutthakan" [Guidelines for Operationalizing the Strategic Plan]. Soon Patibatkan [Army Operations Centre] Memorandum, 30 November 2007.

Ora-orn Poocharoen. "The Bureaucracy: Problem or Solution to Thailand's Far South flames?". *Contemporary Southeast Asia* 32, no. 2 (August 2010).

Prayuth Sivayaviroj. "Army Change Not a Problem". *The Nation*, 8 December 2005.

Prime Minister's Office Order 68/2547. "Nayobai Srang Santusuk nai pheunthi 3 Changwat Chaidaen Tai" [Policy for Building Peace in the Region of the Three Southern Border provinces], 4 May 2004.

Prime Minister's Office Order 206/2547. "Nayobai lae Neaothang Kanborihanchatkan Pheu Serm Srang Santisuk nai Changwat Chaidaen Phak Tai" [Policy and Directions for the Organization of Peace-Building in the Southern Border Provinces], 5 October 2004.

Prime Minister's Office Order 206/2549. "Nayobai Serm Srang Santisuk Nai Pheunthi Changwat Chaidaen Phak Tai" [Policy to promote peace in the southern border provinces], 30 October 2006.

Prime Minister's Office Order 207/2549. "Kanborihan Ratchakan Nai Changwat Chaidaen Phak Tai" [Government administration in the southern border provinces], 30 October 2006.

Srisompob Jitpiromsri. "Updated Statistics: Thailand's Southern Violence from January 2004 through March 2009". *DeepSouthWatch*, 20 April 2009 <http://www.deepsouthwatch.org/node/287> (accessed 15 May 2009).

Star Online. "Sonthi's Meteoric Ascent to Power", 21 September 2006 <http://thestar.com.my/news/story.asp?file=/2006/9/21/asia/15494090&sec=asia> (accessed 12 October 2006).

Suthichai Yoon. "What does Najib Razak Mean by 'Autonomy' for the South?". *The Nation*, 29 October 2009.

Thitinan Pongsudhirak. "Thailand since the Coup". *Journal of Democracy* 19, no. 4 (October 2008).

Ukrist Pathmanand, "Thaksin's Achilles' Heel: The Failure of Hawkish approaches in the Thai South". In *Rethinking Thailand's Southern Violence*, edited by Duncan McCargo Singapore: National University of Singapore Press, 2007.

Voice of America. "Thai Prime Minister Replaces Army Chief", 24 August 2004 <http://www.voanews.com/english/news/a-13-a-2004-08-24-19-1-66357167.html> (accessed 12 October 2006).

Wassana Nanuam and Waedao Harai. "PM Favours Admin Zone for South". *Bangkok Post*, 15 June 2009.

Yuwadee Tunyasiri and Sermsuk Kasitipradit. "Chettha Taking over Security: Forward Command Scrapped in Revamp". *Bangkok Post*, 1 May 2004.

10

FROM MARKETPLACE BACK TO BATTLEFIELD
Thai-Cambodian Relations in the Age of a Militarized Politics

Pavin Chachavalpongpun

The military coup of 2006 that deposed the elected government of Prime Minister Thaksin Shinawatra led to an increasing militarization of Thai politics. This latest political intervention unveiled the calculated strategy of the military. Not only did the coup serve to eliminate the traditional elite's enemy, in this case Thaksin, but it also opened the door for the military to reclaim its control over politics, and consequently, foreign policy. The role of the military in foreign affairs was immense during the Cold War period. The threat of communism in this part of the world allowed the military to entrench its position in the name of defending national security, with the support from the United States, both in ideological and financial terms.[1] But this role was challenged when Thaksin became prime minister in 2001. Throughout the Thaksin administration (2001–06), Thaksin intruded in the military's affairs, diminishing its influence in domestic politics and foreign policy making. Daringly, Thaksin attempted to fragment the army so as to prevent a possible coup. But Thaksin eventually failed. For the military, the only way to regain its political power was to stage a coup against Thaksin. The political turmoil that followed in the post-coup years, in turn, legitimized the military's political position. The military firmly took charge of the uncertain political situation, particularly in dealing with security issues, such as endless street protests and occasional violent confrontations with certain political factions.

In 2008, the pro-Thaksin regime of Samak Sundaravej returned to power through the first election after the coup. The election victory of the People's Power Party (PPP), a reincarnation of Thaksin's disbanded Thai Rak Thai Party (TRT), was a slap in the face for the military elite who were certain that the coup was an effective measure in deracinating Thaksin's political legacy. To destabilize the Samak government, the yellow-shirt People's Alliance for Democracy (PAD) took to the streets of Bangkok, politicizing the issue of Preah Vihear, known in Thai as Khao Phra Wihan. The PAD's protests were launched in retaliation against the Thai government's support for Cambodia in having Preah Vihear listed as a United Nations Educational, Scientific and Cultural Organisation (UNESCO) World Heritage Site. The PAD accused the Samak government, in particular Foreign Minister Noppadon Pattama, previously serving as Thaksin's personal lawyer, for selling the motherland, or *khai chat*, in exchange for certain personal interests of Thaksin.[2] The PAD started an ultranationalist bandwagon rolling, and the military immediately saw the profit in supporting the PAD in exploiting the Preah Vihear issue to discredit the pro-Thaksin government. In this process, the military created insecurity and instability along the Thai-Cambodian border to justify its responsibility as defender of national security, thus guaranteeing its position in politics.[3] In other words, the military turned the "marketplace of Cambodia back into a battlefield". It refused to abandon its aggressive approach towards Cambodia even when Thailand embraced a new pro-elite government under Prime Minister Abhisit Vejjajiva (2008–11). Declaring war with Cambodia became an important component of Thailand's continued militarized politics, a significant trend since the 2006 military coup. It was true that the PAD played a key role in politicizing the issue of the Preah Vihear, but the Thai military was responsible for a series of armed clashes between Thailand and Cambodia. This demonstrated that the PAD worked intimately with the military. But while they shared the same objective of undermining the Samak regime, the military was particularly keen to engage into conflict with Cambodia so as to conserve its position in politics.

The phrase "transforming the battlefield into a marketplace" was first coined during the Chatichai Choonhavan administration (1988–91) in reference to the new foreign policy of Thailand towards Indochina at the looming end of the conflict in Cambodia.[4] Prime Minister Chatichai was eager to shift the Thai position vis-à-vis its neighbouring countries due to two main reasons. First, the regional and international environment was changing, with the Cold War coming to an end and the communist threat dwindling, thus heralding a new era of Thai diplomacy. Second, Thai domestic politics also underwent a drastic change, with Chatichai representing the first elected civilian prime minister since 1976, which symbolized a major step towards democratization. He set up an iconoclastic team of advisers, a combination of academics, technocrats and businessmen, to implement a mercantile foreign policy; this practically reduced the role of the military in foreign affairs. And like Thaksin, Chatichai's move was perceived as a serious menace to the military. He was ousted in a military coup in 1991. Two decades later, the military successfully reversed the Cambodian marketplace for Thai businesses back to a battlefield for Thai generals.[5]

This chapter argues that the 2006 coup created a condition favourable for the military to reinstate the old security-centric foreign policy even when it devastatingly damaged Thai relations with Cambodia. The military realized the need to take back its traditional role of foreign policy making which had been, for a brief period, under the civilian control of Thaksin. As part of the plot, the Thai army relied on its allies in politics to provoke both the Thai nationalists at home and the supposed Cambodian enemies across the border to justify the necessity of armed conflict. The military finally fulfilled its objective; Thailand and Cambodia engaged in a series of armed clashes over the 2008–11 period. The chapter discusses the Thai conflict with Cambodia over Preah Vihear and the ongoing territorial dispute between the two countries as a result of a return of militarized politics in Thailand. It also examines the military's discursive concept of national security, particularly in regards to the transformation of a marketplace policy back to a battlefield. In the final section, it briefly explores the impact of a militarized politics on the Thai view of the Association of Southeast Asian Nations (ASEAN) which, under the leadership of Indonesia as the ASEAN chair for 2011, tried desperately to save the organization's reputation and credibility in its ability to solve interstate disputes peacefully through existing mechanisms.

FACES OF CAMBODIA

Cambodia has long been involved in Thai domestic and international politics, playing different roles over different periods in the two countries' history.[6] In recent memory, following the invasion of Cambodia by the Vietnamese troops in 1978, Thailand was aware of the possibility of becoming the last domino in mainland Southeast Asia. The external environment provided a long-lasting role for the military in overseeing the Thai-Cambodian ties. Thailand went ahead with establishing its diplomatic relations with China, a communist state, in 1975. It hoped that the détente with China and the support given to the Khmer Rouge would contain the advancement of communist Vietnam in the region.[7] The Khmer Rouge survived their expulsion from Cambodia thanks to a steady supply of arms from Vietnam's traditional enemy, China, delivered to the Khmer Rouge by the Thai forces who wanted a buffer against the Vietnamese.[8] In the context of ASEAN, Thailand exploited its position as a frontline state vis-à-vis the communist threat while successfully "Aseanizing" its anti-Vietnam policy. The threat of communism in the neighbourhood offered an excellent opportunity for the military to emphasize its self-important duty as the defender of national security. Because of the nature of international politics at the time, the military was able to dominate the foreign policy making process while portraying itself as the leading state agency in managing different kinds of external threats. Meanwhile, the Foreign Ministry and the National Security Council (NSC) were assigned a supporting role as Thailand interacted with Cambodia throughout the Cold War period. Hence, turning Cambodia into a battlefield and preserving this status served the many purposes of the Thai military, both in boosting its stance in domestic politics and its dominance in foreign affairs.

Since most external threats derived from the immediate neighbours of Thailand, the military became overwhelmingly protective of its foreign policy turf particularly in regards to border affairs. Therefore, Cambodia did not represent the only "battlefield" for the Thai army. Myanmar and Laos, and to a lesser extent Malaysia, were also remade into other battlefields which helped sustain the military's political role.[9] From the ethnic insurgencies, narcotics trade, arms and human trafficking to flows of refugees, these threats were never seriously eradicated, possibly as part of nurturing instability along the borders so as to legitimize the military's influence in border policy. It was known that for decades the Thai military forged close ties with different ethnic insurgents along the Thai-Myanmar border. On the surface, the so-called "buffer policy" was designed to be a bulwark against possible intrusions by the Myanmar army into Thailand.[10] At a deeper level, the Thai military supplied arms to the insurgents and gave shelter to some of the ethnic leaders; this helped prolong the inimical stance, or even war, between ethnic groups and the Myanmar government. The distortion of history and the misuse of nationalism, at the same time, allowed the Thai military to conserve a sense of mutual mistrust and suspicion between Thailand and these bordering neighbours, including Cambodia.[11] The need to turn Cambodia into a battlefield further deteriorated Thai-Cambodian relations. There were many occasions in the past when the two countries froze their diplomatic relationship, primarily due to such persistent mutual suspicion.

When Thaksin came to power in 2011, he came with Chatichai's foreign policy vision of turning enemy lands into marketplaces. He, accordingly, tailored the country's foreign policy based on his business experience. Thaksin empowered Thai ambassadors with the title of Chief Executive Officer (CEO), who not only worked to promote the good ties between Thailand and foreign countries, but also to serve as salesmen. A business-oriented policy seemed to appropriately respond to shifting domestic and international circumstances. Domestically, Thaksin won two landslide elections, thus becoming the first Thai prime minister to see out a full four-year term. Undeniably, he received a huge popular mandate. His newfound confidence induced him to revamp the old system, long under control of the bureaucratic elite. Reducing the influence of the military in foreign affairs was one of Thaksin's top priorities; and the policy of marketplace was deemed a perfect and legitimate solution. Thaksin was an ambitious leader; so he produced ambitious foreign policies. He initiated the Asia-Dialogue Cooperation (ACD), an Asia-wide cooperative framework that connected, for the first time, all regions of Asia. Closer to home, Thaksin successfully formulated a policy of cultivating economic prosperity, or "prosper thy neighbour", in neighbouring countries, through the framework of Ayeyawady–Chao Phraya–Mekong Economic Cooperation Strategy (ACMECS).[12] ACMECS was Thaksin's foreign policy trademark designed to enhance cooperation among countries in mainland Southeast Asia, including Thailand, Cambodia, Laos, Myanmar and Vietnam. But while the objective was to encourage cooperation, particularly in the economic and cultural fields, the real emphasis for Thailand was to place itself at the region's core. In other words, Thaksin was hoping to recreate Thailand as a dominant power in the region, or in his own terms — in the *suvarnabhumi* region, particularly over its less developed neighbouring states.[13] In this latest reinvention, Cambodia characterized a new destination for Thai businesses. And the battlefield in this country vanished.

MILITARIZATION OF POLITICS

After the coup of 2006, the presence of the military in politics was prominent. Even prior to the eruption of the Thai-Cambodian conflict over the Preah Vihear Temple in 2008, Thai foreign policy decision-making returned under the firm grip of the military, during the Surayud Chulanont government (2006–08). There were attempts to delegitimize Thaksin's mercantile policy, for example, in tightening up business regulations by amending the Foreign Business Act (FBA) 1999 — a crude response to Thaksin's sale of his Shin Corporation to Singapore's Temasek Holdings without paying tax. Thaksin was condemned for taking advantage of the loopholes in the FBA.[14] Surayud, a former general, was appointed to the premiership by the coup-makers. He was also Thaksin's adversary. Back in September 2001, Thaksin, as Prime Minister, transferred then army chief Surayud to the ceremonial post of Supreme Commander.[15] Surayud was a royalist and a close aide of General Prem Tinsulanonda, former Prime Minister and President of the Privy Council. Duncan McCargo argues that Prem is the epitome of the so-called "network monarchy", the most important political network in Thailand from 1973 to 2001.[16] One of the main tasks for Prem has been to ensure that key positions in the military and the bureaucracy are occupied by the royalist elite, and that domestic and foreign policies are to be implemented to benefit the network monarchy. Accordingly, Surayud went ahead with downplaying the policy of promoting marketplaces in the neighbourhood. He decisively overlooked ACMECS and exhibited his lack of keenness for the free trade agreements (FTAs) which were much celebrated during the Thaksin era. A new kind of diplomacy *à la* Surayud was then revealed; it was called "ethical diplomacy".[17] The core content of the ethical diplomacy was fundamentally to blaspheme Thaksin's commerce-driven foreign policy and at the same time to glorify the King's philosophy of a sufficiency economy — a supposed antithesis of Thaksin's consumerism encapsulated within the marketplace policy.

When the pro-Thaksin Samak regime succeeded the Surayud government through democratic means, the military was anxious that its position in domestic and foreign policies was in serious jeopardy. Samak quickly reversed the ethical foreign policy back to the commerce-oriented approach in dealing with foreign countries. Crucially, Samak chose to visit Cambodia from 3 to 4 March 2008 as the first country for his introductory tour. But Samak's overt enthusiasm about strengthening ties with Cambodia was ill-received by his political opponents. His visit to Phnom Penh was widely publicized by the PAD as a preparation for possible business deals between Thaksin and Cambodian leaders. This was coupled with a number of cases involving the transfer of government bureaucrats in charge of Cambodian issues without good explanation, including the transfer of the Secretary-General of the National Security Council and the Director-General of the Department of Treaties and Legal Affairs of the Ministry of Foreign Affairs — the action immensely infuriating the bureaucratic elite. On 14 May 2008, a week before the Thai official support for Cambodia's UNESCO bid, Foreign Minister Noppadon and Deputy Prime Minister Somchai Wongsawat, who is also Thaksin's brother-in-law, were invited to preside alongside Cambodia's Prime Minister Hun Sen over the opening ceremony of the newly renovated 152-kilometre National Highway 48 and a 1,560-metre concrete bridge. The road was built with 1 billion baht in financial assistance from Thailand that was initially designated to facilitate the transport of goods from Cambodia to Laem Chabang port in Chonburi through Trat, a project that would transform Cambodia into a renewed marketplace for Thai products. During this visit, Noppadon admitted to have met with Cambodian Deputy Prime Minister Sok An and discussed the development of a joint management plan for the Preah Vihear Temple, which justified the Thai endorsement of Cambodia's UNESCO request.[18]

In retrospect, the dispute between Thailand and Cambodia over the ownership of the Preah Vihear Temple was purposely intensified by anti-Samak government agents.[19] Thailand lost the ownership case to Cambodia in 1962 after both countries took their overlapping claim to the International Court of Justice (ICJ). The issue had been dormant for over forty years but was revitalized by the self-nominated nationalist PAD who took advantage of the dispute to remove Samak from power. Earlier, the Samak government agreed to endorse the Cambodian request to UNESCO. Eventually, Noppadon went on to conclude a Joint Communiqué with Cambodia's Sok An in Paris on 22 May 2008, reaffirming full Thai support for the inscription of the Preah Vihear Temple on the World Heritage list. Upon returning home, Noppadon was greeted by furious PAD nationalists at Suvarnabhumi International Airport. They called him a traitor. The PAD claimed that the government ceded 4.6 square kilometres of disputed land near the temple to Cambodia in exchange for business concessions for Thaksin.[20] Once again, the discourse of "lost territories" was revived to serve a variety of interests of the traditional elite and those in the army.[21] The PAD nationalistic rhetoric, employed to taint the image of the Samak government, also severely impaired diplomatic ties between Thailand and Cambodia and opened the wounds of mutual hatred between the people of the two countries. The reconstruction of Cambodia as a battlefield was underway; it paved the way for the military to recoup its role in foreign policy. Even at this point when Thailand had a civilian government which enjoyed the authority to appoint its own defence minister, the military continued to occupy foreign affairs because of the supposedly volatile border situation. Traditionally, the post of the defence minister is largely powerless. The real power has always been in the hands of the army chief, particularly in the making of a decision on security policy, internal and external.

As the PAD continued to fan the flames of nationalism, the Administration Court stepped in and ruled that Noppadon's Joint Communiqué with Cambodia was unconstitutional.[22] Meanwhile, Sondhi Limthongkul, one of the core leaders of the PAD, proposed a radical solution to the conflict. He said,

> A commission must be set up to invite Cambodia to bilateral negotiations. If the dispute could not be settled, Thailand would, temporarily adhere to the ICJ's ruling, mobilize Thai troops, push Cambodians back from Thai territory, and formally inform Cambodia that, apart from the Preah Vihear Temple, the surrounding land belongs to Thailand, and Thailand would pay any price to protect its sovereignty, even at the cost of war.[23]

The war option was proposed in order to validate the military's role in the bilateral conflict. Under tremendous pressure, Noppadon resigned on 10 July 2008 from the position of foreign minister. His resignation did not terminate the Thai-Cambodian conflict. It just marked the beginning of a new surge in their mutual antagonism as the bilateral dispute became more violent. On 3 August 2008, the first armed clashes broke out near the Preah Vihear Temple, primarily due to the PAD's provocation, resulting in one Cambodian soldier being killed. After Samak was forced to step down in September the same year following a bizarre charge of him appearing in a televised cooking show, Thaksin's brother-in-law Somchai took over the premiership. The PAD and the military elite continued to utilize the Preah Vihear issue to eliminate the Thaksin faction. The PAD managed to mobilize thousands on the streets of Bangkok to protest against the Somchai government for working on behalf of Thaksin in selling out the motherland to the Khmer enemy. Riding on the wave of anger among the PAD nationalists, the Thai military began its first launch of attacks against Cambodia, to further destroy public confidence in Prime Minister Somchai. On 3 October 2008, the second armed clashes took place at Phu Ma Khua, 2.5 kilometres west of the Preah Vihear Temple. It was reported that two Thai rangers were injured from the exchange of gunfire. On 15 October 2008, one Thai and three Cambodian soldiers died in an exchange of rifle and rocket fire when their troops clashed on the border. Hun Sen, in his heated rhetoric, blasted, "Thai troops must stop trespassing on Cambodian land; the contested territory is now a life-and-death battle zone."[24]

Actively supporting the military to degenerate the situation was Kasit Piromya, member of the opposition Democrat Party and a self-proclaimed pro-PAD, anti-Thaksin personality. On 14 October 2008, Kasit, while being interviewed on a television station, attacked Hun Sen with extreme vulgar language. He branded Hun Sen a lunatic leader, a slave of Thaksin and a gangster of Southeast Asia.[25] One day later, another clash erupted along the common border: one Cambodian and three Thai soldiers were killed. Cambodia felt that it had become a victim of the Thai domestic political struggle between Thaksin and the traditional elite. Hun Sen, as he was maintaining close personal relations with Thaksin, retaliated against the Thai elite by publicly lending his support to the Somchai government and the red-shirt movement. This indicated an immensely mutual hatred between leaders of the two countries and explained why Hun Sen adopted a hostile policy towards the Democrat Party when Abhisit later became prime minister. Supalak Ganjanakhundee points out that it was the first time in modern history that a Cambodian leader openly played a hand in internal Thai politics. Normally, it has been the Thai side that influenced Cambodian domestic politics. In the past, Thailand supported the Cambodian opposition to destabilize the regime in Phnom Penh. Hun Sen himself had gained firsthand experience as Thailand backed the Khmer Rouge and the coalition against him in the 1980s. Many of his political enemies sought refuge in Thailand. Supalak said, "Hun Sen probably thinks now is the time to pay back."[26] But Hun Sen's inveterate alliance with Thaksin and his reprisal against the old establishment directly benefitted the Thai military. As bilateral relationship was rapidly deteriorating, the situation along the border became scarily volatile. The atmosphere of volatility gave way for the military to reoccupy its space in foreign affairs. From this perspective, Hun Sen played a part in transforming his own country into a battlefield for the Thai army.

THE INVIOLABLE NATIONAL SECURITY

It was not the dispute over the Preah Vihear that brought down the Somchai government. Exercising its ultimate measure, the PAD seized Suvarnabhumi and Dong Mueang International Airports in late November 2008, creating a state of ungovernability so severely that the military threatened to stage another military coup to end the turmoil. But before this could take place, the Constitutional Court intervened in the crisis, launching an alternative "judicial coup" that resulted in the collapse of the Somchai government. The Court ruled that a PPP member had committed electoral fraud in the December 2007 elections. The Court's president, Chat Chalavorn, said that he was dissolving the party "to set a political standard and an example". "Dishonest political parties undermine Thailand's democratic system", Chat said in the court's ruling.[27] The sudden downfall of the Somchai regime led to a new twist in politics as it allowed the Democrat Party, a minority in the parliament, to form a coalition government through a backroom deal brokered by the military.[28] The assumption of power of the Democrat Party, with Abhisit, an Oxford-educated politician with an elitist background, as its leader, satisfied the needs of the old power, the network monarchy, the senior bureaucrats and the military in the maintenance of their power position. But it also aroused a wave of disgruntlement among the red-shirt members who condemned the judicial coup as yet another self-serving tactic of the Bangkok elite in denying electoral democracy.

During this transition, from Somchai to Abhisit, from late 2008 to early 2009, relations between Thailand and Cambodia went from bad to worse.

This was simply because the Abhisit government intentionally handpicked Kasit, an anti-Hun Sen figure to serve as foreign minister. Kasit was on a mission to purge Thaksin's diplomatic style, including his business-oriented foreign policy, in order to justify his government's anti-Thaksin stance, or even the 2006 coup. The Democrat Party, once joining forces with the PAD in politicizing the Preah Vihear issue, now found itself locked in its earlier hostile attitude towards Cambodia and was therefore compelled to stick with its anti-Cambodia campaign even when it had an opportunity, as a government, to mend the broken ties. It is also noteworthy that due to the fact that the Democrat Party had arrived in power with the help of the military, the government owed much to the elite in the army. With the Abhisit government remaining in the long shadow of the military, the latter immediately prioritized the border conflict with Cambodia, explicating it in terms of a challenge to national security. And with Kasit as Thailand's foreign minister who continued to upset the Cambodian leadership with his offensive language and antagonistic foreign policy, the battlefield in Cambodia was revived. The Democrat-led government went along with the military in reshaping Thailand's foreign policy towards Cambodia to become, once again, security-centric. Protecting Thai territory from greedy Cambodians was declared a major foreign policy change during the Abhisit administration.[29] Such policy served two objectives: to respond to the nationalistic emotion at home spurred on by the PAD as well as to relocate the military back into the realm of foreign affairs.

An aggressive policy towards Cambodia was eventually manufactured directly in the barracks. The defence establishment portrayed the Cambodian danger as real and present. Hence, national security was under threat. The Abhisit government and the military together painted a new face of Cambodia as an aggressor who had an expansionist desire over Thai territories, just like the colonialists and the communists in the past.[30] "Lost territories" has long been a sacred notion. This is because Thailand is the only country in Southeast Asia that was never officially colonized. Yet, while the military incessantly eulogized the wisdom and far-sightedness of past Thai kings for their shrewd diplomacy in dealing with the colonial powers, it also casts another façade of Thailand as a vulnerable kingdom, surrounded by big and small enemies who were hungry for Thai independence.[31] As a result, the compulsion for the military to fend off enemies in order to preserve national security had been on the top of the agenda for almost every regime, whether democratic or authoritarian. The concept of national security has been tightly bound with the legitimacy of the military elite and their involvement in politics. When the nation is under threat, the military's legitimacy is also at risk. They tend to equate the state of national security with that of their own security. Likewise, when faced with any challenge that could diminish their political influence, they are quick to explain it away as a threat to the security of the nation.[32] Owing to the overriding importance of the national security discourse, the military has sought to manipulate it to its own advantage. This is how Cambodia has come to play its part. Ironically, from this standpoint, a nation at war with its neighbour seems to have consolidated the military's place in politics.

Wira Amphai argued that the term "security", or *khwam mankhong*, in the Thai military argot and Thai nationalist discourse has never been clearly defined. The notion "national security", or *khwam mankhong haeng chat*, is particularly elastic; its meaning could be extended as far as to cover the territorial integrity, the security of the monarchy, Buddhism, and even the people.[33] This explains why the military coups in Thailand have been somewhat successful as they claimed to protect national security, yet exactly what they protected remained obscured. The last coup was initially perceived by many Thais as the right remedy for the political deadlock in 2006. The coup-makers averred that national security was in jeopardy and military intervention was essential.[34] The name of the military regime that ruled Thailand in the aftermath of the coup was the Council for National Security (*khana montri kham mankhong haeng chat*), signifying the underlining objective of the coup itself.[35] Cheera Khienvichit, in his study on the concept of national security, emphasized that the definition of national security had been dominated by a small group of military elite, and this definition has changed over time according to the shifting internal and external environments:

> The process of Thailand's national security policy making and implementing has historically been dominated by a small elite. Thai core values began to take root in the mid 19th century when the king and the aristocracy established the concept of nation, religion, and kingship in the national consciousness. Under the domination of the military and the bureaucracy, Thai conceptions of security were influenced by militaristic-authoritarian ideology. Since the 1990s there has been a significant change in national security policy making. The process of security policy making has moved from military leaders to a group of authorities, which consists of the

head of state, military leaders and civilian leaders in related fields. The security making group, which was formed as a committee, is known as the National Security Council.[36]

Thai history has been rewritten discursively in a way that it projects the theme of national security being constantly challenged by the so-called enemies. Paradoxically, the Thai military continued to fight with external enemies in the neighbourhood even when regional cooperation, through ASEAN, was in its most mature phase. From 2008 until today, Cambodia has been the most threatening external enemy to the Thai nation. Although the Cambodian threat seemed to have emerged only in 2008, its roots went further back, to the Thai crisis in the aftermath of the military coup which had witnessed the military's blatant intrusion in politics.

THE TAIL WAGGING THE DOG

The beginning of the Abhisit government was coloured by heightened antagonism between Thailand and Cambodia. For the most part of the government's life, bilateral relations could be described as disturbingly erratic or even bloodily confrontational. Declaring war with Cambodia was a plot found in the 1997 black comedy Hollywood film "Wag the Dog". Now, all the key actors, Abhisit, Kasit, and the PAD performed as spin doctors who constructed a war with Cambodia for their self-legitimization purpose. But unlike in the Hollywood film, war with Cambodia was real. The reality of war assigned a critical role for the military in the safeguarding the national territorial integrity. Even when the pro-Thaksin regimes were removed, the "wag-the-dog" plot was still drawn up to warrant the permanent political presence of the military. In other words, Thai-Cambodian relations were simply a casualty of Thailand's domestic politics in which the military's domination of internal and external policies had to be reassured.

Three months after the military helped stage-manage the Abhisit regime, armed clashes between the two countries resumed. In late March 2009, about one hundred Thai troops briefly entered contested territory near the Preah Vihear Temple. Hun Sen swiftly warned Thai troops of Cambodia's possible forceful counter-attack. Eventually the two countries' armies clashed on 3 April 2009, leaving two Thai and two Cambodian soldiers dead and several injured. Thailand shut Pha Mo E-Daeng cliff and the Khao Phra Wihan National Park and its gate to the Preah Vihear Temple in Si Sa Ket Province. Prior to the fatal shootings, Cambodia had deployed more than 3,000 soldiers at the ancient temple ruins and Thailand had slightly over 2,000 troops on Pha Mor E-Daeng cliff.[37] The armed clashes were encouraged by a new nationalistic boost from Hun Sen's rabble-rousing statement and from Kasit's never-ending insults against the Cambodian leadership. One month after the fatal shooting incident, Cambodia demanded Thailand pay compensation for damage resulting from the confrontation on the border. In its diplomatic note, Cambodia stated, "The attack with heavy weapons by Thai troops on Cambodian territory caused much damage and set a Cambodian market ablaze. The material losses to 319 families, who had lost their livelihoods when the fire destroyed their market stalls, amounted to more than US$2.1 million."[38] Not only did the Thai side refuse to compensate them, Prime Minister Abhisit rekindled the nationalistic impulse by requesting UNESCO review the World Heritage status of the contentious temple when the UNESCO committee was to meet in Spain in late June 2009. Angrily, Cambodian Foreign Minister Hor Namhong challenged the Thai objection, "Cambodia welcomes Thailand militarily, diplomatically, internationally, or through peaceful negotiations. I heard that the second Thai commander on the border put his troops on alert and I would like to tell them that Cambodian soldiers are also on alert."[39]

A few days later during the ASEAN Summit in Hua Hin in 2009, Hun Sen further infuriated Thai patriots by announcing that he would appoint Thaksin as his government's economic adviser. The appointment was made official by virtue of a Royal Decree in the Cambodian capital on 4 November 2009. The fact that Cambodia's cabinet and King Sihamoni endorsed the appointment of Thaksin affirmed Hun Sen's plan, in collaboration with Thaksin, to discredit the Abhisit government. Meanwhile, the government adopted harsher diplomatic measures against Cambodia. On 6 November 2009, Kasit recalled the Thai ambassador to Phnom Penh to protest against Cambodia's official appointment of Thaksin. He also decided to review all bilateral agreements with Cambodia and pull out of maritime talks, which would have covered potential rich supplies of oil and gas in a disputed area of the eastern Gulf of Thailand. Cambodia retaliated by recalling its ambassador to Bangkok and accused Bangkok of overreacting.[40] The Thai military, riding on the notion of national security and the discourse of nationalism, painted a deadly scenario of a possible new round of armed clashes. It built 340 bunkers in villages in Si Sa Ket near the site of the Preah Vihear Temple as a sign of this unease.[41] While the Abhisit government in Bangkok created a stage for the protracted conflict with Cambodia, and the PAD carried on arousing a nationalist sentiment among Thais, the military transformed such an intense atmosphere into tangible armed clashes along the Thai-Cambodian border.

During the Abhisit administration, there were altogether six armed clashes between Thailand and Cambodia; once in 2009, three times in 2010 and twice in 2011 (see Table 10.1).

Since the end of the Cold War, and indeed since the 2006 coup, the Abhisit era witnessed the most frequent, and deadly, armed disputes between Thailand and Cambodia. These were manufactured to serve a variety of political purposes, mainly for the Thai defence establishment. True, the tension with Cambodia was first stirred up as a ploy to overthrow the two pro-Thaksin regimes in 2008. But it was a mistake to assume that the Thai-Cambodian situation would improve under the leadership of Abhisit since the Thaksin cronies were driven out of power. The continuity of fatal confrontations between the two countries unveiled the reality in which the military still gained ample benefits from maintaining a war footing

TABLE 10.1
Armed Clashes between Thailand and Cambodia (2008–11)

Date	Incidents/Consequences
3 August 2008	An exchange of fire near Preah Vihear injured one Cambodian
3 October 2008	Clashes at Phu Ma Kua (2.5 km west of Preah Vihear)
15 October 2008	An exchange of gunfire left three Cambodian soldiers and one Thai soldier dead
8 April 2009	Heavy gunfire erupted and killed two Cambodian and two Thai soldiers
24 January 2010	Exchange of gunfire, no casualties reported
29 January 2010	A brief shootout, no injuries reported
8 June 2010	Exchange of gunfire, no casualties reported
4–7 February 2011	Heavy fire exchanged at Phu Ma Kua, killing two Thai soldiers and one civilian and at least three Cambodian soldiers
22 April 2011	Cambodian troops opened fire on Thai troops near Ta Kwai and Ta Muen Temples; four Thai soldiers and three Cambodian soldiers killed

Source: "Border Clash Kills Four Thai Troops", *Bangkok Post*, 23 April 2011.

with Cambodia; the purpose this time was not to unleash external war to undermine internal enemies, but more to perpetuate the army's power position in politics. There was evidence that demonstrated the military's attempt to intensify, directly or otherwise, the conflict with Cambodia. In late December 2010, the PAD felt that its movement was fast slipping away from the political limelight, and therefore sought to stir up yet another round of disputes with Cambodia to recuperate its political leverage. The PAD sent its members, some from the Thai Patriots Network, together with Panich Vikitsreth, a member of parliament from the ruling Democrat government, to cross over to Cambodia illegally. Consequently, they were all arrested for encroaching on Cambodia's territory — an incident that successfully outraged the anti-Cambodia movement in Thailand.[42] With this incident, the PAD pressed Abhisit to take a tougher line towards Cambodia if those arrested were not all freed, including the military option. Finally, a Cambodian court did let go of five of them, including Panich, while the other two — Veera Somkwamkit and Ratree Pipattanapaiboon — had remained in a Phnom Penh prison. They were charged with illegal entry and espionage. In February 2013, Ratree was finally freed, leaving Veera the only detainee in Cambodian prison.

The PAD deliberately tempted the Thai military to intervene in the conflict with Cambodia. More fundamentally, it permitted the military to resurrect the old political culture in which the army had maintained a tremendous control over civilian rule, particularly in foreign affairs. The crisis at the borderland, which resulted in Thai nationals being arrested on supposed Thai territory, breathed new life to the old discourse of "lost territories" among the Bangkok elite and the defence establishment. Foreign Minister Kasit claimed that these Thais were captured in Thai territory, which somehow contradicted what Veera, one of the captives, had said in a video clip recorded during which Veera and his team were crossing into Cambodia. Veera said with laughter, "We are now in Cambodian territory. Wait, soon the Cambodians will come and arrest us. And we will be rescued by Thai soldiers."[43] Yet, the Cambodian authorities did not find their illegal entry amusing. The arrest sparked a series of armed clashes between the two sides from January to April 2011. The imprisonment of the PAD's members also helped lengthen the bilateral conflict which, at the same time, extended the military's staying power in politics.[44]

The PAD's aggravation proved highly effective. It was followed by fresh armed clashes which lasted for four days, from 4 to 7 February 2011, and became one of the most violent. The Thai army was accused of using cluster bombs to attack Cambodia, an allegation made by the Cluster Munition Coalition (CMC). The CMC claimed the Thai army killed two Cambodian soldiers with the 155-millimetre Dual Purpose Improved Conventional Munition (DPICM) cluster munitions during the border fighting. Thailand is not among the 107 countries that signed the Convention on Cluster Munitions, banning their use. Eventually, Defence Minister General Prawit Wongsuwan rejected the CMC allegation. He said, "No cluster bombs here. We have strictly complied with international laws banning their use."[45] Besides, it was also reported that the Thai military deliberately bombarded the Preah Vihear complex, causing great damage to the eleventh century temple.[46] In April 2011, Thailand and Cambodia again engaged in violent fighting. This time, the two countries were fighting to gain control over two relatively unknown temples hidden deep in the jungle off the main tourist trail — Ta Kwai and Ta Muen Tom in Thai or Ta Krabei and Ta Moan Thom in Khmer. The two temple ruins were practically dragged into becoming a part of the persistent border conflict. Estimated to be at least 800 years old, they are located 15 kilometres apart and around 150 kilometres west of the Preah Vihear Temple, which has traditionally been at the centre of bilateral unrest. Both Thailand and Cambodia have laid claim to the ruins. The two ancient temples are among several elegant Khmer architectural structures built for Hindu deities. Historians believe that both might have been constructed around the same time as Preah Vihear.[47] The Thai military took advantage of the nationalistic emotions that run deep in Thailand. Its aggression vis-à-vis Cambodia was legitimized by the prevailing discourse of "lost territories" that gave birth to nationalist forces, driving the country into deadly conflict with Cambodia.

Indeed, it was evident that since the military turned the Cambodian marketplace into a battlefield, economic ties between the two countries had deteriorated. Bilateral trade volume dropped by 26.24 per cent in the first two months of 2009, according to the statistics from the Thai customs department, just only a few months after Abhisit's became prime minister. And for the whole of 2009, Thailand's exports to Cambodia totalled around US$1.6 billion, compared with those in 2008 which amounted to US$2 billion. In another example, at the peak of the conflict in 2011, the Thai Commerce Ministry admitted that bilateral armed clashes brought trade in the border area to a standstill. The provincial commerce office was instructed to keep an eye on the situation closely in order to warn market vendors of possible impact both in terms of security and trade. Thailand's exports to Cambodia, mostly household commodities, machinery and fuel, are worth about US$1.6 billion each year while the import value is US$97 million.[48] Meanwhile, Kong Putheara, director of statistics department at Cambodia's Ministry of Commerce, agreed that bilateral trade had slowed down due to the large-scale border clashes in February and April 2011.[49] The border conflict simply overshadowed the trading atmosphere between the two countries. Moreover, other joint trade activities were postponed, including the Thai-Cambodian Business Forum which focuses mainly on bilateral cooperation in trade, investment, agriculture, logistics, tourism and human resource development.

BILATERAL VERSUS MULTILATERAL APPROACHES

To substantiate the argument that the military aspired to restructure Cambodia into a battlefield, it is imperative to delve into the foreign policy decision-making process. As earlier discussed, the Thai political domain was "recolonized" by the military following the coup of 2006, which delegitimized the civilian regime of Thaksin and reinstitutionalized the security-oriented policies, both domestic and foreign. From the beginning, the military was not alone in redesigning the Thai neighbour into a war zone. It teamed up with the nationalist PAD and the Democrat Party in aggravating the Preah Vihear issue. At the height of the crisis and with the Thai military's reluctance to pacify Cambodia, not only did Thailand badly suffer from an image problem on the international stage, but so did ASEAN, of which both countries are members. The test to the Thai leadership in the Preah Vihear conflict was as much at stake as that of ASEAN.

Indonesia was ASEAN chair in 2011. The world's most populous Muslim country, Indonesia is naturally the leader of ASEAN. Furthermore, its re-emergence as a born-again democratic country prompted it to play a principal role in ASEAN. ASEAN has recently undergone its own reinvention, with the launch of the ASEAN Charter in 2008 and the rescheduling of its community building now to be accomplished by the year 2015.[50] Such new developments added an immense pressure on both ASEAN and Indonesia to intervene in the Thai-Cambodian conflict, using the existing dispute settlement instruments to prevent the two countries from going to war. But ASEAN's offer to play a mediation role was half-heartedly accepted by the Abhisit government. Compelled to cooperate with ASEAN for the sake of the organization's credibility, the Abhisit government went ahead with consenting to the Indonesian observers being stationed in the disputed area — a decision fully agreed upon by Cambodia. ASEAN Foreign Ministers finally gathered in Jakarta for an Indonesia-facilitated urgent meeting on 22 February 2011 to discuss possible solutions to the border conflict between Cambodia and Thailand. ASEAN Secretary-General Surin Pitsuwan was quick to celebrate ASEAN's success. He said, "ASEAN is certainly rising to the occasion."[51] In reality, Thailand continued its foot-dragging approach and did little to facilitate the ASEAN monitoring team led by Indonesia. While the Abhisit government pledged to work with ASEAN to alleviate the border tension, the Thai military insisted on managing the problem strictly on a bilateral basis. The inconsistency of policy on the part of Thailand showed a complex pattern of foreign policy decision-making in progress. The fact that Thailand failed to involve ASEAN despite its pledge to the organization attested that the military, not the Foreign Ministry, was the key actor who made foreign policy decisions in regard to the country's relations with Cambodia.

Evidence of the military commanding Thai foreign policy towards Cambodia is copious. Both Defence Minister Prawit Wongsuwon and Army Chief Prayuth Chan-ocha declared that they would not attend the Eighth General Border Committee (GBC) meeting with Cambodia in Bogor in April 2011, which was organized by Indonesian Foreign Minister Marty Natalegawa on behalf of ASEAN. Prawit stressed, "No, I am not going. Why should I go for the meeting in a third-party country? Thailand and Cambodia know each other well enough and do not want any other party to get involved." Meanwhile, Prayuth said, "Cambodia's proposal to set up 15 joint border checkpoints in the disputed 4.6-square-kilometre area near Preah Vihear temple was unnecessary. The dispute could be solved through military talks."[52] In addition, the *Bangkok Post* reported:

> Defence Minister Prawit Wongsuwon and commanders of all armed forces have resolved not to allow Indonesian observers to enter the 4.6 square kilometre dispute area on the Thai-Cambodian border, Army Chief Prayuth Chan-ocha said on Wednesday. General Prayuth insisted the top brass wanted the Thai-Cambodian conflict to be solved by the two countries only. He said the army had made a proposal to Cambodia through the Foreign Ministry that if there are to be joint checkpoints in the disputed area a centre should be set up to coordinate their operations. The coordination centre must be manned by Thai and Cambodian soldiers only. It is not necessary to have Indonesian observers.[53]

Thailand's two conflicting approaches, one endorsed by Prime Minister Abhisit in agreement with ASEAN's mediation and the other adopted by the Thai military which concentrated on a bilateral framework, revealed the great extent to which the country was not genuine in solving the conflict with Cambodia. The nature of Thai politics in the post-coup period pointed to the fact that the civilian regime of Abhisit remained weak and subservient to the military. Abhisit's political ascendance with the support from the military could not hide the reality in which the defence establishment was the real force behind the conduct of foreign policy with Cambodia. The success in depicting Thailand as a country surrounded by traditional enemies, in retraditionalizing the discourse of lost territories, and in inculcating the importance of national security, further solidified the military's place in the foreign policy realm. And Cambodia served as a catalyst in this process.

CONCLUSION

Thailand's election of July 2011 had changed the country's political landscape. In an ironic twist of fate, the Democrat Party, endorsed by the traditional elite and the military, suffered a humiliating loss in the election. On the contrary, the party that was blessed by Thaksin, the Pheu Thai, won an overwhelming victory. The new premier, the first female in the country's history, Yingluck Shinawatra, who is the youngest sister of Thaksin, formed a coalition government occupying 300 parliamentary seats out of the total 500. The triumph of Thaksin's faction re-emerged as a threat to the Bangkok elite. So far, Yingluck has attempted to reduce the influence of the military in politics. In so doing, she has transformed Cambodia back to the marketplace. This transformation was complementary to her domestic populist policy. After the election the Yingluck premiership was celebrated in Phnom Penh. Prime Minister Hun Sen sent a congratulatory note to Yingluck and vowed to work with her to alleviate the tension. Hun Sen said, "I am optimistic that with a joint commitment, Your Excellency and I will obviously be able to restore our traditional friendship, good neighbours, and fruitful cooperation between our two countries' peoples. I am ready to work closely with Your Excellency to serve the interests of our two countries and peoples, and to solve all issues peacefully in order to bring good harmonisation to our nations and to contribute to peace, stability and prosperity in the region."[54] Yingluck's much-publicized visit to Phnom Penh on 15 September 2011 symbolized a thaw in the Thai-Cambodian relationship. Thaksin followed up with his own visit to Cambodia from 16 to 24 September 2011, which helped pave the way for a better relationship. In the meantime, a football match was organized on the day Thaksin arrived in the Cambodian capital between the red-shirt team and that of Cambodia, highlighting the fact that Cambodia has very much played a Thai domestic politic game. The détente between Thailand and Cambodia, although it represents a positive turn in their relationship, has certainly made the Thai military anxious of its vulnerable position in politics. The reinterpretation of the 1962 verdict by the ICJ, in November 2013, did not benefit Cambodia nor Thailand in particular, and failed to stir up a sense of nationalism on either side of the border. This could be partly because of an improved relationship between the two countries' leaders — Hun Sen and Yingluck.

In retrospect, the military's domination of foreign policy is not a new phenomenon. During the Cold War when Thailand confronted the communist threat, the military moved to occupy the front seat in the country's foreign affairs. Concerns over national security took centre stage in the formulation of foreign policy; this greatly legitimized the role of the military in the conduct of diplomacy. When Prime Minister Chatichai revised the Thai policy turning battlefields in Indochina into marketplaces for Thai businesses, the military hurriedly rebuffed his idea and soon overthrew him in a coup. The army viewed the marketplace policy as a threat to its eminent role in foreign affairs. Since the coup of 2006, the military revisited the political forefront and once again played an overriding part in the security and foreign policy domain. During this period, armed clashes between Thai and Cambodian troops on the border served to rationalize the military's renewed authority in the foreign policy-making process. Clearly, the Thai army exploited the Cambodian border conflict to preserve its hegemony in Thai politics. To outside observers, on the surface, the conflict between the two countries could be considered as just another violent breakout. At a deeper level however, it indicated an increasingly agonizing state of Thai domestic politics from which the military refused to withdraw itself. As it turned out, the numerous clashes provided another much-needed opportunity for the Thai military to take full control of foreign policy vis-à-vis what was now perceived to be the country's number one enemy. For the army, taking over foreign policy was crucial, as this guaranteed its political role and authority in foreign policy formulation; this was possible because of the coup of 2006 which successfully pulled Thailand back a few decades to the Cold War period where concerns over national sovereignty and territorial integrity were paramount. The military has since gone on the political offensive. The fuss about Indonesia's intervention in the Thai-Cambodian conflict, the mediating role of ASEAN and the preferred approaches to the solution, with the military being firm on its bilateral modality, only underscored the military's desperation to hold on to its position of power in Thai politics.

Notes

1. Christina Kline argued, "When Thailand's rulers made clear their pro-Western and anticommunist orientation, the United States responded with generous financial support." See Christina Kline, *Cold War Orientalism: Asia in the Middlebrow Imagination, 1945–1961* (Berkeley and Los Angeles: University of California Press, 2003), p. 197. See also Daniel Fineman, *A Special Relationship: The United States and Military Government in Thailand, 1947–1958* (Honolulu: University of Hawaii Press, 1997), p. 173.
2. See "Preah Vihear for Koh Kong for Natural Gas/Oil", *Thai Political Facts Info*, 16 October 2008 <http://antithaksin.wordpress.com/2008/10/16/preah-vihear-for-koh-kong-and-natuaral-gasoil/> (accessed 30 August 2011). See also Pavin Chachavalpongpun, "Temple of Doom: Hysteria about the Preah Vihear Temple in the Thai Nationalist Discourse", *Legitimacy Crisis in Thailand* (Bangkok: Silkworm Books, 2011), pp. 96–100.
3. "Prayuth Chan-ocha Wants to Go to War with Cambodia?", MCOT Online News, 15 January 2011 <http://rongkhmer.blogspot.com/2011/01/prayuth-chan-ocha-wants-to-go-to-war.html> (accessed 14 August 2011).
4. For further discussion, see Sunai Phasuk, *Nayobai Tang Prathet Khong Thai: Suksa Krabuankarnkamnod Nayobai Khong Ratthaban Pon-ek Chatichai Choonhavan Tor Panha Kumphucha, 4 Singhakom 1988–23 Kumphapan 1991* [Thai Foreign Policy: A Study of Foreign Policy Making Process under the Chatichai Choonhavan Government, 4 August 1988–23 February 1991] (Bangkok: Institute of Asian Studies, 1997).
5. See Duncan McCargo and Ukrist Pathmanand, *The Thaksinisation of Thailand* (Copenhagen: Nordic Institute of Asian Studies, 2005), p. 51.
6. Pavin Chachavalpongpun, *Reinventing Thailand: Thaksin and His Foreign Policy* (Singapore: Institute of Southeast Asian Studies, 2010), p. 170.
7. Elizabeth Becker, *When the War was Over: Cambodia and the Khmer Rouge Revolution* (New York: Public Affairs, 1998), p. 309.

8. An Asia Watch Report, *Khmer Rouge Abuses along the Thai-Cambodian Border* (Washington: The Asia Watch Committee, 1989), p. 6.
9. The Thai-Malaysian border has almost been completely demarcated, thus representing less problem to the Thai defence establishment.
10. Christopher Roberts, *ASEAN's Myanmar Crisis: Challenge to the Pursuit of a Security Community* (Singapore: Institute of Southeast Asian Studies, 2010), p. 89. See also Pavin Chachavalpongpun, *A Plastic Nation: The Curse of Thainess in Thai-Burmese Relations* (Lanham: University Press of America, 2005), pp. 46–48.
11. See Charnvit Kasetsiri, "Thailand-Cambodia: A Love-Hate Relationship", *Kyoto Review of Southeast Asia* 3 (March 2003), reprint <http://www.charnvitkasetsiri.com/PDF/Thailand-Cambodia.pdf> (accessed 17 August 2011).
12. The key four objectives of ACMECS are: (1) to increase competitiveness and generate greater growth along the borders; (2) to facilitate relocation of agricultural and manufacturing industries to areas with comparative advantage; (3) to create employment opportunities and reduce income disparity among the four countries; and (4) to enhance peace, stability and shared prosperity for all in a sustainable manner. Source: <http://www.acmecs.org/index.php?id=10> (accessed 5 April 2009).
13. Thitinan Pongsudhirak, "Thaksin Bends the Wind", *ISEAS Newsletter*, no. 3 (Singapore: Institute of Southeast Asian Studies, July 2005), p. 2. Also see, Thitinan Pongsudhirak, "World War II and Thailand after Sixty Years", in *Legacies of World War II: South and East Asia*, edited by David Koh Wee Hock, (Singapore: Institute of Southeast Asian Studies, 2007), p. 111.
14. Thanong Khanthong, "Surayud Boxed into a Corner with FBA Amendments", *The Nation*, 20 April 2007.
15. This explains his appointment as prime minister to lead the post-coup government in 2006.
16. Duncan McCargo, "Network Monarchy and Legitimacy Crises in Thailand", *Pacific Review* 18, Issue 4 (2005), p. 499.
17. Address by General Surayud Chulanont at the Foreign Correspondents' Club of Thailand, Grand Hyatt Erawan Hotel, Bangkok, 7 November 2006 (personal copy).
18. <http://antithaksin.wordpress.com/2008/10/16/preah-vihear-for-koh-kong-and-natuaral-gasoil/> (accessed 1 April 2009).
19. Aurel Croissant and Paul W. Chambers, "A Contested Site of Memory: The Preah Vihear Temple", in *Cultures and Globalisation: Heritage, Memory and Identity*, edited by Yudhishthir Raj Isar and Helmut K. Anheier (London: SAGE Publications, 2011), p. 150.
20. "Thai PM's Foes Throw Nationalist Temple Tantrum", *Reuters*, 25 June 2008.

21. See Thongchai Winichakul, "Preah Vihear can be Time Bomb", *The Nation*, 30 June 2008. See also Thongchai Winichakul, "Sia Dindan Pen Prawatthisat Lokphrai Paitaithan Proah Thai Maikuei Sia Dindan" [Lost Territories is a Distorted History which Tricked the Lowly Peasants to Die for their Country because Thailand has Never Lost its Territories], *Matichon Online*, 8 February 2011 <http://www.matichon.co.th/news_detail.php?newsid=1297151137> (accessed 30 August 2011).

22. Thiradej Iamsamran and Ram Indaravichit, *Thodsalak Khadi Prasat Phra Viharn: Wiwatha Guru Sudyod Haeng Thosawad* [Decoding the Phra Viharn Temple Case: Opinion of the Guru, The Best of the Decade] (Bangkok: Matichon Publishing House, 2008), pp. 62–63.

23. "Sondhi Limthongkul's Solution to the Preah Vihear Dispute", *Prachatai*, 2 August 2008 <http://www.prachatai.com/english/news.php?id=732> (accessed 29 March 2009). On 28 July 2008, Sondhi Limthongkul, leader of the PAD, took to the stage at about 9 p.m. to address the crowd rallying near Government House in Bangkok, and proposed the mentioned way-out to the crisis.

24. Richard Lloyd Perry, "Cambodian Threaten Wars over Temple Dispute", *Times Online*, 14 October 2008 <http://www.timesonline.co.uk/tol/news/world/asia/article4940025.ece> (accessed 17 August 2011).

25. His interview can be found at <http://www.youtube.com/watch?v=_UCi-mgmIDs>.

26. Supalak Ganjanakhundee, "Hun Sen Settling Scores but is it Worth it?", *The Nation*, 7 November 2009.

27. Matthew Weaver, "Thailand Prime Minister to Step Down after Court Strips Him of Office", *The Guardian*, 2 December 2008 <http://www.guardian.co.uk/world/2008/dec/02/thailand-protests-somchai-wongsawat> (accessed 27 August 2011).

28. John Roberts, "Thai Military Plays Key Role in Forming New Government", World Socialist Website, 11 December 2008 <http://www.wsws.org/articles/2008/dec2008/thai-d11.shtml> (accessed 30 August 2011).

29. In *Policy Statement of the Council of Ministers*, delivered by Prime Minister Abhisit Vejjajiva, at the National Assembly, 31 December 2008 (personal copy). On p. 8, although it does not indicate Cambodia as the primary threat, it sets the need to protect national sovereignty as his government's second priority, after defending the monarchy. It says, "Strengthen and develop national defence capability in safeguarding the independence, sovereignty and territorial integrity of the state, as well as in protecting the national interest, by enhancing the preparedness of the armed forces, training troops in the conduct of operations, and aligning the budget of the armed forces with their respective missions..."

30. Ker Mumthit, "Thailand Ready to Respond to Cambodian Threat", *Mail and*

Guardian Online, 14 October 2008 <http://mg.co.za/article/2008-10-14-thailand-ready-to-respond-cambodian-threat> (accessed 30 August 2011).

31. Patrick Jory, "Problems in Contemporary Thai Nationalist Historiography", *Review Essay* (Kyoto: Centre for Southeast Asian Studies, March 2008) <http://kyotoreview.cseas.kyoto-u.ac.jp/issue/issue2/article_251.html> (accessed 30 August 2011).

32. Carolina G. Hernandez, "Controlling Asia's Armed Forces", in *Civil-Military Relations and Democracy*, edited by Larry Jay Diamond and Marc F. Plattner (Maryland: The Johns Hopkins University Press, 1996), p, 75.

33. See Wira Amphai, *Khwampenthai* [Thainess], (Bangkok, 1983), pp. 108–109. Quoted in Craig J. Reynolds, "Introduction: National Identity and Its Defenders", in *National Identity and Its Defender: Thailand Today*, edited by Craig J. Reynolds (Chiang Mai: Silkworm Books, 1991), p. 23.

34. *Handbook on Thailand's Political Situation*, Department of Information, Ministry of Foreign Affairs of Thailand, 29 June 2007 (author's copy).

35. "The Council for National Security" was formerly known in English as "the Council for Democratic Reform". Its original name is "the Council for Democratic Reform under the Constitutional Monarchy". The coup-makers later deleted the words "constitutional monarchy" in order not to implicate that the King was involved in the military coup.

36. Cheera Khienvichit, "How Security is Conceived by Key Decision Makers in Thailand?", *Shedden Papers* (Canberra: Ministry of Defence of Australia, 2003), p. 32. See also Muthiah Alagappa, "Thailand The Elite's Shifting Conceptions of Security", edited by Panitan Watttanayagorn, *Asian Security Practice* (California: Stanford University Press, 1998), p. 443, and *National Security Policy 1998–2001*, National Security Council of Thailand <http://www.nsc.go.th/english.html> (accessed 15 May 2003).

37. Wassana Nanuam, Thanida Tansubhapon and Prasit Tangprasert, "Thailand Shuts Tourist Spots after Fatal Clashes", *Bangkok Post*, 4 April 2009.

38. "Thailand Rejects Phnom Penh's Demand for Damages", *Bangkok Post*, 12 May 2009.

39. "Preah Vihear Appeal Targets UN, not Cambodia", *The Nation*, 21 July 2009.

40. Supalak Ganjanakhundee, "Thailand Recalls Ambassador to Protest Cambodia", *The Nation*, 5 November 2009.

41. Marwaan Macan-Markar, "Thai-Cambodia Tension Gives Rise to Schools with Bunkers", *Inter Press Service*, 24 November 2009 <http://ispsnews.net/newsasp?idnews=49385> (accessed 23 June 2010).

42. "Clips Show Panich in Cambodia", *Bangkok Post*, 4 January 2011.

43. See the video clip at <http://www.youtube.com/watch?v=BChWigFiuXQ&feature=related> (accessed 30 August 2011).

44. P. Waddhana, "The Strategy: Taking Cambodia Hostage will Lead to a Military

Coup and War", Agence Kampuchea Presse, 31 January 2011 <http://www.akp.gov.kh/?p=1498> (accessed 30 August 2011).

45. "Cluster Bomb Claim Denied", *Bangkok Post*, 4 April 2011.
46. "Thai-Cambodia Clashes Damage Preah Vihear Temple", *BBC News*, 6 February 2011 <http://www.bbc.co.uk/news/world-asia-pacific-12377626> (accessed 30 August 2011).
47. "Temple Ruins at Centre of Unrest", *Straits Times*, 28 April 2011.
48. "Thai-Cambodian Trade Stalled by Border Clashes", *Business Day*, 5 February 2011 <http://www.bday.net/thai-cambodian-trade-stalled-by-border-clashes/> (accessed 4 November 2012).
49. "Cambodia's Trade with Thailand up 8%", Xinhua, 17 October 2011 <http://www.chinadaily.com.cn/world/2011-10/17/content_13915384.htm> (accessed 4 November 2012).
50. For further discussion on ASEAN's developments, see, Rodolfo C. Severino, *Southeast Asia in Search of an ASEAN Community: Insights from the Former ASEAN Secretary-General* (Singapore: Institute of Southeast Asian Studies, 2006).
51. See <http://www.aseansec.org/25924.htm> (accessed 30 August 2011).
52. Wassana Nanuam and Pradit Ruangdit, "Prawit Rejects GBC Meeting in Indonesia", *Bangkok Post*, 23 March 2011.
53. Wassana Nanuam, "Prayuth: Indonesian Observers not Wanted", *Bangkok Post*, 23 March 2011.
54. "Cambodian PM Congratulates Thailand's New-elected Prime Minister", *China Daily*, 5 August 2011 <http://www.chinadaily.com.cn/xinhua/2011-08-05/content_3416583.html> (accessed 31 August 2011).

References

Alagappa, Muthiah. "Thailand The Elite's Shifting Conceptions of Security". In *Asian Security Practice*, edited by Panitan Watttanayagorn. California: Stanford University Press, 1998.

An Asia Watch Report. *Khmer Rouge Abuses along the Thai-Cambodian Border*. Washington: The Asia Watch Committee, 1989.

Becker, Elizabeth. *When the War was Over: Cambodia and the Khmer Rouge Revolution*. New York: Public Affairs, 1998.

Charnvit Kasetsiri. "Thailand-Cambodia: A Love-Hate Relationship". *Kyoto Review of Southeast Asia* 3 (March 2003) (Reprint) <http://www.charnvitkasetsiri.com/PDF/Thailand-Cambodia.pdf> (accessed 17 August 2011).

Cheera Khienvichit. "How Security is Conceived by Key Decision Makers in Thailand?". *Shedden Papers*. Canberra: Ministry of Defence of Australia, 2003.

Croissant, Aurel and Paul W. Chambers. "A Contested Site of Memory: The

Preah Vihear Temple". In *Cultures and Globalisation: Heritage, Memory and Identity*, edited by Yudhishthir Raj Isar and Helmut K. Anheier. London: SAGE Publications, 2011.

Fineman, Daniel. *A Special Relationship: The United States and Military Government in Thailand, 1947–1958*. Honolulu: University of Hawaii Press, 1997.

Handbook on Thailand's Political Situation. Department of Information, Ministry of Foreign Affairs of Thailand, 29 June 2007.

Hernandez, Carolina G. "Controlling Asia's Armed Forces". In *Civil-Military Relations and Democracy*, edited by Larry Jay Diamond and Marc F. Plattner. Maryland: The Johns Hopkins University Press, 1996.

Jory, Patrick. "Problems in Contemporary Thai Nationalist Historiography". *Review Essay*, Centre for Southeast Asian Studies, Kyoto, March 2008 <http://kyotoreview.cseas.kyoto-u.ac.jp/issue/issue2/article_251.html> (accessed 30 August 2011).

Kline, Christina. *Cold War Orientalism: Asia in the Middlebrow Imagination, 1945–1961*, Berkeley and Los Angeles: University of California Press, 2003.

Marwaan Macan-Markar. "Thai-Cambodia Tension Gives Rise to Schools with Bunkers". *Inter Press Service*, 24 November 2009 <http://ispsnews.net/newsasp?idnews=49385> (accessed 23 June 2010).

McCargo, Duncan. "Network Monarchy and Legitimacy Crises in Thailand". *Pacific Review* 18, Issue 4 (2005).

――― and Ukrist Pathmanand. *The Thaksinisation of Thailand*. Copenhagen: Nordic Institute of Asian Studies, 2005.

MCOT Online News. "Prayuth Chan-ocha Wants to Go to War with Cambodia?", 15 January 2011 <http://rongkhmer.blogspot.com/2011/01/prayuth-chan-ocha-wants-to-go-to-war.html> (accessed 14 August 2011).

Mumthit, Ker. "Thailand Ready to Respond to Cambodian Threat". *Mail and Guardian Online*, 14 October 2008 <http://mg.co.za/article/2008-10-14-thailand-ready-to-respond-cambodian-threat> (accessed 30 August 2011).

National Security Policy 1998–2001. National Security Council of Thailand <http://www.nsc.go.th/english.html> (accessed 15 May 2003).

P. Waddhana. "The Strategy: Taking Cambodia Hostage will Lead to a Military Coup and War". Agence Kampuchea Presse, 31 January 2011 <http://www.akp.gov.kh/?p=1498> (accessed 30 August 2011).

Pavin Chachavalpongpun. *A Plastic Nation: The Curse of Thainess in Thai-Burmese Relations*. Lanham: University Press of America, 2005.

―――. *Reinventing Thailand: Thaksin and His Foreign Policy*. Singapore: Institute of Southeast Asian Studies, 2010.

―――. "Temple of Doom: Hysteria about the Preah Vihear Temple in the Thai Nationalist Discourse". *Legitimacy Crisis in Thailand*. Bangkok: Silkworm Books, 2011.

Perry, Richard Lloyd. "Cambodian Threaten Wars over Temple Dispute". *Times Online*, 14 October 2008 <http://www.timesonline.co.uk/tol/news/world/asia/article4940025.ece> (accessed 17 August 2011).

Prachatai. "Sondhi Limthongkul's Solution to the Preah Vihear Dispute", 2 August 2008 <http://www.prachatai.com/english/news.php?id=732> (accessed 29 March 2009).

Reynolds, Craig J. "Introduction: National Identity and Its Defenders". In *National Identity and Its Defender: Thailand Today*, edited by Craig J. Reynolds. Chiang Mai: Silkworm Books, 1991.

Roberts, Christopher. *ASEAN's Myanmar Crisis: Challenge to the Pursuit of a Security Community*. Singapore: Institute of Southeast Asian Studies, 2010.

Roberts, John. "Thai Military Plays Key Role in Forming New Government". World Socialist Website, 11 December 2008 <http://www.wsws.org/articles/2008/dec2008/thai-d11.shtml> (accessed 30 August 2011).

Severino, Rodolfo C. *Southeast Asia in Search of an ASEAN Community: Insights from the Former ASEAN Secretary-General*. Singapore: Institute of Southeast Asian Studies, 2006.

Sunai Phasuk. *Nayobai Tang Prathet Khong Thai: Suksa Krabuankarnkamnod Nayobai Khong Ratthaban Pon-ek Chatichai Choonhavan Tor Panha Kumphucha, 4 Singhakom 1988–23 Kumphapan 1991* [Thai Foreign Policy: A Study of Foreign Policy Making Process under the Chatichai Choonhavan Government, 4 August 1988–23 February 1991]. Bangkok: Institute of Asian Studies, 1997.

Supalak Ganjanakhundee. "Hun Sen Settling Scores but is it Worth it?". *The Nation*, 7 November 2009.

————. "Thailand Recalls Ambassador to Protest Cambodia". *The Nation*, 5 November 2009.

Thai Political Facts Info. "Preah Vihear for Koh Kong for Natural Gas/Oil", 16 October 2008 <http://antithaksin.wordpress.com/2008/10/16/preah-vihear-for-koh-kong-and-natuaral-gasoil/> (accessed 30 August 2011).

Thanong Khanthong. "Surayud Boxed into a Corner with FBA Amendments". *The Nation*, 20 April 2007.

Thitinan Pongsudhirak. "Thaksin Bends the Wind". *ISEAS Newsletter*, No. 3. Singapore: Institute of Southeast Asian Studies, July 2005.

————. "World War II and Thailand after Sixty Years". In *Legacies of World War II: South and East Asia*, edited by David Koh Wee Hock. Singapore: Institute of Southeast Asian Studies, 2007.

Thiradej Iamsamran and Ram Indaravichit. *Thodsalak Khadi Prasat Phra Viharn: Wiwatha Guru Sudyod Haeng Thosawad* [Decoding the Phra Viharn Temple Case: Opinion of the Guru, The Best of the Decade]. Bangkok: Matichon Publishing House, 2008.

Thongchai Winichakul. "Preah Vihear can be Time Bomb". *The Nation*, 30 June 2008.

————. "Sia Dindan Pen Prawatthisat Lokphrai Paitaithan Proah Thai Maikuei Sia Dindan" [Lost Territories is a Distorted History which Tricked the Lowly Peasants to Die for their Country because Thailand has Never Lost its Territories]. *Matichon Online*, 8 February 2011 <http://www.matichon.co.th/news_detail.php?newsid=1297151137> (accessed 30 August 2011).

Wassana Nanuam, Thanida Tansubhapon and Prasit Tangprasert. "Thailand Shuts Tourist Spots after Fatal Clashes". *Bangkok Post*, 4 April 2009.

———— and Pradit Ruangdit. "Prawit Rejects GBC Meeting in Indonesia". *Bangkok Post*, 23 March 2011.

————. "Prayuth: Indonesian Observers not Wanted". *Bangkok Post*, 23 March 2011.

Weaver, Matthew. "Thailand Prime Minister to Step Down after Court Strips Him of Office". *The Guardian*, 2 December 2008 <http://www.guardian.co.uk/world/2008/dec/02/thailand-protests-somchai-wongsawat> (accessed 27 August 2011).

Wira Amphai. *Khwampenthai* [Thainess]. Bangkok, 1983.

INDEX

Note: Page numbers followed by "n" refer to notes.

A tank parked at Samsen Road, the soldiers carry yellow ribbons as a show of loyalty to the king, 25 September 2006.
Source: All photos courtesy of Nick Nostitz.

A tank parked at Samsen Road, 25 September 2006.

Soldiers guard a crossing, 23 September 2006.

A yellow ribbon at a tank's gun, 23 September 2006.

The nice face of the coup — children pose for photos together with soldiers stationed at Royal Plaza, 23 September 2006.

Associate Professor Giles Ji Ungpakorn at a anti-coup meeting at Chulalongkorn University. Giles led the first anti-coup protest at Siam Paragorn Department Store, the day after the coup, 27 September 2006.

Anti-coup protest at Democracy Monument, 14 October 2006.

The Anti-19 September Coup Network protests at Parliament, 24 October 2006.

A portrait and the final letter are displayed at the funeral of Nuamthong Praiwan, who committed suicide in protest against the coup, 1 November 2006.

An uncomfortable funeral — the military send representatives to Nuamthong Praiwan's funeral, an officer stands next to Nuamthong's widow, and later UDD leaders Prateep Ungsongtham Hata and Dr Weng Tojirakarn.

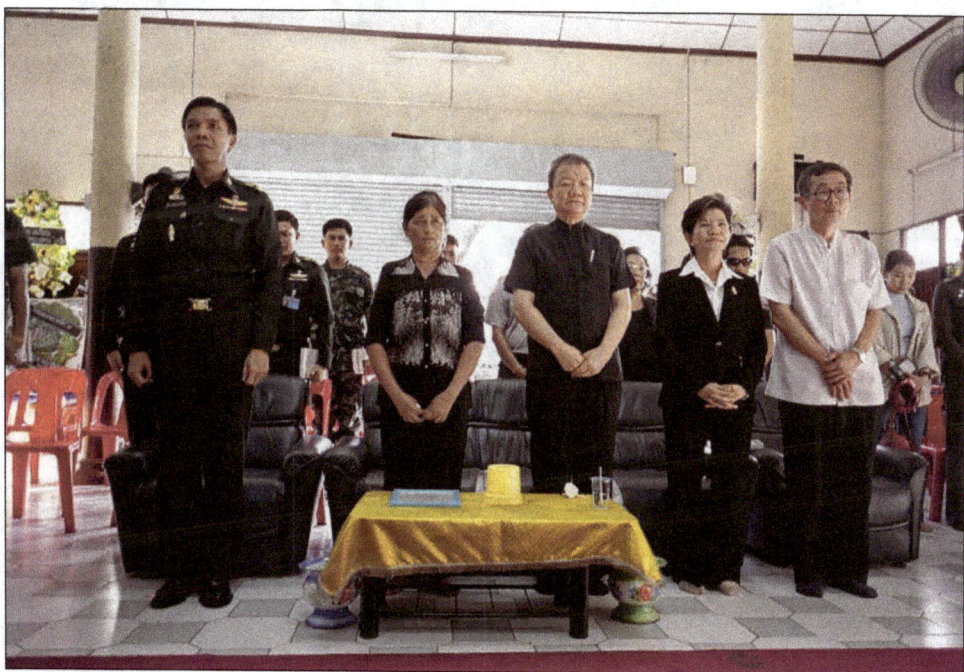

At Nuamthong Praiwan's funeral, former Justice Minister Pongthep Thepkanchana comforts a crying Thai Rak Thai Party supporter, 3 November 2006.

A small stage of the Saturday People against Dictatorship at Sanam Luang, 11 November 2006.

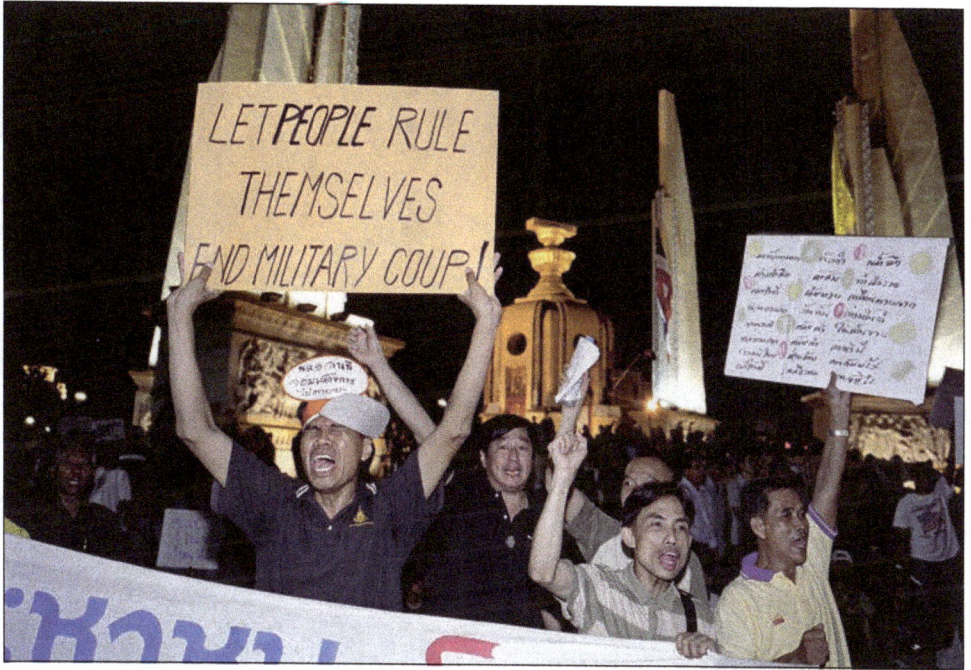

Anti-coup protesters at Democracy Monument, 10 December 2006.

Former Minister under the Thaksin government and deputy leader of the Thai Rak Thai Party Sudarat Keyuraphan is in tears and talks to Thai Rak Thai party supporters after the dissolution of the Party at the Party's headquarters, 30 May 2007.

Distraught Thai Rak Thai supporters at the party's headquarters after the dissolution of the party, 30 May 2007.

Jakrapob Penkair holds a speech at a Sanam Luang stage, 11 June 2007.

UDD protesters try to march to Privy Council chairman General Prem Tinsulanonda's residence, but were blocked by police, 1 July 2007.

Anti-coup protesters at Sanam Luang, 9 June 2007.

General Surayud Chulanont, the post-coup prime minister installed by the military, 8 April 2007.

Anti-coup protesters march by Democracy Monument, 9 June 2007.

The only violent confrontation in the coup period — the "Si Sao Thewet clashes", which occurred when anti-coup protesters managed to break through police barricades and protested in front of Privy Council President General Prem Tinsulanonda's residence, 22 July 2007.

After the clashes, nine UDD leaders were detained for twelve days, 26 July 2007.

A man cuts his arm in a protest action against the military-sponsored 2007 constitution, organized by the 24th of June group. On the microphone is the group's leader, Somyot Prueksakasemsuk, who was in January 2013 imprisoned for *lèse-majesté* violations for eleven years, August 2007.

Samak Sundaravej, leader of the Thai Rak Thai placeholder People's Power Party, and later Prime Minister of Thailand, during an election campaign rally at Sanam Luang, 12 October 2007.